KU-534-621

Law in a Digital World

Law in a Digital World

M. ETHAN KATSH

New York   Oxford
OXFORD UNIVERSITY PRESS
1995

Library
D.L.I.A.D.T.
Kill Ave.
Dun Laoghaire
Tel. 01-2144637

Oxford University Press

Oxford   New York
Athens   Auckland   Bangkok   Bombay
Calcutta   Cape Town   Dar es Salaam   Delhi
Florence   Hong Kong   Istanbul   Karachi
Kuala Lumpur   Madras   Madrid   Melbourne
Mexico City   Nairobi   Paris   Singapore
Taipei   Tokyo   Toronto

and associated companies in
Berlin   Ibadan

Copyright © 1995 by Oxford University Press, Inc.

Published by Oxford University Press, Inc.
200 Madison Avenue, New York, New York 10016

Oxford is a registered trademark of Oxford University Press

All rights reserved. No part of this publication may be reproduced,
stored in a retrieval system, or transmitted, in any form or by any means,
electronic, mechanical, photocopying, recording, or otherwise,
without the prior permission of Oxford University Press.

Library of Congress Cataloging-in-Publication Data
Katsh, M. Ethan.
Law in a digital world / M. Ethan Katsh.
p.   cm.
Includes bibliographical references and index.
ISBN 0-19-508017-3
1. Law—Data processing.   2. Practice of law—Automation.
3. Digital communications.   4. Electronic data processing.
I. Title.
K87.K38   1995
340′.0285—dc20   94-38358

2 4 6 8 9 7 5 3 1

Printed in the United States of America
on acid-free paper

To Beverly
and to Rebecca, Gabriel, and Gideon

Acknowledgments

My ideas about law and technology and my ability to write this book have benefited considerably from assistance provided by many individuals. I am indebted to my colleagues in the University of Massachusetts Department of Legal Studies—Stephen Arons, Dianne Brooks, John Bonsignore, Peter d'Errico, Ronald Pipkin, and Janet Rifkin—for encouraging my research activities and for an ongoing sharing of ideas about the new technologies, and to our staff—Claude Shepard and Tami Paluca-Sackrey—for providing help in innumerable ways. My understanding of the capabilities of information technologies also owes a great deal to discussions with Peter Martin, Tom Bruce, David Johnson, Henry H. Perritt, Trotter Hardy, Ronald Staudt, James Hambleton, and Ejan Mackaay.

I owe particular thanks to Peter Martin and Tom Bruce for enabling me to participate in the Hypertext and Law Workshop at the Cornell Law School Legal Information Institute and for encouraging an electronic version of this book; to the editors of the Villanova and University of Pittsburgh Law Reviews for publishing earlier versions of some material in this book; to the West Publishing Company for providing access to WESTLAW; to Mead Data Central for providing access to LEXIS; to LEXIS Counsel Connect; to Donald Dunn and Bonnie Koneski-White and their staff for courtesies extended to me in using the law library of the Western New England College School of Law; to Michael Crowley and the Mount Holyoke College office of computer services for providing access to their resources; to the Office of Informational Technologies and others at the University of Massachusetts who are responsible for maintaining our link to the Internet, a link that provided access to people and ideas and without which this would be a very different book; and to Hugh Friel, Peter Carino, and Drew Hammond of the University of

Massachusetts President's Office for guiding me in some of the intricacies of the World-Wide Web.

I am very grateful to Helen McInnis and Rachel Pace of Oxford University Press for their interest, encouragement, and advice. More than anyone else, I owe a large debt to my family, to Beverly and to Rebecca, Gabriel, and Gideon. At a time when I was developing ideas about some of the liberating capabilities of computers, they often thought I was enslaved by the machine. They were probably correct, and I hope that I was as well.

Amherst, Massachusetts   M.E.K.
October 1994

Contents

Law in a Digital World

In the future, everything will be digital.

—William Gates

No court can make time stand still.

—Justice Felix Frankfurter

Relationships will be defined more by communications channels than by legal documents.

—Paul Saffo

I believe that we are in the middle of a shift, a generational change really, in the way people use information. On one side of the divide are people who primarily use books as their source of information and who view printed information as the only valid form of information.

On the other side are people who see information as divorced from its format. Be it on a page, on a terminal or in some other electronic form, information is information.

—Robert C. Berring

Introduction: Twain's Challenge and the Culture of Cyberspace

In *Life on the Mississippi,* Mark Twain described his lifelong fascination with the Mississippi River and with the influence that the river had on the people and towns in the surrounding area. Through a series of stories and anecdotes about river life, Twain portrays the river not simply as a moving body of water, as a geographical entity, but as a dynamic component of life and culture in that time and place.

One of Twain's most telling experiences occurred when, as a young man, he was serving as an apprentice to a riverboat captain. While at the helm one day, Twain perceived danger lurking under the surface and, without consulting the captain, suddenly changed course. The captain, a man named Bixby, immediately asked him to account for his action and Twain replied that he had seen an underwater hazard, a bluff reef, just ahead. Bixby, however, declares that Twain has made a mistake and that he should resume the original course. Twain answers:

> "But I saw it. It was as bluff as that one yonder."
> "Just about. Run over it!"
> "Do you give it as an order?"
> "Yes. Run over it!"
> "If I don't, I wish I may die."
> "All right; I am taking the responsibility."
> I was just as anxious to kill the boat, now, as I had been to save it before. I impressed my order upon my memory, to be used at the inquest, and made a straight break for the reef. As it disappeared under our bows I held my breath; but we slid over it like oil.
> "Now, don't you see the difference? It wasn't any thing but a *wind* reef. The wind does that."
> "So I see. But it is exactly like a bluff reef. How am I ever going to tell them apart?"

Bixby responds that he cannot really explain how to tell them apart but that "by and by you will just naturally know one from the other." For Twain, looking back on this some years later, "[i]t turned out to be

3

true. The face of the water, in time, became a wonderful book—a book that was a dead language to the uneducated passenger, but which told its mind to me without reserve, delivering its most cherished secrets as clearly as if it uttered them with a voice."[1]

This is a book about law's journey, a journey that is taking the law in new directions and to new places. Where is law moving from? From many different places. From libraries with large and impressive books. From courts in august buildings. From the paper on which contracts and documents are printed and from the filing cabinets in which they are stored. From the offices in which lawyers interact with clients. From a familiar and stable information environment. Perhaps even from one part of our minds to another.

And where is law going? To a place where information is increasingly on screen instead of on paper. To a place where there are new opportunities for interacting with the law and where there are also significant challenges to the legal profession and to traditional legal practices and concepts. To an unfamiliar and rapidly changing information environment, an environment where the value of information increases more when it moves than when it is put away for safekeeping and is guarded. To a world of flexible spaces, of new relationships, and of greater possibilities for individual and group communication. To a place where law faces new meanings and new expectations.

Law's journey, of course, is also our journey. We are a legalistic culture or, at least, we have been one, and we employ law frequently as both a tool and a symbol. Law is a process that we hope will shape behavior, settle disputes, secure rights, and protect liberties, even achieve justice. It is a social force with many components, something that touches many other institutions and, in turn, is influenced by them. It is a set of rules and doctrines, an institution that embodies cultural values and traditions, and it is also a profession. It can, of course, be much less than this by preserving injustice, violating principle, and denying the realization of rights. Yet, in our personal and business lives, the law is almost always there, generally in the background but, on occasion, alongside us in the foreground.

The new legal landscape that is emerging is, at present, not very easy to see. Part of the reason for this is that the future of law is not to be found in impressive buildings or leather-bound books but in small pieces of silicon, in streams of light, and in millions of miles of wires and cable. Thus, to understand the changes that lie in store for us, it is necessary to look beyond the surface of the law, which still looks fairly familiar and traditional, to much that is hidden from view. Unlike Twain, however, most of us have no experienced captains standing nearby to explain what is real and what is illusion, what facets of the new technologies we should pay careful attention to and what we can ignore, what is a distraction and what is not, what is a significant force for change and what is not, what it means that letters affixed to paper by printing presses increasingly are appearing as flashing lights on a screen or as strings of ones and zeros encoded in electronic form, and what are the bluff reefs and what are the wind reefs.

For Twain, the shimmering and beguiling "face of the water" eventually became reliable and informative, "a wonderful book." Today, more and more of us are spending time staring at the computer screen, something that often serves as a replacement for books and for words on paper. Indeed, in many of its uses, the computer seems to be much more than a "wonderful book," as it allows us to obtain information and work with information in ways not possible previously. Yet, it is important to realize that the fluorescent computer monitor, while revealing and, in many ways, miraculous, is also quite different from a book. It has some qualities of the book but, perhaps surprisingly, it has qualities of the water's surface as well. Unlike the book but similar to the "face of the water," this electronic entrance to the digital world presents us with changing forms and images, with resemblances and illusions, with data that comes and goes, with something dynamic, colorful, and animated. The strength, and at times the weakness, of the book, open or closed, is that it lacks these qualities, that it is an information source that remains constant over time and space, that it is stable and trustworthy, that it is typically black on white, and that it is standardized and uniform.

Some parts of our journey from a print world to an electronic one are quite easy to see. There are, for example, powerful computers sitting on increasing numbers of desks and in increasing numbers of homes. We are aware that microchips affect the operation of many devices we come in contact with daily. Even if one does not own a computer or work with one, no individual can pass more than a few minutes before coming into contact with some process linked to a computer. Cash registers, automated teller machines, gasoline pumps, elevators, and soda machines, for example, rely on microprocessors, and virtually no printed information reaches a reader without passing through some stage in electronic form. Indeed, it is estimated that in the course of a single day, one comes in contact with over 150 tiny computers embedded in cars, exercise equipment, copying machines, and other everyday devices.[2] The late sociologist Rose Goldsen once wrote that "it is still possible to turn off the television set. It is not possible to turn off the television environment."[3] The same can now be said about the computer and the computer environment.

The purpose of this book is to help us understand and come to terms with the nature of the new information technologies and how they are interacting with one of our most central societal institutions, the law. In confronting these technologies, we too are faced with Twain's challenge of understanding clearly what is happening beyond

our field of vision. Some of us are engaged daily in the use of information in electronic form. We employ powerful tools to acquire, work
with, and create information. Yet the impact of the technologies on
legal processes, institutions, concepts, and doctrines—on what is
occurring beyond the "face of the water"—is unclear. Others of us are
sitting on the river's edge, touched at a distance by an electronic
stream of words, images, and sounds that are encoded in digital form.
All of us hear predictions of "information superhighways," of hundreds of channels and choices, of interactive shopping and "electronic
malls," of "information at one's fingertips," and of "electronic
libraries." In such an environment, we all need a sense of what is real
and what is illusion, of what is permanent and what is transitory, of
what will have a deep impact and what can be ignored.

We live in an era of historically significant transitions, of rapid
and deep change occurring in institutions, in practices, in perspectives, and in values. It is a period of significant political change, as
powerful nation-states become impotent overnight, and of considerable social change, as the makeup of families, and even the concept of
a family, becomes different from what it once was. It is an age of
large-scale economic change, as new global entities take root and previously powerful ones decline. Change is global and local, technological and social, collective and individual. Change, in this time period,
occurs so rapidly that it is, even now, becoming a little difficult to
remember the recent time when the USSR and IBM were preeminent
powers in the political and economic spheres, and when three broadcast networks virtually monopolized television.

The law is an intriguing area in which to study change since it has
links to all other important institutions. It is a focal point that sends
out rays that touch economic activity, political interests, ethical values, and individual concerns. For the almost 1 million lawyers in the
United States, the law is a livelihood, and change raises questions of
economic well-being and security. For politicians, change in law
affects the process of allocating resources, of establishing standards
of behavior, and of responding to citizen desires. For citizens, institutions, and corporations, change in legal processes, concepts, and values touches traditional relationships, aspirations for achieving a more
just society, and valuable property interests. As law feels the impact of
the new technologies, change will not be located in only one area.
Rather, as legal change occurs, many different facets of our society
will be affected.

The principal thesis of this book is that change is linked to our
use of new information technologies. These new information technologies are particularly relevant to law because law is oriented
around information and communication. Whatever definition one
gives to the law—whether it is considered a profession, or a method

of resolving disputes, or a process to bring about justice, or a facade to protect the status quo, or a means to secure rights and regulate behavior—it is always concerned with information. What a general once claimed about the military is true of law as well: "If you ain't got communications, you ain't got nothing."[4] Or, as legal philosopher H.L.A. Hart stated in a more scholarly style, "If it were not possible to communicate general standards of conduct, which multitudes of individuals could understand, without further direction, as requiring from them certain conduct when occasion rose, nothing that we would now recognize as law could exist."[5]

Law can be looked at in many ways, but in every incarnation, information is a central component. As one lawyer recently wrote, "from the moment we lawyers enter our offices, until we turn off the lights at night, we deal with information."[6] Information is the fundamental building block that is present and is the focus of attention at almost every stage of the legal process. Legal doctrine, for example, is information that is stored, organized, processed, and transmitted. Legal judgments are actions that involve obtaining information, evaluating it, storing it, and communicating it. Lawyers have expertise in and have control over a body of legal information. As disputes are settled, rights established, values clarified, and behavior regulated, the participants in these processes work with information and engage in a struggle over information. Indeed, one way of understanding the legal process is to view information as being at its core and to see much of the work of participants as involving communication. In this process, information is always moving—from client to lawyer, from lawyer to jury, from judge to the public, from the public to the government, and so on.

Legal scholars have had some interest in the appearance of new technologies generally. The automobile, for example, is recognized as having caused a host of changes in the law—in tort law and in environmental law, for example. Other new technologies, such as nuclear power or biotechnology or medical advances, have caused a reassessment of several areas of legal doctrine. Yet, information technology is different and presents the law with a very different kind of challenge. It is different because, as noted, the law runs on information and because much of law *is* information. Thus, all of law is not affected by the automobile because law is not composed of automobiles. But law is, in almost all of its parts, dependent on communication and information. A change in how information is used, therefore, brings with it the potential for far broader change in law than does any other kind of technological shift.

At the heart of law's relationship with information during the past five centuries has been the technology of printing. In a previous book, *The Electronic Media and the Transformation of Law*,[7] I examined many links between law and communications media, and explored how law has changed throughout history as new communications media have developed. In particular, I pointed out how many of the cornerstones of modern law—the concept of precedent, the evolution of the legal profession, the development of some legal doctrines involving information (such as the First Amendment and privacy, obscenity, and copyright laws)—are linked to the capabilities of printing, the communications medium that has been dominant for the past 500 years.

Printing was the first mass medium and the first medium to enable large quantities of uniform, reliable, and authoritative information to be distributed widely. Printing brought about its own "information explosion" in which there were vast increases in the number of books published, in the size of libraries, and in the number of people able to read. It was also a powerful influence on change in the law. In the centuries following Gutenberg, the modern legal profession developed and a new framework for protecting the individual emerged. Authoritative law became what appeared in books rather than in custom. It was an era in which "Western legal tradition began to be characterized by print. Today, our legal consciousness is still demarcated and mediated by printed texts. Whether, for example, in the formation and interpretation of wills or contracts, or in the review of court trials and legislative proceedings, the law's primary instrument remains the printed document. Wherever we turn, legal reality is shaped largely by the printed word."[8]

We have entered a new age in which print is being displaced by electronic informational technologies, and words fixed on paper are being joined by words (and images and sounds) appearing on screen. Are these new technologies merely more efficient versions of the old? Are they simply new containers that bring the same product to the user in a new way? Do they simply move information faster? Or does the use of information in a new form, particularly by an institution for whom information is a highly valued commodity, change the institution, the user, and those who come in contact with the user? Does it create a new type of institution where it is possible to do new things with information and relate to and interact with information differently? Do these changes make possible new kinds of legal relationships and allow people to interact with law in new ways? Will the law be more or less accessible than it has been? Will law and legal rights be as secure in the electronic environment? Will change in the law occur more quickly and more frequently? Will the role of lawyers change? Will we be more likely to view ourselves as insiders or as outsiders, and will we identify with the law or feel alienated from it? Will the new technologies tend to reinforce the status quo or help empower the disenfranchised?[9] These are, as I will explain later, some of the themes I intend to examine.

Although this book is about computers, it is not about some particular kind of hardware or software on the market today, or about which tools to use or which to buy. Its focus is also not on particular areas of law or legal doctrines involving computers. The capabilities of some computer programs and the content of some rules of law related to communications will be considered, but my main concern is both deeper and broader. New software and hardware appear awesome and miraculous, and yet the changes that are coming about are not linked to any single new capability for working with information. Change in the law is not based simply on the new tools being adopted by lawyers and certainly not on any single piece of software or hardware, but on the degree of difference between these tools and traditional tools the law has used. It is the ripple effect brought about by new patterns of interacting with information and with people that is leading the law, and other institutions, in new directions.

Law and media are two of society's more powerful forces. In any list of influential institutions, law and media rank near the top. It is a bit surprising, therefore, that the links between the two have received negligible attention. If one looks at some of the most perceptive books about the influence of communications or computers on society, law almost never appears in the index. And if one looks at works of legal scholarship, one may find discussions of how the media should be regulated or of constitutional issues of free expression, but almost nothing else. Scholars seem to view the powerful realms of law and media as distinct and independent, each having an impact on behavior and attitudes but having little influence on each other. As Peter Martin has observed, "law and lawyers are profoundly affected by changes in information technology, but for many reasons those effects receive less attention than they deserve."[10]

My view is that law and media are intimately linked institutions. Although law is a powerful social force, it is not all-powerful. It responds to and is shaped by other powerful forces in society. There has, indeed, been much legal writing in recent years about the relationship of law and other forces in society such as economics, politics, religion, race, and gender. A suggestion, such as Oliver Wendell Holmes made a century ago, that "the life of the law has not been logic, it has been experience,"[11] is no longer likely to provoke much debate. What is somewhat novel is to suggest that how we use information should be considered one of the "experiences" that affect the nature and role of law in society.

At the heart of informational and legal change is the shift from printing, from letters fixed on paper, to information in electronic form, to information stored as electrical impulses and as sets of ones and zeroes. In this transition period, and even later, we will not have a paperless environment but we will, more routinely, access information in electronic form, and we will employ tools that allow us to work with and communicate information in ways that are difficult, or not even possible, with letters and numbers fixed on paper. This book is an exploration of what it will mean for law, and for individuals subject to and protected by law, to exist in a digital world—a world where information is created, stored, and communicated electronically. Such a legal world will be different from our current legal world, which remains largely oriented around the printed word. In a digital world, print and paper may still be everywhere, but they will not be the defining or dominant medium. As a result, there will be both new opportunities and new challenges as traditions dissolve, as practices change, and, perhaps most important, as our thinking changes about what information means and what one can do with information.

This is not a technical book about computers, and readers who lack familiarity with computers should not feel apprehensive. This is a book about the influence of computers, about what computers can do and how they will be used, about what they will mean for an institution that for half a millennium has relied on the technology of printing to satisfy most of its informational needs. What is more important than understanding precisely how information is stored on disks or on silicon chips is understanding that information will be stored, organized, processed, and communicated differently in the future, in a form that will have new capabilities, provide many new opportunities, and have important consequences for us. Just as it is possible to appreciate how much change has been brought about by the automobile without having an understanding of pistons or cylinders, it is possible, even without knowledge of the properties of silicon chips, to comprehend how computers will change our relationship with information.

What is most significant about the electronic media is that they allow individuals and institutions to have strikingly new experiences with information. If you had an electronic version of this book, and if you were reading this on a screen rather than in print, you would know that the screen image is still not as clear as the printed image but that the electronic format also empowers you in a variety of ways. You could search through the text in an instant, for example, in order to find a word or topic. You could create links between different parts of the work and, in a sense, rearrange the pages. You could connect parts of this work to other works on your computer or even to computers located elsewhere. You could make notes and highlight text with different colors, all without changing or destroying the original. You could see examples of graphics and hypertext that are discussed later in the book. You might be able to send me your reactions to the book by electronically sending messages to my e-mail address.[12] These and other capabilities illustrate a little bit of how, when information is not fixed to the page, space and distance are less constraining, boundaries often disappear, and information becomes more malleable and flexible than we had thought possible. The existence of an electronic version, created by someone like me, with no training in programming and for whom such an endeavor would have been unthinkable when my last book was published, also reveals that new modes of expression and creativity have become available quite rapidly.

Many readers of this book may not realize that they have already experienced some of the novel capabilities of digitally stored information, information that can respond to and interact with the user. For example, when you dial directory assistance and a voice gives you a telephone number, it may be a digital voice that has responded to your request. Many of us have seen dishwashers that "talk" or cars that remind you to put on a seatbelt. The use of automated teller machines involves sending an electronic request long distances over a computer network and getting information in return. Programming a VCR to record some shows in one's absence is simply telling the computer in the VCR to respond to your individual needs and wishes.

Each of these examples illustrates how machines can acquire new capabilities once they can store and process information in electronic form. Yet, each of these machines is also, in a way, limited. These machines may be marvels compared to what existed a decade or two ago, but they are also not as impressive as they appear to be. They are, for example, usually focused on a single task rather than a range of tasks. The talking dishwasher "knows" something about dishwashers but knows nothing about anything else. In addition, such machines will respond to the one-thousandth stimulus the same way they responded to the first. Unlike even primitive living organisms, the "smart" dishwashers or VCRs of today do not change their responses over time. In fact, any change in response is a sign not that it has learned something but that it is broken. They have been "programmed" to respond to a stimulus but not to change as responses are made. Thus, they are reliable and predictable, which are appealing attributes in a machine, but they are also completely inflexible. I know of no VCR on the market today that, if programmed ten weeks in a row to record a program on Thursdays at 9 P.M., will ask the viewer whether he or she wishes future programs at that time to be recorded every week. Such a machine, which would not be very difficult to design, would reflect and act upon the recording patterns of the viewer.[13]

These electronic marvels are also limited in that they tend not to be linked to anything else. Not only do they not retain information and learn from it, but there is also no sharing of information among these machines. The VCR information stays in the VCR, for example, and the dishwasher information in the dishwasher. Whether you consider these machines smart or not very smart, they are isolated machines, communicating with their owners in a very limited manner and unable to communicate at all with other machines or devices located in the home even though they all, by processing digitally stored information, in a sense speak the same language.

As chips become more powerful and software more sophisticated, and as new links are established to computer networks, more and more machines will learn and will share what they learn. In a digital world, it makes no sense to have machines that are unconnected to each other. Thus, computers are rapidly being transformed from machines that compute into machines that also communicate. For the law, this means not only that the machines of lawyers are connected to each other, but that information about law reaches new places and people. Long-established patterns of distributing information, patterns that are linked to the qualities of printing, are disrupted. This is a considerable force for change since, as Michael Hammer and James Champy have noted, "the real power of technology is not that it can make the old processes work better but that it enables organizations to break old rules and create new ways of working."[14]

In a recent speech, computer scientist Tom Forester asked the following:

> What ever happened to the Information Society? Where is the Information Age? What, indeed, happened to the "workerless" factory, the "paperless" office and the "cashless" society? Why aren't we all living in the "electronic cottage," playing our part in the push-button "teledemocracy"—or simply relaxing in the "leisure society," while machines exhibiting "artificial intelligence" do all the work? . . .
>
> The truth is that society has not changed very much. The microchip has had much less social impact than almost everyone predicted. All the talk about "future shocks," "third waves," "megatrends" and "post-industrial" societies must now be taken with a large pinch of salt. Life goes on for the vast majority of people in much the same old way. Computers have infiltrated many areas of our social life, but they have not transformed it. Computers have proved to be useful tools—no more, no less. None of the more extreme predictions about the impact of computers on society have turned out to be correct. Neither Utopia nor Dystopia has arrived on Earth as a result of computerization.[15]

Forester may be correct that, at present, "life goes on for the vast majority of people in much the same old way." A film made about the home life or business life of most citizens would not have the interest we expect from a science fiction movie. We do not go off to Mars for a vacation; our homes have some intriguing mechanical devices and conveniences, but we are still eating and sleeping and doing recreation in many of the same ways people did these things prior to the computer.

Forester seems to want to see more exotic uses, such as, perhaps, totally electronic courtrooms, where there are no judges at all—peopleless courtrooms as well as paperless courtrooms. Perhaps a society without lawyers. He seems to want a society that is so different, in terms of both the artifacts that make up the society and the way in which business is conducted, that it would look like a science fiction movie. In such a society, machines replace paper, money and workers and, perhaps, even judges, lawyers, and courts.

One theme of this book is that we need to stop thinking in terms of *replacements*, of making traditional institutions disappear, and instead observe the process of *displacement*, of changing patterns of orientation and operation. It is not all-electronic lawyers or electronic judges that we can expect but lawyers, judges, and citizens who interact with machines in new ways and, therefore, cause the process of law to become something different from what it has been. Such displacement may take some time to occur, particularly in institutions such as law where the paradigm of print is powerful and pervasive. Yet, the transition is ongoing and, probably by the end of the millennium, much in the law will not go on "in much the same old way."

In the book and subsequent film, *2001*, a computer named HAL attempts to take over the spaceship and control the functions performed by the pilots. This is the image of replacement, which is embodied in the question of whether computers can replace judges or lawyers. What is occurring, as we travel into cyberspace, actually is a much more complicated process than replacement. Legal professionals, legal methods, legal concepts, and legal institutions are not being replaced, at least not yet, but they are being displaced in that they are accommodating themselves to a new environment, and a new orientation toward information is beginning to color how decisions are made and actions taken.

Most persons view the new technologies through the lenses of convenience and efficiency. New machines are considered to be devices that save time, that allow familiar tasks to be performed more quickly than before. It is, indeed, true that virtually any informational task can be performed more quickly using a computer. Thus, machines are purchased in order to obtain information more quickly, to write and revise more quickly, to calculate one's taxes more quickly, even to draw pictures more quickly. One of the principal suggestions of this book, however, is that the long-term impact on law is revealed by focusing more on the dimension of space than on the dimension of time. The new media do affect time in many ways, but they also affect space in ways that are generally not noted or thought about.

In the realm of space and distance, there are many novel, indeed science fiction-like, developments taking place. We do not travel frequently in outer space but, as I shall describe later, computers are space machines, machines that make space and distance much less of a barrier to sending information and to forming relationships than they used to be. We cannot "beam" individuals between home and office, but we do "beam" information between machines on different parts of the globe. We cannot shrink people or objects, but we can shrink information, in the sense that all of the words in this book can easily fit on an ordinary disk and an entire encyclopedia can be placed on a single CD-ROM. We become able to use distant computers as easily as we use our own, and we can interact with people located far away as if they were next door. We can obtain information that was previously distant, not only in the sense that it was far away but also in that it was inaccessible because special skills were required in order to access it. When computer networks move millions of bits of data in a second and when computers perform millions of operations per second, we find it possible to act, in a sense, as if we have been transported from one place to another.

When I was writing my previous book in the late 1980s, it was clear to me that change was on the horizon but, other than perhaps LEXIS and WESTLAW, there were few spatial miracles that seemed to have taken hold in the law. At present, much still remains on the horizon, but the level of technological activity, particularly in the area of computer communications, has grown enormously. The Internet, largely unknown in 1989, today links more than 130 countries and 25 million individuals, and is growing at a fast rate. Law, as will be described later, has a serious presence on the Internet, in terms of information that can be obtained and people who can share information about law. What may be the most novel legal profession–communications experiment, Lexis Counsel Connect, which is described in chapter 7, uses the new media to, in effect, make the contents of law firm filing cabinets available on a network. All of these developments remove constraints of distance and touch the nature of relationships and the ability to control information.

The emerging digital world is often referred to as cyberspace, a term that was coined by a science fiction writer, William Gibson, in 1984 in his novel *Neuromancer*.[16] In Gibson's vision of the future, individuals will become able to place themselves in a new environment, or at least feel that they are in a different environment, by allowing a computer to control the sensory stimuli—the images, sounds, and smells—that they receive. Since our reality, or our perception of reality, is determined by what we see, hear, feel, and smell, a machine that monopolizes sensory intake and substitutes the sensory stimuli of some other place or time can provide us with an alternative reality and allow us to feel as if we are in a different place or time. By sitting in a new kind of "electric chair," one could leave one's own environment and enter a new environment. One could see, hear, feel, and experience things in "cyberspace" just as one might experience one's physical reality.

I do not use *cyberspace* exactly as Gibson did, nor do I suggest that Gibson's model will come true. I shall suggest some ways of considering cyberspace in chapter 1, but my main purpose in using the term is to emphasize that the electronic media touch us in ways that do transform our environment, provide us with many new experiences, change our perception of reality, and perhaps even present us with a new space, or the equivalent of a new space. In this new environment, "information is the currency—a creative force more valuable than a thousand gold mines."[17]

Cyberspace, as used in this book, is a designation for a mature electronic culture—one where electronic networks are much more fully established than they are today, one where many different kinds of data and stimuli can be instantaneously communicated around the globe, and one where the electronic means at our disposal to acquire and process information are richer and more developed than they are today. What cyberspace represents is a new order, a new vision, a new set of possibilities, interactions, and relationships, all of which we acknowledge are linked to new and powerful means for relating to information.

One of the ironies concerning Gibson's fictional electronic world is that his book was published in 1984. As such, it seems to me to call for comparison with the book that dominated public attention at the beginning of that year, George Orwell's *1984*. Orwell's book was not intended as a prediction of the future, but it was frequently taken as such. For those who believed in it as a predictor, it turned out to be a faulty vision, largely because it was premised upon a critical misunderstanding of the nature of the new media. Orwell assumed that control of the flow of information would be more easily accomplished in an age of electronic media than in an age of print and that the authoritarian world of Big Brother would naturally emerge from this. The reality of the electronic medium, however, is quite the opposite, in that it is among the most volatile and hard to control of the different forms of communication. *1984* did serve as a reminder of the evils of any society where the flow of information is controlled, and Gibson's cyberspace also might be most beneficial to us if it is looked at in a similar manner, as an allegory or metaphor rather than factual prediction.

This book is about a rather large set of questions. Few of them are addressed as separate chapters or sections since they overlap and intersect with each other. They touch issues that are embedded in almost every issue linking law and media, and, therefore, most of the following questions are discussed in some way in several chapters.

What happens to the law when information is more plentiful, more accessible, and more malleable? What happens when information is stored not as letters or words on paper but electronically as zeroes and ones? What happens when those who previously had exclusive access to some information now find that there is much broader access to it? What happens to those who have access to information they never had access to before? What happens to individuals and institutions who become aware of information they never even knew existed before? What happens when information becomes located not in some inert source but in an interactive source? What happens when human sources become accepted as the legitimate source of authoritative information in lieu of the words of some impressive-looking book? What happens when the words and letters of the law are joined by images, tables, icons, and other nontextual sources of communication? What happens when traditional figures of speech are supplanted by new ones and when the search for new metaphors to make our new information environment understandable is completed? What happens when the organization of information is determined as much by the reader as it is by the author? What happens when documents can talk back and answer some of our questions? What happens when your colleagues, the people down the hall whom you consult regularly, are not down the hall but 2,000 miles away?

My goal is less to examine a series of discrete legal policies that are now vulnerable because of the qualities of the new media than to consider how our whole framework for thinking about law and working through problems in a legalistic manner are challenged by media that store, process, and communicate information in digital form. It is not simply that action needs to be taken to deal with privacy, copyright, and similar issues, but that the information environment is shifting and, as a consequence, the manner in which we think and speak about the means at our disposal to deal with these and other issues will be changing as well. Law is not merely a force that is used to exercise authority over others. It is, at the same time, an institution and a process that is affected by the very media it is attempting to regulate. The new media, in other words, change law at the same time that law is used to regulate the use of the new media since the two forces relate to each other in a dynamic and interactive manner.

The book revolves around four broad areas of difference between the print and electronic environments: (1) methods of distributing information (electronic networks versus physical transportation), (2) methods of working with information (actively interacting with machines in addition to reading and writing), (3) methods of graphical and nontextual expression and communication, and (4) new modes of organizing information (hypertext versus linear modes of organization). These changes touch not simply lawyers or courts but citizens who rely upon the law, groups affected by the law, and persons whose work is on the borders of the law. They involve new patterns of interaction and new relationships between the state, citizens, groups, and institutions. They involve computer use at a level beyond the common applications of word processing, databases, and spreadsheets. They do not simply accelerate tasks we are already engaged in but encourage us to think and act in new ways.

The first of these differences between the print and electronic environments concerns the national and international communications links that are rapidly being established and that will make telephone and television, our current electronic means for sending words and pictures great distances, seem fairly primitive by comparison. This is the part of the digital world that has been labeled the "information superhighway," a conduit in which information travels at much greater speeds for much greater distances than on any highway. More than any highway, however, the new media are being linked in a vast network or web. Information can be shared by parties in different places. Information can be moved globally at electronic speeds. Such an environment fosters new interpersonal and institutional relationships. Distances between people and accessibility to information changes. Sources of legal information, traditionally located in bound books, are gradually being displaced into an electronic network consisting of both electronic "documents" and humans.

A second facet of the new technological environment is that users interact with machines differently from the manner in which readers interact with books and with static pages of print. The often asked question of whether computers will replace judges is really the wrong kind of question to ask. Even if "judicial machines" never become available to actually decide cases or interpret points of law, we must still evaluate what role machines will play and what impact it will have that we are not simply reading off the screen but are interacting with increasingly sophisticated machines. WESTLAW, for example, now allows legal information to be obtained by asking questions in ordinary English into a microphone attached to the computer. Further questions can be asked in response to what the computer displays on the screen. This is different from the kind of interaction that lawyers formerly experienced in a law library, and, indeed, it opens up possibilities for nonlawyers to obtain information in ways not previously possible. This is just one example of how, as we develop machines that are more and more capable of interacting with humans, of answering questions, of framing questions, of simulating alternative outcomes of cases, or of assisting in the resolution of disputes, the nature and role of law and legal practice inevitably will change.

A third feature of the electronic culture is the changing relationship of word and image. One of the subtle effects of print was to change how words and images were used. Print, while providing us with many beautiful books of art, tended to support text more than images. It was easier and cheaper to print text than images, particularly colorful images. Partly because of this, the print world of law is a largely imageless world. In the legal worlds of print, "fine print," and "black letter law," there is little other than text. The electronic media, however, are a force that encourages the visual, that deals with color as easily as it deals with black and white, and that allows more opportunities for multidimensional communication. As a consequence, the image will begin to play a new role in our culture. As law succumbs to this force, it learns to communicate in new ways and to represent conflict and relationships in new ways.

A fourth quality of the new media is that they permit information to be organized more flexibly than was possible with print. Books and text encouraged linear modes of organization and analysis and the division of knowledge into discrete disciplines and categories. Indexes and tables of contents provided access to information that had been "bound" and was physically located in a single place. Placing information in electronic form makes possible new forms of organization and new modes of using information. Information that is no longer firmly fixed to paper can be used more flexibly and can be reorganized in novel ways by the user. Hypertext, which permits one to move from any spot in a text to any subject of one's choosing simply by pressing a key or button, threatens many of the habits we use to think about information and to think about law. It raises questions about whether doctrines that assume that information can be contained and controlled, such as copyright and privacy, will continue to be effectively supported.

This book is largely organized as a set of alternating chapters about technology and law. The legal chapters focus primarily on the following: law libraries and accessing legal information, forming and managing contractual relationships, the legal profession, and copyright and privacy. These themes, at least, are the ones that are reflected in the table of contents, which is a convention that came into being after Gutenberg. Tables of contents provide a quick global sense of a book's content, of how it is organized, and of areas that receive the most attention. Tables of contents, however, do not reveal very much about themes that run through the book or through several chapters. My concerns certainly go beyond the topics identified in chapter headings, and I hope that these larger themes become as clear to readers as those highlighted in chapter titles.

I have not attempted to enumerate or identify every area of law touched by the new media. This would require a treatise about virtually every facet of law, just as a volume about the influence of print on law would need to mention virtually every facet of our current legal order. Rather, I have tried to explore some of the currents that lie beneath the "face of the water," some dangers lurking below, and some opportunities for taking advantage of these currents of change. Donald Norman has observed:

> Technology is not neutral. Each technology has properties—affordances—that make it easier to do some activities, harder to do others. The easier ones get done, the harder ones neglected. Each has constraints, preconditions, and side effects that impose requirements and changes on the things with which it interacts, be they other technology, people, or human society at large. Finally, each technology poses a mind-set, a way of thinking about it and the activities to which it is relevant, a mind-set that soon pervades those touched by it, often unwittingly, often unwillingly. The more successful and widespread the technology, the greater its impact upon the thought patterns of those who use it, and consequently, the greater its impact upon all of society.[18]

Entering cyberspace involves understanding these non-neutral facets of technology even more than it does acquiring or using the latest hardware and software. Cyberspace, at least in part, is a state of mind and a set of habits and expectations, and the process of acclimation to this new culture inevitably takes some time and involves some difficulty. It involves understanding that information, more than physical goods, is at the center of any economy of the future, and that working with and adding value to information is becoming the core economic activity. It involves understanding that electronic information can be reworked and revalued in new ways and that novel forms of communication inspire novel kinds of relationships. It involves recognition that one can think about this new informational environment as one thinks about many other spaces, although this is also a space with magical qualities that are not found in physical spaces.

In such a space, change occurs to lawyers and other professionals largely because boundaries vanish and, in a sense, the space in which they work is no longer exclusively theirs. There are changes in how disputes occur and are settled because we interact differently in this space. There are changes in the authority and use of the law because access to this new space is different. There is change in some legal doctrines, such as copyright and privacy, because keeping something from others is more difficult in this space. There is a high level of conflict in this space, rather than harmony and tranquility, because this is an active and creative space, one in which information is more valuable when it is moved than when it is stationary, when it is reworked and changed than when it is guarded and protected. It is a space that calls for effective processes for resolving conflict and managing change.

The late Robert Cover once wrote:

> We constantly create and maintain a world of right and wrong, of lawful and unlawful, of valid and void. The student of law may come

to identify the normative world with the professional paraphernalia of social control. The rules and principles of justice, the formal institutions of the law, and the conventions of a social order are, indeed, important to that world; they are, however, but a small part of the normative universe that ought to claim our attention. No set of legal institutions or prescriptions exists apart from the narratives that locate it and give it meaning. For every constitution there is an epic, for each decalogue a scripture. Once understood in the context of the narratives that give it meaning, law becomes not merely a system of rules to be observed, but a world in which we live.[19]

The world in which we live and our world of law are now being connected in new ways with new forms of narrative and scripture that are electronic in nature. To find the meaning of a change of this magnitude is the challenge of this book.

1

Communicating in Cyberspace: Computer Networks

Tis true, There's magic in the web of it.
—William Shakespeare

"The law is a seamless web," states an old, oft-repeated[1] yet difficult to imagine legal maxim. This metaphor suggests that law not only has an intricate structure but also that all parts of the law fit together smoothly, that each part is linked to every other part, and that the whole arrangement grows and evolves according to plan. More specifically, the seamless web metaphor implies that "the common law could be logically explained and was a part of a greater system"[2] and that "every new decision affects, at least minimally, every legal proposition."[3]

This impressively designed process is embodied in the somewhat similar, albeit more eloquent, words of Oliver Wendell Holmes, whose vision of law was expressed as follows:

> When I think thus of the law, I see a princess mightier than she who once wrought at Bayeux, eternally weaving into her web dim figures of the ever-lengthening past—figures too dim to be noticed by the idle, too symbolic to be interpreted except by her pupils, but to the discerning eye disclosing every painful step and every world-shaking contest by which mankind has worked and fought its way from savage isolation to organic social life.[4]

For most lawyers, judges, and citizens today, law without contradictions and inconsistencies is a vision that is hopelessly romantic and as difficult to imagine as a seamless web. Although law undoubtedly

21

retains some web-like qualities, the modern legal web also appears to contain many loose ends, to be stretched beyond capacity, and to have seams that show very clearly. Gaps in the law are increasingly obvious, and division and specialization, more than unity and generalization, characterize much of legal practice and the law. As Harold Berman noted, "[t]he law is becoming more fragmented, more subjective, geared more to expediency and less to morality, concerned more with immediate consequences and less with consistency or continuity."[5] Or, as Robert Berring claimed, "there is no 'brooding omnipresence in the sky.' The old system of grand structure is gone."[6] Indeed, more than one judge has declared that "[r]ather than a seamless web . . . [the law is] a patchwork quilt."[7]

One way to interpret this loss of faith in the seamless web metaphor is to view it as reflecting a new realism and a greater understanding of the nature of law. The metaphor may never have represented law as it actually existed but, rather, was a myth or symbol and an idealization of our hopes for law.[8] In this sense, the purpose of the metaphor was to encourage a belief in the law's consistency, integrity, and coherency.[9] The metaphor was a symbolic attempt to promote the law's legitimacy and to bring order to the law. The development of the metaphor paralleled the attempts of scholars to portray the law as possessing an all-encompassing structure, to identify links between apparently inconsistent judicial decisions, and to demonstrate that natural connections can be found in seemingly disparate parts of the law.

An alternative interpretation exists, however, as to why the seamless web metaphor may have lost much of its appeal, an interpretation that looks behind the actual qualities of the law to the manner in which these qualities are communicated. This perspective suggests that myths and other strongly held beliefs about law are dependent upon, linked to, and supported by the communications process employed by law. The seamless web, therefore, is not a reference to the process and practice of law as much as it is a characterization of a preserved and organized body of law, one contained and embedded in the centuries-old technology of print. It is a label, a metaphor for an institution whose reflection has been seen for centuries in books and in the domain of print. If, therefore, this characterization of law seems not as compelling today as it once was, it may be because the communications process that underlies the metaphor is shifting. Thus, although it is possible that loss of faith in the metaphor may simply signify the long overdue destruction of a myth, it is also possible to view it as movement away from print-based representations of law and as a growing inability to have faith in a model of law that could only exist in printed form.

A principal theme of this book is that the process of law, and the changes occurring in the law, is not understandable without taking into account how we communicate and work with information. Law is and always has been embodied in some medium of communication.[10] The methods, institutions, and doctrines of law, as well as its metaphors and figures of speech, have always reflected and in some way have been linked to the qualities, constraints, and opportunities of the media used by law—first the spoken word, then writing, and then print.

The shift from print to electronic information technologies provides the law with a new environment, one that is less tangible, less fixed, less structured, less stable, and consequently more versatile and volatile. Ironically, this new environment may, as will be explained, revive thinking about the law in terms of web-like qualities. The context, however, will not be a web-like body of legal knowledge but a new relationship with law, one linked to the new electronic media and to forms of communication that are very different from print. It will be a relationship not with a web that covers and protects, something that has clear edges and boundaries, but a relationship with something even more intricate and magical than a seamless web, something that causes law to question its identity and distinctiveness, its authority and power. The spread of the new web-like form will not bring a restoration of what was envisioned in print, not a separate and distinct presence, but a seamless and pervasive presence, a force that is felt, experienced, and participated in in ways that were never really possible in the past.

The rapid emergence of electronic technologies involves a series of changes in how information is transmitted, used, stored, and presented. Increasing numbers of legal professionals are already familiar with the use of computers for manipulating and processing information.[11] Except for WESTLAW and LEXIS, however, fewer professionals rely on the communicative capabilities of computers, on data networks, and on other new methods of acquiring and transmitting information at a distance. Computers are still purchased primarily to process numbers or work with words. Yet, computer use for communicating, for obtaining information, and for transmitting such information is growing. As this trend continues, and even accelerates, it is inevitably discovered that computer networks link people as well as machines. As will be explained later, this guides us toward a new understanding of the computer and to an understanding that the power of computers to send and receive is at least as impressive and important a capability as the power to manipulate and process text and numbers.

We are currently in a period of transition. More and more people are becoming aware that the computer is an extraordinary communicative device, are acquiring e-mail addresses, are learning how to send and receive information via their computers, and are gaining access to computer-based telecommunication networks. As this transition continues, not only will we develop a new understanding of the novel and powerful modes of distributing information electronically, but we will also realize more clearly that this powerful new medium of communication has significant implications for law as well as for many other societal institutions.

One of the underlying themes of this book is that it is important to look at *how* information is being transmitted and not simply at *what* is being transmitted. Obtaining information from LEXIS and WESTLAW, for example, is a very different kind of process than obtaining information from a print library. Although the information obtained may be the same, different research techniques are involved and new capabilities for processing information are acquired. As will be explained in chapter 3, the differences between print and electronic sources of information are so great that labeling electronic services as electronic libraries is very misleading.

There is, quite understandably, some resistance to trying to understand communications-related change by focusing on media, the means by which information is conveyed, rather than on the information itself. Particularly during the early phase of the development of some new technology, differences in how some task is conducted are not necessarily easy to recognize and, as a result, the qualitative differences between the old and the new technologies tend to be neglected. It is almost to be expected that how the new media differ from the old will be glossed over. Thus, early films were labeled "moving pictures" and were not immediately understood to be a new art form. Or, as James Martin observed, "the first cars were called 'horseless carriages' and looked as though they were designed to be pulled by a horse. It took many years to realize that a good shape for a car is quite different. Radio was originally called 'wireless telegraphy'; it took years to realize that the great application of radio was broadcasting."[12] In the early days of printing, such an outlook led some influential institutions to welcome printing enthusiastically; they assumed that printing was merely a powerful replacement for writing. These institutions failed to understand, however, that printing could not be controlled as easily as writing had been, and they did not recognize that printing also changed the larger environment. Thus, a technology considered to be a "divine art" ultimately contributed to the success of the Protestant Reformation, "a movement that was shaped at the very outset (and in large part ushered in) by the new powers of the press."[13]

More recently, we have labeled the devices that transform electrical impulses into words on paper as "printers," and electronic databases as "libraries." These characterizations, representing obvious frames of reference from the print era, are understandable attempts to place new modes of processing and interacting with information in a familiar framework and to make users feel comfortable with the new technologies. Although these characterizations or metaphors may seem to make sense today, they are patently inadequate. The library metaphor,[14] for example, which will be examined in greater detail in chapter 3, may enjoy as brief an existence as the "horseless carriage" expression, in that it fails to explain the novel and powerful ways in which the new technology differs from the old and gives no hint of the new directions in which the new technologies are leading us. Some day in the future, in other words, the "library" label may seem as imprecise and nearsighted as "moving pictures" does today.

The legal profession is not alone in trying to understand how the movement of information in new ways affects its methods and missions as well as its visible products. Scientists, for example, have recognized that powerful numerical and statistical tools not only facilitate and expand the ability to calculate but also change what science is.[15] Similarly, artists understand that graphical tools not only affect the ability to draw pictures but also change styles and concepts of art. These broader consequences are understandable if one realizes that "[l]anguage, mathematics, law, religion, philosophy, arts, the sciences, and institutions of all kinds . . . are edifices of a sort, like the libraries we build, physically, to store their operating instructions, their 'programs.'"[16] The underlying theme of this book is that new tools for communicating and working with information not only affect our ability to express ourselves, but ultimately bring about changes in what law is and does.

At the end of the current transitional period, print will not vanish, but it will play a substantially different role. As Richard Lanham has pointed out, "[w]hatever happens, however we rearrange our marketplace of ideas—as sooner or later we certainly shall—our sense of what "publication" means is bound to change. We will be able to make our commentary part of the text, and weave an elaborate series of interlocked commentaries together. We will, that is, be moving from a series of orations to a continuing conversation . . . as we move in slow and staggered steps from the printed to the pixeled word.[17]

Print will not disappear, but at some point print will cease to dominate the legal landscape and the legal mind as it has for the past several centuries. Paper and print will continue to be present in our environment, but we will work more frequently with information in electronic, rather than print, form. More important, we will begin to attribute to the electronic medium the attention and status reserved for the culture's primary medium. As Michael Benedikt observed, "just as printing did not replace but displaced writing, and writing did not replace but displaced storytelling, and just as movies did not replace theater nor television movies . . . cyberspace will not replace either objective reality or dreaming or thinking in their historical modes."[18] Thus, words on paper will remain commonplace, but the principal manner in which we think about, describe, and use information will be based on very different electronic models of how information is organized, stored, and processed. We will not be paperless but we may be impatient with paper because, as examples throughout this book will illustrate, paper constrains and confines us in ways that are no longer acceptable.

The new media can be considered to be "displacing" because they not only make available some new tools for working with information but, in a sense, create a new environment. *Displacement* seems an appropriate term for what is occurring because these changes put us in a different space from where we were. The new media do not, of course, physically move us, as did the changes in spatial orientation brought about by the automobile and other modern modes of transportation. But they do cause us to interact with our surroundings differently. The new media change the meaning of distance and provide us with an environment where new relationships with people and groups are fostered, where people can "meet," and where new relationships begin to occur between people and institutions.

This new environment emerges, in part, because the movement of electronic information is governed by quite a different set of rules and expectations than existed in the print environment. Just as the automobile created an environment in which rules and expectations for transportation were novel and unprecedented, the electronic media seem to exist in a context or space where they do not have to play by the same rules as print and, therefore, are not subject to the same constraints as print. This electronic space can be envisioned as an almost magical place, in the sense that various physical laws that restrict movement and limit capabilities appear to have been lifted. The theme of displacement—of being put in a new space—is useful, therefore, because it focuses on context rather than content. As a result, it can serve to shift attention to *how* we use and communicate information and away from *what* the information is. This focus will, I hope, assist in explaining both how the new media are different and why change is occurring as a result.

We are only in the beginning phases of developing the electronic environment or space. Movement in this direction will accelerate as more persons acquire the ability to send and receive information in electronic form and as high-speed electronic networks for communicating information are put in place. For those individuals who currently limit their use of the computer to processing words and numbers, the addition of communicative capabilities represents the next frontier in mastering the electronic technology. Many lawyers are, of course, familiar with LEXIS and WESTLAW, but the electronic communicative environment that is on the horizon involves something vastly different from what occurs when one extracts information from a large and distant database. It involves, for example, a much more extensive and developed network. It involves understanding how persons far away can work on data in your possession, how you can work on data in their possession, and how you can work together on the same data at the same time. As later chapters will indicate, it also involves greater use of nontextual forms of expression, such as images, graphs, and charts.[19] It involves new methods of relating to information, such as hypertext and hypermedia,[20] and new ways of interacting with machines endowed with abilities to respond to the user in some way.[21] It involves appreciating how the tools for working with and distributing electronic data are not simply more efficient and more powerful but are quite different from tools for working with words on paper. It may even involve acquiring a preference for seeing something on the screen rather on the printed page, something that at the moment seems improbable to most computer users. As all these changes in using information occur, new alliances and relationships between people are formed, many of which will touch the law.

In order to explain the nature and impact of the new technologies, I shall frequently suggest that we look at the new media not simply as a means for moving information in new ways but as something that creates a new space, or at least as something that has some of the attributes of a space and can be described in spatial terms. There are at least two benefits to looking at the new media in spatial terms. First, such an approach enables us to understand not only the occurrence of discrete changes in how information is being used and processed, but also the direction these changes are leading both the institution and practice of law. An environmental or spatial framework allows one to see activities not in isolation but in terms of how they are linked to changes in other parts of the institution. A new information place brings about not only changes in specific behavior, but also changes in positions, interests, expectations, relationships, and attitudes. More particularly, the new media are creating change in boundaries, a spatial concept that can be applied to institutions, concepts, and disciplines, as well as to physical territories and nation-states. Using an environmental or spatial perspective enables us to understand not only what is replaced but what is displaced—not only what continues in essentially the same form (or disappears) but what is altered and reshaped.

The second reason it is appropriate to look at the new communications technologies as affecting the law's information environment or space is that there is a clear link between space or distance and the impact of a communications medium. Indeed, much of what any medium of communication does is explainable in spatial terms. Communication in writing and print, indeed communication via any form other than the spoken word, involves overcoming barriers caused by the spatial separation of two or more individuals. At the heart of the new media are capabilities for working with information in distant places and for overcoming constraints that are assumed to be fixed, but in reality are only constraints imposed by limitations of print and writing.

One of the earliest and most insightful commentators on the transformative significance of a new medium of communication, Harold Innis, believed that any new medium changed conceptions of time and space and needed to be looked at in such terms. He wrote:

> A medium of communication has an important influence on the dissemination of knowledge over space and over time and it becomes necessary to study its characteristics in order to appraise its influence in its cultural setting. According to its characteristics it may be better suited to the dissemination of knowledge over time than space, particularly if the medium is heavy and durable and not suited to transportation, or to the dissemination of knowledge over space than over time, particularly if the medium is light and easily transported.[22]

David Bolter, one of the most perceptive current commentators on the electronic media, wrote that "each technology gives us a different space."[23] As will be explained, the electronic media bring change because they, unlike print, are seemingly unconstrained by a variety of physical forces and spatial constraints, and can create a space where Newtonian laws seem to be circumvented.

Computers are commonly perceived as machines that shrink time and that allow various tasks to be performed in less time than when done manually. One of the recurring themes of this book is that we would benefit considerably in our understanding of the impact of the new media if we shifted our focus to the new technology's impact on space and distance. It is the removal of constraints of space and distance that allows new relationships between people, groups, institutions, and information to form. These new relationships are what is moving law in new directions rather than merely accelerating movement in some current direction. The following discussion begins, therefore, with a description of some of the ways that the new media are beginning to provide us with a new kind of space—one that is far less subject to the physical constraints that operate in the print environment.

The Technological Web

Cyberspace is a concept that I associate with a mature electronic culture.[24] Such a culture not only allows one to process and interact with information in electronic form, as will be described in later chapters in this book, but also presents sophisticated electronic means for acquiring and distributing information. It relies on powerful computers to store and analyze data and links these computers together to share data and communicate with each other. Cyberspace emphasizes the network that links computers and supports communication that occurs so quickly that it removes spatial distance as a constraint in obtaining information and even in working with people. It focuses more on the network as a whole than on any particular computer that is tied to the network. It is, therefore, something that is much broader than LEXIS or WESTLAW or any other single large source of electronic information. It suggests an environment where novel electronic interactions foster new relationships with people and information and where communication occurs so quickly and over such great distances that many basic assumptions of institutional life are challenged. In its most controversial characterization, cyberspace assumes that the removal of spatial barriers combined with the high level of online interaction creates a feeling among those electronically connected that they are indeed in the same place even though they are physically separated by great distances.[25] As Howard Rheingold, a popular writer about virtual reality has observed, "at the center of every [virtual reality] system is a human experience, the experience of being in an unnatural or remote world."[26] Or, in the words of Michael Benedikt,

> Cyberspace is a globally networked, computer-sustained, computer-accessed, and computer-generated, multi-dimensional, artificial, or "virtual" reality. In this world, on which every computer screen is a window, actual, geographic distance is irrelevant. Objects seen or heard are neither physical nor, necessarily, presentations of physical objects, but are rather—in form, character, and action—made up of data, pure information. This information is derived in part from the operation of the natural, physical world, but is derived primarily from the immense traffic of symbolic information, images, sounds, and people, that constitute human enterprise in science, art, business, and culture.[27]

Even if one has not yet participated in the online world and, therefore, finds some vagueness in this description of cyberspace, and even if one is unable to accept all of the various meanings of the word, I find it a useful term because it helps to place a clear focus on the communicative powers of computers and on the manner in which changes occur in how space and distance are used and perceived. It is also a term that accepts implicitly the idea that new media bring about new environments, and it recognizes that networks have an impact that goes beyond their normally perceived function of transmitting data at unmatched speeds. It is, finally, a term that may assist us in understanding that individuals encountering cyberspace encounter many of the same challenges that face anyone placed in any new and unfamiliar environment.

As we begin to understand the nature of these networks and the differences between electronic and print forms of communication, and as we strive to come to terms with a model of law that lacks the features of a seamless web, we are immediately faced with a significant irony. This irony is that the communications networks that are rapidly being put into place are themselves increasingly being referred to as a web.[28] Thus, at the same time that the "seamless web" has been losing its power as a useful legal metaphor, our telecommunications system has been acquiring many of the markings of the spider's creation. Computer scientist Vinton Cerf wrote, for example, that "[a] web of glass spans the globe. Through it, brief sparks of light incessantly fly, linking machines chip to chip and people face to face."[29] Similarly, the National Information Infrastructure Task Force Report states: "All Americans have a stake in the construction of an advanced National Information Infrastructure (NII), a seamless web of communications networks, computers, database and consumer electronics that will put vast amounts of information at users' fingertips. Development of the NII can help unleash an information revolution that will change forever the way people live, work, and interact with each other."[30]

The web metaphor, which never resonated very well in print culture, has been embraced in electronic culture. Parts of the web already allow the spoken word, as it moves over telephone lines, to travel across the globe as easily as it travels across the street. It currently permits the written word to be transmitted as easily as a fax or, with slightly more difficulty, as an e-mail message. Using something called the World-Wide Web, several million Internet users with high-speed links to the network are able to see images and hear sounds that originate on distant machines. These capabilities are elementary compared to what will become available, but they can serve as a reference point for beginning to understand the more powerful network that is gradually being put in place to transmit words, numbers, images, sounds, and any combination of modes of expression. This technological web or network, at least when it is fully formed, will touch every medium and form of communication and, as a consequence, every institution.

Prior to the development of electronic forms of communication, every medium was largely independent of every other medium. The spoken word, the written word, and printing each had special strengths and weaknesses, but translating information from one medium into another medium was typically a cumbersome process. Even as recently as two decades ago, print was something largely untouched by electronic forms of communication, broadcasting was distinct from cable television, and television differed from computerized communications. Each form of communication generally existed as a separate industry. The "seams" or boundaries separating these and other forms of communication from each other, in other words, appeared to be natural and were even recognized by law. As one of the foremost copyright scholars, Pamela Samuelson, has commented:

> Copyright law has traditionally treated different kinds of copyrighted works differently. Some kinds of works, for example, do not have the same sets of exclusive rights as do other works. Some special privileges to copy or make certain uses of copyrighted works are available to certain classes of copyrighted works, but not to others.
>
> While there are some historical and public policy reasons for making such distinctions among different classes of works, there are additional important reasons for these distinctions: They reflect differences in the media by which different works have traditionally been made available to the public, as well as the technologies by which the different media are created and the distribution channels by which different media are disseminated to their respective publics. Books, the quintessential work of the print media, are made by printing presses, bound, and sold largely in bookstores. Paintings, sculpture, and photography are quite different media from books, and tend to be produced and distributed in quite a different manner as well. Phonograph records and compact discs are mechanically impressed with encoded information which, when played on a machine, can bring musical performances into one's home. While motion pictures also require a machine to be revealed, they differ significantly as a medium from sound recordings. Yet, they are similar in that they are often broadcast by radio waves, yet another medium whose differences from the printed medium were chronicled by Marshall McLuhan, among others. The point here is that copyright has traditionally conceptualized each entity as being only what it is, and not another thing.[31]

As almost every form of communication becomes electronic, many of the boundaries between media are more difficult to see. What had traditionally been a system of different and distinct media is evolving toward a state of seamlessness and common overlapping qualities.[32] Indeed, when information is in electronic form, it becomes something much less identifiable with any particular medium. In the words of James Beniger: "[T]he progressive digitalization of mass media and telecommunications content begins to blur earlier distinctions between the communication of information and its processing (as implied by the term *compunications*), as well as between people and machines. Digitalization makes communication from persons to machines, between machines, and even from machines to persons as easy as it is between persons. Also blurred are the distinctions among information types: numbers, words, pictures, and sounds, and eventually tastes, odors, and possibly even sensations, all might one day be stored, processed, and communicated in the same digital form."[33]

There are, of course, many bottlenecks or seams remaining in our communications system. It is still not as easy to send electronic data from one person to another as it is to pick up the telephone and speak to that person. Sending data requires some configuration of the following: a computer, communications software, modem or link to a communications network, and the electronic address of the person one wishes to communicate with. In addition, it may be necessary to understand the form in which electronic information can be sent from one computer to another. These are major obstacles compared to picking up the telephone and dialing a number one has dialed many times before. Yet, they are minor obstacles compared to what confronted persons who wished to communicate electronically five years ago and who encountered a much longer and more intricate list of roadblocks and obstacles. For growing numbers of people today, sending data from one computer to another is a process that does occur routinely and, since communications software will remember names, addresses, and numbers, may even be simpler than calling someone on the telephone.

Law is a process in which, using a variety of media, information is moved continuously from place to place. Citizens provide lawyers with information. Lawyers prepare documents and file them in courts and with other agencies. Judges write opinions that are communicated to the profession and the public. Lawyers researching legal problems consult books, electronic sources, and other lawyers. The mass media distributes information about law to citizens. Citizens communicate with other citizens about law. Groups obtain and distribute information about law to members. All of this communication touches what law is and how it works. Indeed, these and other instances of communication constitute a considerable part of the process of law. As Marc Galanter wrote:

> [Law] usually works not by exercise of force but by information transfer, by communication of what's expected, what forbidden, what allowable, what are the consequences of acting in certain ways. That is, law entails information about what the rules are, how they are applied, with what costs, consequences, etc. For example, when we speak of deterrence, we are talking about the effect of information about what the law is and how it is administered. Similarly, when we describe "bargaining in the shadow of the law," we refer to regulation accomplished by the flow of information rather than directly by authoritative decision. Again, "legal socialization" is accomplished by the transmission of information. In a vast number of instances the application of law is, so to speak, self administered—people regulate their conduct (and judge the conduct of others) on the basis of their knowledge about legal standards, possibilities and constraints.[34]

In the past, some of this communication was in spoken form, some in written form, and some in print. Court opinions, administrative regulations, and law-related news typically were in print, whereas communication between lawyer and citizen was oral or in writing. Time, cost, and purpose dictated what medium would be used. Conversations, almost by definition, involved the spoken word. Memos and other documents not intended for wide distribution were written or typed. Print cost more than the written word and took more time to prepare. Distribution of printed materials relied on modes of transportation and was reserved for those situations in which large numbers of uniform copies were needed.

In the kind of communications environment just described, media choices generally were easy. Case reporters and scholarly journals were, quite understandably, in print. The preferred medium for transcripts of court proceedings or of depositions, however, would be writing.[35] Each medium had different economic costs associated with it, different time frames, different audiences, different expectations, and different assumptions.

With the advent of the new media, almost all information and all communication other than what is spoken to someone face to face will have existed, at some point, in electronic form. There may be questions about whether the final form will be electronic or paper, but it is clear that if not now, then in the near future, virtually all information will pass through an electronic phase. Electronic form is the ticket necessary to enter the highways of cyberspace; this functional prerequisite is becoming less and less of an obstacle since, even today, a high percentage of information has been, or is, in electronic form.

As the electronic form is used, the distinct media differences of the past begin to evaporate. A basic theme of this book is that the new technologies destroy many boundaries associated with the traditional media. This can create a feeling of disorientation among new users, as assumptions about something that has been "printed" are challenged and as familiar-looking objects have qualities different from the objects they resemble. Thus, "conversations" can now occur through e-mail and other modes that blur the line between the spoken and the written. Similarly, "documents" may appear on the screen in one form and come out of a printer in another. In a variety of ways, the ability of the electronic medium to mimic different forms allows it to be a supreme impersonator. This can be empowering and helpful as well as something that disorients and misleads.

Telephone Networks and Computer Networks

The key to gaining an initial understanding of computer networks is to focus on one of the most familiar communications devices, the

D.L.I.A.D.T.
Library

telephone. Telephones are found in 93 percent of the homes in the United States. By pressing or dialing seven numbers, one can call in one's local area. By adding three or four more numbers, an area code, one can call any place in this country. By adding a few more numbers, an international dialing code, one can call almost anywhere in the world. Until recently, when telephones became combined with answering machines, fax machines, and other devices, or became able to handle information in digital form, one never thought about consulting a manual to find out how to use the telephone. The "telephone book" was not a book about the telephone but, rather, a book of telephone numbers.[36] Using computer jargon, one might say that the telephone has had a user-friendly interface. More accurately, we should recognize that instruction in how to use the telephone occurs at an early age and that the telephone was historically an instrument with only a single capability.

Telephone communication occurs so quickly and so routinely that we rarely, if ever, consider the extraordinary path taken by the electronic signals as they leave the home or business and travel across town, country, or the globe. The route taken by a telephone call is worth focusing on, however, because it may be the best way to understand that the awesomeness of computerized communication arises both from the power of the highly visible machine sitting on a desk or lap and, even more, from the signal's successful navigation through an invisible and almost incalculable number of linked pieces.

Although cellular telephones and other forms of wireless communication are becoming more prevalent,[37] it is instructive to focus on the physical link that exists between most homes and offices and, indeed, between virtually every location where there is a telephone. It is often said that when one person dials another person and, after a ring or two, the phone is picked up, a "connection" is made. This is accurate in one sense, in that there is an electrical connection formed between the two parties and information begins to travel between the two end points. In another sense, however, all telephone owners are connected to each other at all times. There are, of course, large numbers of calls that bounce off satellites, but many telephone calls still pass along wires and cables and, therefore, anyone making a telephone call is connected not only with the person who answers the phone "on the other end" but with virtually all other persons possessing a telephone. Because of the seamless connections of the telephone network, we do not know the route taken by any single call or whether it traveled by wire or by satellite.

It is, if one stops for a moment to consider it, an enormously impressive achievement merely to have this physical link between millions, if not billions, of different places. Yet, this largely invisible network is the precondition for the communication of data and for the even more impressive technological feat of moving the data correctly from the sender to the intended receiver. In many respects, the actual telephone on a desk, no matter how many buttons or features it has, does not match the technical prowess of the network put in place to support it. The telephone may be the beginning and end point of a voice communication, but the delivery system in the middle—which controls not only how quickly a call is connected but whether it is connected to the right party—is a more impressive feat of engineering than is the device that exists at the end point. As Theodor Nelson, the developer of the Xanadu hypertext system, observed, "people are not surprised that they can reach somebody on the other side of the continent by telephone and yet the idea that they could draw these things from a massive [electronic] library seems very startling."[38]

Although the telephone and its network are remarkable, they also have some notable limitations. The telephone cannot fulfill, or at least cannot fulfill very effectively, many communications goals. For example, the telephone is largely a device for one person to communicate with one other person. Although conference calls are possible, and one could conceivably talk through a speakerphone to a group of persons, such arrangements are not the norm and usually require prior preparation to insure that a group of people are near the telephone at the same time. Telephones, whether for technological or economic reasons, are most commonly used as an individual-to-individual form of communication rather than as a mass or group medium[39] or as a medium for satisfying an institutional goal.[40]

The telephone is also an inefficient means for communicating large quantities of information. Although there have been many experiments involving teaching people from afar using television, video, audiotape, and computers, few, if any, attempts have been made to use the telephone for this purpose. The telephone has at least one virtue for distance learning, in that listeners gathered around a speakerphone would be able to ask questions of the speaker and get immediate feedback, yet even that does not compensate for the cumbersomeness of arranging for groups of persons to be within hearing distance of a telephone at the same time.

Finally, the telephone has no storage capabilities. One can, of course, use an answering machine or tape recorder to store messages or record conversations, but "[e]ven though telephone conversations can be recorded, organizing the recorded material for later retrieval is insuperably burdensome for large quantities of material."[41] Even if saving and retrieving messages became more efficient, the goal of most telephone calls is to hear and interact with a "live" voice. Thus the storage capabilities of telephones are less important than with some other media. It is often the voice accompaniment to the information, as much as the information itself, that makes the telephone call so special.

These limitations of the telephone should not detract from what the telephone does so well, which is allow a conversation in "real time" between people who are at a distance from each other. Nevertheless, focusing on these limitations provides one easy way to understand the power and attraction of computerized communication.

Even regular computer users today may consider a computer to resemble a variety of other objects in the home or office more than it does a telephone. A computer may seem like a piece of paper when text is on the screen, like a supercalculator when numbers are on the screen, like a painting canvas when an image-processing program is running, or like a filing cabinet when a database is operating. Until voices routinely come out of computers,[42] as they will in the near future,[43] it is understandably difficult to perceive the computer as having similarities to the telephone, or indeed as being the preferable instrument for communicating a message from one place to another.

What computers and telephones share is the ability to communicate information over a network at incredible speeds. When a judge asked a defendant in a celebrated case of breaking into computers to explain the term *hacking,* the defendant replied that "[h]acking is the modern art of telephoning."[44] Such a statement reflects the position of a person who sees the computer solely as a communications device, as a means for obtaining electronically stored information in any computer that is linked to other computers. Although the hacker may have an undeveloped moral sense, he sees more clearly than most that the computer and the telephone often occupy overlapping parts of cyberspace.

Yet, just as the computer has overlapping qualities with books and calculators but also possesses additional textual and numerical capabilities, the computer is both more and less than a telephone. One communicating today using a computer gives up some of the personal quality that comes from hearing the human voice on the telephone as well as from obtaining the immediate feedback that occurs as two people are connected at the same time. However, when a computer is connected to a telephone line or to some other electronic network, the user acquires capabilities that are not possible today when the human voice is sent over wires.

1. Computers can send messages to many people simultaneously. Whereas the telephone fosters one-to-one conversations, computers are equally adept at sending messages to one recipient or to many, to communicating with individuals or with groups of people. Until now, "[t]here has been no means for a group of people to adequately exchange information among themselves and reach decisions, other than to meet frequently face to face and talk it out."[45] Repeating a

message many times or sending many copies of a message to many different addresses, however, is a simple task for a computer. Those who are new to electronic communication are often surprised that not only do they have new capabilities for writing and composing but there are options for distribution that did not exist in the print era. The computer can even turn individuals and small groups into publishers in ways that were not possible before.[46]

2. With computerized communication, a person can, with equal ease, send both small and large amounts of information. Having a long conversation on the telephone obviously takes longer than does a short conversation. Electronic messages are sent at such high speeds that it may take virtually no more time to send a long message than a short one.

3. Computers can store increasingly large quantities of information and make possible very fast searches of these growing collections of data. The computer uses information in digital form, and this underlies all of the machine's powerful capabilities. On the other hand, the telephone is still largely an analog device. Although new methods of organizing and searching voice recordings are emerging, it is still much more cumbersome to store and use such material than digital material.

To some extent, these more flexible and powerful capabilities for storing, copying, reusing, and distributing some kinds of information are a consequence of great differences in how we traditionally have used and relied on print, writing, and the spoken word. Until the last century, it was not possible to store sounds. We have a fairly long experience, however, with storing print and writing. Sound in stored form, therefore, is part of the new environment, and this sound will be presented to us in fairly novel ways. Once sound is in digital form, it can be combined with other information in electronic form. As computers evolved, they acquired new capabilities for working with words. Further increases in power have provided graphical capabilities. The process of attaching sound to documents may appear unnecessary and strange, but this may simply reflect assumptions that are a result of our print tradition. There are no longer any technological reasons that electronic documents cannot have sound and text as easily as they have images and text.

4. Time and place are not as constraining with computerized communications. There is no requirement that the recipient of a message be in a particular place at a particular time when one sends a computerized message. Such messages are retrievable from any place at any time. Telephone messages frequently lose value when they are left in answering machines because the purpose of most telephone calls is not simply to leave a message but to interact and quickly exchange information. "Telephone tag," the game of leaving messages

on answering machines, is an irritating inconvenience with voice communication. For electronic communication, however, the asynchronous quality, where a message is read, considered, and responded to at some time after the message is sent, is a benefit. A recipient of an electronic message will have some time, at least, to reflect on the content of the message. Thus, what is annoying for voice communication is generally considered a virtue for electronic communication since electronic communications can be read at one's convenience. In addition, electronic communication rarely interrupts meetings or conversations as telephone calls do. Nevertheless, whenever there is a need for an instantaneous answer, the telephone may remain a more appropriate instrument than the computer.

Using labels and categories such as mail, publishing, or broadcasting can become frustrating with electronic communication because any information that is in digital form can become any one of these types merely by pressing a few buttons using appropriate software. It is often helpful to refer to the existing media for purposes of explanation, but it is also problematic to do so. As Henry Perritt wrote, "[t]hese technologies blur at their margins, and, with the advent of networks that handle information at varying levels of abstraction, sometimes become indistinguishable."[47]

Although both computers and telephones rely on a network to send and receive information around the globe, the additional power and flexibility of the computer will often make it the technology of choice over both the telephone and print. The computer will not replace the telephone, but it will displace it, in that the computer will be used for some purposes the telephone now satisfies as well as for many other purposes, such as publishing, that go far beyond the capabilities and use of the telephone.

Models of Communication

There has been extraordinary growth in computerized communications over the past few years. For example, in spite of mediocre software and a user-unfriendly environment, the number of networks linked to the Internet[48] increased from 217 in July 1988 to 14,121 in July 1993. Between July 1993 and September 1994, as the Internet received more publicity, software improved, and commercial possibilities became clearer, the number of networks more than doubled to 39,977. The number of packets sent has increased from 152 million in July 1988 to more than 23 billion in November 1992 to more than 72 billion in September 1994. The number of host computers linked to the Internet increased from 28,174 in December 1987 to 1,136,00 in October 1992 to 3,212,000 in July 1994.[49] The number of World-Wide

Web servers increased from about 500 in the fall of 1993 to almost 10,000 in the fall of 1994. It is estimated, as of the fall of 1994, that approximately 25 million persons have Internet access of some kind, either through universities, businesses, or commercial services such as CompuServe or America Online, or through some other arrangement.

These are astonishing indices of the growth of communication over networks, and the attraction of this form of communication might be clearer to nonusers if one compares the basic model of telephone communication with the several different models of distributing information electronically. The basic telephone model consists of a human calling another human. At its simplest, this model has two humans and two telephones (or two humans, two telephones, and an answering machine) linked together. In such a model, the human uses the first telephone to call the second telephone which is answered by either another human or the answering machine. The answering machine is basically a temporary storage area for messages, automatically answering the telephone and allowing the intended recipient to retrieve the message later.

Computer-mediated communication can occur in a similar manner. In the simplest use of the computer for communication, an individual uses the machine in a manner similar to a telephone, composing a message and sending it over the network to another computer, which stores it until a second human looks at the information. This type of communication is called electronic mail (e-mail) since it appears similar to sending a letter or message via the postal service. Because it is in electronic form, the message is easily stored, replied to, or forwarded to others. In the typical e-mail model, the receiving computer is like an answering machine in that it receives and stores messages until the recipient can look at them. The receiving computer differs from an answering machine in that the computer receives every call, whereas an answering machine is only an alternative receiver to a human.

Because of the ability to send the message over great distances almost instantaneously, it might have been just as appropriate to employ a term that emphasized a connection to the telephone as to suggest a link to the postal service. In the future, when sounds may be sent as part of an e-mail message, and when we become accustomed to hearing sounds emanating from the computer, this connection to the telephone will become more obvious and the mail analogy may appear anachronistic.

E-mail requires a computer with a modem or some other link to a computer network, and communications software. The software structures the electronic environment, dialing the telephone number or network connection of the computer where the recipient has an e-mail address, acknowledging electronic signals, and automatically handling other chores that are necessary to move signals over a network.[50] An e-mail address is the equivalent of a "mailbox" or place where messages are collected until they are looked at by the recipient. Most of the popular commercial services, such as CompuServe, Prodigy, or America Online, in addition to providing other services, provide users with electronic addresses. The addressee can have his or her personal computer dial the host computer and send the host an account number and a password to gain access, and the e-mail messages will then appear on the screen. These messages can be read, distributed to others, downloaded to the addressee's computer, or, if desired, printed on a printer.

Although e-mail's similarity with ordinary mail is often questionable for the one-to-one forms of electronic communication, it is even more inappropriate to use the term *e-mail* to designate a general category covering other forms of electronic communication. Once information is placed into electronic form, it can be communicated in ways not before possible. Some e-mail may have the tone of a letter or in-house memo, but some may not. More important, computer-based communication is different from both mail and the telephone because data in electronic form can be copied easily and distributed so much faster than information in any other medium. Thus, the simple e-mail model of electronic communication just described is only one of several new communication patterns among people and computers. The telephone model is fairly rigid and resistant to new uses, whereas the computer is both more powerful and more flexible.

There are already in large-scale use several important models for electronic distribution and publishing of information that go far beyond the e-mail model.

Model One (e-mail to multiple parties). Figure 1 represents one person using a computer to send the same message to several persons. This involves little extra work for the sender and minimal extra demand on the computer's resources. Such capability for broadcasting or distributing messages is a common feature of communications software used for e-mail. The sender of a message merely creates a list of electronic addresses. The software then automatically does all the "labeling," "addressing," and distribution.

This model moves computerized communication closer to writing or print since it is similar to typing the notation "cc:" at the bottom of a memo or letter, sending copies to a list of people, or using mail-merge features of a word processor to send the same letter to many different persons. When done electronically, however, copying and sending is much easier than when the same task is done with a letter or memo. Most e-mail software allows an individual to use a distribu-

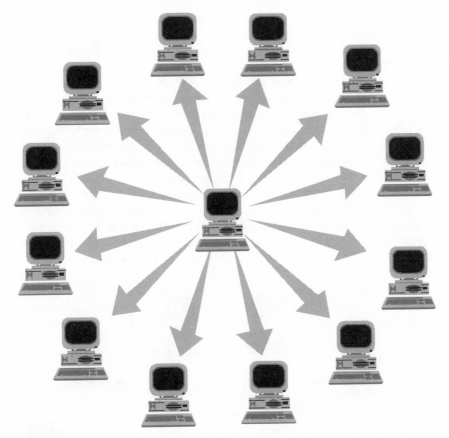

Figure 1

tion list with many names and addresses; sending a message to all of these persons is as easy as sending a message to one person.

Model Two (groups). Figure 2 represents a second model which further expands the ability of one individual to reach a potentially large audience. Whereas the first model was a one-to-many model, the second model is a many-to-many model. In this model, an individual composes a message and sends it to a special electronic address at some computer connected to the network. The computer where this address is located has a list of addressees to which it forwards a copy of any message sent to it. This computer does not originate messages, but forwards any message sent by anyone on the distribution list to all others on the list. Such an arrangement means that anyone who sends a message to the central computer will have the message copied and distributed to the whole distribution list. This model tends to foster a much more active flow of information than the first model since every sender of a message is, in effect, publishing the message to all those on the distribution list and each reply to a message is forwarded to the whole list.

With this model, senders of messages may not even know how large the distribution list is or who is on it since all an individual has to do is send one message to one electronic address. One can distribute a message broadly without preparing a distribution list of one's own. Being able to send a message to the central computer is like having access to a mailing list without having to print copies of the mailing, without having to affix mailing labels, and without having to take the material to the post office. Thousands of subject-oriented groups are currently using this model on the Internet.[51]

Our language is struggling to find an appropriate term for this process that turns computerized communication into a medium resembling mass communication. There seems, on the surface at least, to be a basic similarity between this model and print; in both, one

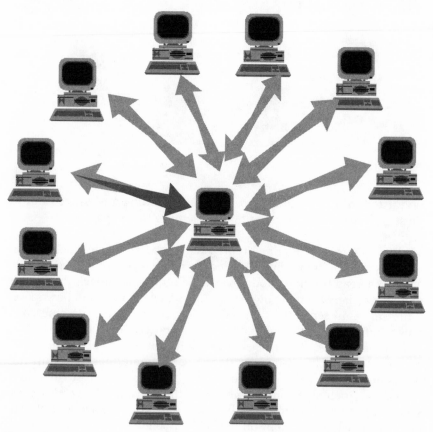

Figure 2

machine makes a lot of copies of a message and distributes them. There are, however, notable differences from print. There are, for example, different economies of scale for this model of electronic communication. With print, per-copy costs decrease as press runs increase. With electronic distribution, this may not occur and it may be no more cumbersome and may take little more time for the central computer to send the message to 5,000 persons than to send it to 5 or 500.

The difficulty in choosing a widely acceptable term or phrase for such communication is also partly a consequence of the fact that the model is so much more flexible than writing or print and, therefore, can resemble more than one familiar form of communication. For example, the model supports small groups as well as entities with many members. When the central computer is forwarding messages among five or six persons, the pattern of discussion can resemble an extended luncheon conversation. When twenty or thirty persons are circulating messages, the model might be thought of as a small conference. When larger numbers of recipients are involved, there are analogies to newsletters, journals, or newspapers. As this indicates, the model operates in a wide variety of forums, some of which have print antecedents and some of which do not.

It is often stated that the computer can turn anyone into a publisher. Such a statement usually refers to the capability, provided by word processors and desktop publishing software, to create documents and newsletters with sophisticated designs and typefaces. Thus, the statement suggests that everyone can become a publisher because it no longer costs a great deal to create a printed "look." Using desktop publishing software, small groups can create documents that appear to be typeset. An electronic network, however, turns everyone into a publisher in a different and more meaningful way. The network provides the facilities for individuals to distribute their messages efficiently and cheaply, both widely and narrowly, to large groups as well as small. Using today's technology, the message sent from another computer actually may not have the "look" of print when it appears on the screen, but it may have been distributed to hundreds, if not thousands. Such widespread distribution is possible because the process is much faster and much more flexible than that used for distributing the printed word.

Figure 2 clearly represents a publishing model of electronic communication in that it makes it possible for an individual or group to share and distribute ideas and information widely to other individuals and groups. It is not, however, a publishing model with all of the same components as print publishing. For example, although the central computer that forwards messages can be an effective distributor, there may be no editor, since the machine may be programmed to distribute every message sent to it. Indeed, the value that is added to information in typical print publishing may differ considerably from the value that is added currently in electronic publishing.[52]

For print, there is a principal or paradigmatic publishing model; an author provides a publisher with a work and, after editing, the publisher sells the work to as many purchasers as possible. The economics of print are fairly straightforward, at least compared to the model of electronic publishing, because the publisher knows how many copies must be sold for the work and the firm to be profitable. Electronic publishing is still developing, but it appears clear that there will be many different models, some of which are quite different from the main print model. In general, distribution options increase because of both the ease of copying and the speed with which such information can be transmitted over a network. This is particularly true for distribution patterns that are diffuse and decentralized, such as in Figure 2, where individual recipients of electronic information frequently copy the information and begin a new distribution process by forwarding it to others or by sending it to another computer with a different distribution list.

As is described in the next section, the electronic publisher may distribute nothing, instead providing access to a single copy that, because of the computer's capability for making exact copies, is brought over the network from the large computer to someone's personal computer. The image on the screen is not the original but a copy. Copies multiply as they are read, and multiply even more if they are circulated by the reader to others. One writer has recognized that "[a]ll digital machines copy in order to communicate. They are essentially repeaters, able to regenerate perfect copies with abandon."[53] The language that is often used in reference to computerized communication, therefore, can be misleading since it may fail to take the copying-communications process into account. For example, to say that a file is sent from one computer to another is not accurate since it is always a copy of a file that is transmitted and not the original. The fact that communication necessitates copying and that powerful tools exist for working with and altering copies in digitized form is both a catalyst to creative work and, as will be explained later, a source of the problems facing contemporary copyright law.[54]

Electronic distribution affects formats as well as distribution patterns. As a result of the typically cumbersome and expensive methods used to distribute print publications, periodicals are divided into issues and a certain number of issues are printed each year. This also makes later access easier when a yearly index is prepared. However, although bundling a publication into issues and volumes seems natural, it is really a consequence of the influence of the print environment. Journals in electronic form, for example, can distribute articles as soon as they receive editorial approval. Similarly, indexes may not be needed as searching techniques improve, and page numbers need not be assigned if the information will remain in electronic form. In summary, the electronic environment not only changes the tools used for distribution but changes assumptions about material that is distributed and allows for new models in presenting information. Many of the arrangements for and assumptions about adding value to information will break apart as information and publishing are electronified. Some types of electronic bundling of information and some methods of bundling electronic information will look like their print ancestors and some will not.

Model Three (online services). Figure 3 portrays many computer users individually communicating with another computer, and obtaining information from that machine. Unlike some of the previous models, computer users in this model do not use the large computer to communicate directly, or share information, with other users. Compared with the model represented in Figure 2, whoever operates the central computer may exercise considerably more control over communication. Examples of this model are large commercial databases, such as LEXIS/NEXIS, WESTLAW, DIALOG, online library catalogs, and other electronic information services. Internet Gopher and World-Wide Web sites operate somewhat differently but could also conceivably limit or restrict access.[55]

The model represented in Figure 3 has been, thus far, the most economically viable model of network publishing. The main reason for this is that it contains a point of access that can be controlled, allowing charges to be levied before access is granted.

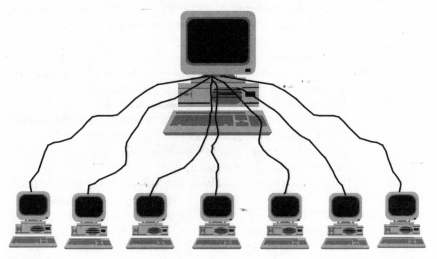

Figure 3

Once machines are linked together, users may obtain information from a distant machine without actually being aware of where the information is coming from. Because information in electronic form can travel so quickly between computers, users can think that they are connected to one computer when, in fact, they have been routed to some other computer. Selecting from a menu, a user can also shift quickly from one computer to another. For example, a person wishing information that is available through the DIALOG database can dial DIALOG directly and obtain the information or, if he or she has access to WESTLAW, can access DIALOG databases by selecting them from the WESTLAW directory menu. Users of the Internet have access to files on thousands of different computers through Gopher[56] or the World-Wide Web,[57] software that allows users with no technical knowledge to access information distributed around the world.

Such systems come quite close to seamlessly linking computers. Users of Gopher or the World-Wide Web typically obtain information from distant machines without being aware of where the information they are looking at has been stored. It is worth recognizing that the Internet is built upon an assumption of seamless communication. The Internet is not itself a network but a collection of more than 30,000 networks that are linked to each other and can share information with each other because of agreements about how information will be transmitted. The seamlessness is evident from the fact that many frequently assume that they are "connected to the Internet" even though what is occurring is that one is connected to a network that has links to other networks, all of which together make up the Internet. What is shared is not a single network but a set of communications protocols that may make it seem that there is only one network.

A familiar nonlegal example of virtually seamless communication among computers is the use of a banking card to obtain money from an automatic teller machine located outside of a bank's local area. This transaction takes place almost as quickly in a remote location as it does when the transaction is made using the bank's own teller machine, even though there is complex interaction and communication among computers that may be thousands of miles apart. It is an activity that, for most persons, is as easy as making a telephone call. This transaction is a function of efficient networking among financial institutions and suggests that other, nonfinancial information might eventually be accessed routinely as well.

We are not yet at a point where other information transactions are as simple to complete as ATM transactions, and, indeed, most individuals would be fairly satisfied if they were simply able to dial a single computer, access it, and retrieve information from it in an easy and routine matter. Although this is a difficult chore for many, increasing numbers of persons feel quite comfortable today jumping from one remote computer to another and obtaining information using what is an electronic version of "interlibrary loan." In print libraries, interlibrary loan allows access to materials held in another library. The links between sources of information on a computer network allow not only borrowing from a second library but a feeling of presence in the second library—located at some distance to the first— where one can browse and retrieve needed information.

The above models do not cover every form of electronic communication. Experimentation with hybrids and combinations—the continuing expansion of electronic networks, combined with the flexibility of information in electronic form—will inevitably encourage both experiments and entrepreneurs. I have not discussed the closest parallel to print publishing, the distribution and sale of disks and CD-ROMs. Although information on disk can be employed, copied, and processed as effectively as information obtained over the network, the electronic network can be used to connect to other networks, providing individuals with opportunities to distribute information in ways not possible with disks and CD-ROMs.

Many readers may be familiar with one or more of the models just described. All law school students learn how to retrieve data from LEXIS or WESTLAW (Figure 3). Many law firms and businesses have local area networks (LANs) that connect computers in the firm and allow attorneys to send e-mail and other information to each other in electronic form. Some individuals may subscribe to CompuServe or Prodigy or some other service that provides them with both an electronic address and access to a large database of information. Academics are increasingly familiar with the Internet, which also supports all of the models identified.

Communication using computers can only increase as software becomes easier to use and automates many tasks, as screens become able to show clearer images, as faster networks are employed in lieu of telephone lines, and as computer users become more knowledgeable about using electronic data and see the benefits of obtaining data in electronic rather than printed form. All of these developments exert pressure on the law because of changes in the flow of, and ability to control, information. If law is a method of dealing with information, of structuring and organizing it, of storing it, of evaluating it, of regulating access to it, and of communicating it to the public, then a more powerful and efficient network, which touches all of these functions, makes it less and less likely that past practices will provide the basis for future practices and that modes of organization that were successful in the past will continue to be successful in the future.

The next chapter describes, in a more generic way, two perspectives on space that can provide understanding of why change occurs as new information technologies are employed. The first concerns physical or geographical distance, which, quite evidently, becomes not as great a constraint in obtaining information or in developing new working relationships as it was in the past. The second focuses on informational distance, a concept that allows us to understand why some information is hard to obtain or use even though we may be physically close to it.

2

Electronic Information Places

If the dull substance of my flesh were thought,
Injurious distance should not stop my way;
For then, despite of space, I would be brought,
From limits far remote, where thou dost stay.
No matter then although my foot did stand
Upon the farthest earth removed from thee;
For nimble thought can jump both sea and land,
As soon as think the place where he would be.

—William Shakespeare

In 1987, scientist Peter Denning wrote:

Computer networks that nurture networks of people are the culmination of a process of evolution that can be said to have five stages: (1) file transfer, (2) remote connections, (3) distributed computation, (4) real-time collaboration, and (5) coherent function. At the first stage, a network is able to transfer files of information among computers, but without guaranteeing delivery time; this stage is sufficient to support electronic mail, bulletin boards, news services and jointly authored papers. At the second stage, the network enables a user to connect to remote resources, such as instruments, computers, or databases, and employ them in real time as if they were local. At the third stage, the network is able to support distributed computations that include computing processes and resources at widely separated nodes; an example is a user interface process on a workstation, connected to a numerical process on a supercomputer, connected in turn to a graphics display system. At the fourth stage, the network directly supports collaboration by permitting real-time conferences of users at different workstations, who can communicate as

49

if they were gathered around one workstation—that is they can tap into a "common universe" in which they can talk, point to and share objects, edit and run programs, and examine outputs. At the fifth stage, the network is a coherent system comprising people and the resources contributed by them; each person can look in at this world from his workstation. The network will provide services to help people locate, use and contribute resources, and to translate between the terminologies of the disciplines.[1]

We are, at present, still some distance away from an easy-to-use, flexible, widely accessible, and broadly used network of electronic communication. Most of Denning's stages have been realized, but only for the relative few. The Internet is a structure that is habitable but not as hospitable as it ultimately will be. Network-based information places may one day be as efficiently used and as accessible as ATMs (perhaps even accessible *from* ATMs), but the Internet is not yet such a place. Yet, it has experienced extraordinary growth in spite of some user unfriendliness and other limitations. In the near future, hardware that currently is considered to be state of the art will become commonplace and will process and move data faster on equipment that uses graphical screens and other user-friendly devices. In addition, software written to take advantage of this hardware will be smarter and will better understand areas of difficulty for users. This will eliminate a variety of current bottlenecks and make acquiring and transmitting data considerably easier than it now is. Increasing amounts of information will be available only in electronic form, and this will certainly enlarge the market of electronic communicators. As a result, growing electronic links between persons and persons, persons and computers, and computers and computers may be the most significant development of the next stage of the computer era.

Denning's perspective is useful because he recognizes that the new technologies provide users with a space as well as a delivery system. Computer networks are not simply data networks and they are not merely a set of "channels" added to our existing information systems. They are people linkers and group creators. Libraries provide access to information and link people with information. The spoken word links people with people. Computer networks efficiently link people with other people as well as with information sources. This is a fact that underlies many of the changes being brought about by the new media. Computer networks can foster new relationships with information, as might occur in a library, but they can also foster new relationships among people, groups, and institutions, as might occur in some other setting.

The following section describes two perspectives on space that can provide understanding of why change occurs as new information technologies are employed. The first concerns physical or geographical distance, which, quite evidently, becomes not as great a constraint in obtaining information or in developing new working relationships as it was in the past. The second focuses on informational distance, a concept that allows us to understand how every medium requires different skills of users and why some information is hard to obtain or use even though we may be physically close to it. Each medium creates its own form of informational distance that affects who uses information and in what manner.

It is reasonable to expect that by the end of the decade, large numbers of persons who will have a desire to transfer or obtain data from some point thousands of miles away will be as comfortable doing so as they are calling another person on the telephone. New tools will be available to assist in extracting information efficiently and easily from remote databases and other electronic sources of information and that will make today's tools seem primitive. For many individuals, the network has already become the medium of choice for sending and receiving data from colleagues and associates. Although the preferred nonvoice technology today may be the fax machine, which is far easier to use although less flexible than computer-based communication,[2] by the end of the century the computer will be recognized as a desirable means for sharing and communicating information. People will understand that communication in this manner opens up opportunities not available with mail, the telephone, fax, or, most importantly, many traditional forms of print.

There has been a great deal of attention focused on the "national information infrastructure," a set of networks that, it is hoped, will carry data more quickly, more efficiently, more securely, and more reliably than telephone lines. This is an enormously important and challenging undertaking, one that is currently ongoing and is involving government much more directly than it has been involved in most recent computer-related developments. Many details of governmental involvement in the new electronic networks are still not clear, but in 1991 Congress passed the High-Performance Computing Act, authorizing the development of the NREN, the National Research and Education Network.[3] Encouragement of high-speed communications has been a high priority of the Clinton administration since it took office. It is not unreasonable to expect that, over several years, data transmission speeds on fast networks will increase from 45 megabits (45 million bits per second) to 1 gigabit (1 billion bits per second). With such an increase, approximately 30,000 pages can be transferred in a brief moment, rather than 50 single-spaced pages.

The speed with which data can be accessed or transmitted does not necessarily create an effective or coherent information place. For users, entrance to and exit from an electronic information place is through the computer monitor one stares at and, as will be described later, slower progress is being made in how information is presented on screen than in how it is transmitted. The technology, in other words, has conquered physical distance quite impressively. Once one finds that the information he or she is seeking exists somewhere in electronic form, it is not very difficult to view it and obtain it very quickly, if not instantaneously. There is a different kind of distance, however—what might be labeled informational distance—that also interferes with efficient exchanges of information. One can be physically close to some information or have the means to obtain it even if one is physically distant from it. Yet, if the information is in a language one does not understand, or its presentation is unnecessarily ambiguous, the information will not be found or it will not be of value since it will not be understood.

Informational distance remains a considerable challenge. The ability to conquer physical distance is quite important and the negation of physical distance may account for the astonishing growth of the Internet. E-mail has become popular because this is such an attractive method for exchanging information quickly over great distances that individuals have been willing to learn the skills that are necessary for overcoming informational distance. The Internet, at least when one uses tools such as Gopher or more graphically oriented software tools such as Mosaic, Cello, or Netscape, does reduce the informational distance problem. Cyberspace, however, given its inherent malleability, can be a much warmer place than it is. We will, at some point, have such an electronic information place that is not disorienting to enter, where fewer technical skills will be needed than are needed today and where information that is presented on the screen will have more value and meaning. Today, however, the emphasis is on speed, on the quantity of information accessible, rather than on the quality of the information experience.

During the summer of 1992, I participated in the Electronic Conference on the Influence of E-Mail on the Legal Profession.[4] Due mostly to the initiative of Trotter Hardy of the College of William and Mary School of Law, and David Johnson, an attorney with the Washington, D.C., firm of Wilmer, Cutler and Pickering, fifteen attorneys, professors, and law librarians discussed, over a three-week period, the implications of using electronic mail in law practice. All communication among the participants took place electronically. Participants sent comments to a computer at the College of William and Mary. This computer in turn forwarded these messages to every other participant. Most academic participants had e-mail addresses on the Internet and others received their e-mail through private services such as MCIMAIL or CompuServe.

At the time of the conference, the participants were unsure of the impact e-mail would have on the profession. All of the practitioner participants used e-mail, but they were at the electronic vanguard of the profession. The most obvious benefit to the practitioners was that e-mail allowed communication and sharing of information internally with other members of his or her firm. Additionally, some attorneys used e-mail to communicate with clients and others.

The underlying concern of practicing lawyers "attending" this e-mail conference was how e-mail might be employed to save time. This is the attraction and main value of computers generally for lawyers, since greater efficiency and increased output in a shorter period of time often results in direct economic benefits. There is no expression that is understood as clearly as "time is money," and computer use, therefore, will continue to increase among lawyers as long as the machines are perceived to reduce the first part of the "time is money" equation or increase the second.

Ingenious attorneys will undoubtedly translate the ability to exchange information at incredible speeds into income-producing opportunities. Efficient networks, in this sense, can be viewed as simply reinforcing and adding to the capabilities of stand-alone computers, which automate tasks and increase the speed with they can be accomplished. Time savings and claims for efficiencies and economies thus provide the basic incentive, rationale, and justification for investing in new technology.[5]

As is true of almost any technology, unintended and unanticipated effects and consequences are inevitable. A central theme of this book is that change occurs not only because time is less of a constraint but because space and distance are no longer obstacles to performing many informational tasks. The societal and institutional effects of the new media seem to be less clear and less widely understood for communications technologies, however, than for some other technologies. Nuclear power, for example, not only provides individuals with energy but may have health or ecological consequences. Automobiles not only provide transportation but have affected the environment, urban economics, and family life. In each of these cases, not every implication of using the technology may be fully understood, but the technology is broadly recognized as doing more than simply satisfying society's demand for cheaper energy or a more flexible mode of transportation. With new communications technologies, unfortunately, the social impact is harder to measure and is much less obvious. Yet, as Langdon Winner has pointed out, "every thorough-going history of the building of technological systems points to the same conclusion: Substantial technical innovations involve a reweaving of the fabric of society—a reshaping of some of the roles, rules, relationships, and institutions that make up our ways of living together. . . . For as you build infrastructure . . . different patterns of association and activity take shape around those systems. The technology is never the sole cause of the changes one sees. But it is often the occasion and catalyst for a thorough redefinition of the operating structures of society and of the daily experiences of people in their work, family life, and communities."[6]

The view that computers can satisfy needs more quickly and efficiently and yet not change the people or institutions that use the technology is not very realistic. An individual user's needs may be satisfied in a more economical manner, but, as information begins to be used in new ways, computer-based communication will also cause important changes in institutions. In other words, at the same time that individuals and firms are trying to ascertain whether they are accruing any economic benefits from their investments in technology, other kinds of dividends or effects can be occurring to the institution or to the public. The key reason for this is not that new forms of access to information allow users to do things more quickly or more conveniently but that they do them differently than before. Speed and convenience may be the attraction for new computer users and the justification for purchasing hardware and software, but most users at some point find themselves using information differently, possessing information that they would not have had previously, asking questions they might not have asked previously, and working with people they might not have had contact with before. As Peter Martin has recognized, "[i]nevitable changes in methods of information distribution and scholarly communication are likely to threaten not only the ways of working (which we find so comforting and take so much for granted that we identify them with work itself), but also important values that we see, quite rightly, as embodied in institutional structures that rest precariously on obsolete technology."[7]

As a greater variety of information becomes available to us without our going anywhere for it, new opportunities and ways to use information arise that were not previously available.[8] Individual expectations change as new abilities to acquire, process, and distribute information appear. Even more important, pressure for social and institutional change builds. The library or other source of information is brought closer; some groups or individuals may now have access to some information for the first time.[9] These kinds of changes are not always easy to discern or to gauge since the first steps and experiments in using electronic information may be quite tentative.

To understand how and why law and the legal profession are changing, it is necessary to recognize that the changes that are occurring inevitably will go beyond more efficient management of time. Even if lawyers are able to extract large economic benefits from the technology by being able to do more in less time, other significant changes in law can be expected to be occurring, albeit out of general

view and without much awareness. Speed and time savings may be
the driving forces behind the growth of electronic communication in
law, as elsewhere, but the keys to understanding any structural
changes that may be occurring lie along a different dimension, that of
space and distance.

In this regard, even though no breakthroughs were announced or
even novel uses of e-mail described, the electronic e-mail conference
was an intriguing experiment. What was highlighted was not the message and *what* was said, but the medium and *how* things were said.
The technology allowed a participant to feel as if he or she were
attending a conference—a novel and revealing experience. The participants engaged in an active give and take with a rather high level of
interaction. It seemed to me, at least, to be as easy to send a message,
to "say" something and to have it heard by all the participants, as it is
to say something while seated around a conference table in a seminar
room. Indeed, in some respects it was easier, since one did not have to
worry about interrupting someone else or of speaking out of turn. It
also may have been more fruitful; this electronic "conference center"
allowed the participants to be more reflective than would have been
the case in a face-to-face conference.

The experiment suggested that networks would become an agent
of change not because tasks could be completed more quickly, but
because new opportunities would be opened up as constraints related
to space and distance were eliminated. The institutional and social
impact of such electronic communication becomes more comprehen-
sible by focusing on relationships between people and between institutions that, because of spatial constraints, could not have existed in a
print culture. Electronic communication does, of course, compress
time, but what is most important or influential is that it also com-
presses space and, at times, creates new virtual spaces.

Obtaining information from a database or sending a message to a
colleague across the country requires less time using electronic means
than traditional means. Corporations that own databases or provide
e-mail services are able to charge substantial fees that they then justify on the basis of such time savings. Additionally, most software
aimed at the legal market promises a like gain in efficiency. The more
significant and influential part of electronic communication, however,
from an institutional and long-term perspective, and one that should
be looked at apart from any capability for reorienting time, is that all
of our assumptions about space are being turned upside down. We
can, or will be able to, use information without being in the same
physical place as the information. We can also form relationships
with people in ways that were not possible when we were located in
different places and were not electronically linked.

Instead of asking how much time the new media can save, the

questions those interested in the law should be asking are what kinds of law-related interactions are becoming possible in this new electronic space and how are interactions with information being changed. Every traditional source of legal information, from the colleague down the hall to the collection in the law library, is touched in some way and will need to be explored as "cyberspace supplants physical space."[10] As already noted, spatial constraints are being relaxed—but there are different kinds of spatial constraints. More specifically, there are constraints involving relationships with people and constraints involving relationships with information. The law library, and the books in the law library, are central symbols of the law's concern with information during the past 500 years. The new media represent the equivalent of an earthquake hitting the library, not because the electronic library may replace the physical library but because the role of the library, whether it is electronic or print, is shifting as information becomes accessible from new sources. This, of course, affects not only the law library and legal professionals, but citizens whose distance from the law is shifting as well.

The time-saving features of computers may only provide an illusion that legal traditions and practices are being handled more efficiently and that they are being strengthened.[11] As it fosters new relationships between both people and information, cyberspace is likely to fuel a broad spectrum of change. The following analysis, therefore, provides a spatial equivalent to a "time frame," a perspective for seeing why new uses of space are pushing the law in new directions. Pressure for change occurs each time that an electronic message is used in place of some other kind of message or, even more important, each time that an electronic message is sent when one would not have been sent previously. Both the individual's and the profession's orientation toward space and distance, toward legal institutions and legal information, is reoriented in some way. At some point the cumulative effect of this will become quite apparent, as will changes in who the lawyer is and what law is.

The process of change that will occur as spatial constraints affecting the structure, organization, and practice of law are relaxed is not something that can easily be measured or monitored. It requires us to look at law not simply as a set of rules or as a group of persons who provide a service, but as an institution that can be understood in spatial terms and as an institution that has, over time, adjusted to traditional spatial constraints in a variety of ways. It requires us to look not at the reasons that lawyers or legal institutions are adopting some technology but at what actually happens to the individual and the institution when the technology is used. One should focus attention, in other words, not simply on whether the needs of the purchasers or users have been met, since that may only reveal changes in the "bottom line" and whether or not the technology will continue to be used, but whether the purchaser's behavior changes, whether new relationships are formed, whether there is access to and use of new and different kinds of information, and whether patterns of interaction change.

The kind of spatial focus that provides a foundation for understanding future changes in law has two elements, one that concerns actual physical distances and one that considers a different kind of distance—one relating to access, use, and presentation of information and how these activities are affected by the nature of the medium of communication being employed. The following sections briefly discuss constraints of physical distance and informational distance that are inherent in a print culture. This discussion provides the background for a consideration of the kinds of changes that are likely as law feels the effects of a process of information acquisition and distribution that is considerably different from what currently exists.

Physical Distance

For those using a computer that is linked to a network of some kind, it is no longer always necessary to go somewhere to obtain information or work with someone. As Michael Benedikt has observed, it is now possible to "wander the earth and never leave home."[12] This is hyperbole, of course, but it is true that distance is much less an impediment to the formation and maintenance of personal and business relationships than it was in the past, and it is virtually no obstacle at all to the acquisition of information. The new media allow one to interact with persons in ways that were not possible when distance prevented the formation of a working relationship. Electronic communication still does not allow a user to literally "reach out and touch someone," as the telephone company has advertised, but it does allow relationships to form that were not possible before when distance prevented, or sharply limited, the sharing and communicating of information. As the spatial barriers to information flow fall, it becomes possible to reach out and work with someone or provide a service to and interact with others. There is a potential impact on any person or institution for whom the distribution, selling, or processing of information is part of some relationship. Such activities no longer take place in the same context they did previously because people can interact with others in new ways. It may be debatable whether highly personal relationships can be established at a distance,[13] but it should not be difficult to recognize that many new and different kinds of business and legal relationships will occur because of the new capabilities to communicate.[14]

The new media not only connect people with other people who

are located at a distance, but they connect people with distant information. For example, over the Internet, one can obtain information from any one of thousands of computers around the world that are linked to it. With portable computers and wireless machines, such sources of information eventually will be available from airplanes or from the tops of mountains. Such capabilities change not only our ability to obtain information but how we think about or speak about many sources of information. For example, we may eventually stop distinguishing between having access to electronic information and simply having the information. We will refer to physically distant electronic information in the same way we now refer to material that is on a shelf in our home, in a book in the library, or in a file on our office computer. Indeed, in some contexts, particularly when one needs up-to-date information, access will be preferable to ownership.

Libraries are being particularly challenged by such changes since the accrediting agencies of libraries often take into account the "holdings" of libraries. It is relatively easy to count the number of books in a library, but figuring out what one is "holding" when one has access to electronic materials is becoming a problem. Current guidelines of the American Association of Law Libraries and the American Bar Association, for example, prohibit counting materials that do not appear as separate items in the library catalogue. This prohibits a library from including in its holdings all the files on WESTLAW or LEXIS that are accessible from its computers, although some libraries have attempted to do so. This may or may not seem reasonable, but this is the type of restriction that inevitably will be modified. Such a restriction constitutes a preference for information in one form over another, something that may at times be appropriate. However, it also limits innovative attempts to use the new technologies to expand access to information and it ignores the changing value of access and ownership.

As distance becomes less of an obstacle to both dealing with people and dealing with information, change will occur not only in our traditional sources of authoritative information—books—but in how we think about these sources. One computer executive has argued that "[t]he information age will not be here until you can access the Library of Congress from your desk."[15] The Library of Congress is, indeed, already making some parts of its collection available electronically,[16] but we are moving in the direction of having available from one's desk a source of information that is much more diffuse, scattered, and potentially larger than what exists in the Library of Congress. In a print world, it matters that the Library of Congress is in one place and that other sources of information, however useful they might be, are in many different places. In an electronic world, the physical location of information is an obstacle that can be overcome and, indeed, the miracle for the user is that dispersed information can, when it is seen on screen, appear to be in one place. If one thinks of cyberspace as a place, of course, the information is in fact in one place.

Those who previously had the ability to restrict access to certain information by controlling physical places, or benefited in some way from the fact that people and the information they needed were in different places or that information was available only in a distant place, find themselves vulnerable to change. Both working relationships and informational relationships can be expected to change as spatial barriers that limited communication between individuals, between practitioners and teachers, between lawyers and clients, between courts and lawyers, and between citizens and the government begin to fall.

Informational Distance

As just noted, the new media allow new kinds of interactions between people separated by distance and also allow information to be acquired and distributed in new ways. It is much less clear, however, how the new technologies touch information and people who are separated by a different kind of distance. Communications theorist Joshua Meyrowitz has pointed out that people can be physically close to some information and yet not have access to it.[17] In such instances, information is not under lock and key, but it is in a form that is difficult to retrieve, use, or understand. Such information is encoded not by sophisticated cryptographic methods but by the use of professional languages or by the use of some medium that requires special skills that only a few may possess.

Informational distance refers to how inaccessible a medium makes information. The medium may be difficult to use or the information may be presented in a difficult-to-understand format. Consequently, some information may be less accessible than other information, not because it is far away or because it is conceptually complex but because of inherent qualities of the medium in which it is organized and stored. For example, Meyrowitz notes, "any writing system is more selective and exclusive than spoken language."[18] Further, he argues:

> Throughout history, the vessels in which ideas have been stored have come to be seen as the shape of knowledge itself. Yet to understand the impact of new media, we need to be able to distinguish between the inherent complexity of specific ideas and processes and the superimposed complexity of the means through which we encode and describe them. It is conceivable, for example, that if the only way people learned to tie their shoelaces was through descriptions in print, tying shoelaces might be viewed as a skill that was "naturally" restricted to the highly educated.[19]

Law is, of course, inherently more complex than tying shoelaces. As will be explained soon, access to and use of legal information, or at least some kinds of legal information, may be difficult not simply because of its complexity but because of the skills necessary to find and use the information in printed form—because of complexity of form, not because of complexity of content.

Because media may create barriers to information flow that are as significant and as impenetrable as physical barriers, in any discussion of the effects of communications technology it is necessary to be aware of how different media change modes of access to, and use of, information. Meyrowitz points out that "media, like physical places, include and exclude participants. Media, like walls and windows, can hide and they can reveal. Media can create a sense of sharing and belonging or a feeling of exclusion and isolation."[20] For this reason, he suggests that

> physical settings and media "settings" are part of a continuum rather than a dichotomy. Places and media both foster set patterns of interactions among people, set patterns of social information flow.
>
> Thus, while places create one type of information-system—the live encounter—there are many other types of situations created by other channels of communication. This wider view of situations as information-systems, rather than as places, is especially relevant to the study of electronic media because electronic media have tended to diminish the differences between live and mediated interaction. The speech and appearance of others are now accessible without being in the same physical location. The widespread use of electronic media leads to many new social situations.[21]

For those using electronic networks, it has become clear that the distance between people has been narrowed much more quickly than the distance between people and sources of information. For those seeking an answer to some problem, e-mail or an electronic list of the kind described in chapter 1 have become a primary information source. Electronic lists allow people to ask their question to hundreds, perhaps thousands, of persons. In this process, one uses the most valuable informational source on the network, the accumulated knowledge of the people connected to it. One can do so as if he or she were having a conversation with thousands of knowledgeable individuals, and the question can be rephrased or followed up if the answers are not specific enough.

Electronic information sources such as LEXIS and WESTLAW contain enormous quantities of information. In the future, however, they will be competing not simply with print libraries but with people networks. To compete successfully, such services will have to realize that they are not simply "electronic libraries" competing with print libraries but are information sources competing with a wide range of other electronically based information sources, whether they be people or machines.

Informational distances and media settings are particularly relevant to the study of professions because a professional, by definition, controls a body of knowledge. When access to information requires special skills and informational distances become greater, institutional roles become more distinct and professional authority grows.[22] Conversely, professional authority tends to decline when informational distances are smaller. The status and authority of law and lawyers, therefore, are related not simply to what they do but to what they know, and to how distinct the information they possess and control is from generally accessible information.[23] It is related, for example, not only to the physical separation of law libraries from other libraries but to the distance created by legal language, by digests, by key numbers, and by other tools of access to the storehouse of legal information. As new links to legal information develop, change will occur that affects the law but that is largely unrelated to the content of the information. The role, authority, and domain of the lawyer become vulnerable as the "distance" that exists between law and citizen, between lawyer and lay person, and between legal and nonlegal bodies of information narrows. As Henry Perritt wrote "in the long run, adoption of information technologies will blur the boundaries between citizen and agency and between agency and court. Blurring of these boundaries may necessitate rethinking the definitions of some of the basic events that define the administrative process, public participation and judicial review."[24]

By opening up new possibilities for interacting with people and information, electronic communication changes our perspective on both physical and informational distance. Many constraints limiting interpersonal and informational relationships will be removed as the law and the legal profession gradually adapt to the new communications environment. This does not necessarily mean that the new environment or the new technologies will be accepted eagerly, rapidly, or uniformly. Institutional change does not occur at the same rate as technological change, and there are considerable pressures on the profession to resist change.

Lawyers are comfortable with traditional ways of obtaining and processing information and have spent much of their professional lives adapting to and successfully exploiting the constraints of physical and informational space imposed by print. The new media not only require that one learn how to use new tools and employ new skills but they contain challenges to traditional concepts, orientations, and habits of work. The rewards, or even the need, of immersing oneself in the new electronic environment will probably be less clear to many individuals than the very apparent difficulties of acquiring new skills, and of using machines that are relatively costly, are still not used by everyone, and do not present information as clearly in their infancy as they will when they mature.[25] In addition, some spatial cornerstones of law, such as courthouses and libraries, are, often in a literal sense, carved in stone. There is pressure being exerted on what occurs in these edifices, but their physical prominence alone causes change to occur more slowly.

We are still in an early stage of electronic communication; the networks we can see and use, miraculous in some ways, are fairly primitive in others. Most individuals are still content with computers that have no, or very limited, communicative capabilities. For those who do use computers to communicate, many confuse extraordinary capabilities to acquire information from great distances with a much less impressive information space formed on the computer monitor. However, although an increasing number of lawyers are using computers, few perceive the new technology as a necessary instrument for establishing new relationships with people or with information. We are, as I have argued, still obsessed with time but rather blind to issues of space. Yet, even in this early period, one can try to apply a "space frame," a spatial orientation, that at least suggests the direction of change and allows us to understand why change in some areas is occurring faster than in others. Most important, the following analysis is designed to show that electronic networks are not simply pathways that move data faster and more efficiently. Electronic networks also bring new ways of thinking, disturb old habits, and, as a consequence, require us to confront basic concerns of the law.

The main value of using a spatial perspective to explore the impact of the new technologies is that it highlights and clarifies the differences between the print environment and the electronic environment while providing a means for understanding why change is taking place. Viewed in such terms, the process of adapting to the new media has similarities to coming to terms with an alien environment or culture. In both situations, one needs not only to learn some discrete skills but to become sensitive to a new range of possibilities and a new set of appropriate attitudes and behaviors.

The concept of an environment should be familiar to all computer users. Every computer comes with software that defines an operating "system" or operating "environment." Software designers understand that one aspect of their role is to create a user-friendly "look and feel" that provides functional capabilities in tandem with an effective and even inviting mode to use these capabilities. Indeed, as the commonly used "desktop" metaphor suggests, designers view the electronic environment as having at least some qualities in common with a familiar workspace.[26] Yet, as one designer has noted, "[d]esigning human-computer experience isn't about building a better desktop, it's about creating imaginary worlds that have a special relationship to reality—

worlds in which we can extend, amplify, and enrich our own capacities to think, feel, and act."[27] As will be discussed in chapter 3, it is critically important to understand this view of software. Software structures the nature of the electronic environment, shapes what cyberspace looks like, and defines the user's constraints and opportunities. Interaction between software and hardware creates an environment that tells the user what is possible and what is not, and as such limits are understood and obeyed, it frames the kinds of activities that are undertaken and the role that is performed.

Figure 4 is intended not as an objective, precise, or drawn-to-scale map. It is a model, a visual device that suggests one way in which a new medium can have an impact on law that is understandable in spatial or environmental terms. It is a macro-level sketch of some of the elements of our legal system as they have come to function in the print environment. Each of these elements has a fairly well defined role and position in the legal process, and coordinated communication occurs among at least some of these components. In visual terms, each of the elements is separated from the others, and some elements are also closer, in both a physical and an informational sense, to each other than to others. These elements of law do not merely exist, but they exist in a relationship to each other. The lawyer, for example, stands closer to the court than does the client. The lawyer also stands *between* client and court. As result, the courts may speak to citizens, but they do so at a considerable distance.

The lack of links between some elements and the distance separating the elements both signify something. For example, the distance between elements generally enhances the legal profession's identity

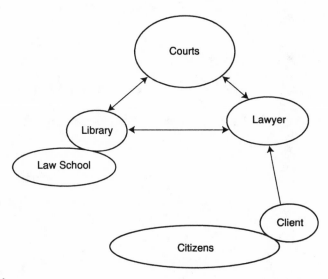

Figure 4

and independence. As we consider possible areas of change in the new electronic environment, this visual portrait can be expected to change. Will the elements currently in the diagram be as prominent in the new environment? Do new patterns of communication arise that affect the distance between the elements and the relationship between elements? Do new entities, currently outside the boundary of this universe, move inside the boundary?

In addition to looking at the legal space as a whole, each of the elements might be considered individually as a separate environment. Within each element there are organizational structures and processes that reflect physical and information distance. Within each element there are distinct modes of interacting with people and information. Within each element, one can ask both what kinds of constraints may be lifted as electronic forms of communication are employed and how difficult will it be to maintain barriers and boundaries.

The following chapter applies some of these concerns to one of the elements, the law library. The library is an appropriate place to focus an exploration of legal spaces because it may be the most obvious legal artifact of print culture. It is a place that physically differentiates the citizen from the legal professional. The law library is also a place where one of the earliest uses of computers in law occurred and where legal use of computers for communication is quite high. It is, therefore, an intriguing setting for trying to understand more clearly than we do now what the impact of electronic networks will be on legal roles and relationships with information.

3

Law Libraries and
Legal Information Places

> The impact of LEXIS and WESTLAW is not simply a matter of a
> new technology simplifying or speeding up a preexisting process;
> it involves a change in the structure of legal literature. . . . in law,
> more than any other discipline, the structure of the literature
> implies the structure of the enterprise itself.[1]
>
> —Robert C. Berring

The earliest and perhaps the most familiar use of electronic communication by the legal community involved electronic legal research.
The emergence of LEXIS in the early 1970s and of WESTLAW several
years later enabled lawyers and law students to obtain legal information very quickly from the LEXIS database in Ohio or the West database in Minnesota.[2] For the past several years, every law student in
the United States has had free access to these services, and their use
generally in the practice of law has been increasing. These databases
contain huge quantities of information. They are more up-to-date
than any print library and in some areas, such as coverage of cases
and judicial opinions, are more comprehensive than any print library.
Each electronic service contains "unofficial" opinions that, for one
reason or another, will not be published and that some courts have
even said should not be relied upon.

There has been an understandable tendency to assume that
LEXIS and WESTLAW are libraries. The companies themselves refer
to the databases as libraries. Both companies promote their services
as an alternative to manual research in the physical library and as a

significant time saver compared to traditional library research.[3] Although costs continue to be high, both companies argue, with some validity, that after factoring in the amount of lawyer and librarian time that is saved, this mode of research can be cost-effective. Similarly, most assessments of LEXIS and WESTLAW have tended to focus on whether the quality of research is comparable to what can be produced in the print library. Finally, for WESTLAW at least, many of the indexing features of the print collection, such as key numbers, have been imported into WESTLAW and suggest to users that these electronic information places are substitutes for a library's print materials.

Debates about the value of LEXIS and WESTLAW have largely focused on either economic concerns or whether the quality of material retrieved electronically is equivalent to material located using traditional print methods.[4] The generally unstated question and concern underlying almost every discussion of electronic legal research is whether the electronic services can now or at some point in the future substitute for print, and whether some parts of the library can be exclusively electronic and paperless. The following analysis looks at what is occurring in a somewhat different framework and assumes not that one *will replace* the other but that one is *already displacing* the other, that the growth of electronic sources of information changes the nature of information seeking activities because the context of information seeking is different. Whether a search leads to different results depending upon whether one is seated at a terminal or moving through the library stacks is important if one is doing research in an actual case. Such a concern does not, however, provide much insight into the long-term impact on law of electronic information resources that inevitably will occur as increased reliance is placed not merely on LEXIS and WESTLAW but on network connections generally.

To understand why displacement involves changes that are very different from those presented by cost or research quality studies, it is again helpful to look at libraries as environments or spaces. When this is done, the focus of attention becomes not how much something costs or whether one has found a particular item, but the nature of the architecture and whether the space one occupies to do such research creates new options for interacting with people or information.

The growth of cyberspace does not necessarily mean the end of the print library, but it does suggest a different and less central role for the print library. The growth of high-speed networks makes it very clear that we will see substantial growth in the use of electronically acquired information. We will have access to increasing numbers of databases and sources of stored information, through networks and at speeds that do not exist today, utilizing search and data retrieval programs not yet on the market. We will increasingly view people, who may be far away but linked to us electronically, as a new form of colleague whom we recognize as a source of authoritative information. We will have access to information, therefore, that might ever exist in a physical library but that is located on the network—a place that is much more diffuse and diverse than the physical places it is displacing.

There is one reason, above any other, that electronic research techniques and demand for information in electronic form will continue to grow. This is that data in electronic form can be used so much more easily and for so many more purposes than can data in print. Data in electronic form is reusable almost instantaneously, can be combined with other data, and can be edited, copied, communicated to, and worked on with others. Value can be added to information in many more ways using electronic tools.[5] Meaning can be found by employing perspectives and modes of analysis and presentation that are difficult if not impossible with words fixed on paper. Again, print collections will not disappear, but the extent to which print versions of electronic material are maintained will certainly change. These changes can be expected to cause some controversy and generate some access problems for those untrained in, unfamiliar with, or not possessing the technology. Yet, as more people become familiar with cyberspace, as more materials become accessible only in electronic form, as more electronic relationships are formed with both people and information, electronic space will become the focal point of the profession, and the legal profession will be forced to come to terms with the new technologies and the new environment.[6]

A law library is not merely an entity with links to the profession and to other elements in the legal process, but it is itself a spatial setting, an environment. For example, print law libraries are invariably architecturally impressive spaces. They also typically are quiet spaces: spaces where individuals, rather than groups, are likely to be at work. In the library, everything is categorized, materials in each category are located near each other, and every item is assigned a particular space. Within categories, various methods of organization are employed so that access and use are possible. Library materials are physical objects can be used by only one person at a time. Librarians, experts in the nature and use of these materials, systematically organize the collections and, since they are physically located in the same space, assist users. Users must be familiar with the library's organizational structure as well as at least some of the ways that have been established to make the organizational structure accessible.

Print law libraries typically are self-contained and physically separate from other libraries. In universities with law schools, the law library is located in the law school building apart from the general university library. The separateness of the law collection can be overcome by ordering a copy of some book that already exists in the general university collection, by ordering something through interlibrary loan, or by going to another library. As a practical matter, however, physical separateness reinforces the informational distance that is created by the content and organization of any law collection. Law is a distinct enterprise not only because of the nature of law and the work that lawyers do, but because the boundaries of law are reinforced by the manner in which legal materials are kept separate and by the spatial distance that one must overcome to encounter nonlegal materials.

The physical separateness of the law library is matched by a substantial informational distance. A lay person wishing to use a particular court opinion, for example, not only may have difficulty reading it but will have difficulty finding it. Finding legal cases often requires users to navigate the access route provided by digests, descriptive word indexes, and key numbers. What appears to most lawyers to be an efficient and ingenious mode of access is a roadblock to the lay person. Consequently, legal cases, which arguably are the most important part of the legal collection, are also the part of the collection with the greatest informational distance. This separation of the legal from the nonlegal, through physical and other means, also provides an extra measure of status and authority to the law and to those who work with it.

Peter Martin of Cornell Law School has written eloquently of the various functions performed by a law school library. He notes:

> Just as the information resource denominated "library" presumes a community of interest, it also creates communal space. Indeed, there is no space more sacred in my school than the reading room of the law library. Often, and not just when raising money from nostalgic alumni, we speak of it as the heart of the school, a laboratory for students and faculty. The location of faculty offices in close proximity to the library collection was a critical design element in our recent building program. In truth, the library *has* been the law school's laboratory, shared by faculty and students, offering resources that students use side-by-side and see their faculty using.[7]

The electronic environment described next challenges our concepts of both physical and informational distance. It is a different kind of space, and because of this will bring about new relationships and interactions with people and information. Thus, to feel comfortable in such an environment, one needs not only to master particular skills but to adapt to an environment that plays by a very different set of spatial rules and satisfies informational, professional, and personal needs differently. It requires recognizing that the physical nature of the print library frames how print information is organized and used and that many assumptions about using and accessing information implicitly take into account the physical space in which print information is located. In electronic space, the informational context changes. Indeed, as I shall explain shortly, the spatial context is so different that it is highly problematic, perhaps even counterproductive, to even continue calling the new environment a "library."

Electronic Environments and Physical Distance

Electronic sources of legal information are often thought about as simply being alternatives or supplements to print libraries. Although these legal databases can be accessed from almost anywhere by any computer, it is still common to find law libraries with specially designated machines for either WESTLAW or LEXIS. Law librarians tend to be responsible for training in electronic legal research methods and to be most familiar with information available electronically. This arrangement emphasizes the common thread between print and electronic collections: that material in one may resemble material in the other and that those most skilled in using electronic collections are probably librarians. This arrangement also helps to conceal the fact that they are very different kinds of environments and that they fulfill overlapping but not identical informational goals.

Although they have approximately twenty years of experience with online legal research, experts are still uncertain how to teach students to become competent online researchers. Most agree that many students and practitioners do not have adequate skills.[8] Yet, part of the problem in teaching research skills is in looking only at skills and not looking at the environment in which those skills will be used. In teaching traditional library skills, one is able to assume that the student has had experience with books and the print environment. The instructor need not, therefore, be very explicit about the rules governing the physical environment or the relationship of physical laws to the print library. The electronic environment, however, is a radically different kind of environment, and if the user does not possess an understanding of its special features, he or she will not thrive when exposed to it.

Consider, for example, the following environmental or spatial differences between the print library and the electronic information resource:

1. The print library is a physical place, whereas the electronic library is not. Print libraries must obey physical laws—one is either in the library or one not; a book is either available for use or not. The physical structure housing the library does more than allow information to be stored in it. It also serves as the interface to the stored information. It provides certain cues to users and, in a subtle way, informs the user about the research task that is being undertaken.

A print user sees and even feels the progress that is made as a search for information proceeds. As one pulls books off the shelves, looks in indexes, and turns pages, one "gets closer" to "locating" the search objective. The print user also learns something about the organization of the field that is being researched. As Robert Berring pointed out, as one looks for legal material in the print environment, one acquires a framework for understanding law, a framework that is reinforced and built upon as one moves from one step of the process to the next.[9]

Electronic sources of information, at least at present, contain little to suggest a framework or organizational structure for law. This is not surprising since, as will be described later, the task of organizing material in cyberspace is as often the job of the user as it is of the supplier of information.[10] Today's electronic services often fill the screen with information and data but provide no visual feedback to the user that compares to that conveyed by the spatial configuration of the print library. The electronic sources tell the user how many "hits" there have been, how many sources of information contain a certain word or concept, but almost nothing else.

In WESTLAW, the initial directory screen employs a print metaphor, asking users to select a choice by typing in the "page" number of that choice. When one selects a page number, the first screen disappears and a new screen listing the files in a particular directory appears. However, going to one of these virtual pages cannot convey the same sense that one has when picking up a book, which has a cover and a finite number of pages, and turning to a particular page. Going from electronic page to electronic page provides none of the subtle informational cues one obtains while moving from library aisle to library aisle or from one set of reporters to another. The user of the print library is in both an impressive and a somewhat informative space, whereas the person who is logged on to an electronic library today, at least, is for all intents and purposes in a vacuum. It does not have to be this way and, as I shall explain presently, it probably will not be this way for very much longer. At present, however, it may be easier to find a needle in the haystack of an electronic collection but, since one obtains almost no feedback on the process of needle finding, the next search will probably be conducted in as blind a fashion as the first.

2. The user of the print library is rooted to one place. This may seem so obvious that it is not worthy of mention. The user of the electronic source of information, however, is not so rooted. Once one escapes the architecture of the print library by using electronic networks, he or she also is freed of the physical laws that normally limit mortal humans.

A user of an electronic collection is really in two places at once—

in the place where the computer is located and in cyberspace, where the electronic information place is located. After electronically entering cyberspace, the user goes somewhere without actually being there. Using an electronic database can be disorienting because the user receives little or no feedback about what is occurring and, more important, because illusions—events that seem to violate physical laws—occur routinely. The experience makes many users feel weightless and evokes in some the same feelings encountered in looking at an illusion or an Escher drawing, of something that seems familiar but, as one looks at it closely, turns out to be a representation of something that cannot exist.[11]

The objects that one sees on screen seem to be the same as familiar physical objects. When one looks more closely, however, which unfortunately many do not, it becomes obvious that this is an illusion and that the electronic version of an object has properties not possessed, or lacks properties possessed by, the physical object that it replaces. Thus, as one uses the electronic media, for example, one finds words and images that are animated and that could not function in the same way in our physical world.

Consider, as just one example, the first screen of choices one encounters after logging on to LEXIS. LEXIS labels the choices that appear in Figure 5 as "libraries." Although this undoubtedly provides some comfort and familiarity to users today, labeling these sources of information as libraries is also problematic. To the unsophisticated searcher, it suggests that the different choices lead to different collections, to different bodies of information like the different collections in two print libraries, or to different materials in two parts of one print library. This can be confusing, however, particularly to new

```
                        LIBRARIES -- PAGE 1 of 2
Please TRANSMIT the NAME (only one) of the library you want to search.
- For more information about a library, TRANSMIT its page (PG) number.
- To see a list of additional libraries, press the NEXT PAGE key.

PG NAME    PG NAME    PG NAME    PG NAME    PG NAME    PG NAME    PG NAME    PG NAME

-------General Legal-------- --Public Records-- --Helps-- Financial --Nexis--
MEGA   1 ALR    6 LAWREV 6 ASSETS 6 INCORP 6 EASY   1 COMPNY 17 NEWS   14
GENFED 1 BNA    6 MARHUB 6 DOCKET 6 LEXDOC 9 GUIDE 13 NAARS  12 TOPNWS 14
STATES 1 ABA    6 LEXREF 6 FINDER 9 LIENS  6 PRACT 13 QUOTE  17 LEGNEW 15
CODES  1 CAREER 6 HOTTOP 1 INSOLV 5 VERDCT 9 TERMS 13            CMPGN  15
CITES  6 BEGIN  6 CLE    5                                       WORLD  18
LEGIS  1 CUSTOM 9
----------------------------Area of Law----------------------------------
ADMRTY 2 ENERGY 2 FEDSEC  3 INSURE 3 MEDLNE 16 PRLIAB 4 STTAX 4 UCC    5
BANKNG 2 ENVIRN 2 FEDSEN  3 INTLAW 3 MEDMAL  3 PUBCON 4 TAXANA 6
BKRTCY 2 ESTATE 2 FEDTAX  3 ITRADE 3 MILTRY  4 PUBHW  4 TAXRIA 6
COPYRT 2 ETHICS 2 GENMED 16 LABOR  3 MSTORT  5 REALTY 4 TRADE  5
CORP   2 FAMILY 2 HEALTH  3 LEXPAT 3 PATENT  4 STSEC  4 TRANS  5
EMPLOY 2 FEDCOM 2 IMMIG   3 M&A    4 PENBEN  4          TRDMRK 5
```

Figure 5   LEXIS Library Selection Screen

users, because an electronic database such as LEXIS does not con-
form to the same physical laws as print libraries. Print libraries are
organized around the physical fact that every copy of some work
must be in some place and, indeed, can only be in one place. Every
book is assigned one and only one call number. All the copies of a
given work are under the same call number and are located in the
same place in the library. Indeed, the call number indicates something
about where the book will be located in any library.

LEXIS libraries operate by very different rules and to those who
have been conditioned to the spatial constraints of print libraries,
using LEXIS and other electronic sources of information can be disorienting. Disorientation results from the fact that the choices in Figure 5 do not really represent different libraries, in the sense that they
are separate collections, but most closely resemble special exhibitions
that one often finds in libraries, in which different parts of a collection that relate to the theme of the exhibition are brought together.
What LEXIS can do that print libraries cannot do is create an infinite
number of such subgroups and combinations. A LEXIS library resembles this kind of exhibition because it organizes a part of the LEXIS
collection topically.

A print law library must obey Newtonian laws. Thus, to create an
exhibition and put materials on display that are located in different
realms of the library, the materials must be removed from the places
where they normally reside. Two or three concurrent exhibitions
might cause a problem, therefore, if there was some overlap in the
materials needed for the different exhibitions. In addition, materials
included in an exhibition cannot be loaned to patrons unless the
library owns more than one copy of the material.

LEXIS, WESTLAW, and other databases do not need to grapple
with this kind of constraint. They can organize and reorganize
"libraries" many times because they are really only providing alternate routes of access to one or more files. They can provide as many
"exhibitions" as they wish without affecting access to any files in the
exhibition. Files in any LEXIS library are always "in" since nothing is
ever checked out of the electronic "library." Everything is, in a sense,
"on reserve" yet everything can also be "taken out."

Choosing the appropriate electronic "library" is more challenging
than deciding whether to look for a book in one of two print libraries
since the content of one electronic library may overlap with another.
Indeed, to one who approaches LEXIS with a print orientation, the
laws of physics appear to be violated, since one object appears to exist
in many different places. The *New York Law Journal* file, NYLAWJ, for
example, appears in seven different libraries—Banking, Genfed, Leg-
new, NY, NEWS, Realty, and States. It also appears in various group
files in each of these "libraries." That one file is in six or more places

at the same time is, of course, an illusion, but it is an illusion worth noting, since the apparent ability of the electronic media to escape physical laws presents users with many other, similar kinds of illusions. Effective electronic research requires understanding, getting used to and adapting to such apparent illusions,[12] coping with a kind of weightlessness and escape from the pull of gravity, and recognizing organizational structures that could not exist with physical objects.

Such illusions have received little attention because users are presented with illusions from the very first moment they touch a computer keyboard. The main illusion, of course, is that there are letters and numbers on the screen, at least letters and numbers that are the same as letters and numbers on a written paper. Using the keyboard or providing input in some other way involves manipulating electrical impulses. Pressing the key for *A* on the keyboard sends a different electrical pattern than pressing the letter *B* and causes a different set of lights to flicker on the screen. Is the user, when he or she presses keys on the keyboard, typing "letters" or merely turning on different patterns of electrical impulses? The flexibility inherent in the computer derives from the fact that there are no tangible images that might have to be erased, only electrical impulses that might need to be changed. We typically move past this illusion very quickly, although it does occasionally trouble some new users. I was once told by a new user, for example, that he was having difficulty adjusting to the fact that pressing the spacebar on the keyboard caused the letters on the screen to move. This contradicted his experience with a typewriter where pressing the spacebar caused the carriage or typing ball to move and where, of course, letters on the paper could not move from place to place.

3. The manner in which an electronic database appears to enlarge its collection by rerouting access to files and increasing the number of different "libraries" it contains is more than matched by the manner in which databases can grow instantaneously merely by establishing electronic links to other collections. It is easy to mistakenly assume that files one sees on a screeen are stored on the same computer or share space in the same computer. That belief builds upon some notion that what is presented to us on screen as a single entity actually exists as a unit. In an electronic world, where space is conquered at electronic speed, what appears as a single entity will increasingly be many different entities linked together electronically. A LEXIS library on electronic media and law could, in theory, consist of several files, some of which are in the LEXIS computer in Ohio and some of which are located elsewhere. It would appear on the screen, however, as a single "library."

WESTLAW does something similar through its arrangement with DIALOG, a large commercial database of general information, and

Dow Jones. WESTLAW subscribers can access DIALOG and Dow Jones from the WESTLAW menu and use them in a manner somewhat similar to how LEXIS subscribers use NEXIS. Although the link between WESTLAW and DIALOG may not be as seamless as the link between LEXIS and NEXIS, what is important is how practical it has become to offer users information that can come from locations that they may be unaware of.

Figure 6 shows one of the menus on the University of Massachusetts Department of Legal Studies Gopher.[13] This information is accessible to most persons with Internet addresses. It appears to the user to provide information stored at the University of Massachusetts. As Figure 6 illustrates, however, none of the data is located at the university. Whenever one of the menu items is selected, information is obtained from a computer located somewhere else. There is, therefore, almost no limit to the size of "collections" linked together in seamless fashion.[14] Users may be unaware of this, however. As computer scientist David Gelernter has noted, "[o]ne computer can only be so fast but the aggregate power of a *group* of computers is limited only by the size of the group." One can paraphrase this and state that one computer can store only so much information but the aggregate size of a *group* of computers is limited only by the size of the group. This capability makes it possible not only to access huge quantities of information but, as will be described in chapter 8, to create new works by linking together parts of files or works located on different machines into what appears to be a single work.

The seamless linking of scattered computers in order to permit access to information contrasts with the nonseamless linking of libraries in the print world. Linking exists in print libraries under the guise of "interlibrary loan." Spatially separate institutions do cooperate to supplement each other's collections. Electronic interlibrary loan is fundamentally different, however, since the conquering of space makes the process neither "interlibrary" nor a "loan." Multiple sources

University of Massachusetts
Department of Legal Studies

Internet Gopher Information Client 2.0 pl10

1. Americans with Disabilities Act	[source: Villanova Law School]
2. Citizen's Guide to Using the Freedom of Information Act	[source: Wiretap gopher in Cupertino, California]
3. Copyright Law/	[source: Cornell Law School]
4. Health Law Resources/	[source: St. Louis University Law School]
5. Laws Relating to the Net and Computer Use	[source: Electronic Frontier Foundation]
6. U.S. Constitution	[source: Cornell Law School]

Figure 6

of information merge into one source; users do not even feel that they are consulting multiple sources. In addition, there are no "loans" in the electronic universe; what appears on the computer screen is a copy, which may be kept and stored or discarded from memory. Unlike the print environment, where a library never has its whole collection physically present in the library, since part of every lending library is always on loan, everything in the electronic library is always "in." Nothing is ever removed from the library by patrons.[15]

4. Because of physical space limitations in print libraries, librarians must decide what materials will occupy the available physical space. This raises the premium on both the quality and the relevance of the stored material. If physical space is limited, higher quality and more relevant materials will receive preference over lower quality and less relevant materials, and, in a law library, materials related to law will receive preference over materials related to some other field. It is natural, therefore, in an era of print collections, to have libraries devoted to specialized fields. Also, for efficient access, the physical space must be organized. The physical arrangement of different specialized collections has reinforced boundaries between disciplines and collections. For law, it focuses the attention of users on materials the profession considers necessary and makes it less likely that attention will be directed toward nonlegal literature. As Spencer Neth commented, only partly facetiously, law students asked to describe a biological process such as the fertilization of an egg are more likely to quote from a judicial opinion involving such a process than to consult a scientific work in a medical library some distance away.[16]

The "librarians" of electronic space are under less pressure to organize their collections. As a result, when print models of organization are applied in the electronic environment, they may even appear arbitrary and constraining. During most of the 1980s, for example, law schools did not have the same access to NEXIS that they had to LEXIS. During this period there was a clear division between electronic law and nonlaw materials, much as the distinction that exists in the print realm between legal and nonlegal libraries. The attention of law students was focused on legal materials as it had always been. When access to NEXIS was finally provided, the decision may have been a competitive action by the Mead Data Corporation, but there was also a technological imperative behind it. With space no longer a constraint, the lack of access to nonlaw materials that are part of the same collection becomes harder to justify. Eventually, it will be understood that one connected to cyberspace is no longer really in a law library but in an environment that can be organized by the user to fit his or her needs.

One of the reasons it is misleading to label the collections in Figure 5 as libraries is that there are no librarians. One may or may not be accessing LEXIS or some other database from a computer in the physical library, but control over the organization of information is shifting from the librarian community to the programming or software community and to the individual user. The information place that is established on screen is shaped by the software and by modifications to the software that can be made by users. Software can make the information place a usable place or it can make access difficult. Librarians have some expertise in arranging physical space so that access to information is enhanced. The librarians of cyberspace, what some have called "cybrarians," may emerge eventually, but this will not occur until it is understood that it is the qualities of electronic space and not the qualities of physical space that frame the access and use of information.

The qualities of information in cyberspace are not self-evident, and they often are masked by many superficial similarities with print libraries. They have been recognized, however, by a professor of architecture, Michael Benedikt, who, because of his training, is probably more sensitive than most to the nature of physical space. Benedikt writes that in cyberspace

> the principles of ordinary space and time, can, in principle, be violated with impunity. After all, the ancient worlds of magic, myth, and legend to which cyberspace is heir, as well as the modern worlds of fantasy fiction, movies, and cartoons, are replete with variations of logic of everyday space and time; disappearances, underworlds, phantoms, warp speed travel, mirrors and doors to alternate worlds, zero gravity, flattenings and reconstitutions, wormholes, scale inversions, and so on. And after all, why have cyberspace if we cannot (apparently) bend nature's rules there?[17]

Similarly, computer programmers understand that their creations allow them a degree of flexibility that traditional craftspersons do not enjoy. Sherry Turkle asked students learning programming, "What are your favorite books and can you say why?" One student's answer was particularly revealing: "Winning science fiction. In science fiction, you can start from scratch. It's like writing a program. Even in Logo programming, children can create worlds that operate by Aristotelian principles instead of Newtonian ones. No physical constraints. Make a whole new world with its own rules."[18]

As a result of the different kind of space that users find themselves in when using electronic sources of information, the use of the word *library* to describe this space may be more confusing than illuminating. The word *library*, when it was first used by LEXIS, may or may not have been assumed to fit the dictionary definition of a library and to be an appropriate use of the term. Given the great difference between electronic "libraries" and print libraries, however, I would suggest that it is necessary to begin to view the word *library* differently, to consider it as a metaphor rather than as a label—a device to encourage people to think about one object in terms of some other, more familiar object. Yet, if one considers the word *library* in this manner, it is apparent that it is an inappropriate figure of speech because it may mislead users about the nature of the space they are in.

A metaphor is a "cognitive hook"[19] that can help a user to understand something unfamiliar by using terms related to something familiar. In this case, it has been assumed that applying the term *library* can facilitate using the computer in lieu of the technology it is replacing, and can allay the anxieties of users. The reason for this is that metaphors and other figures of speech can shape how experience is conceptualized.[20] Metaphors, according to George Lakoff and Mark Johnson, are

> pervasive in everyday life, not just in language but in thought and action. Our ordinary conceptual system, in terms of which we both think and act, is fundamentally metaphorical in nature.
>
> The concepts that govern our thought are not just matters of the intellect. They also govern our everyday functioning, down to the most mundane details. Our concepts structure what we perceive, how we get around in the world, and how we relate to other people. Our conceptual system thus plays a central role in defining our everyday realities. If we are right in suggesting that our conceptual system is largely metaphorical, then the way we think, what we experience, and what we do every day is very much a matter of metaphor.[21]

A similar view has been expressed by a designer of software interfaces, who notes that "a word which is used in a metaphorical way is just the tip of the iceberg. A metaphor is an invisible web of terms and associations which underlie the way we speak and think about a concept. It is this extended structure which makes metaphor such a powerful and essential part of our thinking. Metaphors function as natural models, allowing us to take our knowledge of familiar, concrete objects and experiences and use it to give structure to more abstract concepts."[22]

Metaphors can thus clarify, but they can also obscure. Lakoff and Johnson point out that "[i]n allowing us to focus on one aspect of a concept . . . a metaphorical concept can keep us from focusing on other aspects of the concept that are inconsistent with that metaphor."[23] This is the troubling aspect of using print metaphors to describe information located in cyberspace. Because the electronic and print environments operate according to different rules, the use of print metaphors shapes the user's thinking in a way that is dysfunctional and that does not help the user become oriented to an electronic environment. Although some assume that "if the interface presents representations of real-world objects, people will naturally know what to do with them,"[24] because of the spatial differences, the library metaphor actually provides little insight to the user.

One of the most perceptive analysts of the role of metaphor in helping or hindering new computer users, Brenda Laurel, has pointed out a similar problem with a very common metaphor used in software, that of the "desktop." Laurel notes that there are

> two ways to fall off the desktop. One is when you start looking for other things that "go" with it and you can't find them—filing cabinets, telephones, blotters for doodling and making notes or even an administrative assistant to make some calls or type some letter. The other way to fall off the desktop is to find something on it that doesn't go with everything else, thereby undermining or exploding the mimetic context—for example, a trash can that gobbles up your trash seemingly at random and ejects your disks.[25]

The novice electronic legal researcher might be considered to be in some kind of freefall as well as he or she tries to adapt to a "library" that lacks many of the gravitational forces that help one function in a print library. To stop this freefall, the user needs new types of support in addition to training in skills. This support may be in the nature of new metaphors,[26] and certainly includes new software that provides more feedback to the user.[27] In this regard, the following analysis of Professor Robert Berring is particularly insightful since Berring uses spatial terms such as *structure, location, situation,* and *setting*—terms that implicitly recognize the importance of context. Berring writes:

> The full-text on-line legal databases are a new form of legal literature. The new literature is more or less identical in content to the old West system, but it is accessible in an entirely new way. If we concentrate on the question of access to the case law, we can begin to understand how radically the legal databases break with the literature of the past. . . . The Digest was the internal, mediating structure within the old mode of discourse. . . . the location of issues and cases in the old paradigm was part of their meaning. Because the cases were accessible through the Digest, they were always presented to the practitioner as situated. The situation was a substantive context, a setting that told the searcher the meaning of the case as much as it did the opinion itself.
>
> Free-text searching in legal databases, however, deprives the researcher of context.[28]

As the electronic culture matures, our language will eventually respond to the proliferation of informational contexts by providing us with more specialized and appropriate terms. Our language will then reflect the new kinds of informational spaces, and imprecise or inaccurate metaphors will no longer have the same kind of influence on our thinking and perception that they have had for the past twenty years. As print-related terms are used less often, the lens through which we view electronic space will put the novel qualities of cyberspace into clearer focus. Assumptions that have been made as to who should control or organize cyberspace will be reassessed.

This new space will then be seen not simply to be an extension of the print world's impressive achievement, the library, but as an extension of many different information sources that are used in daily life. Cyberspace can be considered to be as much an extension of one's personal library or of one's rolodex as it is of the law library. The screen, our pathway into cyberspace, can be as much a link to far-flung colleagues as it is to stored documents. No single metaphor seems adequate since individuals are more able to shape the use of the network and create it in their own image than was ever possible with the bricks and mortar needed to shape the physical spaces required in the print world.

The attempt to understand cyberspace by creating metaphors is both necessary and frustrating. We already have a long list of metaphors for cyberspace, such as the common ones of a highway or frontier, and the less common ones such as a church, a luncheon table, kudzu,[29] or, more negatively, a compost heap.[30] Although all of these metaphors, such as calling cyberspace a library, have some appeal, none of the metaphors are perfect because there is something about this kind of electronic activity that is novel. By making distance an obstacle to be overcome rather than an impenetrable barrier, cyberspace reveals itself as a more flexible space than any physical space and, therefore, as a space that is quite different from the libraries that have been one of the centers of law for some time.

Electronic Environments and Informational Distance

The electronic environment not only changes physical distance and external models of organizing information but also affects internal modes of thinking about information. The person interacting with a computer, particularly when this computer extends his or her access to information in ways that our language has difficulty describing, is engaged in a different kind of experience from the person who is interacting with a set of books in a print library. Admittedly, it is difficult to think of online sources of information as being anything but a substitute for books. Everything about the manner in which electronic databases have been presented to users suggests that they are, in all ways, merely alternatives to print materials.[31] One who employs a spatial context, however, sees the online environment more broadly as an environment that encourages different attitudes about, and new relationships with, information.

Informational distance relates to the manner in which information is used and to the tools and skills needed to access information. Through working with information in an electronic environment, the user experiences something quite different from that experienced in the print environment. The print experience involves not merely taking information off a page, but understanding and using indexes, turning pages, being cognizant of the length of chapters and the weight of the book, being influenced and giving meaning to bold, underlined, and other typefaces, and being aware that every other copy of the book that one is looking at is identical to it. It involves habits of learning, of reading, of implicit understandings of what can be done with information. Print users accept the fact that to pass on to others what one has read is not easy. Paraphrasing is not exact and hand copying or photocopying what is being read may be fairly cumbersome. The electronic media provide new means to work in a group and to share both what one reads and what one writes. Everything that is read, or written, can easily be forwarded and, as a consequence, begins to provide users with a new orientation toward the process of reading and using information.

Although Gutenberg printed the first book that used movable type in the West, he did not create the information environment of print. That environment emerged gradually as books became smaller and more manageable, as libraries grew, and as new devices, such as indexes and title pages, and new typefaces became commonplace. Charles Goodrum has pointed out that it took a generation before a Venetian printer, Aldus Manutius, rejected the idea that

> a book had to look like a manuscript. He was convinced that the invention was being applied in the wrong direction. Instead of huge, wood-bound lectern folios, he believed a book should fit in a saddle-bag so that it could be moved and read at leisure. He shrunk the pages, invented cardboard covers to be used instead of pine, decided that the Roman type would never squeeze together enough to make a hand-holdable volume so he invented italics which take up much less space yet retain their legibility. Finally, he was committed to making the book as beautiful a piece of hard print as the manuscript had been as a work of hand art. He designed clean, austere pages that have never been surpassed for their grace and visual harmony.[32]

Consequently, it should not be surprising if, at this time, the electronic environment has not yet adapted to and developed equivalent, or even more powerful, tools to reduce informational distance and to deal with the uniqueness of the online environment.

For several reasons, the online environment is likely to be an area of enormous change in the near future. First, almost any new personal computer sold today is many times more powerful than the average computer it is replacing. Second, almost any new modem sold today allows information to travel in and out of the computer at several times the rate of modems that were prevalent a few years ago. Third, looking ahead three or four years, transmission rates of the evolving global network will be many times faster than transmission rates of the current Internet, and many individuals and groups will have direct access to the network. Fourth, even before that, new technology may allow for fast transmission rates over regular telephone lines.[33] The hardware that will make up the electronic environment in the not too distant future, therefore, will at the very least bring information in at faster speeds than it does today.

Once this hardware is in place, the key influence on what the electronic environment looks like to users and on how one accesses and relates to electronic information will be software.[34] Cyberspace is in a sense like any other space, in that it can be redesigned and made more habitable. This is largely the role of software. Software allows and regulates interaction with the electronic environment. Software controls whether the mode of interaction is through words, through arcane commands, through a mouse that one can use to make a choice by pressing a button or, in the future, through the human voice. Software controls how much information is presented to the user and what the user is expected to know in order to successfully navigate through a computer located many miles away. Software is the guide, the architect, even the interior decorator, of cyberspace. It is not totally erroneous, therefore, that some software refers to the background design as "wallpaper" and that we speak of "leaving" or "exiting from" software.

The landscape of cyberspace, therefore, is not preordained. Its appearance and its usefulness change not only as hardware changes, as words become easier to see on the screen, as color becomes popular, or as speeds of transmitting and processing data increase, but also as new software appears that illuminates the space and provides feedback and guidance to users. Software builds on technological developments. It can be designed to allow and encourage the use of images when images are appropriate, to recognize mistakes and suggest solutions, to provide help to users, to welcome users, and to understand and anticipate the needs of users.[35] Software needs to exploit and facilitate the use of the unique capabilities of the powerful hardware and provide guidance to users who approach letters on the screen as if they were reading a printed book.

Communications software thus far has presented users with a rather sterile, uninviting, and unhelpful environment.[36] This unfriendliness has been overshadowed by the rapid advancement of computer hardware. The accessibility of remote information by electronic means, in however awkward or cumbersome a manner, still is impressive, perhaps even miraculous. In 1974, the first broadly advertised personal computer, the Altair, had no keyboard or means to connect to other computers. It was programmed using switches and provided feedback to the user not from a screen but from a panel of lights. William Harrington, who was involved with LEXIS at its earliest stage, recalls that "searches typically ran five minutes, often twenty or thirty minutes, and sometimes more than an hour—and still the lawyers thought the system marvelously fast. One demonstration search, run on a terminal in a hotel suite in St. Louis during an ABA convention, ran four hours! Wilson and Harrington took the interested lawyer . . . to dinner, while the search was running, and it was not finished when they returned. Still, the lawyer was impressed with the efficiency of the system, which had found a case his firm had overlooked after weeks of conventional research."[37]

Two decades have brought quite extraordinary progress. Yet, there remain considerable difficulties in using online sources of information that are not inherent in the technology but are a consequence of software that developed in an earlier period and that does not exploit present capabilities or opportunities. As Mitchell Kapor and Jerry Berman wrote:

> "Transparency" is the holy grail of software designers. When a program is perfectly transparent, people forget about the fact that they are using a computer. The mechanics of the program no longer intrude on their thoughts. The most successful computer programs are nearly always transparent. . . . Personal computer communications, by contrast, are practically opaque. Users must be aware of baud rates, parity, duplex, and file transfer protocols—all of which a reasonably designed network could handle for them. It's as if, every time you wanted to drive to the store, you had to open up the hood and adjust the sparkplugs. On most Internet systems, it's even worse; newcomers find themselves confronting what John Perry Barlow calls a "savage user interface." Messages bounce, conferencing commands are confusing, headers look like gibberish, none of it is documented, and nobody seems to care. . . . The network becomes needlessly exclusionary.[38]

If information distance is to be reduced, therefore, software is the key. Concerns over software will have to change "from what the software does to how it does it."[39]

The relationship between informational distance and software can be illustrated by the manner in which one acquires information from WESTLAW and LEXIS. Looked at narrowly in terms of what information is needed to find something, the electronic world might appear to reduce informational distance considerably. The user no longer needs to have knowledge of legal categories, indexes, digests, or key numbers.[40] Users can find materials using words or combinations of words. Nothing would appear to erase informational distance as much as this, which speeds up searching and makes electronic searching a much easier task than print searching.

Unfortunately, word searching is not really very easy, nor is it conceptually simple.[41] For example, thinking up all appropriate words is not particularly easy, and only recently has an online thesaurus been provided to help users struggling to find appropriate words.[42] This, however, is only a small part of the problem. Even more important, what is necessary to conduct an effective word search is to arrange the words in a certain way. Whether one finds 3 cases or 300, or whether the number of relevant cases found will be 3 out of 500 or 300 out of 500 depends on whether words are linked by "ands" or "ors" or "withins" or "not withins," or whether the words are inside or outside a set of parentheses. Even if legal databases were provided cost-free to the general public, they might be relatively useless to lay people because this boolean scheme is difficult to master and there are considerable differences in the rules and conventions for searching different databases. Although software could be redesigned to help searchers, this does not appear to be a very high priority of database vendors.[43] Nor, unfortunately, does the role software plays in structuring space seem to be recognized by those who study legal research methods, since there has been negligible discussion of software issues in debates over problems involved in teaching electronic legal research.

A user logged on to most commercial databases today can feel close to relevant material but informationally distant from it. What is necessary to overcome the information distance that exists today is for software design to progress in the next twenty years as much as hardware has progressed since the Altair of 1974. It is not unrealistic to expect continuing and substantial improvement in software design. As this occurs and as electronic space becomes more inviting, and as rates for using commercial sources decline, usage can be expected to increase rapidly and information distance will diminish. This has considerable implications for both citizens and lay people as well as for legal professionals.

Relationships of Nonprofessionals to Legal Information

Control over a body of information is part of the definition of a profession.[44] Access to legal information in the print environment requires specialized training in research methods. Many feel that the legal profession's complex storage and retrieval techniques make lay people too dependent upon lawyers; the antidote consists of books and manuals that attempt to summarize various legal procedures in simple English.[45] With print, in other words, the only practical means for reducing informational distance between citizen and the law is to create an alternative genre of literature that explains procedures and concepts in simpler language and that avoids traditional legal materials almost entirely.

There are no recent attempts to develop completely new methods of accessing print materials that might be easier to use than traditional search-and-retrieval methods. To attempt such a task would be a forbidding, if not impossible, undertaking. The new information technologies, however, do make it possible to break down informational distances in ways that were not possible or economical with print. In an electronic information environment, there will be a different distance between legal and nonlegal information than there is in a print culture, and there will also be a different distance between those who have controlled legal information in the past (the legal profession), and those who have not (clients and citizens). There are several reasons for this.

Electronic Materials Do Not Rely on Print Categories. As noted earlier, access to information typically occurs in a manner that is different in the electronic environment from what it is in the print environment. A key obstacle to access in the print environment is a lack of knowledge of the subject matter and of the manner in which the subject matter has been organized. With print, one ordinarily needs to know something about the subject matter in order to find out more about it. The knowledge threshold is much less in the electronic environment, however, and if there are difficulties in accessing electronic information, they are much less related to what one already knows, since words are more important than categories in searching databases. What currently is a limiting factor that is more important than awareness of content and categories is the poor design of software.[46]

This is a significant point. Barriers to using print materials are, in a sense, inherent in the medium used to store information. The barriers currently standing in the way of or lending confusion to accessing electronic materials, however, to a considerable extent are a consequence of poor software design which will gradually be remedied. As computer scientist David Gelernter asserted, "[t]he software revolution hasn't yet begun; but it will soon."[47] Many problems that are experienced in accessing electronic information, in other words, are software related rather than content related. Electronic research has some inherent problems, but it is also a process that is immature and evolving and not fixed. As software begins "to change more than any other element in the computer paradigm,"[48] the relationship between users and information will change as well.

The introduction by WESTLAW of natural language searching is quite intriguing in this regard. It was made available in October 1992 and is considered by many to be more of an alternative to than a substitute for boolean searching.[49] The natural language option, called WIN ("Westlaw Is Natural"), allows one to substitute questions in standard English for searches previously conducted using the boolean model. A WIN search will present the user with between 20 and 100 cases in a ranking order of relevance that is related to the number of times the main search terms occur in the documents found. LEXIS introduced a natural language option, called Freelance, in early 1994.

WIN is WESTLAW's second attempt to reduce the complexity of boolean searching. The first was EZACCESS, which helps unfamiliar searchers find material that has a word or combination of words in a case or document. Although EZACCESS is easy and does provide access, the kind of access it provides is limited. Some of the flexibility provided by regular boolean searching is lost, and it is therefore essentially unusable and unreliable except for a quick and superficial look at some area by someone unfamiliar with the syntax required for a WESTLAW boolean search.[50] Indeed, persons who have difficulty remembering how to use "and," "or," "within," and so forth but who are generally familiar with the boolean model would probably find WESTLAW's WESTMATE for WINDOWS software an easier and more helpful alternative than EZACCESS.

As already noted, WIN may or may not be able to satisfy the needs of persons who are already capable of conducting boolean searches. It is an interesting development, however, because it is an alternative that moves users one more step away from the great informational distance inherent in print. No longer does one need to know legal categories or remember arbitrary connectors that vary from database to database. What WIN does, or some descendant of WIN will do, is remove indexing methods (the roadblock of print) and computer language (boolean searching) as distance-creating artifacts.

One descendant of WIN (or at least a talented sibling) is voice-recognition software Westlaw demonstrated in early 1994. Users of this software[51] can ask WESTLAW questions rather than typing in the questions. This is not something that will enhance the searching skills of persons already using WESTLAW, but like any improvement in the computer-user interface, it expands the market of potential users by reducing the informational distance between user and source.

If WIN is successful and as software becomes smarter and easier to use, the impact will be much wider than merely reducing confusion about electronic searching. Using the spatial perspective, one can view improved software as having the potential for reducing distance between those who need or desire legal information and the information that traditionally has been "distant" from them. WIN and other software improvements should be able to resolve the problem of different databases' having different commands and rules for searching. One might use the same means to access legal information, medical information, and financial information. Such an information system retains a role for professionals, such as lawyers, who work with relationships in a complex environment. The role, however, will be linked to the complexity of data and not the complexity of access.[52]

Looked at in this way, what WIN has the potential for setting in motion may be less significant for members of the legal profession who have difficulty with the boolean system than it is for nonlawyers. The impact of WIN, in other words, may be on a group that was so distant from legal information that it did not even exist as a market. Nonlawyers can now move closer to law-related information in electronic form as WIN decreases the distance between searchers and databases. Control of information by the profession may be considerably more difficult in such an environment, particularly if efforts are made to market WESTLAW more broadly than it is now marketed and if rates are reduced. This transformation can occur even if WIN turns out not to meet some needs of the legal profession. Although lawyers may need a means to find cases that is at least as reliable as boolean searching, which itself has difficulties,[53] other consumers of legal information may not have such a constraint and may find that WIN satisfies all of their needs.

If the network eventually becomes the place containing the body of knowledge upon which the authority of the profession relies, it may turn out to be a place where space reserved exclusively for professionals is not as easy to design and where it is not as easy to exclude nonprofessionals as it was in the print environment. Electronic space appears to be a place where it is much easier to "bypass hierarchies."[54] It is also a place that is much less exclusive and easier for nonprofessionals to enter. More nonlawyers have probably read legal materials on the Cornell Law School Legal Information Institute Gopher and World-Wide Web servers during the last two years than have entered the Cornell Law School library reading room in all the years since its founding. This is not meant to be a criticism of print libraries. Print libraries are not always "user-friendly" places, and law libraries are less user friendly than general libraries. Overcoming the distance that exists in libraries is a large part of the function of the reference staff. We tend not to recognize many of the obstacles that exist in libraries because librarians are accessible and libraries are familiar places. Libraries, particularly those we frequent, appear to us to be "user friendly," but that is more a consequence of many years' exposure to libraries rather than of their innate nature.

Legal material retains a barrier in terms of style and language. Yet, there are other obstacles and boundaries that will diminish in importance. As software becomes more usable and more able to anticipate and respond to the needs of users, as costs of access to legal materials decline, as the law learns to communicate using visual modes, and as electronic resources become more accessible to nonprofessionals, informational distance is reduced and pressure for change begins to build. As Thomas Bruce, co-director of the Cornell Legal Information Institute, stated, "the audience for legal information is not at all what we thought it was."[55]

The Network Is More Diffuse and Heterogeneous Than the Print Environment. In general, the electronic network opens up a much broader source of information for users than does a print library. The electronic network can be viewed as a larger, more inclusive, and less differentiating space than is the physical environment, where different kinds of informational activities use different tools and are clearly separate activities. In the physical environment, for example, calling someone for advice is a completely different kind of activity from reading a book, which in turn is different from searching for something in a public library, which in turn is different from reading a newspaper at home. The network provides many resources and techniques to obtain information that are not as clearly delineated. For example, the same or very related tools are employed to consult individuals as to consult a database. Our large electronic space lacks the clearly defined boundaries around many activities that we are accustomed to. This is what is implied when it is said that everything is at one's fingertips. Instead of moving from one kind of information-seeking activity to a distinctly different one, the network may be viewed as providing users with a variety of options, some providing the equivalent of turning on a television news program or consulting a popular magazine article, and some the equivalent of conducting serious research in a library.

In addition to being an information space that links sources of information that were separated in the print era, electronic networks considerably expand the number of sources of nontechnical law-related information available to users. All networks involve sending and receiving messages in somewhat similar ways, and the lines of demarcation that qualitatively separated print sources are much more difficult to locate. The Internet, commercial services, and individual bulletin boards are quickly becoming linked to one another. The source of electronically acquired information of any kind, therefore, can be a person or group that has been contacted via e-mail, textual information, hypertextual information, an interactive piece of software, or, more distantly into the future, interactive video. Once one finds one source, that source will lead to other sources, not by the use of arcane commands but by using a menu or relying on some other software that anticipates the user's needs.

Some of these sources of information may compete with traditional print sources, but most will probably be novel alternatives. Electronically accessible archives of groups such as the Electronic Frontier Foundation (EFF) and the Computer Professionals for Social Responsibility[56] provide a wide variety of information related to the goals, concerns, and activities of these groups, ranging from legal documents used in cases, to articles, newsletters, position papers, and other material not readily accessible in a print environment. Such sources may soon be far more numerous than what is readily available in print for most citizens and more accessible as well.

Expert Relationships with Information

Easier or expanded access to information and the opening up of new sources of legal information may be desirable for society and may be enthusiastically welcomed by citizens, but legal professionals may react to such developments with some ambivalence. Easy and expanded access, for example, may not be the primary consideration of either law or legal professionals. The professional is much more concerned than the lay person with the accuracy and authoritativeness of information than with easy, or even cheap, access.[57] The law has thrived in the print environment because there were accessible sources of standardized and trustworthy information. There are several levels of agents in the print environment, such as editors, publishers, and librarians, who in a sense certify material before it can enter the print library. For this reason, the mere presence of something in a law library's collection has traditionally been an indication that the work had some degree of authority and authenticity.

The new information environment has fewer certifying agents. Because electronic space can grow faster and more cheaply than physical space, collections can grow faster and can also grow more easily without standards being applied to what the collection contains. Relatively few professional librarians have control over legal information stored in electronic space on the Internet. The bias of the network tends to be inclusive rather than exclusive, and distributed computing, as mentioned earlier, fosters this by allowing users to treat separate collections as if they are one. This is highly convenient but it is also not always clear where information originates or how to evaluate information that would not have been readily available from print sources. Although there is no shortage of references to "electronic libraries," the organizing role that has been performed by bibliographers and librarians is left largely to software designers or to individual users. This raises problems because, at least at the moment, "most computer interfaces are not designed to allow the user to question data validity."[58] This challenges law because, as Virginia Wise has perceptively observed:

> [T]he increase in the volume of information makes it more necessary than ever for users of information to be critical consumers of the information available to them, knowing how to evaluate the raw data for authority, accuracy, bias, and incompleteness. Perhaps because law as taught is so much about authority, students are accustomed to thinking of legal sources of information as authoritative, but that habit ill-trains them for evaluating the various forms of locating

information. Moreover, something about the sameness of computer screens often cripples students' ability to distinguish between sources, disabling them from making judgments of better or worse that they are so used to making in most other facets of their professional and personal lives.[59]

The manner in which users obtain information also contributes to this. Electronic information is always obtained through copying. Often in a manner consistent with requirements of the copyright law and sometimes in a manner that violates it, information moving over the network may not be simply copied but is used, worked on, adapted, and in a variety of other ways altered in some fashion. There is, on the electronic network, a proliferation in sources of information as data is copied and moved and value is added to it. Current systems provide few cues about authenticity. They do not adequately explain whether the item one is seeking exists in one place only, and there are multiple routes of access to it or whether the informational source is a copy made of the original or some other copy. It is not as easy as it once was to be certain that what one is looking at is necessarily the same as some piece of information with the same name that was obtained from a different source. Similarly, there are no bibliographical tools available to inform a user that some item that has been found is the latest version. At least at present, whatever the process, the trustworthy character of print, where all copies are identical, seems impossible to match in the electronic environment.

This may be both a problem and an opportunity for law and for lawyers. It is a problem because "[o]rganizations are networks of information flow; therefore, directing flow to the right places, filtering it in useful ways, and even preventing it from flowing to certain locations improves organizational performance. . . . the primary goal from this perspective is not to produce more information, but rather to reduce the amount that any one subsystem must process."[60] This is a much harder task for institutions that relied on print-based traditions and processes to focus attention and to regulate and manage the flow of information. Yet, those who recognize and understand the differences between print and electronic space will understand why the role of the legal professional is changing and what kinds of tools can be employed to exploit the new electronic space. The lawyer's relationship with printed information was a relationship with information in a stable, authoritative, and trustworthy form. Information was something that could be found or discovered and then analyzed, interpreted, and applied. Cyberspace cannot help but gradually bring about a different attitude toward information since information will be less stable and will be updated much more often than can occur in the print environment. At the very least, this requires much greater sensitivity to and capabilities for dealing with change. As one teacher has argued, "Managing change is itself a technique, and a technique that can be taught like any other, but it is commonly ignored as teachers assume that the information retrieval techniques of today (or, even worse, of yesterday) will be those of tomorrow. In order to avoid this trap, instruction should emphasize the skills and strategies of dealing with change. . . ."[61]

Mastering change involves understanding that law is slowly moving away from a model where the nature of printed information is mimicked in various institutional processes. In an era of print, when one could assume that information was fixed in a tangible medium, an orientation naturally developed toward the lawyer as one who understood the nature of the print-web, was proficient in extracting information from it, and was knowledgeable in applying it. The lawyer in the electronic era—a person I shall describe later as a "digital lawyer" who operates in an environment where experts are more easily accessible but trustworthy information might not be, where physical and informational distances are different from what they were, where citizens are not as distant from law and lawyers are not as distant from clients, and where law will not be as distant from experience as it once was—can be expected to assume a much more challenging and dynamic role toward information and information processes.

The rearrangement of boundaries that have contributed much to the structure and operation of law is part of a larger process in which processes are displacing things and traditional symbols are losing meaning. The legal significance of this will be examined again in chapter 5 in a discussion of contracts and the management of relationships. More generally, however, it is clear that what is touching the law is at work in the larger society as well. In the words of Kevin Kelly:

> The Atom is the icon of 20th century science.
> The popular symbol of the atom is stark: a black dot encircled by the hairline orbits of several other dots. The Atom whirls alone, the epitome of singleness. It is the metaphor for individuality: atomic. It is the irreducible seat of strength. The Atom stands for power and knowledge and certainty. It is as dependable as a circle, as regular as round. . . .
> The internal circles of the Atom mirror the cosmos, at once a law-abiding nucleus of energy, and at the same time the concentric heavenly spheres spinning in the galaxy. In the center is the *animus*, the It, the life force, holding all to their appropriate whirling stations. The symbolic Atoms' sure orbits and definite interstices represent the understanding of the universe made known. The Atom conveys the naked power of simplicity. . . .
> The Atom is past. The symbol of science for the next century is the dynamical Net.
> The Net icon has no center—it is a bunch of dots connected to

other dots—a cobweb of arrows pouring into each other, squirming together like a nest of snakes, the restless image fading at indeterminate edges. The Net is the archetype—always the same picture—displayed to represent all circuits, all intelligence, all interdependence, all things economic and social and ecological, all communications, all democracy, all large systems. The icon is slippery, ensnaring the unwary in its paradox of no beginning, no end, no center. Or, all the beginning, all end, all center.[62]

"[T]he story of the law," write Collins and Skover, "is one of distancing text from context."[63] That has been the story for several millennia, since law became more focused on what was written than on what was said and since what was written became more important than what was said. The electronic environment, as it matures, will displace those who assume that information automatically is authoritative and that exclusive access to information can be maintained. The role of the lawyer may continue to involve the management of change, but this will be a more dynamic and continuous process than it has been in the past. It will reflect a model of law "as connecting rather than disconnecting" and as a "flow of dialogue"[64] rather than as a seamless web hovering above life. It will be a more multidimensional[65] process in which those who will be successful will be those who understand the nature of electronic space since it will be less through physical spaces and more through electronic space that many of the concepts, practices, and approaches of law and legal practice will be defined.

4

Interacting in Cyberspace

I am in a familiar place. Have I been here before? I feel I know this place, yet even as I turn something appears to have changed. It is still the same place, but not quite identical to what it was just a moment ago. Like a new performance of an old symphony, its intonation is different, and in the difference between its present and its past incarnations something new has been said in a language too subtle for words. Objects and situations that were once thought to have a fixed identity, a generic "self," now possess personality, flaw and flavor. All permanent categories are defeated as the richness of the particular impresses upon me that in this landscape, if I am to benefit fully, attention is both required and rewarding.

—Marcos Novak

After establishing the Apple Computer Company in 1979, one of the first actions taken by Steve Jobs and Steve Wozniak was to have a logo designed. This logo, an apple with red, yellow, orange, and green layers, is still the company's symbol. Its vivid colors attract the eye and it is often a focal point of Apple's advertising. There is one element of the logo, however, that is sometimes not noticed or remembered. This is that one side of the apple has a jagged edge, suggesting that at least one bite has been taken from it.

The missing piece is an obvious allusion to Adam and Eve's bite from the fruit of the tree of knowledge. That early bite, which the book of Genesis simply states was a "fruit" but which folklore has transformed into an apple, provided the Garden's inhabitants with a new perspective on who they were and a new awareness of the nature of their environment. Adam and Eve's action, one might say, brought

92

about the human race's first information explosion, and made them aware of a whole range of stimuli and sensory information. They faced an environment that, in an instant, seemed to contain vastly more information than it had previously. All of their understandings of who and what they were changed in an instant. Perceptions of themselves and of their environment changed as, in the words of the author of Genesis, "the eyes of them both were opened, and they knew they were naked."[1]

The story of the bite from the tree of knowledge may or may not be accepted as literal truth, but it remains a provocative device for revealing what can occur as one is exposed to information in a new form and as one's informational environment changes. It reminds us that we can and should look at technological changes from the perspective of individuals who must confront new circumstances, new understandings, new challenges, and new perceptions of themselves. The story involves not merely the acquisition of information but the removal of perceptual boundaries. In addition to being aware that a new technology changes *how* information is produced and also *how much* information is produced, there are changes in how each individual interacts with information in a new form. A new technology provides us with a new informational space in addition to a range of new tools and, over time, this changes individual perceptions of the environment, expectations about the environment, and the skills needed to acquire and use information successfully in the new environment. These changes in an individual's relationship with the informational environment may not occur as instantaneously as they occurred in the Garden of Eden, but we too, if one can carry the analogy one step further, may wonder not only about our new powers but about how exposed we are, about how vulnerable are a variety of generally unchallenged assumptions about the nature of information, and about how many bites it will take before we become aware that our identity is changing.

The first part of this book focused on the consequences of bringing distant information closer. This chapter examines what occurs when users engage new sources and forms of information and begin to interact with them in new ways. What we face in the coming years is a change not merely in how many sources of information are available but in how we interact with information. The new media not only bring more information closer but change the manner in which users interact with information. In so doing, the new media create new links and new distances between existing elements in the legal process and a new frame for the individual's relationship with the law.

If law is looked for in books, certain expectations and habits of thought are employed. If law begins to be thought of as residing somewhere in electronic space and as a set of informational transactions, we will begin acting and thinking in somewhat different ways. The

D.L.I.A.D.T.
Library

medium employed by the law colors how distant we are from it and whether it is accessible or remote, friendly or hostile, tolerant or demanding. It affects when we can navigate through the law by ourselves and when professional assistance is needed. It shapes whether we are satisfied with traditional modes of conflict resolution and with existing artifacts of legal culture or whether we will begin to feel that new practices are needed.

Communications technologies help structure the relationship between the individual, the ruling authority, and law. This is an issue that is at the heart of the story in Genesis. Indeed, from a legal perspective, the theme of one's relationship to the law may be the central theme of the biblical story. Adam and Eve, by committing an act of rebellion, initially found themselves naked and powerless before the only law that existed in their world. Eventually, however, they realized that they were not powerless but that they had new opportunities to make law as well as respond to it. Their protective and confining umbrella had been removed and the ongoing and eternal struggle to construct something new began.

Unlike the Garden of Eden, where the total human population was quickly transported together into a new environment, we are traveling into cyberspace one at a time. Important changes have not been experienced by everyone or been seen by all. Cyberspace is already a reality to some, whereas to others it is a term of science fiction. We are vulnerable rather than "naked," but this is a more subtle condition and one whose meaning and impact are more difficult to describe.

The umbrella that has been removed from us, the one that is leaving us exposed, is the umbrella of print. I use the word not simply to refer to the books and other tangible artifacts we still see, but to the expectations we have come to have about how information is and should be used. Printing provided something novel for law, something that could embody information in a tangible, standardized, and mass-produced form, a form that could provide identical information in many different places. This was a miraculous achievement. As we increasingly interact with information in electronic form, however, we are becoming aware that information is being packaged differently and that "mere" packaging affects how content is used. For law and for other institutions as well, the gradual replacement of one umbrella by another, the shift from printed to electronic sources of information, involves a series of changes as the manner in which we think about information shifts from the model of the printed book to something that more appropriately reflects the qualities of electronic communication. Traveling into cyberspace involves moving away from a view of information and law as being fairly static and fixed to a model where information is hard to hold on to, where it can be accessed quickly and easily but possessed over time only with great difficulty. We will, of course, continue to use information by reading, thinking, and responding to it in some way. Many skills that came into wide and general use in the print era will continue to be valuable as information becomes increasingly accessible in electronic form. Yet, interaction with information in electronic form will present us with new options and make new demands on us. What we read, how we think about information, and how we respond to it will gradually change. More particularly, as we take from the knowledge trees of cyberspace, we will be challenged to develop new skills and habits of thought, patterns of acting and patterns of thinking, that will be reflected in institutional processes and practices.

One of the fundamental reasons for change in how we interact with information is that we are being liberated from many of the constraints that are inherent in the printing process. Time and space, as has already been described, are becoming much less formidable obstacles than they once were. This is liberating in that it will allow us to use our creative energies to develop new modes of distributing and presenting information. This may also be viewed as disrupting established patterns of acting and thinking, and of presenting us with new contexts and many new choices, many of which touch traditional values, beliefs, and substantial economic interests. Although we have not been as ignorant of our general surroundings as Adam as Eve may have been of theirs, the new capabilities and opportunities provided by the new media will pose questions for us too about how to cope with a new informational environment and about what changes in accepted behaviors and abilities are required to respond to a changed relationship between humans and machines.

This chapter examines three fundamental changes in the information environment that are linked to new modes of interacting with information:

1. Movement toward information that is less stable and permanent.
2. Movement away from mass production and distribution of information.
3. Movement toward machines that respond to and anticipate user actions.

The next chapter explores how the new media can be used to structure relationships and how the use of contracts may change as a result.

From Movable Type to Moving Type

Printing relied on letters and alphanumeric symbols as the basic element for producing books. A printer's workshop contained thousands of pieces of type, each consisting of a letter or symbol. Selected pieces of type could be arranged and rearranged in seemingly endless ways. Once the small pieces of metal were placed in some order, they could be used to impress the same message on any number of pieces of paper that were fed through the press. Printing, therefore, created not merely many copies of a work but large numbers of *identical* copies of the work. The capability of print to produce multiple uniform copies has been suggested as being an even more important quality than the ability to print large numbers of copies.[2] Prior to printing, copies made by hand inevitably contained errors and thus fostered a cultural skepticism about whether words on paper could be trusted as representing the author's views accurately. Printing, however, as one scholar has noted, "replaced precarious forms of tradition (oral and manuscript) by one that was stable, secure and lasting; it is as if mankind had suddenly obtained a trustworthy memory instead of one that was fickle and deceitful."[3]

This quality of printing brought about a major transformation in how people related both to the spoken word and to works embodied in print. These changes also served as a cornerstone of basic elements of the legal process. The idea and the operation of a *common* law, or *equal* protection of the laws, or a strong system of precedent,[4] is greatly assisted when lawyers have a common point of reference, are able to consult exact copies in different places, and have complete faith that the language that they are quoting is identical to language in the document consulted by others. By standardizing the body of legal information, printing enabled law, in the form of words on paper, to acquire an authority that had been lacking in the scribal period when "word of mouth" was often considered to be more reliable than words on paper. Without this element of trust, it is not likely that a model of law as dependent upon "law in the books" would have evolved as it has during the past few centuries.

The manner in which the qualities of a communications medium affect law is the theme of Michael Clanchy's *From Memory to Written Record: England 1066–1307,*[5] an exploration of changes in English law that occurred in the eleventh to fourteenth centuries. Clanchy describes how the spoken word retained its authority even as writing and literacy became more common in the pre-print era. Oral contracts, for example, were often preferred over written ones. This may seem odd since agreements today are considered tentative until they are "put in writing." At that time, however, because of the nature of writing, the idea of relying upon or consulting a written document was not common. Memory was considered to be more trustworthy than something written, and "practical questions were answered by oral testimony and not by reference to documents."[6] In other words, if there was a dispute over land ownership and a written charter needed interpretation or was contradicted by what was remembered, memory took precedence over written proof.[7] The "principle that 'oral witness deserves more credence than written evidence' was a legal commonplace."[8]

The intriguing opportunities presented by placing contracts into electronic form and of structuring relationships using electronic links will be discussed in the next chapter. Written contracts are, along with the "written" judicial opinion, paradigmatic artifacts of the print period of law. The different treatment that contract law gives to oral and written contracts is a complicated matter, but what is noteworthy is less the details of when oral contracts can be enforced than the frame of reference that assumes that anything written is more reliable than anything spoken.

It is a bit ironic that a process identified with *movable* type may have had its largest impact by creating a final product that was much more fixed and stable than the work of scribes. What was brought into being by type that could be rearranged in innumerable ways were works that could not be changed as easily as something that had to be copied by hand. Thus, forgery and careless copying, which were commonplace in the scribal period, became less common. Although printed works were not "etched in stone," the large number of standardized copies provided works that were not easily changed and that contributed a sense of authority and authenticity that had been lacking earlier. Any user of print materials could assume that the printed work contained the words of the author, and it was irrelevant whether the author was alive or dead, or living nearby or in some distant place. Lawyers and citizens could assume that the words on paper were not merely a representation or manifestation of the law but were the law itself.

Our interaction with information is increasingly not with fixed letters on paper or with units of type but with flickering dots on a screen and with units of electricity that the eye cannot see. Typing on a computer keyboard presents the illusion of continuity with a typewriter, and word processors present the illusion of working with actual letters and words, but what is occurring as one presses keys is not the fixing of an image on paper but the manipulation of electrical impulses, and the turning on and off of dots of light on the screen. Those who use word processors appreciate the ability to delete words, to move them around, to "cut and paste." Those who work with graphics have even more impressive capabilities for changing appearances. One who shrinks a picture or enlarges a font size can do this because electrical impulses and not letters or pictures are being modified. This provides great support for creative endeavors since it is possible to experiment with and try out many approaches. It also, however, has an impact on the finished work since, in the future, some works may never be considered to be finished. Instead of being safeguarded by the fixed and protective cover of the printed book, they are entered through a much more permeable frame—one that may even, as will be described, invite a reader or user to interact with and alter the original.

In his extraordinarily insightful work, *Turing's Man*, David Bolter describes the lack of finality that infuses the world of programmers. He writes:

> Turing's man lacks the emotional intensity of his predecessor. He invests less of himself in his games because the games he plays are not irrevocable. They are meant to be played to a conclusion and then reset and played again. The programmer indeed cares about the game's outcome, but he is saved from ultimate failure by its impermanence. A computer program that fails can usually be corrected and rerun. In another sense, this is a disadvantage, for a programmer can never forget that every solution in the computer world is temporary, makeshift, obsolescent. . . . the ease of transferring data and the huge amounts of data transferred mean that nothing in the computer world remains long in one form. Every programmer knows how easy it is inadvertently to destroy hours of work with the touch of the wrong button. But no program is intended to last long anyway. If it is useful and often used, then someone will soon modify it for his own plans, which differ slightly from the original purpose. Eventually, it will be thrown out altogether, when new equipment or software makes it obsolete. A philosopher or poet of the nineteenth century might aspire to be read for hundreds of years to come. An inventor might hope to make a machine whose utility would extend for decades. A computer programmer or engineer measures his achievement in years, often months.[9]

These differences between print and electronic communication provide some of the fuel propelling our rapidly changing society. Information can be produced, obtained, and distributed more quickly than ever before, and this accelerates, or provides a pressure to accelerate, any process oriented around information. Print had provided law with an environment that was conducive to moderated change, an environment where it was possible for judicial opinions to be, at the same time, something that was "final" and also something that could be reworked, reinterpreted, and used as a determining factor in future cases.

The book has been a comfortable and common symbol of law because it supports a sense of finality and even irrevocability, of something that is the same wherever it is observed. The pages of print, once they are published, are the same no matter how often the book is opened and are the same for all who possess the book, no matter where they are located. As we work more and more with the "bytes" of the new technologies, change is occurring on several different levels, causing many electronic artifacts to lack in some way the fixed quality of words on paper. An electronic work, for example, may be different each time it is opened and it may be configured to look different for each user. The fixity of the printed word is accepted by many as an almost inevitable part of the information environment and thus affects how we think of information and interact with information. As will be discussed later in connection with copyright law, it colors what we assume about the creation and the ownership of information. Substituting information in electronic form for information in printed form, however, gradually makes us aware that a broad range of constraints on the use and reuse of information are being lifted.

It is intriguing that a considerable effort during this early part of the transition period has been devoted to making electronically produced information look as if it had been printed. Desktop publishing software and laser printers have made it quite simple to produce documents that look as if they were printed. Office memos that used to be handwritten or typed now often appear as if they were "typeset." In this context, however, appearances are highly deceiving. Just because machines are called "printers" does not mean that they produce material that is identical in all ways to material that emerged from the traditional publishing-editorial process. The focus on desktop publishing reveals that there is still, in this transition period, a preference for paper documents. The appearance of the letters on the page, however, may be all that such documents have in common with traditionally printed materials, As will be described in the next section, for example, electronically "printed" information is often personalized and individualized, different for every recipient, and something that contradicts one of the basic contributions that printing made to modern society.

Electronic tools empower users to change, edit, modify, and manipulate information much more easily than is possible with print. Finality and fixity do not come naturally to electronic materials. In general, many of the processes of working with information are accelerated and, as indicated in the previous chapter, electronic information travels along different routes in order to reach users. The consequence of this is that those working with electronic information have new tools to acquire, process, and distribute information. At the same time, authors, creators, and publishers have less power to control the image that all users will look at since some of the controls that affected how individuals assessed and thought about printed information are no longer in place.

During this transition period we have acquired tools that bring large quantities of information to us from any place at any time. The new media remove, or at least weaken, various boundaries that separate and differentiate. We engage in increasing numbers of information transactions since information can move over wires or through the air rather than on trucks or trains. The electronic media remove many constraints on using information or finding information, and electronic information can circulate widely without the assistance of editors and publishers. There has, however, been little attention to what occurs if the resultant information lacks some of the qualities of print that have made it reliable and trustworthy.

A manager of one of the largest legal databases has described this concern over the reliability of electronic information as being

> one of the seminal problems of the information age. Those of us engaged in developing bigger and hopefully better information retrieval technologies recognize that *authenticity, currentness, originality*, etc., of any given quantum of information is a significant problem for the user, and one of our jobs is to assist the user to determine each of these qualities for a quantum of information that his search has retrieved. The mere fact that a document is retrieved as a result of a Boolean or natural language query is no more than *prima facie* evidence of relevance!
>
> Many voices have been heard in other fora bemoaning increasing serials subscription costs and wishfully thinking that the Internet will solve the professional and scholarly journals problems for us by removing the editorial middlemen, thus making all that original research available to us for free—or at least a very much reduced price. Yet it is precisely those journals that have provided the *authentication* of research and *validation* of published results.[10]

In this transition phase, it is not completely clear how persons and institutions that require certainty about the sources of electronic information will be satisfied. There are some technological fixes to this problem, such as digital signatures, but these may require those who have such concerns to expend more attention and energy to this problem. We already have authentication rituals for writing, such as requiring a notary seal or witnessed signatures, but many users do not understand that something similar will be required for some electronic material in order to obtain a satisfactory level of authority.

The speed with which new information replaces old in an electronic environment has not brought about Adam and Eve's acute sense of embarrassment, but the rapidity of change and the loss of some steadying guideposts of print have been disorienting and perhaps even destabilizing. We have received a flood of information, but only gradually is the sense of awe at the technological feats inherent in such achievements being tempered by an awareness that the *movable* quality of information in electronic form brings with it other changes as well that, in the short term at least, may be quite disruptive to law on a whole series of levels.

The problem with authority and authenticity is not an insurmountable problem, but it is also not an insignificant problem. It is clearly a problem of the transitional phase we are currently in where we have been blind to some value provided by information in printed form. In this early period, we have sacrificed much of the value added by editors and librarians in order to take advantage of the speed with which access is provided by the electronic media. In our current euphoria over the magical tools that have become available, the value added by print publishers has largely been unnoticed. As Michael Heim observed, the book industry "provides readers with various cues for evaluating information. The publishers legitimize printed information by giving clues that affect the reader's willingness to engage in reading the book. Editorial attention, packaging endorsements by professional or colleagues, book design and materials, all add to the value of the publisher's imprint. Communicating in contemporary cyberspace lacks the formal clues. In their place are private recommendations, or just blind luck. The electronic world, unlike the traditional book industry, does not protect its readers or travelers by following rules that set up certain expectations."[11]

We are, to use a widely used phrase, at the "electronic frontier." There is general euphoria about the openness and freedom of this frontier space, of capabilities for working with information that do not exist in print space. The frontier area, however, also lacks many of the guideposts that have made it possible to conduct business using the traditional media. The emphasis in the past decade has been on moving and extending the boundaries of the frontier and providing access to the frontier area. This certainly is desirable, but there is also the necessity to devote serious attention to the manner in which life is led on the frontier. Those concerned with law need not only to extend the frontier but to organize it. Law is not simply a body of information or knowledge, but a body of authoritative information,[12] and the legal process cannot be dependent upon a medium of communication whose reliability is open to question. Authority and authenticity have been embedded in print materials. They are not yet embedded as well or as clearly in electronic materials.

There are, it might be argued, different kinds of print materials— some, such as legal materials, bearing a high level of trust, and others, such as the *National Enquirer*, having very low levels of trust. The point, however, is not whether the words of the author are true but that the words that appear can be assumed to be the author's words. There are many examples of plagiarized books, but even in these cases we can hold accountable the person whose name appears on the book's cover. Electronic distribution poses new problems of accountability and trust because the user interacts with the electronic material in a new way. As will be described shortly, the person sitting at a computer, looking at the screen, and using the mouse or keyboard may be involved in one of many possible activities. Unlike reading, which may change the reader but does not change the material being read, the interaction with the computer will change both the user and, in many cases, the material that is being interacted with.

The Decline of the Mass Media

Because printing encouraged the production of large numbers of identical copies, it became the first *mass* medium. One who reads a book or newspaper or watches a television program knows that many people, at other times and places, will see the same image and be presented with the same information. The economics of printing encouraged this since printing is a process where the cost of printing each item declines as the number of copies printed increases. For broadcasting, the value of a program increases as the number of viewers increases. Such modes of communication are most easily used by large organizations that are communicating with large audiences. The mass media are less easily or economically used by smaller groups. Electronic communication, however, is more flexible than print or broadcasting. When information is distributed over a network, the process is hospitable to individuals and groups as well as those seeking large audiences.

One reason for this is that electronic information is not so much distributed by a producer as it is obtained by a user. The paradigm of electronic publishing is different from the paradigm of print publishing in that the goal of the latter is to allow the reader to possess a copy, whereas the goal of the former is more commonly to provide access to an information source. As I shall explain in a later chapter, this will frequently lead to a preference for access to information over ownership or possession of information.

Any information on any connected computer is, in theory, accessible and, therefore, is "published" as soon as it is placed on the computer. Electronic publishing over a network requires a means of access, but there is no burden of distribution on the creator or producer. Whereas print publishers estimate the number of purchasers and then decide how many copies to print, the electronic publisher that relies on the network makes no such estimates and needs only to produce one copy. This change in the manner in which we obtain electronic information involves us not only in a change in patterns of distribution but in a change in how we think about accessing information. An interesting example of what is involved in such a change can be seen in proposals to bring to several hundred channels to television users. Television, whether broadcast or cable, is a mass medium in which sound and images are distributed at prearranged times. The number of choices at any given time can be equated with the number of channels, and viewers must select a program from an available channel. Cable television provides many times the number of channels than broadcasting because the wire is able to accommodate more information than the spectrum that is used to send signals through the air. If the number of available channels is increased from 40 to

500, the market may be more splintered than if there are only 5 channels but the economics of mass merchandising will still be in force.

When the first proposals for a 500-channel system were made, jokes were told about how big the dial would have to be or how big *TV Guide* magazine would have to be. Such comments reveal not a real problem of logistics but simply how greatly the television model of distributing information has affected our thinking. In reality, we are moving toward a system where one might say either that there are an infinite number of channels of communication or, indeed, that there are no channels of communication because the concept of channels makes no sense when considering electronic communication. The technological feat of providing so many new and accessible sources of information forces us to change our frame of reference, our language, and the concepts that we typically have employed to describe viewing moving images on a screen.

The public discussion and concern over hundreds of "channels" may represent as good an example as any of how our minds change as we become acquainted with new opportunities. The opportunity to access hundreds of sources of information via a television set is certainly novel. The age of broadcasting and even the age of cable have not prepared us for an electronic space in which access to information and access to people is as easy as it is becoming. Access to 500 channels is, therefore, difficult to understand given the experience with television. Yet, 500 channels may not be difficult to understand if one stops thinking in terms of television and mass communication and, instead, employs a telephone model or a bookstore model or a public library model or simply a space, such as an apartment building, where there are several hundred apartments. When we speak of channels it is implied that there are a finite number of channels. The movement to electronic communication moves us beyond the fixed and constrained model of broadcasting. One could argue that anyone possessing a telephone has millions, if not billions, of channels available in the form of telephone numbers that could be dialed. The computer user linked to a network, database, or information service also could claim to have staggering numbers of channels available. The browser in a bookstore or library has thousands of "channels" available. What inevitably occurs, however, as the number of channels increases, is that the whole concept of "channels" becomes obsolete, which is why we do not think in terms of channels when talking on the phone or browsing in a library.

As citizens become increasingly able to select from an array of informational alternatives, the information each of us receives will be very different, both in appearance and in content, from messages received by others. There will no doubt continue to be frequent occasions when the same image or information will be distributed to millions simultaneously but it is also not too far fetched to declare, as some have done already, that "the era of mass media is past"[13] and that identical information distributed to all will no longer be as dominant a condition of modern life as it has been. Our sources of information are proliferating, and increasing amounts of communication will be individualized or "groupified" rather than massified. It is no longer possible to expect everyone in an area to focus on the news presented by the local newspaper when there are increasing numbers of cable channels and electronic sources of news. In commercial matters, we are targeted, indeed bombarded, by direct mail marketers who know a great deal about us, who can tailor messages to many different groups of people,[14] and who link us with others on the basis of interests rather than geography. As e-mail becomes more popular, this will become even more common and, unless electronic filtering methods are improved, more troublesome as well.

The junk mail phenomenon involves receiving letters that are "personalized" and are directed to us on the basis of information that others possess about us. A more significant long-term trend is that we are no longer as constrained to wait for information to come to us, but have new capabilities for seeking out information that meets our needs and for selecting more efficiently from among an expanding informational universe. We will be able to instruct machines about the kind of information that is of concern and interest to us. In a mass media world, the decision of what constitutes "news" is now done by persons other than ourselves. These decisions, of selecting "newsworthy" events from among all of the events that occur in the world, are made by editors and reporters and determine what current information is available to us. The ground is moving out from under this model as more information becomes accessible electronically and as individual desires can be accommodated in ways that were not possible in the past.

Those with access to the Internet, either directly or through connections provided by CompuServe, Delphi, America Online, or other commercial enterprises, can already obtain much information in ways that were not possible even a year or two ago. Individuals can have White House press releases and summaries of Supreme Court decisions automatically sent to their e-mail addresses. Individuals with interests in foreign affairs can receive news distributed by foreign governments. The decline of the mass media, although it may hurt those industries that profited from mass distribution, is rapidly spawning new entities that will profit from satisfying informational needs using the new means of distribution. Current suppliers of information are not unaware of this. The competition between cable companies and telephone companies to serve as the informational conduit to the home, and the scrambling between existing publishers, the traditional news media, and entertainment providers to enter new markets, is just one example of this.

The question of who will win these and other ongoing competitions to survive and thrive in the new informational environment will be an ongoing one. The history of printing suggests that those who controlled the previously dominant technology may not be prepared to exploit the new environment. Habits of thought and frameworks for understanding the communication of information may be too ingrained to allow new ventures to be developed and succeed. Yet, beyond the question of who will win is, perhaps, a more important question of what it will mean for us and for law when this new informational environment begins, certainly before the new millennium, to flourish.

The print model of mass distribution has been "imprinted" upon our conception of information. If one assumes that the evolution of modern law also has been deeply touched by the link to authoritative words on paper, then the future character and organization of law also will be different from what it has been in the past. Much of the authority of the lawyer, for example, can be traced to the need for an interpreter of information that was accessible only in printed form. The lawyer, like the newspaper, has been a vehicle of communication and interpretation in an era where there have been relatively few vehicles for transmitting information between government and citizen. The newspaper industry has begun to understand that it faces many new challenges in an electronic environment where patterns of communication are changing and are much more diffuse than they were previously. Governments are struggling mightily to preserve some measure of control over the flow of information in an environment where conduits of communication are proliferating. Law, however, seems much less aware of its own vulnerability to changing patterns of communication and interaction with information that allow audiences to be reached in new and different ways.

Changes in the manner of distributing information are momentous in many ways. It is quite obvious, for example, that large economic interests are at stake. Industries that are slow to realize that *mass* communication is not an inevitable and permanent mode of providing information to large numbers of people but is rather a stage in the evolution of opportunities for communication will be increasingly vulnerable. There is, for this reason, an ongoing reorientation of advertisers and journalists to the novel capabilities of the electronic media, in addition to the shifting competitive strategies of broadcasters, cable companies, and telephone companies. There is a much less commented upon shift involving individuals, as more sources of information emerge and more information is easily accessible from novel and nontraditional sources.

Modern Western law, as an agency of the state, often has been attacked as being linked to the organs of mass media, as using the mass media to promote the legitimacy of law and of other powerful institutions. Whether or not one subscribes to this theory, there is a link between law and mass communication that exists at a deeper level. The legal profession might be viewed as actually being an organ of mass communication, as being the means by which law is communicated from state to citizen. There is variety in the messages about law provided by lawyers, just as there are different messages about contemporary issues presented by different newspapers. Yet, it is still true that the lawyer is a principal source of legal information, an intermediary who guides the process of learning about legal matters and who serves as a significant conduit for legal information. The traditional news media have learned during the past decade that their captive and rather passive audience has essentially escaped, not because the audience actively sought change but because new technologies cut many of the chains that bound viewers and networks. This fragmentation, however, is not limited to television or newspapers but is a more general phenomenon that is touching all institutions that are dependent upon information.

Machines That Recycle Information

Our ability to understand the different natures of electronic and print information paradigms suffers, as I have already suggested, because metaphors and frames of reference that are commonly employed to explain human-computer interactions actually provide little to guide us. Print-related metaphors, for example, that call the screen a "desktop" or the material on screen a "document" or a "file" provide no real insight into what it means to be able to interact dynamically with computerized data. Although we are accustomed to reading, browsing, looking at, or consulting print documents and files, we do not really interact with them in the same way that we interact with electronic sources of information. Nor is television a suitable context for placing human-computer interactions into an understandable perspective. Television may stimulate and provoke both thought and action, but there are, at least currently, no real opportunities to interact with a show that is being watched. One may have many choices in what to watch, but interaction with the standard television set is limited to pressing the on-off button and the channel selector.

Print and other traditional mass media are one-way media, capable of delivering information *to* readers and viewers but unable to receive information *from* users, at least at the time they are receiving information. Reading can be a highly engaging, provocative, and stimulating experience, but it is, and has been for the past few centuries, a solitary and private experience. Publishers may know how many copies of a work have been sold, but they usually do not know who has bought a copy or when the copy is being read. Anonymity, therefore, is a condition that comes fairly naturally to print space. Interacting with a distant computer involves not only taking *from* the machine but giving something up *to* the machine. At the very least, the computer, and possibly others, possesses information on who is using the machine and when. This is a key difference between print and electronic media that, as will be explained later, affects a wide range of law-related issues, from privacy to copyright to the nature of the legal profession. In addition, as we provide information to the computer, either intentionally or simply as a consequence of using the machine, our relationship with information changes. A reader of a book may take some kind of action depending upon what has been read, but the book will remain as it was when it was bought or borrowed. Human-computer interactions, on the other hand, may change the user and, at the same time, the data on the computer are also changed in some way.

It is somewhat unfortunate that the one-way nature of reading and viewing has, at least thus far, established the conceptual framework most users employ in thinking about how information is obtained from computers. From the perspective of most users, the act of reading from a computer monitor seems similar, if not identical, to the act of reading from the printed page. For such persons, obtaining information electronically may at times seem preferable to print since it is faster and easier and they need no longer go to a library or search through musty old newspapers to obtain some desired piece of information. Or it may at other times seem inconvenient when compared to print, since the computer screen may not be as readable as the page of print and the computer is not yet as portable as books or newspapers. In either case, however, the model used for comparison is print and the computer is seen, like a book, to be a container of information that is sent or delivered to the user.

I have already suggested several reasons why the process of accessing electronic sources of information is quite different from the process of accessing printed information, and how the new medium changes the distance between individual and information. The interactive qualities of the new media change the relationship between individual and informational sources even further and provide another reason why we shall have to leave print models behind as we think about or describe how one works with electronic information. The main reason for this is that the interactive quality of electronic communication turns a process in which information flowed only to the recipient into a process in which information flows both to and from recipients. Electronic space is not hospitable to one-way communication, the pattern of communication that is typical of print. Rather, it opens us up to a process that retains some qualities of print and television but that also is interactive in ways that are reminiscent of face-to-face conversations where both participants to the conversation walk away different from what they were before.

To a considerable extent now, and to a much greater extent in the future, the typical mode of obtaining information will involve not simply the receipt of information but an exchange of information—an information transaction—in which one gives up information as part of the process of receiving information. It is not much of an exaggeration to claim that "daily life is nothing but a string of transactions from credit card purchases to phone calls. . . . each action adds to a spreading electronic wake that we leave behind as we go through life. A few bits of matched data can tell volumes about us all, a conclusion implicit in the informal motto of the marketing industry: 'We know more about you than your mother.'"[15] In electronic space, in other words, there may be no mere passive "readers" or recipients of information. Every act of reading, merely because of the manner in which it occurs, becomes part of an exchange in which, in ways that are not yet completely clear to us, one must provide information in order to obtain it. Users of electronic information systems cannot be mute or passive readers since it is largely through dialog that information is obtained. Electronic *interactions,* in other words, are almost always also information *transactions.*

The interactive nature of digital communication adds an element that is not present in the print environment. In print space, or even television space, information coming in is observed by the recipient and, perhaps, acted upon by the him or her. In simplest terms, one has no expectation that the book the reader is reading or the program the viewer is watching can change as it is being read or watched. Electronic space is different in that, at least potentially, the user changes as he or she receives information and the environment changes as information is received from the user. Just as the user is obtaining information from some source, the source is receiving information from the user. This may take a moment to understand since our framework for understanding the process of communication is still rooted in print space where such a dynamic interaction cannot occur. It is a highly significant point, however, since the most novel element in the human–computer interaction may not be that the user is more active than the person using some other medium or that one can select from a host of options presented by a machine that may be thousands of miles away or that everything is occurring much faster than before. Rather, it may be that the machine providing information to the user is, at the same time, getting information from the user and is acting upon and perhaps communicating that information to other parts of the network.

One obtains possession of print materials either through borrowing, where he or she receives something without giving up anything, or through a purchase, where he or she receives something by giving up money. In either case, the consumer can be virtually anonymous and obtains information through a fairly clear and discrete transaction. For a publisher to get "feedback" about a purchaser or for a network to get information about viewers, some special method or line of communication must be designed. In electronic space, however, although information is being acquired at a distance, it is difficult for the user to hide since one must, at a minimum, send some information to some source before receiving any information. Anonymity is exceedingly difficult to preserve in electronic space since some bit of information about oneself is commonly revealed as part of communicating on line. We might be obtaining information for free, but we must at least "sign on" to some system. More significantly, when information is being sold, the provider is always interested in receiving more than money. Indeed, as will be explained, anyone selling anything in an "information economy" is interested in receiving information along with the purchase price.

In this transition period, where there is already considerable recognition of the value of obtaining information from and about consumers but when most consumers are not yet on line, methods of obtaining such information are relatively inefficient. Consider, for example, the marketing technique of providing "rebates" to persons who purchase a particular product. Rebates are an advertising technique that offers a purchaser a sum of money if proof of purchase is sent to the manufacturer. Many, if not most, consumers view such rebates as a discount, a reduction in the price of the product. Yet, rebates might more accurately be considered as a separate transaction in which a consumer provides information about himself or herself in exchange for a sum of money. Rebates are a means for manufacturers to find out who has purchased their product and, frequently, to obtain some economic and lifestyle information about the purchaser as well. In exchange, the consumer is paid a sum of money.

Manufacturers are eager to purchase such information about consumers so that it can be used in analyzing purchasing patterns and evaluating marketing strategies. Purchasers can be directly targeted when new products are developed. Such information can be merged with other information and perhaps even sold to other companies collecting information about consumers. Yet, the rebate process is also not particularly efficient. Many consumers do not fill out rebate forms. Other consumers may understand that in this information transaction what is being provided to the manufacturer may be of greater value than what is being given to the consumer and are reluctant to reveal information about themselves.

Rebates in their current form probably will not survive for much longer. Placing paper forms in packages and asking consumers to fill out and send the forms back is cumbersome, slow, and inefficient. In addition, all of the information sought by the manufacturer can now be acquired instantaneously through electronic means. Purchases may still be paid for by cash or check, but common purchases are increasingly becoming electronified and, as this occurs, the consumer gives up information as well as money in exchange for a product.

The clearest example of how this process occurs is provided by the cards distributed by many supermarkets that afford consumers "discounts" if they allow the cashier to scan the card prior to paying for a purchase. The card allows an information transaction to occur in which, in effect, the consumer sells information to the store. The information consists of data about one's purchasing habits. The price being paid by the store is the difference between the regular purchase price of the item and the so-called discount price. In exchange for a shopper's not purchasing anonymously, an instant rebate is provided by the store.

Such information transactions are extremely valuable to supermarkets in that they can obtain a clearer sense of who is buying what. Marketing effectiveness can be enhanced by direct marketing techniques that are oriented around the consumers' purchasing habits, which the "discount" card allows the store to learn. All of this occurs because the information that is provided to the store is in electronic form and can be merged and processed with other information obtained by the store. Further, depending upon laws governing such transactions, such data can be sold to other enterprises interested in such information. The store, in other words, like any other business in today's information economy, understands that collecting information should often be as high a priority as collecting money. Indeed, as will be discussed in more detail later, the store may be said to be as much in the information business as it is in the grocery business.

As we take advantage of the conveniences provided by electronic communication, we need to understand that anonymity is not maintained as easily in electronic space as it is in print space. Interactive electronic contacts between individuals and machines, such as typified by the electronic rebate just described, open up possibilities for owners of the machine to collect information about consumers in a way that virtually all consumers today are unaware of and, given how often we use electronically coded cards to make purchases or provide identification, in a way that is virtually impossible for the consumer to prevent.

When used efficiently, computers may be said to eat information

at the same time they give up information. In a print-oriented economy, it is traditionally noted that "time is money." Time savings will
still be a value or goal in an electronic economy, but the main rule in
using interactive information technologies is not "time is money" but
"information is money." Computer use has not brought about time
savings as fast as many purchasers have hoped for. Part of the reason
for this is that the use of computers places us in a space where things
begin to happen that could not have happened in print space. Information starts to be created and collected in an accelerated way and, if
a use can be found for the information, some economic value will be
created. There is, therefore, as one begins to use computers to obtain
and provide information, a whole series of new opportunities that
should start to present themselves if one understands the primary
rule of electronic space—that "information is money."

Automation is another label often placed on the process of relying
on computers in lieu of other means of working with information. The
scanner used by the cashier may be described to consumers, for example, as simply automating the checkout process. Describing what is
occurring in this manner, unfortunately, may hinder rather than clarify
understanding of what occurs as one technology displaces another.

Automation is generally considered to be the replacement of
human labor by a machine. The purpose of automation, it is generally
assumed, is to lower costs, to save time, to remove possibilities of
human error and variation, and, in general, to exercise greater or
more efficient control over some process. Although all of this can
occur, such a perspective leaves out what is becoming one of the principal goals of automation, which is to acquire information in electronic form. As already noted, the value of possessing information in
electronic form is that it can quickly be combined with other information and be used for tasks quite different from the task in which the
information was collected.

What is neglected in the common view of automation is that information technologies invariably generate information as they do their
work, and the information that is generated does not stay put or simply
feed back in a perpetual loop, but is put to some use because it is now
in a form that is easily usable and often even valuable. Interaction with
computers encourages the recycling of information and changing existing information or creating a new information product. As this occurs,
as information is created and used, what is taking place involves much
more than efficient management of some facet of some institution or
enterprise. The language of automation suggests too much of a closed
system. Bringing information technology into an arena, even with the
purpose of automating some process, often fails to have a confining or
limiting effect but, instead, is revealing and opens up the system. Information technologies, if it is possible to generalize about them, typically

are not a good means to compartmentalize operations or to exercise rigid control. This is so because the technology that regulates the flow of information is at the same time creating information. Someone will want that information. Much of this information will escape, either by design or by accident, and it escapes because it is in a form that is easily used, easily copied, easily analyzed, easily manipulated, and easily combined with other data.

A professor at the Harvard Business School, Shoshana Zuboff, suggested that we need to create a new word for what occurs with the electronic media, that instead of *automate*, we might employ the word *informate*, which to her has a more active meaning and suggests that new information is generated at the same time that some process is being regulated.[16] This "informating" quality of the new media accounts for the growth of information-related activities, something that has occurred even though our tools for capturing electronic information are less developed and efficient than our tools for producing or processing information. When automation is understood to be part of an informating or interactive process, it is also understood to be a catalyst for making information more plentiful, to be something that accelerates the flow of information, that allows information to be put together in new ways, and, hopefully, that encourages creativity. It is a process that fosters expression and makes control over expression difficult and it is a process that makes the protection of privacy difficult as well.

Some of the most frequently asked initial questions about using electronic media involve whether humans can be replaced by machines. This is the "automating" paradigm at work, as lawyers and citizens inquire whether machines can replace judges[17] or whether machines will replace lawyers.[18] As traditional informational activities are electronified, some tasks performed by humans will indeed be performed by machines. We will engage some "expert systems"[19] and some processes endowed with artificial intelligence. These tasks, however, should be viewed in the larger "informating" context, as being part of a process in which individuals are continuously creating information as they interact with the new media. The digital-age lawyer or judge, as will be described later, is not a machine but a person who is sensitive to this process of working with machines and is focused on using the information that is generated by it.

When human-machine interactions are approached as opportunities for generating information and adding value to information, it becomes obvious that cyberspace is a location where good environmental habits may be highly rewarded. Since any interaction with a machine is a transaction that creates data, the ecological imperative of reusing and recycling information presents a particularly desirable model to follow because data that is created in one context can be used in some other context. Indeed, the magical properties possessed by electronic space allow one to efficiently recycle information and to perform feats of transformation that are not possible with physical matter that is recycled in our physical world.

My goal in this discussion has been to focus on the more dynamic movement of information in electronic space. If the metaphor for information in print space is a library, a separate space where information can be stored and consulted, where there is a separate location where every book can reside—the metaphor for electronic space might appropriately be ecological—where information is a commodity that we use, that may have value for a limited period of time but whose life can be extended indefinitely through the ecological principles of recycling and reuse. The entry into cyberspace is presenting us with an intangible product whose recyclable value is becoming increasingly obvious. This raises many difficult questions for privacy law, copyright law, and the legal profession—questions that will be discussed later in this book. It also raises intriguing but less obvious questions for the continued use of paper documents, such as contracts, which are examined in the next chapter.

5

Contracts: Relationships
in Cyberspace

THE BIG PRINT GIVETH, the fine print taketh away.
—Steve Cavrak

It is difficult to think of any legal artifact that is more familiar and commonplace than a contract. Tenants and landlords, consumers and merchants, employees and employers, business partners, even some husbands and wives, have rights and responsibilities that are defined by contract. Contracts touch us all and shape many relationships between ourselves, people we know well, and people we may not know at all. They bring the law into our presence in a direct and tangible way and often establish a framework for what we own, how we work, and where we live. It is not surprising that one of the first courses taken by every law student focuses on the law of contracts. Familiarity with general principles of contract law and some work with contracts may be one of the only things that all lawyers, regardless of specialty, have in common.

Contracts not only are a common artifact of modern life and a core area of law but reflect values and expectations of Gutenberg's revolution. There is, most obviously, the connection that is revealed in the expression *fine print*. "Fine print" is most commonly found in standardized contracts that are used with large numbers of customers or employees. Print was, as has been noted, the first mass medium, and the standardized contract might be considered to be an example of the law's use of the mass medium. The party offering a standardized contract is a publisher exploiting the capabilities of print. The power to control the wording and design of the contract in a way that

114

serves the interest of the publisher more than the reader reflects not only the greater bargaining power of one party but the general power of all print publishers to control a document's appearance.

The impact of print on the nature of contract law and on our use of contracts, however, goes beyond the mass production of agreements with unreadable or unintelligible language. Contracts are a means of using information to create and structure relationships. The ability of parties to manage their relationships by relying on pieces of paper is intertwined with changes brought about by printing in how individuals interact with information. Printed contracts of any kind needed not only a technology for reproducing information but a set of attitudes that saw value in relying on, interacting with, and trusting information on paper.

Many, if not most, contracts are not printed but are simply agreements between two or more parties that have been reduced to writing. Yet, such contracts also operate under the spell of printing. They are not employed in the same way or for the same purposes as written agreements were in the pre-print era. We possess many examples of business transactions from ancient times, indeed from as far back as the first examples of writing on clay tablets. Yet, printing changed the manner in which we rely on words on paper and the context in which we use written contracts. Written contracts now, more than in earlier times, are considered to be necessary to structure future business relationships and transactions and to be the best evidence of what was intended at the time an agreement was made. This is true even though, according to contract law, the piece of paper is only evidence of the contract, the actual contract being the "meeting of the minds" that was reached before the document was drafted.

This chapter explores opportunities presented by the new media for structuring relationships. This is a subject that clearly does not possess the newsworthiness of discussions of how the new technologies affect some deeply held value, such as privacy. And it lacks the immediacy of some public policy issues, such as whether restrictions should be lifted from some previously regulated industries—the telephone and cable industries, for example. What is important about the following discussion, however, is that it tells us about an element of law that many citizens take as for granted as the air we breathe. Our attitude toward words on paper, our use of words on paper, and our expectations about words on paper are so deeply ingrained that it is difficult to stand back and look at what a change in technology means for the manner in which we orient many of our relationships. Yet, how we structure relationships and how we can use the new technologies for this purpose are critical questions because one of the primary effects of new patterns of communication is to create new links and relationships, both personal and commercial.

Underlying the following discussion of contracts is the larger question of how we will continue to relate to other kinds of paper documents and print resources on which the law now places so much faith. We interact with information on paper so routinely that little if any thought has been given to what it will mean when the words of the law, and perhaps the pictures and sounds of the law, become accessible using a mode of communication that involves a very different kind of interaction from what we have had with information in printed form. Words on paper, whether in the form of a contract or a will or even a judicial opinion written by a judge, are the nutrients that sustain the law. Such documents are not simply instruments for communicating information but are the end point of some kind of process of communication and a means to focus attention, interests, and concerns. As at least some legal documents become located in electronic form, however, we will begin to look upon the activities affected by such documents differently. We will have not only new tools but a new outlook on how some relationships and behaviors should be structured and monitored.

In Michael Clanchy's *From Memory to Written Record: England 1066–1307*,[1] there is a story of a dispute between St. Anselm, the archbishop of Canterbury, and Henry I. To resolve the legal dispute, both parties sent envoys to Pope Paschal II. When they returned and the letter to Anselm was being read aloud, Henry's envoys objected and claimed that the Pope had given them an oral message that contradicted what was in writing. Who should be believed? The audience apparently was split, with some maintaining that any documents with the Pope's seal should have priority and others indicating that the spoken word of three bishops was preferable to "the skins of wethers blackened with ink and weighted with a little lump of lead."[2]

Clanchy, as noted earlier, provides an exhaustive array of examples of how, in the centuries before printing, oral proofs and testimony were preferred to written proof and testimony. He concludes that "the principle that 'oral witness deserves more credence than written evidence' was a legal commonplace. . . . To make a record often meant to bear oral witness, not to produce a document."[3]

Our faith in words on paper has come about not only as skills of reading and writing have increased but as we have acquired a whole set of assumptions about how those words are produced and about the relative significance, usefulness, and reliability of any written document compared to possibly contradictory language that might exist only in memory. For the past few hundred years, a legal doctrine called the Statute of Frauds has discouraged the placement of contracts in oral form.[4] Oral contracts, according to the Statute of Frauds, have the dubious status of being legal but not enforceable. The message, clearly, is that any and all points of interest to the parties should be included in the contract and that the preference is for the contract to be on paper. Paper is considered to be such a stable, firm, and trustworthy container for language that it is assumed to be able to hold and govern any and all concerns of the parties. Viewed in this way, information that might exist beyond the boundaries of the document is generally as useful as if it did not exist at all.

After several hundred years of growing familiarity with and use of written and printed documents, the handshake and the oral promise may technically qualify as contracts but fall largely in the arena of nonlegal relationships. Indeed, the handshake is generally considered to symbolize reliance on trust rather than on a legal agreement. The legal environment has declared its preference for one medium over another. Whether the contract is written or printed, the law typically considers oral reassurances to be irrelevant. Printing contributed to our being brought to this point, a point where electronic alternatives to using writing and printing are beginning to surface.

What will be the impact of the new information technologies on such a basic and commonplace legal instrument? Thus far, the intrusion of the new information technologies into the legal environment has touched contracts in three ways. First, the consumer marketplace has produced software that allows lay people to produce some contracts without the aid of a lawyer. There are several computer programs on the market that contain forms that can be printed out, filled in, and used as contracts. These are usable in a variety of fairly commonplace transactions such as between landlords and tenants. They have not attained the popularity of some other kinds of mass-marketed legal software, such as tax preparation or will programs, but they can be expected to be used increasingly for relatively simple transactions. As will be described later, this type of software may be important not simply because it provides easy access to legal forms but because it will evolve into a device that provides information about the contract and about the context in which it is used and about when further assistance may be desirable. It may have an impact on fine print by decreasing the informational distance between consumer and legal document and by providing some legal advice and information about commonplace contracts. It may, as a program called Negotiator Pro does, provide guidance to parties involved in negotiating contracts.[5]

A more sophisticated use of information technologies is the document-assembly or document-drafting programs lawyers use to put together more complex contracts. Such programs create a draft of a contract out of pieces of contracts that have been worked on in the past. In larger law firms, any contract that is drafted becomes a potential component for a future contract. Document-assembly software builds on the copying and editing capabilities of computer programs and turns the lawyer into an information worker who builds in a more obvious and automatic way on a similar task that has been done before.

In both of these examples, the end result is a contract that comes out of a "printer." The computer helps to produce the contract, perhaps even to give advice on how to fill in the blanks and what the blanks mean, but the contract is on paper rather than in electronic form. The computer is used as a tool, creating contracts that appear the same as written contracts and that are indeed the same as written contracts.

More ambitious is the use of Electronic Data Interchange (or EDI), which is intended to allow contracts to be in electronic form.[6] An authority on EDI, Benjamin Wright, notes that, "at a simple level, the objective of EDI is to replace paper. The creation, shuffling and storage of paper is cumbersome and expensive. By eliminating paper, EDI allows information to be exchanged between trading partners more rapidly, more efficiently and with far fewer errors."[7] The purpose of EDI, in such situations, is to create something in electronic form that is as legally binding as a paper agreement containing the signatures of the parties. Wright estimates that 40,000 companies now rely on EDI in some form. Certainly, EDI and other uses of electronic communication as a substitute for paper will continue to grow. It has been estimated, for example, that "seventy-five percent of banks' requests for other banks' issuance, advice, confirmation, or negotiation of credits are sent electronically."[8]

However impressed we might be with the new tools for producing paper contracts or paper-like agreements in electronic form, the focus of attention for those concerned with the electronic media should be broader than just the production of contracts that cause the parties to an agreement to relate to each other in the same manner as parties traditionally related to each other. If the new media are an environment and not merely a set of tools, it is necessary to ask in what direction the new media are moving the structuring of relationships. Just as the electronic distribution of information changes our conception of a library and displaces the traditional role of print information in law, is it possible for the new media to displace the role of the contract in legal transactions?

To answer this question, it is necessary to move beyond the electronically generated paper contract, and even beyond typical EDI where contracts exist in electronic form but could be printed out if the parties wished to do so. It is necessary to consider what it will mean to employ contracts in electronic form, contracts that exist only in cyberspace and that also cannot really be duplicated on paper. The reason that such contracts can exist only in electronic form is that they are interactive and dynamic. Such contracts produce and create information and incorporate information provided by the parties as the contract is performed. Such contracts will not replace written or printed contracts, but they will create a new environment that will change how we look at written or printed contracts and what we expect of them. The displacement that will occur not only will affect how contracts are used but will, as will be described later, touch the role of the lawyer, and the distance that lies between individual, lawyer, and the law. At their core, however, they will affect the nature of relationships, how they are structured, and how disputes that arise between parties are resolved.

The road that leads toward electronic contracts involves not merely the acquisition of new skills or the development of new software but a shifting orientation about what it means to interact with information and to use information to create and manage a relationship. It will involve understanding implicitly that opportunities and concerns are different when something is in electronic form. It involves a different set of expectations about how to structure transactions and even how to deal with conflict. Increasingly, during the past decade, the field of law has been using modes of conflict resolution that rely less on the traditional adversary model of litigation. The law's accommodation to what is called Alternative Dispute Resolution has required it to look clearly at the process used to settle disputes and not simply at the result or outcome of the dispute. The employment of a new form of relationship management will require something similar.

The examples given previously of technology's impact on the drafting of contracts illustrate the machine's ability to perform some tasks much more quickly than human labor. The machine seems to save both time and money. The end product of using technology in this manner, however—the actual document produced—is changed little, if at all. Focusing on these early uses of the technology, therefore, may suggest that little is taking place beneath the surface. Certainly, it does not lead one to a clear understanding of the kind of change that will occur when the medium employed can efficiently link people in different places and can evaluate information and generate new information for the parties to use. Automation, as mentioned earlier, does not simply speed up a process or replace an existing process but changes the environment by producing information and by encouraging attempts to use and add value to the information that is produced. As this occurs in the contract setting, expectations about contracts will change and we will begin to understand more clearly the rather far-reaching kinds of changes that will touch how relationships are formed and structured.

As discussed in connection with libraries, I would suggest that the most effective way to understand the changes that the new media are bringing to contract law in particular and to the world of paper documents in general is to become aware of and focus on issues of space as well as time. It is not surprising that programs to save time would have a great attraction for both lawyers and clients. Yet, the contract is something that exists in space as well as time. It links people through space as well as over time. A spatial perspective may not be an obvious way to observe how change will take place, but it is an appropriate one.

Existence in Space

Paper has a tangible quality that provides contracts with a discrete and independent existence. Paper provides a space where time may be captured, and capturing a moment in time is one of the basic goals of a contract. The contract creates a record of the point at which there was a "meeting of the minds." It is not difficult to see that paper's ability to capture time and space reinforces the contract law ideal of an agreement that contains the whole relationship between the parties. Paper, which itself has the clearest and most discrete margins, is thus a most appropriate ally for establishing the type of relationship presumed by classical contract law to also have clear margins. As one scholar has asserted, "the discrete transaction commences sharply by clear, instantaneous agreement and terminates sharply by clear, instantaneous performance."[9]

We now possess a medium that can do more than record an event and allow us to refer back to it. Electronic information does not simply exist frozen in time but evolves over time. It achieves this, in part, by turning the boundaried space of the paper document into a space that is not limited by clear margins, and by continuously performing the magical feat of lifting letters and numbers off the page and substituting new letters and numbers. In the space in which electronic contracts will exist, new information is not merely accommodated but becomes a focal point of the parties. As a result, time is not and cannot be frozen as it can be in print space. As the electronic media are employed to manage and monitor relationships, therefore, the same kind of focus on a particular time and place that paper and print have encouraged becomes vulnerable.

The differences between print space and electronic space cause us to use information differently and, ultimately, to think and speak about information differently. Thus, whereas the main way in which we relate to print is by reading, the new technologies encourage interaction, a somewhat broader activity with expanded opportunities for working with information.[10] Quite frequently, we may simply look at something on the screen and read it, but increasingly often we will be employing the keyboard, mouse, or some other input device to obtain information in novel ways. At such moments, we are not simply "acquiring" information electronically or "reading" electronic information, but we are interacting with the new media. During the process of obtaining information in this manner, we may also give up information, either inadvertently or in response to explicit requests for information. Also at this time, the machine we are using may be linked to many other machines and may be acquiring data from other users and from other sources of information. The data we are interacting with, in other words, is likely to be dynamic and changing. This creates a very different kind of environment from that provided by the printed book, which is stable and fixed and provides us with the same image today as it did yesterday. Almost any electronic source that is looked at for information will inform you that something about the information process has changed since it was last consulted. In LEXIS, for example, virtually every time one looks at the results of a search that was performed a few hours earlier, he or she will be reminded that the database has changed and that new cases or materials have been added.

It is certainly true that print libraries change over time, that new books and journals are added to the collection, that new volumes of case reporters are published, and that new pages are added to loose-leaf services. Yet, there is a different, more dynamic, and more accelerated process of change that adheres to electronic space. Those who use electronic sources become accustomed to receiving updated information as they are working, or, as in a spreadsheet, seeing new numbers replace old numbers before their eyes. With print, there is the assumption based on hundreds of years of shared experience that reading may change the reader but it does not change what is read. Electronic space operates on different assumptions. The mere process of interacting with a distant source, and the speed with which information is updated, means that what one consults one moment may not be the same as what one consults the next. Electronic documents, in a sense, almost ask for updating and, therefore, cannot bind people over time in the same way that a stable print document can. We may continue to refer to them as "documents," just as electronic sources of information may continue for some time to be called "libraries." Yet, we will gradually realize that these "documents are no longer merely an electronic analog to paper, but rather dynamic, modular, multimedia entities. . . . Documents can carry with them information about their origin and identity, as well as executable code that knows how to manipulate or render them."[11]

Electronic information that is shared and updated puts the parties involved in a new place and a new kind of relationship. One of the intriguing emerging examples of this, according to Benjamin Wright, is "vendor managed inventory. Before VMI, a buyer such as a retailer would analyze its sales, and based on its analysis place orders for new inventory. Under VMI, the responsibility for analyzing sales and for deciding when the buyer will receive new product shifts to the seller. The buyer sends raw sales data in electronic form to seller. Seller then makes judgments as to which products are more likely to sell in the future and decides which products to send. This shift in responsibility changes the allocation of risks and responsibilities between buyer and seller."[12] The reason it changes the relationship is that technology employed in this manner puts the seller in a new place and closer to a particular place on the sales floor than even the retailer may be.

We are still connected in almost an addictive way with paper-based information. and it will take some time before paper loses its status as the preferred medium for reading about almost any kind of information. This is partly a consequence of the clearer image paper presents and partly of the convenience in holding and transporting paper and books. Yet, the preference for paper is more than a matter of convenience and style. It signifies the importance of paper as a cultural artifact and reflects our common understanding and acceptance of what is authoritative. Paper, at least until now, has been where trustworthy information has been located. Our culture and our law have already sorted out under what circumstances a signature signifies authority. We are only now working through issues such as whether an e-mail message is a "writing" and whether a signature is needed at all.

As we become more reliant on information in electronic form, we will not turn off the printers and forgo looking at paper copies, but we will gradually understand that it is the paper version that may be lacking in some way. Paper will be employed when it is useful and convenient, but it will not carry with it the symbolic force that it enjoys today. Increasingly, it will be realized that any "printout" of something that exists in electronic form is going to be different from, and often less authentic than, what appears on the screen. This will not always be true, of course, but it will be true often enough to cause a shift in our automatic respect for and preference for paper. Paper copies of information may have the same words as something that exists in electronic form, but they will not be considered in the same way as the original or employed in the same way that the original is now treated.

As we proceed into cyberspace, therefore, the screen will become used more frequently not only as letters on the screen become more readable but as the most valuable source of information is recognized to be the electronic version of the information that is sought. In other words, at some point, or at least for some kinds of information, we will not treat the paper version as the authentic version and the electronic version as a next-best substitute, but we will understand that what appears on paper or is printed out is merely a copy of something that originally and primarily exists in electronic form and that must be consulted in electronic form.

This transformation in what is the medium of choice for information transactions is revolutionary and it is the kind of revolution that will occur in stages and over time. There are many different kinds of information and each will involve the kind of changeover in attitudes and expectations just described. For many kinds of information, where currency and timeliness are of primary importance, it is already recognized that paper does not provide the most useful information. Bank statements, for example, are understood to be out of date when they are received. A correct balance means a current balance and this can only be obtained electronically.

Information in electronic form focuses more attention on the present than on the past, and on the process of change more than on what once existed. Paper allows us to easily divorce the present from the past, to consider the past as something discrete and almost unconnected from the present. Information in electronic form, however, does not exist as discretely in either time or space, although it does allow us to trace connections back to various points in time and perhaps even to obtain more information about what was occurring at a previous point in time than does paper. In terms of contracts, this might seem to reinforce and facilitate the task of determining what was intended by the parties. This would be true if there continued to be as great a concern with past intention as traditional contract law has. What is more likely, however, is that as new forms of communication are employed, new concerns will arise and the focus on the past will be less emphasized. Process and dispute solving and reestablishing relationships may, for example, prove to be valued much more than determining what was intended at the time some contract was formed.

"Electronic documents," James Martin has written, "should not be imitations of paper documents."[13] Contracts in electronic form can, as will be described, be differentiated from paper contracts in a variety of ways. These differences, on one level, merely provide parties with a new and more powerful set of tools than had been available with more traditional media. Looked at in this way, electronic contracts will provide a new mechanism to form a relationship and to guarantee some kind of future actions—to essentially do the same thing as paper contracts, only in a faster manner. Yet, the overall effect of these individual differences also pushes us in new directions by causing us to think differently about the information and people we interact with. The electronic contract does not exist in space as does the paper contract and it cannot, therefore, focus our attention in the same manner as the paper contract. When the electronic contract brings the parties together, its concern is less a document that exists in space than a source of information that exists over space. This changes the way in which we think about the present and future, and about how disputes and controversies that may arise should be handled.

Existence over Space

The interactive electronic document substitutes capabilities for connecting the parties over space for the capability of paper to exist in space. With paper, the parties to the contract are necessarily in different places, albeit looking at identical copies. They may or may not engage in an ongoing communicative process, but their relationship is, according to contract law at least, shaped by and focused on what has been agreed to "on paper." The computer, however, links us together and engages us in a dialogue or an ongoing series of communications in ways that are not really possible with paper. The electronic form is communicative as well as interactive and can be used to create an equivalent to an open telephone line or, even more than that, a technology that effectively puts the parties in the same space.

The electronification of text does more than merely move words off paper and onto a computer monitor. It can be viewed as creating a new environment. It does not merely replace paper but displaces both the paper contract and the parties and brings a reassessment of the nature of the relationship between the parties and how this relationship is to be ordered. For this reason, displacement requires us to look at the larger environment and to acknowledge that constraints of time and space are continuously being lifted, and that events occur that even appear to violate physical laws. The parties to a contract, for example, who may be located in different parts of the world, can pretend that they are in the same place, can work together, and can even look over one another's shoulder.

Although the electronic contract lacks the discrete quality of the paper contract, it possesses an ability to link the parties that is not possible with paper. When we use paper and print as our informational framework, as we have been conditioned to do, we tend not to think in terms of interactive or communicative possibilities because paper is mute. We can, of course, write a response to someone or redline a draft and send it back, but print, more often than with electronic communication, creates discrete one-way informational experiences rather than ongoing ones. The electronic medium talks back in novel ways. In the current period, it is true that the medium may have little to say or little intelligent to say. And I do not want to suggest that in a few years we will have the kind of conversations with machines that individuals might have with each other. But I do view the process of interaction with machines and with people connected to each other by machines as potentially involving a give and take—not simply asking a question of a machine and getting an answer but working with the machine, clarifying issues, rephrasing questions, and, ultimately, getting what is needed. As this occurs, our attitudes and expectations about agreements and relationships will change as well.

By providing a new link between the parties, the dynamic contract becomes something that can monitor the relationship in addition to specifying obligations and conditions of performance. The contract can contain warnings, alarms, notes from one party to another. This kind of contract can overcome many different kinds of boundaries that are inherent in paper contracts. Informational boundaries, for example, limit contracts to what appears among the clauses of the contract. Whereas under some circumstances one might want everything to be contained in the contract, in other circumstances the electronic contract can be a dynamic and hypertextual document, referring to and linking to other sources of information more easily than can something on paper. The contract can respond not only to the parties but to changing conditions of some kind and then inform the parties of these new events or conditions. The electronic contract, in other words, connects the parties to each other and, if desired, to other people and to other sources of information in ways that are difficult to imagine with paper.

Interactive electronic contracts will not make the lawyer's role any easier. Instead of using one's skills to fashion a document that physically exists and is self-contained, lawyers may be pressured to become more involved with the ongoing relationship between the parties and with problems that arise from the relationship. Under this view, the contract in electronic form becomes one star in a constellation of relationship-shaping devices, ranging from project management software to dynamic electronic contracts to traditional paper contracts, some of which are interactive and some of which are not. The move from paper, therefore, to a more communication-intensive medium brings many challenges to the profession and some pressure to change. As will be explained later, there are opportunities for information-sensitive members of the legal profession to establish a new level of expertise, to develop some boundaries is a largely boundary-less setting, and even to stake out some claims for control over a portion of cyberspace. For members of the legal profession who neglect the new forms for linking people and institutions together, such changes will prove damaging.

It may be difficult for some to imagine the kind of dynamic contract I have been outlining. Indeed, calling it a contract or document may be part of the problem in trying to understand the capabilities it might have and the opportunities it presents. The static or mute quality of paper permeates the idea of a contract and of a legal document. Thus far, in the electronic era, the association of paper with contracts has generally been reinforced by the use of software that focuses on producing information that will appear on paper. In this respect, such software, whether it be word-processing software or document-assembly software, may be misleading us about what is likely to occur in the future.

The clearest view of the future might be obtained by looking not at any of the most familiar types of computer programs, such as word processors or databases, but at a category of software called "groupware."[14] Such programs are designed to help groups of persons to work together even if they are located in different places. In a sense, groupware is a highly enhanced type of communications program, enabling users to share information easily, to allocate responsibilities, and to coordinate activities. Unlike many other programs, groupware "facilitates key economic activities instead of simply recording the results."[15]

The raison d'être of groupware is to manage and enhance group dynamics, to foster the type of communication that will allow the goals of the group and its members to be achieved. Groupware "may play secretary and clerk, managing the file, transporting it to the appropriate location, making copies, tracking transmittals. It may play meeting facilitator, focusing the group on open issues and cementing consensus around closed issues."[16] Groupware is not a substitute for a contractual agreement, but it may obviate the need for many kinds of formal agreements by providing mechanisms for checking on whether someone has done what was promised, by alerting parties of changed conditions, and, in general, by providing a sense that the parties are as much together as they are apart.

One of the benefits of using groupware as a model is that it suggests that in the future a contract might be viewed not as a piece of paper or as an agreement made at a particular time and place but as a continuing and ongoing process of collaboration. This characterization of contract may seem, to some, to be too far removed from common understanding of what a contract is. It might be argued that such a view of contract moves beyond the realm of contract into a different form of coordinated activity. Interestingly, however, there are no universally accepted definitions of contract. Most characterizations of contract focus on promises and offers, acceptances of offers, breaches of the terms of the agreement, and enforcement and interpretation of the agreement. A fairly recent definition of contract, however, looks at it a little differently by focusing on the relationship formed by the agreement. Under this definition, a contract is "the relations among the parties to the process of projecting exchange into the future."[17] The value of this definition is that it "establishes an interrelationship among the parties that is broader than their promises and agreement. The agreement is fleshed out by its social matrix which includes such matters as custom, cognizance of the social and economic roles of the parties, general notions of decent behavior, basic assumptions shared but unspoken by the parties, and other factors in the particular and general context in which the parties find themselves. This definition also underscores that the economic core of the contract is an exchange between at least two parties and that contract is an instrument for planning future action."[18]

This is a definition that might cover the kinds of novel qualities that may come about as we begin to encounter electronic contracts. Such contracts are not merely electronically drafted agreements or agreements on paper that have been stored in electronic form. Rather, they are interactive and inherently different from any agreement on paper. Indeed, they could not really exist on paper.

In ancient and medieval times, transfer of ownership required not the passing of "title" or the signing of a deed but the "two parties would come upon the land, each with his witnesses, and the one would hand the other a twig or piece of turf which would symbolize the land passing from the possession of the one person to the other."[19] Similarly, contracts for the future performance of some action were not common, and promises and agreements to do something at a future time were not legally enforceable. Commercial transactions required that the actual exchange of land, goods, or money take place. What was important was transfer of the goods and actual possession and not the performance of some abstract obligation.

In a most interesting analysis of law in "performance cultures," societies that did not rely on writing, Bernard Hibbitts relates that many different communicative forms were relied upon to bring cohesion to groups that could not rely on writing. Contracts, in such cultures, were not thought of in the same manner as modern contracts. Hibbitts concludes that there was "the performative inclination to think of law not as things but as acts, not as rules or agreements, but as processes constituting rules or agreements. A performative contract, for instance, is not an object, but a routine of words and gestures. A witness to a contract testifies not to the identity or correctness of a piece of paper, but to phenomena seen and heard."[20] In such situations, the contract is embedded in the behavior and actions of the parties more than in either fine print or large print.

Although this model of the interactive contract may seem to be a radical departure from the familiar paper-focused contract, it is a model that, some have argued, actually fits more closely the way contracts, agreements, and relationships are structured and carried out than does the all-inclusive paper contract. Several legal scholars have asserted that the assumptions of contract law are not supported by the reality of business transactions and, therefore, that the requirements and remedies provided by contract law are almost irrelevant in the marketplace.

The principal proponent of what has come to be known as "relational" contracts, Ian Macneil of Northwestern Law School, has suggested that contract law reflects a "heroin-like addiction to discrete transactions"[21] but that when one looks at actual agreements, it is difficult to find situations where context is not significant and where all that matters is text. One way of viewing the changes now occurring, therefore, is to see the law moving to a model that is more consistent with reality and practice. Such a model would focus less concern on enforcing discrete contracts and place more attention on maintaining and reinforcing the relationships established through contracts and other means. The shift will place a greater focus on how relationships are structured, on what components of the relationship are emphasized when disputes arise, and in how disputes are resolved when they do arise. There will be less concern with interpreting states of mind or clauses of documents and more attention focused on promoting outcomes, creating and sustaining relationships, and adding value to the information that is produced by the parties. This may require the meaning of the word *contract* to expand somewhat. Yet, as noted previously, the word has never had a definition accepted by all, and ways of viewing agreements can change in response to external conditions. The main challenge to such contracts, if indeed they will be called that, is to exploit the novel capabilities of the electronic medium to allow people to communicate and work together even if they are in different places, while maintaining a sense that agreements and promises can be relied on.

One difference in approach between the "relational" model of contract and the more traditional model embodied in contract law can be seen in the following example given by Richard Speidel:

> Suppose the parties are in the fourth renewal of a five-year contract for sale. The written agreement is silent on whether there is a duty to negotiate in good faith in light of changed circumstances, and there is no applicable trade usage. In the past fifteen years, the parties willingly negotiated in good faith when an unanticipated change occurred on ten occasions. In the second year of the fourth renewal, one party refuses to negotiate despite changed circumstances and threatens to terminate the relationship. The other claims a breach of contract.
>
> Relational theory would identify and assess the parties' pattern of behavior over time (the "is") and, in all probability, conclude that their behavior produced an internal norm of cooperation and adjustment (the "ought"). Taking the next step, one might conclude that the norm became a term of the contract and that a failure to negotiate is a breach. UCC section 1–205(1), however, might not permit this last step: "A course of dealing is a sequence of previous conduct between the parties to a particular transaction which is fairly to be regarded as establishing a common basis of understanding for interpreting their expressions and other conduct." There is no written "expression" to interpret, and the issue is not simply how to interpret the pattern of conduct. Rather, the question is whether a refusal to engage in that conduct, properly interpreted, is improper. Although UCC section 1–205(3) states that a course of dealing is relevant to "give particular meaning to and supplement or qualify terms of the agreement," the emphasis is still on some "term." Thus, the pattern

of previous conduct is, arguably, relevant to interpreting or supplementing a term in the agreement, not to supplying that term.[22]

Paper contracts bind parties to an act. The electronic contract binds parties to a process. To some, this change in focus may seem revolutionary. Yet, it will probably appear to be a lot less revolutionary to those whose actual business activities involve the negotiation and carrying out of contracts. It may surprise many to learn that most studies of the use of contracts in the business world have found that most violations of contracts that appear to be binding are not litigated. Stewart Macaulay, for example, found that "industrial managers and merchants seldom litigate to solve disputes about contracts, preferring to use other techniques of dispute avoidance and settlement."[23] The reason for this is that

> parties treat their contracts more like marriages than like one-night stands. Obligations grow out of the commitment that they have made to one another, and the conventions that the trading community establishes for such commitments; they are not frozen at the initial moment of commitment, but change as circumstances change; the object of contracting is not primarily to allocate risks, but to signify a commitment to cooperate. In bad times parties are expected to lend one another mutual support, rather than standing on their rights; each will treat the other's insistence on literal performance as willful obstructionism; if unexpected contingencies occur resulting in severe losses, the parties are to search for equitable ways of dividing the losses; and the sanction for egregiously bad behavior, is always, of course, refusal to deal again.[24]

Possibilities for legal enforcement of the fine print or the large print of a contract are, no doubt, something that all parties are quite aware of. Yet, litigation is rarely the preferred alternative when problems arise. Consider the following case put forward by lawyer A and, more important, the nature of the responses of lawyers B and C:

> *Lawyer A:* I have recently been involved in two fairly complex joint venture negotiations in which the parties (both pairs) had a great deal at stake, i.e. the transactions were of tremendous strategic importance to all sides. In both cases, the parties came in thinking that they had locked each other in for long periods of time (precisely because the venture was of such importance) with punitive termination penalties, long terms, and the like. And in both cases the folly of this approach became apparent, and we ended up with something just short of termination-for-convenience for all parties—on the grounds that the venture might, for reasons that nobody could easily foresee, become disadvantageous for either of the parties, and that if the parties couldn't continue to operate the venture in a mutually beneficial way there was, as a practical matter, no way to really force anyone to stay in. This strikes me as a generic problem (and not unlike a pre-nuptial

negotiation where exit possibilities are up for bargaining), and it is difficult to see where, except in situations where there is an extreme imbalance in the bargaining position of the two sides, one would want to structure the relationship differently.[25]

Lawyer B: I have a tendency to favor relatively "easy" termination provisions. However, my big concern is who owns the IP [intellectual property] rights and what else happens once we've easily got out of the agreement. Often there can be joint inventorship/ownership on patents etc which affects the rights of the parties to exploit the patent, unless well controlled in the agreement. . . .[26]

Lawyer C: The "war story" that I see again and again is excessive concern, initially with "ownership" as if it were a binary off/on matter. When the possibility of non-exclusive licensing back gets explored, clients tend to begin to understand that it takes a lot more than a property interest to create value—and that all sides are generally better off if they permit the other sides to maximize the value they create.[27]

The attitudes of these attorneys recognize that many contracts are already interactive in the sense that a productive relationship is not something that is formed at a particular moment and fixed on paper but is something that develops and evolves. The attorneys also understand that the relationship is worth more than any single deal.

Ian MacNeil pointed out that

the ultimate goal of parties to a discrete transaction is to bring all the future relating to it into the present or, to use a rare word, to presentiate. They can then deal with the future as if it were in the present. . . . Only 100 percent complete and binding planning can do this. Presentation thus does not occur—or to be more accurate, can occur only very partially—in a primitive contractual relation. The incompleteness and lack of precision in planning for the future resulting from custom in a primitive society leave the future where it is; waiting to happen. Obviously, the difference in viewpoint is likely to affect the way people respond to what the future actually brings.[28]

Looking at contracts with this emerging perspective may seem fruitless, counterproductive, even irrelevant, to some. The contract, after all, is a document that is intended to bind one to promises made at a particular time and place and not to change over time. Its whole purpose would seem to be to create something fixed and binding and that is not opened and reopened. It is something that should enable one to plan for the future based on what was agreed to in the past. It would, therefore, seem to be an area of law that, more than most, should resist migration to cyberspace.

In 1861, Sir Henry Maine asserted that the evolution of society could be described as being a movement "from status to contract."[29]

What is embodied in such a claim is that the manner in which relationships are formed and structured evolve over time.[30] The interactive and networked quality of the electronic media will eventually move us again in conceptualizing the link between law and relationships. This step may be viewed either as expanding the traditional conception of contract or as creating a new category. It is not yet clear whether the electronic contract is a small step forward and merely a different tool to achieve the same end as a paper contract, or whether it represents a new and different paradigm.

It is not surprising that most persons think that the paper is the contract. The paper is stable, has a tangible form, and has clear boundaries. The presentation of information in electronic form moves us gradually into a new environment where the clarity and stability of paper are not present and where the production of information begins to displace reduction. This considerably more dynamic environment looks beyond the seemingly stable form of physical objects, such as a paper contract, to the behavioral patterns that underlie the contract. It focuses on the "interconnected web of relations"[31] and on how the establishment of links changes the parties or objects that are linked. As Kevin Kelly has observed, "a distributed, decentralized network is more a process than a thing. In the logic of the Net there is a shift from nouns to verbs. Economists now reckon that commercial products are best treated as though they were services. It's not what you sell a customer, it's what you do for them. It's not what something is, it's what it is connected to, what it does. Flows become more important than resources. Behavior counts."[32]

As electronic information displaces print, it will be clear that there are possibilities for other kinds of documents and processes, such as interactive briefs and client interviewing and information systems, that would be more interactive and up to date in electronic form.[33] It also suggests some broader implications, in that more dynamic models of regulation in many different areas may emerge. Charles Mooney, for example, has suggested that "the attributes of information technology call into question more than the source, style, and structure of law. . . . information technology provides an opportunity to rethink the substantive underpinnings of the regulatory and supervisory approaches toward financial institutions that were developed in the first half of this century."[34] In the area of securities regulation, for example,

> information technology seems to have had remarkably little impact on the basic approach of the SEC's regulation and supervision. . . . it may be worth asking whether information technology could provide a new model for regulation and supervision. In lieu of traditional approaches such as notice and reporting requirements, spot audits, and the like, one can imagine a financial intermediary as a patient in

the hospital's intensive care ward (an apt and easy bit of imagery in the case of some financial institutions). Electronic "nodes" would be attached to all of the financial intermediary's "vital organs." The regulators would monitor the intermediary's "vital signs" on a "real time" basis. They could immediately (or almost immediately) discover changes (such as withdrawals of capital or shortfalls of customer securities). Indeed, the complete financial condition of the intermediary would be continuously exposed.[35]

In general, the new technologies put law in touch with an information environment that is more dynamic, interactive, and multidimensional, and that can more accurately represent the kinds of complex and delicate relationships that permeate our lives. As one computer scientist has written,

> All around us things change their identity. The atoms that make up the universe swirl and collide and keep swirling and colliding. Everything is in flux. Everything flows. The universe unfolds as a river runs. . . . We can put black-and-white labels on these things. But the labels will pass from accurate to inaccurate as the things change. Language ties a string between a word and the thing it stands for. When the thing changes to a nothing, the string stretches or breaks or tangles with other strings.[36]

6

Beyond Words: Visualizing in Cyberspace

Lascivious paintings generally have more influence that dispassionate arguments.
— Statement made at the trial of *Madame Bovary*

We live by symbols.
— Oliver Wendell Holmes

"In the beginning was the Word," states the New Testament. It might be added that even after the beginning, there were relatively few voices with relatively few words competing with the divine voice for attention. Today, we live in an age of media abundance, where it is relatively easy to hear the voices of persons located anywhere on the planet, to access words and images stored in computers thousands of miles away, to send and receive faxes while one sleeps. Even when we are alone and away from home or office, handheld and cordless devices, ranging from telephones to computers, intrude upon our solitude and allow us to see, hear, and communicate with others.

One of the consequences of having access to so many different means of communication is that we often must choose among media, and make decisions about *how* to communicate as well as *what* to communicate. All forms of communication are not equal, and decisions are continuously being made about whether to employ one medium or another. Such choices, which previous generations did not have to make, are significant because they reveal one's understanding of and sensitivity to the strengths and weaknesses of different media.

The choice of whether to send a note via e-mail or "snail mail" (a term often used by e-mail enthusiasts to refer to the U.S. Postal Service) is not one of the great decisions of modern life, but every choice of this kind makes it very clear that different forms of communication have different conventions and that each uses a different tone or style. We implicitly understand, for example, that handwritten notes are more personal than printed ones, that telephone calls are more personal than letters, and that an actual visit is more personal than a telephone call. We are aware that films and plays generally have more emotional impact than the scripts that are used to make the film or play. We sense that to send someone a written memo usually establishes a more formal, perhaps even hierarchical, relationship than does a telephone call.

In the beginning, words, whether of human or divine origin, were spoken. Over time, words acquired a degree of permanence, as spoken words became stored first in writing and later in print. As will be explained in this chapter, the digitization of language presents us with something new, with information that can appear as traditional printed text or can be transformed in an instant into an image or even a sound. The placement of information into electronic form adds complexity and choice to communication and raises many questions about how we express ourselves, about what words mean, and—the focus here—about how the longstanding relationship between word and image is changing.

McLuhan's claim that the "medium is the message"[1] was exaggerated, but it is not unfair to say that every medium *has* a message. Indeed, most media have several messages that color how and when they are used and what impact they have on users. Most people realize, for example, that hearing about an event is different from seeing the event or reading about it. Seeing an event on television is different from being present at the event. When the telephone company suggests that one should "reach out and touch someone," it is really proclaiming that the telephone can overcome distance, that it can do so instantaneously, and that it is superior to other media when two persons are not in the same place and one needs to hear a voice at virtually the same moment that it is spoken. We are generally aware that some media allow information to travel faster than others, and some can communicate large quantities of information more efficiently.

Other differences among media are more subtle. For example, a message sent via one format may be trusted more than if the identical message was sent some other way. Many readers may be more willing to accept a claim if it appears in this typeface in a book than if it is handwritten or appears in a traditional typeface in a manuscript. Similarly, some media are more suitable for communicating some kinds of information more than others. Feelings and emotions can be excited more easily through the visual media than through print, whereas abstract ideas traditionally have been the province of print. We are only gradually learning that if one wants to keep the contents of some message confidential, it may be risky to send it electronically or put it into electronic form. In a variety of ways, the significance, value, and even the meaning of a message are affected by the manner in which it is sent.

Many decisions about using a particular medium are, of course, based on economics or on other factors, such as convenience or ease of use, that are unrelated to the content of the communication or the communicative qualities of the medium. We may send or acquire information in some way not because it is the most appropriate method for what is being communicated but because it is the cheapest. Some forms of communication may simply be unavailable or inaccessible. Even in such cases, however, it is probably understood that there are various options for communicating with someone and that, if cost were not an issue, there would be a preferred choice.

The rapid pace with which new technologies are introduced leaves us with little time to acclimate to them. At the same time that we acquire and embrace these new technologies, we are challenged to understand them and to become aware of how they will affect us, our families, our institutions, and our society. The new media routinely present us with magical acts, such as when we interact with machines thousands of miles away or perform extraordinarily complex calculations almost instantaneously. Such feats challenge our understanding of the physical world as they overcome previously existing constraints of time and space. We develop new assumptions about what is possible as we begin to understand, for example, that the air is not empty space but is saturated with data that some new technologies, such as televisions, cellular phones, and other wireless devices, can transform into knowledge and information. We are coming to view "traffic" in terms of what moves through wires and through the air as well as what moves on highways. And just when we assume that we have mastered some new technology, it may be declared obsolete and be replaced with something with greater or different powers.

It is often a considerable challenge to identify the qualitative differences among media. For a new medium, whose strengths, weaknesses, and potential uses may not be apparent, this is a particularly difficult task. Frequently, a new technology will be perceived not as something with unique characteristics that will create new institutions and change old ones, but rather as something that simply extends the capabilities of an existing technology. As pointed out earlier, the first cars were labeled "horseless carriages" and computers were called "typewriters with memory." Some computer programs that allow a user to create colorful images on screen are still called "paint" programs even though it is possible to use such programs to produce images more resembling a poster or photograph than a painting, or to create images that resemble neither posters, paintings, nor photographs. Using such labels may alert consumers to some features of a product, but they also mask the revolutionary character of the new technology. Referring to some computers as "notebooks" or "powerbooks," for example, understates the broad range of the machine's capabilities by hiding how much more flexible electronic tools are than a notebook or any other kind of book. The computer and the telephone are still considered by most people to be independent devices even though we will soon talk to people far away by speaking into the computer and small telephone-size devices will accommodate both voice and data communications.[2]

We are currently in a developmental or transitional period, when large numbers of people are experimenting with the new technologies, and equally large numbers have little or no direct contact with them. Such an era may be the most difficult time to obtain an accurate image of how a medium will be used a decade or two later. Many uses for the technology will not have been discovered and important capabilities may not yet have been developed. During such periods, even the inventor of a technology may misread the technology's strengths and capabilities. Alexander Graham Bell, for example, thought that the telephone could be used to broadcast musical concerts, much as the radio has been used. In the 1400s, among the first and most enthusiastic users of early printing technology were the clergy, who assumed that the church's teachings would be strengthened by printing large numbers of religious books. As noted earlier, they could not have predicted that printing was radically different from writing, that it was not as controllable as writing, that opponents of the church would be able to distribute large numbers of critical messages, and that the Reformation would owe much of its success to the manner in which Luther employed the printing press.

Adding to the difficulty of understanding the special character of a new technology are modern marketing techniques. Advertisers are aware of the seemingly paradoxical fact that it is often harder to sell a more innovative product than a less innovative one. A radically new product that is "ahead of its time," and that makes more than merely marginal improvements over the product it is intended to replace, may be threatening to many users and thus may fail in the marketplace. A highly innovative product, therefore, may be less of a commercial success than some other product that is only slightly different from what existed previously and does not require much retraining or change in work habits. Because of this, advertisers of new products not only will hail new functions and capabilities, but will emphasize that there are many common qualities shared by the new with the old. Indeed, traditional qualities may be stressed more than the novel, unique, and different capabilities of the new medium so that potential purchasers will not think that their skills have become obsolete.

Producers want users to feel comfortable with new products and to believe that they can employ many of the same skills they have used in the past, albeit in a more efficient or flexible way. Ease of use, ease of learning, and consistency with the past are qualities that can affect sales as much as new features and capabilities. Without strong connections to the traditional way of doing things, a product may not be considered to be "user-friendly." New software, for example, must be seen to have some links to traditional tools or users will think, quite correctly, that they will need to learn not only new skills, but new habits of thought and new approaches to information. Thus, new devices, such as mice or trackballs or pens that write on the screen, may not be exploited fully at first even if they are more efficient than the keyboard. Such devices suggest not only that a new skill must be learned but that there are new ways and new possibilities for relating to the machine other than through keys and language.

One of the most intriguing areas where traditional work habits and thinking habits are colliding with technological change concerns images. The first years of the personal computer revolution were preoccupied with the machine's ability to process words and compute numbers. For most users, the machine seemed to be a replacement for the typewriter or adding machine. More recently, however, increasing numbers of computer users have learned that it is possible to "compute" images as well as numbers and words. Just as placing words in electronic form opens up opportunities for interacting, communicating, and creating with language, placing images into electronic form encourages new ways of working with and approaching the visual. The personal computer, during the first decade of its existence, revolved much more around words and numbers than images, and many computer users still are not accustomed to routinely seeing pictures on a monitor. Indeed, computer monitors, at least until recently, seemed to be the mirror image of television, welcoming words and numbers but not images, just as television screens communicate more through pictures than through text. The computer is changing quickly, however, and in the future it may actually be the computer that will deserve the "image factory" label more than the television and that will touch deeply the ancient link between word and image.

The personal computer, as I shall explain in a moment, is not yet the powerful graphical force that it is destined to become. Indeed, the history of the personal computer, particularly in legal contexts, has been exclusively textual and this has blinded many to its graphical potential. The transition that we are experiencing, however, goes beyond the speedy movement and processing of words and numbers. It involves moving away from a culture that cultivated and emphasized text toward a culture that will not neglect words but that will be much more involved with and supportive of images and visual communication. It involves understanding that the electronic media are capable of mimicking printed text but that they are actually moving us in a direction that is not generally associated with print.

The major difference between the images on a television screen and the pictures on a computer monitor is that television allows one to *see* images, whereas the computer allows one to *work* with them. The computer user, unlike the television viewer, can do more than simply turn something on or off. He or she has tools for processing images, copying them, manipulating them, interacting with them, and creating them. The computer is becoming a more impressive multimedia machine than television in that opportunities for creating and working with images will be much greater. Text, images, and sound are being brought together, and the person looking at these multiformatted screens of information will be more than a fairly passive "viewer." We will have new abilities to select and choose information since, as George Gilder has noted, "interactivity, almost by definition, is a computer function, not a television function."[3] Most significantly, however, we will be able to create in new ways, to design what appears on the screen rather than accept what appears on the screen, and to create images that do things we at present have almost no experience with.

The key element in the computer's wide-ranging capabilities for working with words, images, and sound together is that information exists in electronic form. Print is stable and permanent and this, indeed, has been one of its virtues. Printed data exists as ink on paper. Once words are printed on a page, they stay there and do not change form. It is not easy to imagine a book that, as it is opened, somehow changes how the letters look. This is, however, almost exactly the kind of transformation that does occur with electronic data as one stores, uses, and then re-stores the data. Electronic data has a much different and more active kind of existence than print since changes are continuously occurring as it moves from being stored on a disk to being communicated on a network to being viewed on the screen.

Electronic data is not stored as we see it on screen, as text or image. It is stored as electronic impulses, or as a collection of zeroes and ones, and only at the last moment is it transformed into something that human sense organs can understand. Because of the manner in which electronic data is stored and processed, technology is necessary to transform it into something recognizable to the eye or ear. Letters and pictures are not simply hiding on a disk in some superminiaturized form. Their existence, at all times other than when they appear on the screen, is in some other kind of configuration.

Storing data as electronic impulses or as a set of binary numbers opens up enormous possibilities for interacting with and transforming the data. With print, one can cut up the page or, with copying machines today, one can make copies of it. But pictures stay pictures and words stay words. It may be difficult to comprehend how a computer can turn a picture into words—but that is because we think of data as pictures and words, as they exist in print, as something tangible and fixed. If we were more cognizant of the fact that numbers, letters, and images can all be encoded in electronic form, the flexibility that is inherent in the digital form would be more apparent to us.

Some of this flexibility is apparent today when spreadsheet users, simply by pressing a button, can display a column of numbers as a bar graph, pie chart, or some other image that may communicate meaning more clearly than a list of numbers. If they do not like the shape or appearance of one kind of graph, they can press a different key and see the data refashioned into a different kind of graph. Software can be designed to add more choices, to add a musical accompaniment or an animated graphic to text or numbers. In other words, once data is in electronic form it assumes a chameleon-like quality that is unattainable with information fixed in print on a page.

As will be explained shortly, words, much more than images, thrived in the environment of print. Law has reflected this preference for the word over the image. It has created vast libraries of books, all of which contain text almost exclusively. The law has a strong attraction to the black-on-white color scheme, whether in clothing, in words on paper, or even in using a metaphor, such as "black letter law," to capture the either-or character of rules.

Print and the Vanishing Image

Gutenberg's bibles were the first books printed in the West and were also beautiful and impressive examples of the printer's craftsmanship. Yet, although Gutenberg was both creative and masterful in creating a new technology, neither he nor his colleagues experimented very much in the design of their work. In terms of appearance, the first printers simply employed the existing model of what books looked like. Because they were interested in selling books, the first printers tried to emulate the style of scribes and to produce books that had a familiar appearance. Gutenberg's bible and other early printed books mimicked the "look and feel" of manuscripts, employing an appearance that readers were familiar with. In size, style, and typeface used, the first printed books tried to "pass" for manuscripts. It was felt that this was necessary in order for the public to buy books, to use books, to perceive the printed book as something that was "user-friendly," and to enhance the demand for printed books.

Early printers were obviously aware that printing would make more books available, but they were too immersed in scribal culture to be able to foresee that printed books ultimately would look different, be read differently, and be used differently. Thus, although they employed a new process for producing books, the early printers wanted printed volumes to look like manuscripts and did not attempt to create a new style or format for books. Only gradually did styles change and did printed books begin to look different from manuscripts. They began to include title pages, justified margins, alphabetical indexes, and a clear statement of who the author was. These changes facilitated access to printed works, and gradually cultural and institutional developments occurred that had not been possible with manuscripts and that could not have been foreseen by Gutenberg.[4]

As print culture matured, it began to differ from scribal culture in much more than the number of books available or even in how they looked. Printing was not simply writing in some accelerated or more efficient form but something that brought change on several levels. There were not only more and cheaper books, but higher literacy rates, changed reading habits, and changed attitudes toward the authenticity and trustworthiness of words on paper. In general, there emerged a different informational environment and a different relationship to information contained in a printed book than there had been to information in manuscript form.

Why was printing not simply mechanized writing? Why was the impact of printing 1,000 books so different from asking 1,000 scribes to each copy 1 book? And why, as the machines turned out thousands, indeed millions, of books,[5] did word seem to benefit more than image? The main answers to these questions follow.

1. Print standardizes. Unlike a thousand manuscripts, printed copies are all the same. Indeed, the most basic feature of print is that it produces many identical copies of the same material.[6] This is important for law, in that it makes it possible for a geographically diverse community to have common assumptions about what is lawful and not. Without a medium such as printing, the underpinnings of such a system would be lacking.

2. Print provides a clear point of reference. Print suggests to us a place where solutions to problems can be found, namely in rules or other material in printed books. Law, in the form of printed books, can be the starting point, if not the focal point, of a decision-making process. Printed law can be pointed to whenever possible distractions such as politics, ideology, or personal values begin to influence the judicial process. Law even tends to occupy a distinctive place, whether in a court, a law library, or a law office.

3. Print encourages and facilitates organization. Growing bodies

of printed information required a means for finding material about a particular legal issue. Efficient access, in turn, required mapping and organizing the law and developing tools for finding the law. Internal boundaries were established as new areas of law grew and categories of law that are familiar to us evolved. Professions were also organized as they gained control over areas of knowledge and monopolized tools to access this knowledge. In addition, external boundaries separating law from other disciplines and the legal from the nonlegal were clearly delineated.[7]

4. Print abstracts. Print enables the law to construct its own universe and to create and rely on relationships that are fictional or hypothetical and only exist as they are described in the books of the law. Words can represent and describe legal entities that have no tangible counterparts. Rights can be established and assigned. Abstractions are critical to the law, and their use is facilitated by the exclusion of images.[8]

5. Print stabilizes. Print publishing is not instantaneous. Electronic communication speeds up publication by replacing the physical transportation of information with electronic distribution. Updating can be continuous and immediate. Printing still produces a physical object, and change, in the form of a new edition, can be a fairly cumbersome and time-consuming process.

One of the more subtle changes in the appearance of books after printing involved how images were used. As books became organized in a more standardized manner and pages of print became smaller and neater than the average manuscript, readability became more of an issue than it had been with manuscripts. Printing presses could, of course, handle pictures, and books of art often were published. Indeed, this was the era in which linear perspective in art emerged and the use of linear perspective was popularized through printing.[9] Yet, the emphasis of most printed works was on text, and the ancient and continually shifting relationship between word and image became more focused on words and less on images. The link between word and image that writing had nurtured over centuries gradually eroded. As a result, one scholar concluded, the illustrated book, "the book in which text is accompanied by paintings depicting a scene in the text, is a medieval conception. The Renaissance did not adopt it and adapt it; it rejected it. The history of the illustrated book in the fifteenth and sixteenth centuries is an account of a losing struggle for survival. By 1550 the illustrated book [was] dead."[10]

If one looks at the literature of the law closely, it is apparent that the law is an institution in which images have less value than words. They may have some symbolic value but little functional value. The literature of the law is enormous and contains millions of pages of words that describe, prescribe, predict, persuade, characterize, explain, and represent. The vehicle of explanation, persuasion and representation, however, is virtually never nontextual. Bernard Diamond, a professor of law and psychiatry, has suggested that

> [i]t is as if a deliberate effort were being made to dehumanize the law, to transform the law into an abstraction that has no relationship to an individual. I would like to see law reports illustrated with photographs of all the participants, including the victim, the defendant, the attorneys, and the judge. Perhaps then the student might understand that the legal process is concerned with real live human beings. To my knowledge, no modern law book is illustrated except those dismal anatomical texts used for reference by personal injury lawyers. This has not always been so. I own a 1562 Flemish criminal law book illustrated with many beautifully detailed engravings depicting every crime described in the book.[11]

Printing undoubtedly helped popularize some artists and made available reproductions of paintings.[12] However, the team of scribes and artists that previously produced manuscripts together gradually was dissolved and the manner in which they worked together was fractured. Although both authors and artists independently benefited from the distribution of many copies of their work, "[r]elationships between text and illustration, verbal description and image were subject to complete transpositions and disruptions."[13]

The changing appearance of books during the Renaissance represents, in a sense, a divorce of text and image, the development of a new style of expression, and changed habits of thought. One effect of the mechanization of book production, therefore, was to change some creative opportunities for artistic expression and visual communication. There was still some concern over the visual, but in law, at least, this centered less on illustration and decoration than on the development of new typefaces for printed text. Typeface design does reveal some sensitivity to the importance and influence of appearance. Yet it also indicates that the principal focus was on the text and that whatever roles were previously performed by illustrations, or by word and image acting together, were eroding.

There are, of course, many books printed with illustrations and pictures.[14] In most such books, however, the "pictures do not appear *in* the text, they are full-page engravings standing by themselves. The text accompanies the pictures; the pictures are the principal thing in the whole publication, the text is a very secondary matter. The Renaissance artist does not see his work as subsidiary or subservient to a text, neither does a Renaissance writer wish to have his composition interpreted and made visible through another man's imagination, beyond the reader's."[15] Printing not only fixed words on paper but created a format that was fixed in the sense that text interspersed with images was not easily accommodated. When Galileo, in 1610, wrote about observing the moons of Jupiter, he placed a sketch of the planet and its moons in between words, in the middle of a sentence, assuming that it was only natural to provide an image at that point. The image placed in between words was not something separate—an illustration or figure supporting the words—but was, like the words surrounding the image, simply part of the paragraph. In Edward Tufte's words, "the stunning images, never seen before, were just another sentence element."[16] This was not something that future authors could expect to do.

This point is "illustrated" by Ernst Goldschmidt in his recounting of the publication of Erasmus's *Praise of Folly*. Erasmus had written

a book full of irony and wit, not a solemn rhetorical exhortation, a book replete with allusions to the life and silly superstitions of the common people, to the ridiculous pomposity of the clergy, to the pretensions and frailties of us all. If ever there was a book which can be said to be "full of picaresque detail," here it is. The *Praise of Folly* was first published in Paris in 1511. By 1515 Erasmus was settled in Basel in the house of his publisher John Froben, who brought out a new edition of the book in that year. Froben at the time employed among other designers of title-borders, of initials and other ornaments, a gay young artist not quite twenty years old, called Hans Holbein. Holbein was extremely amused when he read the *Praise of Folly* in the 1515 edition, and he filled the margins of his copy with hundreds of brilliant little drawings, which are so superb and became so famous that four centuries have not allowed this painter's joke to perish, and Holbein's book is still preserved in the Basel Museum. There can be no doubt whatever that Erasmus was shown this book. I feel convinced that he chuckled over it. I cannot imagine that his host and printer Froben should not have suggested the publication of the *Encomium* with Holbein's sketches reproduced in woodcut. It is perfectly certain that if he did so, Erasmus put his foot down and prohibited the idea. No such edition reproducing Holbein's drawings saw the light before 1676. That Erasmus appreciated Holbein's art is evident from the fact that most of the numerous first editions of his writing issued by Froben are decorated with title-borders and initials by Holbein. But Erasmus's text enlivened by pictures? Unthinkable. The *Praise of Folly* stood on its own merits. For the "literate," for those who could appreciate its style, its neat sarcastic phrases, its evocative word-pictures, no further "illumination" was needed. And the "illiterate," who laugh at funny cuts, had no business with the *Encomium* Moriae.[17]

There are, of course, many books with both text and pictures or text and numbers, and there are large numbers of very beautiful books devoted solely to art. The strength of printing, however, particularly in a field such as law, lay much more with words than with images, and the most commonly printed books—whether fiction or nonfiction, of mass appeal or limited appeal, contained only text.

Printing images, particularly colorful images, was and is, even today, both a more expensive and a more complicated process than printing text. Books of art inevitably cost more than works consisting solely of text, and most authors know that including something other than text in a manuscript may be discouraged or limited by the publisher.

In most books today, there are only words. Verbal skills are critical because there is nothing other than the selection and placement of the words to provide meaning. The words on the page are the sole link between author and reader. This may seem to be an obvious observation, but it is important to note because other media, which supplement words with other communicative devices, can be less dependent on verbal precision than is writing or print. The spoken word, for example, is accompanied by gestures and inflections that can indicate that some words are to have a meaning completely opposite to what has been said. The meaning of something that is spoken does not depend exclusively on the words that are employed; body language and tone of voice communicate meaning and emphasis. This is why reading a transcript of a conversation will almost inevitably suggest that the speakers are inarticulate and unable to speak in complete or grammatically correct sentences. Yet, the speakers probably understood each other very well. Rules of grammar and syntax were not critical to convey meaning because they were helped by many nonverbal cues to communicate information. Similarly, transcripts of lectures are almost never suitable for publication without a great deal of editing and rewriting because the style of the spoken word is so different from the written.

Unlike a speaker, who can sense whether an audience needs something to be restated or rephrased, an author knows that his or her words will be fixed on paper. Words on the printed page stand alone and demand our undivided attention. There is little, other than the words and how they are strung together, to indicate what they mean. Thus, printed text exists isolated and independent, separated in time and space from the author, and provides no visual or auditory cues to compensate for ambiguity or lack of clarity. Indeed, the need for this kind of precision is one reason why rules of grammar and spelling became more formalized after printing than they previously had been.

The cultural adaptation to printing involved more than confronting an information explosion in which more books were published and available. It required acceptance of new grammars, new modes of discourse, new styles of expression, new appearances and designs, and new assumptions about information. Such changes occurred only gradually, as print culture displaced scribal culture, and as print-oriented styles of expression and habits of thought emerged. Similar changes are occurring today as electronic technologies displace print. It is not that fewer words are being produced. Quite the contrary. It is, rather, that a subtle new relationship between user and information and between word and image is evolving.

Computers and the Reappearance of the Visual

We are in an era that is comparable to Gutenberg's in that new capabilities are available but how they will ultimately be used is difficult to determine. It is not surprising that our generation is as oblivious to the cultural, institutional, and psychological ramifications of the electronic media as early printers were to the consequences of printing. We can see an information explosion occurring, a quantitative increase in the production of data, but are much less able to accept the computer as something that will change habits of reading, communicating, and even thinking about information. We continue to assume, for example, that words on the screen are no different from the same words on paper, just as at one time in the past it was assumed that words on a printed page were no different from words in a manuscript. We often aim to produce documents that look as if they have been printed. Although the electronic media do have undeniable similarities to print, they are not simply an extension of print. Indeed, although there are surface similarities, there are also quite profound differences and these differences account for the pressure on institutions such as law to change.

One of the most intriguing areas of difference between print and the new media concerns the support provided to visual communication. Printing encouraged the exploitation of the word, and partly because of this, law, journalism, and other enterprises concerned with words and language flourished. At the same time, however, visual communication received much less support and nurturing. The manner in which images appear in the literature of the law suggests that lawyers and judges believe that virtually all of their communication needs can be satisfied through words. It is probably difficult for many in the law even to imagine any ways in which visual communication can enhance the communicative capabilities of the law. I shall describe in this chapter some ways in which this might occur, but what is perhaps most important to understand is that there will be ongoing pressures from the computer for law to accommodate itself to the visual and to employ new means to communicate. Although it may be difficult to imagine all of the possibilities for change, the likelihood of change in how the law communicates is very strong. Thus, it is important to understand why the electronic media differ from print, and why the future of the personal computer will involve a reordering of the use of word and image and more support for the image than has been true in the past.

Cultures and institutions do not simply make a conscious determination of when words and text are to be preferred to image or symbol. Rather, our beliefs in this area are conditioned, at least in part, by the media employed in different fields of endeavor. In law, this medium has been print and the reliance on print has structured not only how images are used but how they are understood. The electronic media, however, are removing many of the economic and technical constraints that operated to separate text and image. Images can be powerful communicators, and a medium that supports graphical communication will encourage users to employ images. The entrance of images into a space dominated by text can also be expected to be disruptive in some ways.

What kind of machine is the computer? As noted earlier, we should be wary about extrapolating from early uses of any technology. This is particularly important in evaluating the graphical capabilities of computers because the personal computer, in its earliest form, was even less hospitable to images, and less able to nurture a word–image relationship, than print had been.

The computer is an excellent text manipulator and, during the 1980s, found a large market in the legal profession. Just as early printers had an economic incentive to print and sell books with religious themes[18] because the clergy was literate and used books, software producers saw a large legal market for programs that could manipulate words and numbers. The law is a text-oriented universe and it is not surprising that machines with powerful capabilities for processing text would find the law to be a lucrative market. Indeed, the law can be viewed as at least as prominent a market for software that could manipulate text as religion was for printed books in the mid-fifteenth century.[19]

Text-oriented software, such as word-processing and database programs, was welcomed because it made lawyers more efficient in arranging text, creating forms, assembling documents, and storing information. Text processing and data manipulation could be done both more quickly and more cheaply than before. Since what came out of the "printer" mirrored what had always come out of law offices, namely documents filled with text, there was little pressure to think of text in new ways or to see that to compete successfully in the future would require coming to terms with the new capabilities that mature computers would make available.

The law market, in the infancy period of the personal computer and to a large extent even today, was gulled into thinking that the computer was simply a more powerful text-generating machine than the printing press and the typewriter. Indeed, since it was possible to make documents look as if they had been typeset (and the machine providing this print-like output was called a printer), the pressure to identify printed text with electronically generated text, and printing and computers generally, was nearly overwhelming. Because of this, there was little change in the manner in which attorneys thought about information even though there were changes in how they worked with it. The manner in which personal computers were used during most of the 1980s, therefore, tended to reinforce the law's reliance on words and text and revealed little about the ultimate impact of the electronic image on law.

The pressure to think of the computer as a text-oriented machine rather than as a device that opened up quite new and different modes of communication stemmed from two sources. First, as mentioned earlier, one of the foremost goals of computer users in the 1980s was to create documents that looked as if they had been typeset. The whole desktop publishing industry was oriented toward putting a typesetting machine on everyone's desk. Just as Gutenberg employed a style that appeared scribe-like, desktop publishing software was designed to provide consumers with something they were familiar with and with something that was valued.

The second reason that computers were assumed to be nongraphical in nature stemmed from the technological limitations in many early personal computers. Many early personal computers, for reasons that I shall explain in a moment, had difficulty putting images on the screen. For much of the 1980s, it was easier to manipulate what came out of the printer than it was to manipulate what appeared on the computer's monitor. One could, using many word-processing programs, instruct a printer to print large or small letters in almost any imaginable typeface. Yet, on most machines one could not change the appearance of letters on the screen. There was, in other words, great divergence between what was printed and what was seen on the screen. Compared to what could come out of the printer, the screens of most computers showed only unadorned text, in only one typeface, and with no margins. Text on a computer screen was readable, but it was presented in so uninviting a manner that few could imagine wanting to read lengthy material off of the screen.

In terms of what appeared on the screen, the word processor had little more graphical capability than the typewriter. This was certainly not troublesome to the legal profession, however, since it was words the profession was primarily interested in. The typewriter had contained virtually all of the symbols and letters that were needed by the law, and a machine that had all the capabilities of a typewriter plus the ability to expedite editing and rewriting appeared to be an enormous advance. That only letters could occupy the screen was of little concern to anyone. Indeed, even if word-processing programs could have included graphical capabilities, the legal market would not have welcomed it. Given the law's attitude toward images, there was simply no need for computers to have such capabilities.

The limited graphical capabilities of early word processors was a hindrance to some occupations, such as advertisers, graphic artists, or designers, who worked with both words and images. Occupations that needed nontextual capabilities gravitated to Apple Macintosh machines, which had an ability to integrate text and graphics. Lawyers tended not to use the Macintosh, because the law had little need for image processing and because IBM-compatible machines, due to technological considerations I shall describe, typically could process text more quickly than the Apple machines.

The lack of graphical capabilities in early word processors was not simply a consequence of lawyer preferences or market demand. It was also the result of a technological standard adopted by IBM that affected how information appeared on the screen. There was during the 1980s an important technological distinction between IBM computers (and IBM clones) and Apple Macintosh computers, which accounted for artistic users' gravitating toward the Macintosh and text-oriented professionals' adopting the IBM standard. The IBM personal computer, in its original bare-bones version, showed only text on the screen.[20] The screen was divided into a grid, with eighty columns and twenty-four rows. In each one of the 1,920 spaces, a letter, number, or symbol could be placed. One had no choice in how the letters looked. They were, in essence, preformed and all the computer did when a key was pressed was send an electronic signal to place one of the letters or characters in the box on the screen. Thus, whenever one typed and letters appeared on the screen, they looked similar no matter which brand of word processor was employed or which brand of IBM-compatible computer was used.

Apple wanted more flexibility and recognized that the division of the screen into eighty columns and twenty-four rows was arbitrary. Images on a computer screen are not created by putting a single complete picture on the screen similar to the way a printing press might press a woodcut against paper, but the by the lighting up of dots of light, called pixels. Any picture one sees on a computer monitor is really just many pixels arranged in a pattern. Since the pixels are very close together, the eye is fooled into thinking that there is a single picture on the screen.

The quality of a computer screen depends on how many pixels are lit up. In general, higher-priced screens have more pixels, and the higher the number of pixels per inch, the greater clarity any image or letter will have. Lower-priced monitors will have fewer pixels and the edges of letters and images will appear less smooth. When Apple wanted screens to be able to show more than letters, it abandoned the text-mode screen with the 80×24 grid. By lighting up different patterns of pixels, the Macintosh screen could show pictures and letters in a variety of shapes and sizes.

IBM owners who wished to have images could purchase extra equipment called graphics cards so that images could appear on the screen. These cards were not required for word processing or many other business uses, but they were required to play computer games, which were the most common early use for graphics screens. All of the prominent word-processing programs for IBM computers, at least until 1990 when a new version of Microsoft Windows software was introduced, employed the text screen for typing and editing. Although word-processing programs provided users with hundreds of options for manipulating, editing, arranging, and printing text, there was one choice that users were never given. They were not able to edit using a graphics screen. Typing and manipulating text was always done in text mode on the 80×24 grid.

Apple's decision to allow text and image to share space on a screen gave it many capabilities that were largely unavailable to IBM users. The added flexibility of the Macintosh, however, came at some cost. This cost was speed. Tasks performed on a Macintosh screen tended to take longer than similar tasks performed on an IBM screen. The reason for this was that sending messages to individual pixels any time a key is pressed required much more computing power than placing letters or numbers on the 80×24 text screen. Plugging a pre-formed character into one of 1,920 boxes is relatively easy compared to lighting up a particular pattern of pixels on a graphics screen. On a monitor sold with many computers today, there may be 1,024 columns and 748 rows of pixels. Such a screen has more than three quarters of a million pixels. To alter the shape or size of a letter or image on this screen might require replacing or rearranging hundreds of thousands of pixels. This was a task that early computers could do, but it inevitably took longer to complete such a task than it would take to rearrange letters on a text screen. If there was a picture on the graphics screen along with the words, the task would take even longer. Computer users value speed of response very highly—perhaps more highly than any other quality—and if a user had no great need to see nontextual images on the screen, the slower response times of graphics-mode software placed it at a competitive disadvantage to text-mode software. During the 1980s, the Macintosh had a reputation of possessing a broader range of capabilities than IBM machines but also of responding more slowly because of its graphics capabilities.

Further complicating the text–graphics competition was color. Monitors progressed from having no color capabilities to being able to show 4 colors, then 16 colors, then 256 colors, and, more recently, millions of colors.[21] Color monitors are pleasing to the eye and color can

D.L.I.A.D.T.
Library

be used to communicate information. The text user may benefit from having several colors available, but he or she has no great need for a large number of colors. Persons who work with images, however, may have a need for many different shades of a particular color. Certainly, realism is enhanced by shading, and this requires many colors.

The problem for the graphics world was that the use of colorful options slowed down processing even more. Having four or sixteen colors available for text enhanced the appearance of the screen with no significant loss of speed. The availability of four or sixteen colors, however, did not satisfy those interested in images. Color monitors require the computer to send a message not simply to turn a pixel on or off but to indicate which of any number of possible colors should be lit up. Color came to the Macintosh world somewhat later than it came to the IBM world because color imposes so many additional burdens on hardware and software and, unless, the computer becomes more and more powerful, it will operate more slowly with a color monitor than with a monochrome monitor.

The text–graphics competition was not really much of a competition during the 1980s. The IBM text world controlled most of the personal computer market,[22] partly because graphical capabilities were of little significance to businesses and other institutions more concerned with words and numbers than with pictures. In the legal world, IBM's text mode was supported by most software producers and was reinforced by LEXIS and WESTLAW, the two most prominent legal databases. These collections completely excluded images from their databases. Judicial opinions in print, for example, may include a graph or drawing or picture. In LEXIS and WESTLAW, however, such nontextual information was absent and was replaced with a message to consult the print version. If a judge had placed a word or phrase in italics, the electronic version would contain a note, "empahsis added," with no clear indication of exactly what the judge had done. West had even deleted its famous key symbol, which appears hundreds, if not thousands, of times in every volume of judicial opinions printed by the West Publishing Company. The lack of the key symbol was not particularly troublesome and the deletion of nontextual material was understandable, due to the technological constraints that existed. It is interesting, moreover, that the inability to show pictorial representations was of relatively little concern to anyone. Most of the law seemed able to live quite happily in an imageless world.

Even if the text screen had been able to show some images, there was another significant problem with including images in the LEXIS and WESTLAW databases. Just as showing text on a screen is easier and faster than showing graphics, it is typically easier and faster to send words between computers than it is to send images. In general, words travel faster than images because files of words are almost inevitably smaller than files of pictures. Indeed, when one compares the size of files containing words with the size of image files, one often finds that a picture is literally worth a thousand words. The earliest modems, the piece of hardware that allows electronic data to travel over the telephone lines from computer to computer, allowed data to move at 300 baud (or bits per second). The next generation of modems operated at 1,200 baud. These were replaced by 2,400-baud modems and then by modems operating at 9,600 baud, 14,400 baud, and higher speeds.

The higher the baud rate the faster data moves. With 300-baud modems, text scrolls down the screen very slowly. Users can read words faster than a 300- or even a 1,200-baud modem can bring in information. Information coming in at 2,400 baud is probably faster than most persons can read and at 9,600 baud, the screen is filled with text in about a second.

Important changes have occurred to personal computers in the past few years and the victory of the text screen during the 1980s has turned out to be a very shortlived one. Computers are rapidly becoming more powerful and are able to process many more instructions per second than ten years earlier. Increased computing power eliminates many of the constraints involved in working with images or a graphics screen. More software has become available that is designed to work with images, and this suggests that the marketplace sees a use for images. Even word processors are adding graphical features and are competing as much on these capabilities as on their prowess in manipulating text.

The power of most computers sold today eliminates many of the slow response time problems that hindered working with graphics. At the same time, high-speed modems and direct links to computer networks that move data at even higher speeds are reducing the time it takes to send images from one computer to another. Techniques have also been developed to compress or significantly shrink the size of files containing images. All of these changes have made it possible to replace the text screen with a graphics screen and yet not have a machine that performs much more slowly than it did before. The computer itself, it should be recalled, is simply dealing with information stored as electrical impulses and as combinations of zeroes and ones arranged in some order. It is only at the very last stage, when something appears on screen or comes out of the printer, that a shape recognizable by the human eye is formed. For the computer's internal operations, therefore, there is no significant distinction between word and image, or text and graphic. The only difference is that the graphic may involve a larger and more complex arrangement of zeroes and ones than text, and more computing power may be required for the graphical to appear on screen as quickly as a letter or word. The continuing exponential increase in computing power, however, is making this constraint of the personal computer's first decade disappear.

As a consequence of the increase in computing power, the personal computer is moving out of its textual phase and is providing a much more flexible environment, one that is much more hospitable to images. It is not losing its ability to process text, but it is acquiring new capabilities as it becomes more powerful. It is able to do new things that are a sharp departure from what personal computers were able to do in their infancy and a sharp departure from the capabilities provided by print. It is setting the foundation for devoting increased attention to visual communication. Law could, conceivably, resist using these new capabilities and continue its exclusive relationship with words. What is more likely to occur, however, is that the law will join some other disciplines and professions in entering a more lighted and colorful environment. It will begin to discover uses for communicating visually, begin to employ graphical images more frequently, begin to see various advantages to visual communication, and, perhaps slowly, begin to adapt to a more visual model of law.

The transformation from text screen to graphics screen, from lack of capabilities to new opportunities, became most apparent with the appearance of Microsoft Windows software in 1990. Microsoft Windows software is routinely sold with IBM-compatible computers today and when such a machine is turned on, one sees a screen populated by both words and images. Such a screen is a graphics screen, with many little symbols and icons that could not have appeared on the text screen of the 1980s. We are presented with opportunities with such a screen that much of the experience of the 1980s did not really prepare us for. Nor did the long history of print prepare us for exploiting the new opportunities.

The Nature of the Visual

Whatever skill or expertise one has with words, whether in reading or in writing, is a consequence of many years of schooling and practice. There may be considerable and continuing controversy about how to teach children to read and write, and at what age to begin, but there seems to be no question that reading and writing should be a primary focus of the elementary curriculum. There is also general acceptance of the idea that literate individuals need the skills of both reading and writing. Indeed, the two skills are considered to be so intertwined and so closely related that it is difficult today to imagine possessing one of these skills without the other.

It is to the credit of our educational process that we view reading and writing as being almost a single skill. At one time, mainly in the pre–print era, it was widely understood that reading and writing were quite different skills. At that time, reading was one skill and writing another, and there were far more people who could read than could write. It is still possible to read fairly well and yet be a mediocre writer. Reading requires being able to recognize the shapes of the letters, to understand the sounds they represent, and to be aware of the meaning of words. Writing is a more difficult and complex skill, since the writer must be able to recall as well as recognize words and to arrange them in a coherent manner.

Reading is an act of consuming what others have created, whereas writing is itself an act of creation. Consuming what already exists is inevitably less of a challenge than creating something new. Writers, more than readers, must possess a sense of style, tone, and form and must consider rules of grammar and syntax as they link words together. This is why writing is taught separately from reading and why good reading ability does not necessarily translate into skillful composition. There obviously is overlap between reading and writing skills, in that both benefit from an expanded vocabulary, and the act of reading may benefit the act of writing, and vice versa. However, almost like eating and cooking, each also makes some special demands on individuals, and exercising one ability does not necessarily improve the other. It is for this reason that so many more years have to be devoted to nurturing the ability to create using words and letters, and why many individuals with many years of schooling still cannot write very clearly.

The processes of reading and writing, of consuming the works of others and of creating one's own works, also occur with visual communication. Most persons, however, have enormously different expectations about their capabilities for visual reading and writing than for reading and writing words and letters. For example, we are all assumed to be visual consumers, whereas very few are considered able to create visually. The educational process devotes relatively few resources to visual communication. This is because we are all assumed to require no training in order to see and to consume the visual, whereas visual creation is presumed to require innate talents and to be almost unteachable. We thus treat visual consumption and creation as distinct and almost unrelated skills. Indeed, the attitude we possess about the relationship between the two sides of visual communication is similar in many ways to the attitude toward reading and writing that was held in the pre-print era. However, just as cultural attitudes toward literacy changed as the new technology of printing spread, it is likely that cultural attitudes toward visual communication will change as well.

We live in an increasingly visual culture and are exposed to ever-growing quantities of pictures, images, icons, charts, figures, graphs, scales, tables, diagrams, maps, sketches, blueprints, and colorful and animated graphics. The changes that came about in reading and writing after Gutenberg, as more people learned to write as well as to read, occurred as individuals recognized value in how they related to words on paper. As new electronic tools promote the graphical, will new energies be focused on both understanding and creating through visual means? Will an increasingly visual culture devote more attention to the visual and teach about it just as print culture recognized that reading and writing text were fundamental skills that should occupy fundamental positions in the curriculum? Can the new media narrow the gulf between "visual reading" and "visual writing," between visual consuming and visual creating, in the same manner that print narrowed the gulf between textual reading and writing? Is it likely that the new technologies can effect a new balance between visual consumer and visual creator? And if this occurs, what impact will it have on a text-oriented enterprise such as law?

Visual communication has been so neglected that it may not even be clear what is meant by the phrase. I use it to refer to data, other than letters and words, that are seen by the eye and have meaning. There is a very large amount of such material ranging from simple symbols to complex graphs, from grammatical marks such as periods or exclamation points to electronic icons, from realistic photographs to animated abstract symbols, from the practical to the mystical and spiritual. Visual communication can be employed for "composing and understanding messages at many levels of utility from the purely functional to the lofty precinct of artistic expression."[23] It can be superficial or profound, something with instantaneous impact or something that requires time-consuming analysis.

Why does the educational system not focus on either visual consumption or visual creation in the same manner that it focuses on reading and writing? One reason is that seeing is assumed to be simply a physical act. The act of reading is a visual act that not only must be learned but is assumed to involve cognitive and perceptual skills as well as the physical sense of sight. It is difficult to find a visual act other than reading, however, where the perceptual and cognitive are seen to play an important role. Other than reading, almost everything else that we see and learn from is assumed to be largely a consequence of physiology, of how well the eye functions.

Formal training in the visual tends to be neglected because it is commonly assumed that "the process requires little energy; the physiological mechanisms are automatic in the human nervous system. The fact that from this minimal output we receive vast amounts of

information in many ways and at many levels provokes little amaze-
ment. It all seems natural and simple and suggests that there is no
need to do more with our abilities to see and to visualize than just
merely accept them as natural functions."[24] Thus, although educators
refer to a concept of "reading readiness," a set of cognitive and perceptual skills that need to be present before children can effectively be
taught to read, there is no comparable concept of "visual readiness"
and little understanding of nonphysiological factors in how and what
we see. As Gombrich pointed out,

> we hear a lot about training the eye or learning to see, but this
> phraseology can be misleading if it hides the fact that what we can
> learn is not to see but to discriminate. If seeing were a passive
> process, a registration of sense data by the retina as a photographic
> plate, it would indeed be absurd for us to need a wrong schema to
> arrive at a correct portrait. But every day brings new and startling
> confirmation from the psychology laboratories that this idea, or
> ideal, of passivity, is quite unreal.[25]

For different reasons concern itself very much with providing
skills to individuals so that they themselves may create and communicate visually.[26] Whereas training in seeing is considered unnecessary
because everyone without a physical handicap is presumed to be able
to see, training in producing the visual is deemed unnecessary because
so few are assumed to be capable of visual creations. Many consider
visual communication to be related to art and aesthetics, and it is
assumed that some artistic talent is necessary to be an effective visual
communicator. Such ability is also assumed to be an innate talent
rather than a learned skill. It is assumed that a special artistic talent is
necessary that most individuals do not possess and cannot learn.

These assumptions about what is innate and what is not, and
what can be taught and what cannot, may be much less valid than
they are assumed to be. For example, is it true that all people see the
same things and see them equally well? What one sees or what one is
capable of seeing often goes beyond eyesight or vision quality. Some
people do see better, or at least differently, than others. Their eyesight
may not be superior, but they may be more perceptive and see sub-
tleties that escape others. They may be more capable of understanding a message contained in the visual. There is visual material of varying complexity, and appreciation of this material may not be possible
without building onto the physical ability to see. If reading involves
cognition as well as recognition, isn't there some comparable process
of cognition and recognition that occurs as we are presented with
graphical information?

The process of learning to see, of making sense out of a set of visual cues, is one that is engaged in continuously, both in one's personal and one's professional life. For some occupations, such as medicine, training in seeing is indeed part of professional training. Subtle changes in color and pigmentation, which may not be perceptible to the lay person's eye, can suggest danger to the trained eye. For other professions, however, such as law, training focuses exclusively on the "mind's eye"—on envisioning rather than on vision, on abstract thinking rather than on our sense of sight. The new technologies do not demand that any less attention be devoted to reading and writing or that reading and writing be considered anything other than critical and fundamental skills. They do, however, point to the need to be familiar with appropriate mechanisms of expression, some of which will entail greater use of the visual. As such a change occurs, the word-image relationship will necessarily change as well, and expertise in and understanding of the visual will need to be taught even in a field such as law where it has been completely absent. Such a development will require an important admission, namely that legal capabilities are or will be intertwined with seeing, and that what one sees is a function of perception as well as of physiology.

Innate artistic talent measured by the ability to draw pictures on a canvas is no longer a prerequisite for being a successful visual communicator. Even currently available graphical tools do much of the drawing for the user, assuming the user knows what kind of final product is desired. The machine, for example, does the drawing of a graph if you press the right keys or mouse buttons, just as the machine "prints" letters and words if you press certain keys. Even when pictures are the end result desired, the electronic process of creation provides models that can be altered and adapted, rather than created "from scratch." In some programs, aesthetic quality, such as the use of color or typefaces, or "visual persuasiveness" is suggested to the user, or evaluated electronically, in the same manner that electronic spell checkers or grammar checkers evaluate and suggest modifications to what one has written. We are only beginning to work through a new framework for evaluating the nature of creative work[27] and are only beginning to have sophisticated image-processing tools available at a price comparable to word-processing software. There is, needless to say, a time lag before such tools become as accepted as word processors, but they are no more difficult to use and, as is gradually being recognized, there are occasions when text will simply be inadequate compared to the electronic image. Some word processors, indeed, no longer process words exclusively but have added capabilities for displaying and working with images as well.

When should visual means be employed instead of words? What is inappropriate use of the visual and what is appropriate use? The

new technologies, by opening up a realm of expression that has generally been suppressed in law, require the law and lawyers to deal with
and develop a set of norms, a professional language of the visual, a
grammar and syntax of the graphical, a set of common understandings of what types of visual communication are acceptable, what
unacceptable, and why. This is an enormously difficult, challenging,
and time-consuming task, and one that will cause troublesome problems for the law. The question of what role visual communication
should play in the law is one we are largely unprepared to answer and
is as difficult a question to answer as the question of what role print
would play in the law after Gutenberg, if such a question had indeed
been asked in the late 1400s. In other words, we have no experiences,
traditions, customs, or norms to draw upon as we do with text when,
for example, we wonder whether the colloquial or the humorous or
the poetic can appropriately be included in a legal communication.

The computer facilitates and greatly expands the use and production of the visual, but it does not insure that such forms of communication are used effectively or appropriately. The ease with which we
can change images and the manifold choices we have in selecting how
something will look mean that we need to understand how to choose
and employ the visual. We need to be clear about the purposes of
communication and give the same attention to the visual as is given
to the verbal. We need to understand what value to attribute to the
visual when it is so easy to manipulate images and distort originals.[28]
The law is a process of structured communication. It is a formal institution, and part of the process of legal education is training in a particular style of professional discourse.[29] The expansion of modes of
expression that emphasize the graphical thus poses a large challenge
to this hegemony of text.

One noted legal scholar has written that "[s]peech may be uplift-
ing, enlightening, and profound; but it is often degrading, redundant,
and trivial. Speech may be abstract and theoretical, a near cousin to
thought; but it is often concrete and immediate, filled with calls to
action, intertwined with conduct. Speech may be rational, contemplative, orderly, organized, and soft; but it is often emotional, raucous,
chaotic, untidy, and loud. Speech may be soothing and comfortable;
but it is often vexatious and noisome. Speech may confirm and
affirm; it may be patriotic and supportive of prevailing values and
order; but it may also be challenging, threatening, and seditious, perhaps even treasonous.[30"] Speech, in other words, may be quite varied.
The law, however, is highly selective in how it uses words. Lawyers
understand that there is an accepted and appropriate tone and style
to legal writings and to judicial opinions. Legal writing is relatively
formal, and almost always prosaic rather than poetic. There are some

specialized words that may be used only within legal circles. Writing style is obviously important to the law, and legal writing is a subject of study in every law school.

In coming to terms with the varieties of language, the law has developed norms and conventions for how and when language is used. Legal speech, for example, is typically much more "rational, contemplative, orderly, organized, and soft" than it is "emotional, raucous, chaotic, untidy, and loud." It is language that has been placed under professional control. This is the result of years, if not centuries, of evolving customs, traditions, norms, and expectations. The visual represents a whole new and unfamiliar mode of discourse. In the past, the law has relied more on exclusion of the visual than on accommodation to it or regulation of it. Print has certainly been an ally in this exclusionary policy, since print itself has, as noted previously, welcomed images much less eagerly than it did text. As the new media invade the law, however, and as law and other institutions recognize value in visual communication, exclusion will no longer be as desired or as feasible a policy. The law will have to contend with shaping the use of the visual and also with challenges to traditional textual styles.

Visual communication, like text, can be employed in an enormously varied and flexible manner. Pictures can be realistic and functional, or impressionistic and abstract. They can be garish or subtle, and as varied in tone and style as text. They can be formal or informal. They can accompany text and serve as an illustration of text, or they can be communicative by themselves. They can be static, as when they appear on the printed page, or, in an electronic era, they can be moving. Not everything can be communicated through visual means just as there are some things that cannot be communicated through words. Not every use of the visual is appropriate for the purposes of the law, but the law currently suffers more from too little use of images than from too much.

The varied possible uses of visual communication mean that different facets of the law will likely employ the visual in different ways. Some parts of the law will eagerly and fairly quickly embrace visual tools, whereas other parts will seek to maintain an exclusionary policy. The process of infiltrating the law, in other words, will be uneven. Some cracks in the law's exclusionary policy toward the visual, however, have already occurred. Fear of the visual, at least in some legal arenas, is being replaced by demand for the visual. Certainly, more use of the visual will occur as the technology matures and new applications that further facilitate the use of the visual are developed.

Where, in the currently textual world of law, might visual communication be welcomed, or at least considered? One way of understanding the potential attraction of the visual to the law is to consider a few of the ways the law uses information and the ways in which the visual capabilities of the new technologies may affect these uses. Law has kept visual communication at a distance, yet there clearly are areas of law in which communication would be enhanced and facilitated through use of the visual.

Persuasion

Much of law consists of advocacy and persuasion. Trials, negotiations, even meetings with clients, involve more than mere explanation or description. Many legal settings require that information be used to persuade the listener or reader of the value or correctness of a position and to move some distance from a previously held position. To succeed in persuasion requires that information be viewed differently after the presentation than it was before. Thus, persuasion is a consequence of both the information presented and the manner in which the information is presented.

Persuasive impact can be enhanced by skillful rhetoric and by employing words, either on paper or orally, and it can also be heightened by the effective use of visual information. "We catch on fast," Pamela McCorduck has noted, "when someone draws us a picture."[31] Effective visual communication may at times employ sophisticated technology, or it may involve a relatively simple arrangement of information. Figure 7, for example, consists of a very simple visual presentation of words and symbols. Yet, it is also an extraordinarily effective arrangement and illustrates how even simple graphical tools can be much more effective than text alone, whether written or spoken. The table in Figure 7 was employed by the lawyers for defendant John Gotti, in his 1987 trial for racketeering and conspiracy, to inform the jury about the character and believability of several witnesses. This exhibit was the last piece of evidence viewed by the jury before returning a verdict of acquittal.[32]

Images often may not be a substitute for words, but words often also may not be a satisfactory substitute for images. The entry of images into the law need not bring with it a neglect of the verbal. Rather, a new awareness of the power of the visual entails new challenges, since one must possess both verbal and visual skills and an understanding of how the two can work together. The trial is a process in which persuasion is central and the use of electronic images, visual displays, and electronic animations and simulations have become quite common.[33] Yet, persuasion is a goal not solely of the litigator but of advocates generally. This is a large area for law, and the persuasive capabilities of the visual may be enough to break apart the fortified walls that the law has erected to guard against entrance of the visual.

CRIME	CARDINALE	LOFARO	MALONEY	POLISI	SENATORE	FORONJY	CURRO
MURDER	X	X					
ATTEMPTED MURDER		X	X				
HEROIN POSSESSION AND SALE	X	X		X			X
COCAINE POSSESSION AND SALE	X		X	X			
MARIJUANA POSSESSION AND SALE							X
GAMBLING BUSINESS		X		X		X	
ARMED ROBBERIES	X		X	X	X		X
LOANSHARKING		X		X			
KIDNAPPING			X	X			
EXTORTION			X	X			
ASSAULT	X		X	X			X
POSSESSION OF DANGEROUS WEAPONS	X	X	X	X	X		X
PERJURY		X				X	
COUNTERFEITING					X	X	
BANK ROBBERY			X	X			
ARMED HIJACKING			X	X			
STOLEN FINANCIAL DOCUMENTS			X	X	X		
TAX EVASION				X		X	
BURGLARIES	X	X		X	X		
BRIBERY		X		X			
THEFT: AUTO, MONEY, OTHER			X	X	X	X	X
BAIL JUMPING AND ESCAPE			X	X			
INSURANCE FRAUDS					X	X	
FORGERIES			X	X			
PISTOL WHIPPING A PRIEST	X						
SEXUAL ASSAULT ON MINOR							X
RECKLESS ENDANGERMENT							X

Figure 7   *United States v. Gotti et al.*

In considering this chart, Edward Tufte notes that it "invites reading both horizontally and vertically; neither direction enhances the reputations of those testifying against Mr. Gotti and his colleagues, as the eye detects curious patterns and unbroken runs of X's. Mr. Polisi, for example, has something of a streak going. Those marks indicating each crime by each witness are not modest or shy, and they dominate the spreadsheet grid (although only 37 percent of all the possible combinations are marked). Placement of particularly obnoxious activities at the top (murder) and bottom of the list (pistol whipping a priest) exploits the visual prominence of those positions." Edward Tufte, *Envisioning Information* (Cheshire, CT: Graphics Press, 1990), p. 31.

Measuring and Monitoring

⅃ text can capture reality at a particular moment but, since it ₑₘains fixed, it is not an effective medium for obtaining feedback on ongoing changes. The fixed quality of print has been one of its virtues, endowing print and those who use it with an aura of authority and trustworthiness. It has shaped thinking about precedent, which represents authority in a stable and trustworthy medium, and it has colored thinking about copyright,[34] which protects creative works fixed in some medium.

Printed text is less effective at measuring or monitoring continuing, ongoing, or rapidly occurring changes. Measuring and monitoring traditionally have been labor-intensive human activities as well as activities that rely upon rapid feedback and communication. These processes consist of people gathering information, communicating that information, and assessing whether change has occurred. In an interconnected electronic space, monitoring should be occurring continuously and the impact of various actions on other actions should be available in "real time."

Such measuring and monitoring capabilities of computers really have no mechanical parallel or antecedent in the print era. Whatever measuring and monitoring was necessary was a human activity. In law, for example, lawyers would draft a contract and may then have received some periodic feedback as to whether the contract was being fulfilled. In a different context, probation officers would fulfill their responsibilities by requiring periodic visits of persons on probation.

One of the ways our environment is changing significantly is that data can be acquired, processed, and distributed continuously. As discussed earlier, electronic contracts eventually will be more than paper contracts in electronic form. They will monitor performances and alert parties and their lawyers about problems with performance or about a need for modifying an agreement due to changing conditions. Electronic ankle bracelets, which originally were developed to monitor the movement of cattle and prevent them from going astray, are, in some locations, employed to monitor persons on probation. All such uses raise not only questions of privacy but issues of displacement, of what it means to have so much more information than previously and opportunities to use such information in new contexts.

Measuring and monitoring are not functions that the law excels in or even has engaged in to a great extent. Computers, however, can simulate the future, measure change over time, and receive and evaluate data in ways that were never possible with print. What is important to recognize in connection with visual communication is that the medium's visual capabilities provide intriguing possibilities for alerting us about change and about the direction of change. Images and numbers can be employed to show change in ways that are not possible with print. Increases and decreases can be demonstrated visually through changes in the size, shape, or color of objects on screen. In the contract context, for example, lack of performance might send a red flag to the attorney for one of the parties. This could be an actual image of a red flag, and the red flag, if ignored, could grow larger over time, something that would be both meaningful and attention getting.

Recording

The visual media present us with new opportunities for recording legal events. Ronald Collins and David Skover have pointed out that "we live in an era of 'paratexts,' in which words and images, as captured by electronic recording, compete with print to represent legally significant events."[35] These "paratexts" are visual recordings, nontextual recordings of experience. What occurs, as information is captured on videotape or on disk, is a process they label "enframing"—

> an activity that brings a person, object, event, or idea into presence and simultaneously sets boundaries around the representation of these things. When we enframe an event, we bring it into presence by describing it in some way (for example, by an oral or written account) as we describe this event, we fix the terms by which we understand it. In the case of the oral or written account, we locate the event within a setting of words, thus fixing our understanding of the event in terms of the words selected to describe it. Had we chosen instead to draw a picture, the same process would occur, but within the field of pictorial representation.
>
> Any technique that reproduces reality enframes or shapes reality. . . . Enframing, therefore, is a quality of any mode of representation, and varies according to the selected mode. Different modes of representation, with their different types of enframing, will set different boundaries. . . . oral, written, print, and paratextual modes of representation enframe reality in radically different ways. Thus, a shift from one mode of representation to another produces far-reaching consequences for law, which currently is highly dependent on texts of one sort or another.[36]

Much of the legal process consists of the examination of recordings. These recordings may be a recollection, a kind of recording that has been made in one's mind as one has seen an event. They may be a contract or deed, a written record of some transaction. They may be a transcript or some other written record of a process that has taken place. They may even be a judicial opinion, a recording of the judge's views. There are various rules about the use of each of these kinds of recordings and there are varying levels of resistance to using visual technologies in their place. Videos of events, such as the video of the Rodney King police beating, have largely been welcomed as an enhancement of

the legal process. Videotaped wil
increasingly being considered. Vid
other hand, unheard of.

The law's ambivalence about us
text is understandable if one understan
than replacement that is taking place. Mc
new medium is never an addition to an old
old one in peace."[37] A new medium changes rei
tances. Thus, it is fear of change at this level that probably
the resistance of the U.S. Supreme Court to the presence of television
cameras in the Supreme Court chamber. It is not concern with deco-
rum and dignity in the courtroom, as is commonly assumed, but a
recognition that the camera is a force for change on any process on
which it focuses its lens.

Interestingly, the Supreme Court has for several years been distributing its opinions electronically. What it has not recognized is that
electronic distribution also will change the distance between the
Court and the public. Currently, the Supreme Court controls a communications process, designating the content of information to be
submitted by parties, the manner in which it is submitted, and the
time at which announcements of decisions are made. It is a process of
communication in which only one side has power to make demands
on the other. The process of communication, in other words, both
symbolizes and reinforces the Court's power.

The process of communication also distances the Court from its
various constituencies—the public, the news media, and the attorneys
and parties in a case. The Supreme Court, and appellate courts in general, is far removed from "people's courts." The Court limits itself to
consideration of legal questions, never communicates directly with the
people in the case, and hears about the human concerns of the parties
only second hand, if at all. The focus at the Court is on the abstract
and the general, more than on the individual or the particular.

Print is a great ally for the Court in this process because it
inevitably works as a distancing medium, as a mechanism that assists
the Court in controlling what is discussed and communicated. Print
requires us to look at experience that has been abstracted into words.
It allows us to envision something, to conceptualize something, to
reason abstractly about something, to approach an issue with some
degree of detachment. The use of words, embodied in a document,
focuses attention on the words, gives them an importance of their
own, and allows them to be separated from their author. In any decision, for example, the judge writing the opinion is named and can be
held responsible, but the opinion can also be treated as existing
almost independently of the judge and be given a life of its own. The
judge at some point recedes into the background and the printed
opinion occupies the foreground. The judge is an unseen force, hiding

behind the printed opinion as much as he or she might hide behind the judicial robe.

Print, therefore, operates as a subtle but highly significant force in the process of making the judicial process appear to be objective, neutral, and impersonal. It affects the whole environment and not simply a single part of the process. It shapes the process as does the architecture of the courtroom, which elevates the justices above the public and sets the tone for proceedings, or as a judicial robe, which deindividualizes the judge and reminds the judge of the nature of his or her authority. Both architecture and dress stress the formality of the occasion and reveal how problems are being appraised. They are not simply inconsequential symbols that are relics of the past. One can argue whether they are needed or not or desirable or not, but it is clear that they affect both public perception of the judiciary and how the judiciary perceives itself and its role.

All of these artifacts create distance between judges and others. Maintaining distance is a key concern of the Supreme Court, and print may be a more powerful definer of distance than either robes or architecture. Print is as encompassing as architecture or dress, since it touches judicial habits of thought at almost every stage of the Court's process. It sets boundaries as to who may communicate with the Court, what may be communicated, and how it may be communicated. It allows the judge to fade into the background, which is of critical importance, since one of the goals of the Court is to encourage decisions to be thought of as "the law" rather than as the creation of an individual justice or group of justices. If it takes some degree of magic to achieve this, then print might be thought of as one of the major props that are necessary for this to occur.

Television in the courtroom would displace the current position of the Court. The justices, heretofore represented on television by low-resolution sketches drawn by courtroom artists, would be entering our homes more frequently and in a more personal manner. Introducing television to an institution such as the Supreme Court may therefore be seen as being akin to changing the architecture of the Court and changing the dynamic by which the Court communicates to others. It changes the distance that is assumed to exist between Court and public and the relationship the Court has with the public and other groups affected by it.

There can be disagreement about both whether the Court has been too removed from the rest of society and whether the legal process will be more responsive if there is less distance. What is clear is that the new visual technologies, as they work their way into institutions, complicate the distance-setting process. The Court may understand that bringing television into the courtroom has an impact on the distance-setting mechanism and that it will have an even greater struggle than it now has if it wishes to keep itself as independent as it has been but without being perceived as too greatly isolating itself. In the new communications environment, it risks losing its legitimacy if the distance that is established is too great, and it faces an identity crisis if it does not find other means to enable it to maintain the kind of distance that supports its traditional sources of authority and methods of operation.

There is another interesting side to the Court's resistance to television cameras that suggests the futility of absolutely refusing to admit cameras. During the same period that it has resisted the visual, the Court has been accommodating itself to the computer's extraordinary capabilities in distributing words and text. Court opinions are drafted using word processors and are distributed in electronic form. They are electronically accessible within minutes[38] and almost instantaneously converted to a draft of the version that will appear in *US Reports*.[39]

The Court undoubtedly views its new computers as text processors, as a means of efficiently and quickly distributing words. This is an attitude, as mentioned earlier, that sees the computer and word processor as being simply a powerful extension of print, of doing what printing did and something more. The computerization of the Court, however, does much more than this. The computer is the Trojan horse that contains the visual perspective the Court has been so vigorously resisting. The visual need not necessarily enter through the front door and with great fanfare, as would occur with a vote to allow television cameras to enter. It is also possible for the visual to enter through an electronic side door, without much notice, and yet, over time, leave a permanent mark upon its traditions, practice, and values without there being any awareness or recognition of what has taken place.

Representation

Law, it has been written, is a "builder of worlds."[40] These worlds, however, have been largely worlds created out of words and language. At the very least, words are one of the crucial building blocks of the law. As Harold Berman wrote, law involves a "belief in the power of certain words, put certain ways, to bring about certain effects denominated as legal. This kind of magic is necessary if law is to work."[41]

Law is a body of information that needs to be communicated to various audiences. It is engaged in a continuous process of construction, and much of this process consists of representing legal ideas, concepts, and relationships. Judicial opinions, as already noted, are a type of recording of one person's reasoning processes, but they are also considered to be something more, a representation of law and legal principles. It is not because they reflect a single individual's wisdom and insight but because they fulfill the function of representing the law that they are stored and organized. The judge's name is part of the opinion but generally a subsidiary part. If opinions were simply recordings, the particular judge would be emphasized. As a representation of the law, the opinion moves the judge into the background and the language and ideas become the focus of attention.

Traditionally, words have been the almost exclusive vehicle for representing the law. There are, of course, various highway signs or even red, yellow, and green streetlights that effectively represent simple rules. The law also has relied on visual symbols, such as robes and uniforms, to communicate power and authority. But the need to communicate complexity has largely been fulfilled through words and text. Words are the law's vehicle for representing and explaining, and if complexity has required the use of difficult terms or concepts, or even the development of a language that only one with professional training could understand, that has not been resisted.

Interestingly, law has employed a few graphical allusions. References to "points of law" or "lines of decisions" provide a slight hint that how law is understood may depend on how it is viewed and that there are various spatial arrangements that could assist in evaluating data. What is novel about the new media is that the new visual tools expand our language of description and allow us not only to "draw parallels" in our minds but to manipulate and interact with many different representations of complex relationships and activities. As these tools are employed, they can change how we use and understand law.

Donald Norman has argued in a recent book that one of the basic keys to effective communication is "matching the representation to the task."[42] He uses as an example two fairly simple games, one the game "tic tac toe" and the other a game called "15." All readers are probably familiar with the rules of tic tac toe. In the game of 15, the rules require each player to alternately pick a number from 1 to 9. Once a number has been picked, it cannot be selected again. One can win the game by selecting three numbers that add up to fifteen. If the remaining numbers bring one's total to more or less than fifteen, the players start the game over.

It is not particularly easy to describe in words how 15 is played. Even after reading the above description of 15, readers may still be having some difficulty understanding how the game is played. Norman indicates that tic tac toe is a spatial game and our original understanding of that game comes not from reading a set of rules but from seeing and recalling a pattern of lines and X's and O's. Norman then uses the following graphic to show that 15 can be learned quite easily if it is conceived of graphically. Indeed, in looking at Figure 8 one sees that the two games are really the same. One wins 15 only if a horizontal, vertical or diagonal configuration equals fifteen.

4	3	8
9	5	1
2	7	6

Figure 8

According to Norman, "the form of representation makes a dramatic difference in the ease of the task, even though, technically, the choice does not change the problem. . . . The power of a representation that fits the task shows up over and over again. Bad representations turn problems into reflective challenges. Good representations can often transform the same problems into easy experiential tasks. The answer so difficult to find using one mode can jump right out in the other."[43]

We have not yet reached the point where we automatically review our alternatives for representing complex, or even simple, relationships. It is therefore not difficult to find examples of the law's resistance to graphical communication, examples that illustrate how poorly words function in some contexts and how unfamiliar and unaware we tend to be with the language of the graphical. The following, for example, appeared in the Supreme Court's decision of *Board of Education of Kiryas Joel Village School District v. Louis Grumet*, decided June 27, 1994:

> SOUTER, J., announced the judgment of the Court and delivered the opinion of the Court with respect to Parts I, II-B, II-C, and III, in which BLACKMUN, STEVENS, O'CONNOR, and GINSBURG, JJ., joined, and an opinion with respect to Parts II (introduction) and II-A, in which BLACKMUN, STEVENS, and GINSBURG, JJ., joined. BLACKMUN, J., filed a concurring opinion. STEVENS, J., filed a concurring opinion, in which BLACKMUN and GINSBURG, JJ., joined. O'CONNOR, J., filed an opinion concurring in part and concurring in the judgment. KENNEDY, J., filed an opinion concurring in the judgment. SCALIA, J., filed a dissenting opinion, in which REHNQUIST, C. J., and THOMAS, J., joined.

What does this mean? If we are trying to communicate with simplicity and with richness of detail, is not this the opposite? Should it take a half-hour of concentrated thinking to figure out what relationships are stated here? Is there a better way to reveal those relationships?

It is not easy to determine what is the most appropriate table, chart, or graph to show these relationships in a way that allows virtually instantaneous understanding. The most important point is that the route for doing this is not text alone, and this will be true for representing many kinds of relationships in law, many that are considerably more complex than this one.

Pamela Gray has suggested that the more complex informational environment in which we reside requires that we employ new tools that will enable us to relate efficiently to this information. She writes,

> There is a vast number of units of legal information, which are relative to each other, and a lot of different ways of arranging and processing them. The law has been fashioned in this way by many legal experts over hundreds of years. It is the product of a collective legal intelligence which functions holistically. However, there is now far too much legal data for retention and processing by an ordinary person. When there is an attempt to scale up a legal application, cognitive problems arise for the knowledge engineer who must master the law, and for the user who wants to understand it. If the corporate system of legal intelligence is to be simulated in such a way that its various forms of expertise can be accessed coherently, then interactive graphics, which represent the legal logic framework, must be provided as a cognitive aid for the user. This visualization of the corporate legal intelligence is a method of making the program transparent, in order to facilitate communication between the system and the user. As such, it may be regarded as a representation of artificial legal intelligence itself.[44]

The new technologies bring us closer to graphical means of communication, and well-designed software will assist the user in overcoming handicaps in representing information. One proponent of the use of hypertext in law, a subject that will be discussed in chapter 8, has argued that we should exploit capabilities for creating

> flowcharts, pictures and other graphical information. Elements of a picture can be turned into interactive "buttons" that trigger further actions or take the user to pertinent subsets of the material. For example, data related to a specific state might be accessed by clicking on that state in a map. The regulation applicable to one part of a complex piece of machinery might be accessed by selecting the appropriate portion of a picture of the equipment. The logic of a statute can be laid out as a flowchart, with each section available in more detail with the click of a button. The availability of graphics allows and encourages the use of flowcharts to show visually the relationships between various arguments and entities—and allows elements of those pictures to serve as navigational aides.
>
> By giving the user a powerful new type of control over an interactive screen, hypertext systems create the potential for a large array of new "information topologies." The world of printed text is linear—all ideas are presented at a particular place in a long string of text. Jumping from place to place is difficult at best. The world of the computer database is planar. It consists, in essence, of a series of boxes or cubbyholes. The world of the outline program—providing a structure that can be opened and closed—is a three dimensional tree, because certain branches can be hidden behind the main topics at any time. With the development of hypertext systems, we have been

provided with the ability to create and navigate through a more complex, multidimensional space. Because the user can create links of
any "shape" between any two pieces of information, our documents
(which will in effect have become software programs) can take the
form that most naturally fits the shape of the ideas themselves (or, at
least, the way in which most of us naturally think about them). With
hypertext systems, lawyers are finally able to build models of the
legal domain that are complicated enough to do justice to the materials we wrestle with every day.[45]

In a similar way, Stephen Jay Gould has argued that

> [p]rimates are visual animals. No other group of mammals relies
> so strongly on sight. Our attraction to images as a source of under-
> standing is both primal and pervasive. Writing, with its linear
> sequencing of ideas, is an historical afterthought in the history of
> human cognition.
>   Yet, traditional scholarship has lost this root to our past. Most
> research is reported by text alone, particularly in the humanities and
> social sciences. Pictures are poorly reproduced, gathered in a center
> section divorced from relevant text, and treated as little more than
> decoration.
>   Pictures are not peripheral or decorative; iconography offers pre-
> cious insight into modes of thinking that words often mask or
> ignore. Iconography becomes even more revealing when processes or
> concepts, rather than objects, must be depicted.[46]

Timothy Terrell has suggested that we are at a stage in the evolution of law in which we are poised to move beyond two-dimensional
understandings and representations of law. In an article titled "Flatlaw: An Essay on the Dimensions of Legal Reasoning and the Development of Fundamental Normative Principles,"[47] Terrell refers to a
short allegory about English society titled *Flatland*, written almost a
century ago by Edward Abbott. *Flatland* was a place

> inhabited by two-dimensional creatures. . . . the relative social status
> of any individual in Flatland was established by the number of sides
> in the individual's figure. Thus, soldiers and the lowest classes of
> workmen were isosceles triangles, and among their group relative
> status was determined by the acuteness of the smallest angle in the
> triangle. But women, according to Abbott (and the not so charming
> Victorian view), were simply straight lines, and hence had the
> sharpest, and most dangerous, "point" of all. Professionals were four-
> and five-sided figures; the narrator of the tale was himself a square.
> Hexagons, septagons, and so on, represented increasingly important
> individuals, with the pinnacle of the society being the figure in which
> the multisidedness of the individual gave way to one curved perime-
> ter: a circle. Priests were circles. Not surprisingly, one common
> ambition of the members of this society was that their children have
> more sides than they had themselves.[48]

Terrell, in an observation that summarizes several thousand years of legal history, states that "Flatlaw is not an easy place to reach. But it is an even harder place to leave behind."[49] Although Terrell focuses on legal reasoning and does not directly associate two-dimensional thinking with print culture, this observation is a most effective summary of both the status and the attraction of law in a print culture, and explains our ambivalence about the passing of the print paradigm.

The new graphical tools facilitate, in the words of Edward Tufte, an "escape from flatland"[50]—an opportunity to see relationships where no link was previously visible, and a force for seeing things in different ways. Changes in perspective and in representing reality are, like law, linked to the tools that are available for expression and creation. Samuel Edgerton pointed out that art changed radically in the fifteenth century as artists discovered how to use geometry to create the illusion of depth and perspective. He noted that

> [I]t should not be overlooked that almost coincidental with the appearance and acceptance of linear perspective came Gutenberg's invention of movable type. Together these two ideas, the one visual, the other literary, provided perhaps the most outstanding scientific achievement of the fifteenth century; the revolution in mass communication. Linear perspective pictures, by virtue of the power of the printing press, came to cover a wide range of subjects and to reach a larger audience than any other representational medium or convention in the entire history of art. It is fair to say that without this conjunction of perspective and printing in the Renaissance, the whole subsequent development of modern science and technology would have been unthinkable.
>
> Hence the real contribution of linear perspective seems to have been more to the advancement of science than to the history of art. If perspective often seems inimical to the impatient and introverted aesthetic sensibility of artists today, it certainly appealed to the more extroverted, acquisitive attitudes of the Renaissance. In the early Quattrocento, it was the processed goal of artists to know as much about their physical surroundings as possible in order to lend conviction to their moral message. As linear perspective fixed their eye more intensely on the natural world, these humanist craftsmen became quasi scientists. As their perspective pictures proliferated, especially through the medium of printed books, more and more people from all walks of life began to be aware of the underlying mathematical harmonies of nature which perspective articulates.
>
> So far as science is concerned, can there be any question that the special geniuses of Leonardo da Vinci, Columbus, and Copernicus were given a very special catalysis at this time by the new communications revolution of linear perspective? Indeed, without linear perspective, would Western man have been able to visualize and then construct the complex machinery which has so effectively moved him out of the Newtonian paradigm into the new era of Einsteinian

outer space—and outer time? Space capsules built for zero gravity, astronomical equipment for demarcating so-called black holes, atom smashers which prove the existence of anti-matter—these are the end products of the discovered vanishing point.

Or, are they? Surely in some future century, when artists are among those journeying throughout the universe, they will be encountering and endeavoring to depict experiences impossible to understand, let alone render, by the application of a suddenly obsolete linear perspective. It, too, will become "naive," as they discover new dimensions of visual perception in the eternal, never ultimate, quest to show truth through the art of making pictures.[51]

It is, as computer scientist Marshall Brain commented, "hard to have graphical dreams in a textual world."[52] The law has thrived in flatland and it is understandable that it is ambivalent about escaping from it. We are, however, gradually moving beyond "flatland." We are encouraged, particularly by these new electronic tools, to look as well as to think, to create animated and interactive models that allow us to view complexity and to see patterns in relationships of many kinds. The journey out of flatland may not be rapid, but it has begun and the landscape is changing even if the law's eyes are still largely closed and its thoughts remain fondly focused on where it has been.

7

Digital Lawyers: Working with Cyberspace

Most of what lawyers do is store, categorize, organize, retrieve and analyze data. Microcomputers and networks have revolutionized the way people in other businesses perform these tasks, but they have barely made a dent in how lawyers do their jobs.

—Fred Bartlit

In the 1990's the key challenge of survival for legal expertise will depend on service quality and a capacity to use data and information technology tools.

—Richard Volpato

For some readers, a "digital lawyer" may bring to mind a high-tech executive gift—the legal equivalent of a digital watch or digital thermometer, something that one could consult in a variety of circumstances but that would also be small enough to keep in a pocket or briefcase. Such an electronic device would allow users to obtain legal information and even legal advice by viewing a small screen or by choosing among several digitized "voices of authority." An enhanced version might have wireless links to some electronic network and empower electronic agents to seek sources of information somewhere on the network.[1] It is not clear how large a market there would be for such a device or how useful it would be, but a little machine, a "portable lawyer,"[2] that provided some answers to a specified range of legal questions is certainly technologically feasible.

Some version of this kind of electronic legal tool, either as a hand-

172

held electronic device or as a more sophisticated networked oracle dispensing legal information, may, in the not-too-distant future, populate the shelves of some consumer electronics stores. It is already possible to purchase software that advises one how to prepare tax returns and fill out simple wills, health care proxies, and various kinds of forms and contracts. A large machine—an electronic kiosk in Phoenix, Arizona, called "QuickCourt"—provides legal information, helps citizens fill out court documents, and prints out the appropriate court forms.[3] QuickCourt, which looks like a soda machine and has been called a "divorce machine,"[4] uses a touch-screen along with audio, video, and graphics to communicate with users.

Such programs may not be capable of high-level legal reasoning, but they are becoming increasingly sophisticated and may provide a degree of competition for some lawyers, particularly those whose legal practice has traditionally extracted value from "paperwork" in not very complex transactions. Thus, these programs are not insignificant or necessarily marginal, and they eventually will have some impact on narrowing the informational distance between citizens, lawyers, and the law. Yet, the primary focus of this chapter is not an electronic robot or artificially intelligent tool embodying a sophisticated neural network[5] but a human being—a lawyer who is not digital but who interacts with digital information, is acutely aware of the electronic environment, is highly sensitive to the changing economic role and value of information, and understands the emerging opportunities presented to those who use electronic modes of communicating and processing information.

Sensitivity to the value, qualities, and capabilities of information in electronic form is probably the distinguishing characteristic of the digital lawyer. Such lawyers will understand that supplying the right information quickly is more important than ever before and that both the ability to access information and expectations about response times are changing. Such lawyers will be aware that the "library" of cyberspace, the new location of authority and of authoritative legal information, can be virtually any computer or any individual connected to the network. They will recognize that responding to client needs efficiently requires sharing information electronically with clients. Such lawyers are likely to depend heavily on data communications to clients and on a "network" of colleagues, consultants, acquaintances, and experts, perhaps even through "personal digital assistants"[6] that reside in a client's pocket. They will think less in terms of owning or possessing legal information than of exploiting links to legal information that they have in place. These communications links not only will change relationships between clients and lawyers but will make lawyers aware that their goal should be to build "communities of knowledge, not storehouses of information."[7]

In addition to being linked to and involved with the network, the digital lawyer will understand and even welcome the fact that much information will not be in a fixed and stable form—that, indeed, it may exist in a continuously changing interactive medium. Thus, the digital lawyer will be comfortable with electronic contracts—not simply electronic versions of paper documents or contracts transmitted electronically, but dynamic contracts that monitor relationships as well as establish them.[8] In general, the digital lawyer will view the new media as a means to fashion new and more complex relationships and interactions among persons and groups separated by a distance. The digital lawyer will both see things differently and see different things, since he or she will have some expertise in employing graphical and other electronic nontextual capabilities to describe, characterize, and represent conflict, and will be more comfortable with and more likely to employ new modes of resolving conflict. Such a lawyer will understand that, like digital images, situations that appear to be black or white can be reprocessed and manipulated into something that, when seen from a different perspective, is composed of many different shades of gray. Such a lawyer will recognize that the new technologies are not neutral and will be an ally of the legal profession only if lawyers change their ways of thinking about information.

The digital lawyer will be aware, as will be described on the following pages, that information-related transactions and conflicts are proliferating, that options for managing conflict are increasing as well, and, perhaps most importantly, that informational consequences must be considered when resolving conflicts.[9] The digital lawyer is focused on the goal of using information efficiently and profitably, which means being sensitive to the fact that as one uses information electronically, he or she also is creating new informational byproducts that can have great value. The digital lawyer will be aware that if the new opportunities that surface in the highly competitive electronic information environment are not exploited successfully, the profession will become an increasingly vulnerable and threatened institution.

These qualities of the digital lawyer do not make such lawyers visibly different from today's lawyers, although the preference for information in electronic form will make such lawyers' use of and dependence on technology more obvious.[10] Yet, the digital lawyer should not be confused with a lawyer who has simply automated many tasks and invested heavily in hardware and software. The essential difference between the digital lawyer of the future, which may turn out to be the only kind of lawyer to thrive in the future, and today's attorney lies only partly in access to technology and in skill in using technology. Rather, the core change in the digital lawyer is an understanding of the value of information in an environment where new tools for processing and communicating information make adding value to information and using information to develop new relationships the central concern of the economic system. Thus, the digital lawyer understands that one cannot fully serve the client or meet the client's needs unless the lawyer is sensitive to and meets the client's informational needs as well. He or she understands that the underlying informational value of the dispute may dictate nontraditional courses of action in order to do what is in the client's interests informationally. The digital lawyer knows that although the new media present opportunities to save time, the most novel characteristic of these technologies may be in how they operate on space and distance. He or she is still aware that "time is money" but is more focused on the fact that "information is money." In sum, the successful digital lawyer knows that he or she is in the information business as well as the legal business and that he or she is competing with others in the information business, some of whom are lawyers and some of whom are not. Indeed, such lawyers may come to feel, at times, that they are more in the information business than in the legal business.

The New Legal Environment

The digital lawyer may be largely in the future, but a hint of what is to come can be observed in an electronic service, Lexis Counsel Connect, which was begun in 1993.[11] Lexis Counsel Connect is attempting to accelerate the journey of large law firms into cyberspace and to help acclimate the corporate segment of the legal profession to the electronic information environment. It is an enterprise that is intriguing not only because of its electronic nature but because it encourages a rather novel orientation toward information and the value of sharing information.

Lexis Counsel Connect can be described as an electronic information place for large law firm lawyers. It has elements of a private club, such as membership fees, and it is exclusive in that only lawyers may belong.[12] It also resembles a conference center in that serious online discussions take place about various professional topics of interest to the members. One could also characterize it as being, in part, an ongoing professional seminar or a continuing legal education meeting in which one is educated by one's peers about some legal matter. Indeed, Lexis Counsel Connect most frequently uses the professional seminar as a metaphor for what it is doing. Finally, it is a marketplace, where expertise can be described and decisions may be made about whether to hire a firm to provide legal representation. The president of Lexis Counsel Connect has even employed the metaphor of a "shopping center" to suggest that various kinds of information can be obtained using the service.[13]

As an electronic information place, where interactions and links among people separated by distance can occur as if they were in the same place, Lexis Counsel Connect is more than a conference center, shopping center, or any other physical place in that it can, at the same time, be all of them. If it survives, therefore, it can also be the precursor of some professional arrangements for which we have no precedent. The primary focus in Lexis Counsel Connect is on fostering relationships between corporate counsel and law firm lawyers, but the technology makes possible various kinds of new linkages among the lawyers themselves. For example, some members of Lexis Counsel Connect may decide that they are lawyers sharing common facilities, in that they "see" and interact with each other almost daily, and they will build upon such a perception. Indeed, there is no reason that a firm of lawyers could not be established with Lexis Counsel Connect or some other electronic network serving as the principal space of the firm or as the means for allowing the lawyers to collaborate in a productive manner.[14]

Membership in Lexis Counsel Connect provides the following:

1. Capabilities to send and receive e-mail from Lexis Counsel Connect members as well as from persons on the Internet and subscribers to commercial services such as CompuServe and AmericaOnline.
2. A wide range of online discussion groups about many areas of law and legal practice. Corporate counsel are encouraged to post questions that they are confronted with and lawyers post answers to such questions.
3. Law-related information and access to periodicals.
4. Limited access to Internet services and information.
5. Law firm-generated information that will be described later in this chapter.
6. New links to and opportunities to use LEXIS-based resources promised for the future.

Lexis Counsel Connect assumes that lawyers in large law firms already find themselves in a new informational context and, as a consequence, that law firms that persist in doing business in the traditional manner eventually may find themselves out of business. It may be the first law-oriented venture that uses the new technologies to try to create the kind of informational environment in which digital lawyers can be comfortable. It is an experiment that attempts to provide the client-lawyer and inter-law firm electronic links that digital lawyers will require. It assumes that using electronic tools to work with information is one means of succeeding in what is a more competitive environment than previously. It illustrates the opportunities that may open up for lawyers able to exploit the new technologies as well as the vulnerability of lawyers in an electronic environment and the risks for those who resist the new media.

Lexis Counsel Connect's link to cyberspace is most apparent in its existence in electronic form and in its promotion of electronic communication among lawyers, clients, and others. One can find parts of Lexis Counsel Connect in physical locations and one can find most of what Lexis Counsel Connect does being done somewhere in some physical place or even on some other electronic network.[15] There really are no physical places, however, that foster all of the kinds of communication that are found in Lexis Counsel Connect. Even more importantly, perhaps, Lexis Counsel Connect is an endeavor that embodies values of an electronic culture and attempts to exploit the technology to preserve and enhance an institution—the large law firm—that has resided for decades as a comfortable and perhaps complacent inhabitant and beneficiary of print.

Lexis Counsel Connect's most intriguing quality is an attitude about the value of information that encourages sharing information in ways that do not really have a place in print culture. One of the effects of electronic communication is to remove distance as an obstacle to communication, and Lexis Counsel Connect exploits this capability in a novel way. It not only links attorneys in various firms and places together but links them to the firms' filing cabinets or, at least, to materials firms have produced that in a print world would often remain in the files of the firm. Firms are encouraged to place documents that they have produced online. These documents include memos and articles on substantive developments in the law—briefs, forms, and contracts prepared by the firm—as well as other kinds of information.[16] The end result is an environment in which "(1) the customers can demand the creation of a more efficient market for legal expertise, (2) the suppliers of information are tied together electronically, and (3) both can draw on stored expertise in the form of memos, checklists, and document models from across the entire profession."[17]

This unlocking of the filing cabinet runs counter to a more familiar and traditional attitude of controlling and limiting distribution and is often perplexing to lawyers who hear about it. Yet, it is a practice that is consistent with a new perspective on information that is encouraged by the new technologies, one that assumes that "days of hoarding hard-won legal expertise are over. Being a valuable lawyer in a networked world involves sharing information with others, so that you become a valuable node on the network—a source that clients come back to again and again."[18]

Lexis Counsel Connect is the brainchild of David Johnson, a lawyer for the Washington, D.C., firm of Wilmer, Cutler and Pickering, and Steven Brill, the editor of *American Lawyer* magazine. Johnson is one of the most imaginative and knowledgeable persons in the law-computer field, and Lexis Counsel Connect appears to reflect his sensitivity to two very different kinds of pressures that lawyers must address if the legal profession is to sustain itself in the new information environment:

1. Increasingly vulnerable and ineffective institutional and informational boundaries. The legal profession is losing its ability to exercise control over access to and use of legal information.
2. An increasingly active and volatile information environment. Information transactions not only occur at an unprecedented rate but are accompanied by a high level of conflict.

Boundaries

All modern institutions are confronted with boundaries that do not exclude or contain information as effectively as they did previously. Nation-states, for example, are learning that controlling the flow of information has become more difficult in an age of electronic media than it was in the age of print.[19] Economic institutions find that protecting trade secrets, patents, and copyrights is more difficult than in the past.[20] Increasing numbers of disputes involving intellectual property reflect not simply new and easy methods of copying but problems with assumptions inherent in copyright law and distinctions, such as between ideas and expressions or between original and derivative works, that are employed by copyright law.[21]

Professions also face problems with boundaries.[22] One of the qualities of a profession is that it exercises control over certain kinds of information.[23] Indeed, professions appear to divide up their service areas in a manner similar to the way boundaries divide territory. Thus, Andrew Abbott wrote: "The central fact about [professional] jurisdiction is its exclusive character. While intermediate settlements are not unusual, in general one profession's jurisdiction preempts another's. Conversely, it is also true that no profession can hold infinite jurisdiction. But if jurisdiction is constrained in these ways, it follows immediately that any profession's move implies moves by others. A change in the balance of jurisdictions leads to a chain of effects eventually absorbed by environing professions."[24]

The identity and power of a profession and its control over a certain market are the consequence of several factors that create boundaries and that set the professional apart from the nonprofessional:

1. The profession is identified with a theoretical body of knowledge. It is assumed that academic training is required in order to master this information.
2. The state cooperates in protecting this informational boundary by holding persons liable for "unauthorized practice of law"[25]

and by allowing the profession to regulate itself. State-granted authority to exercise jurisdiction over an area of knowledge and over some kinds of transactions has served as a protective umbrella for the legal profession. It is one reason that the legal profession has thus far been less vulnerable than many commercial enterprises to the impact of the new technologies. Lawyers do operate in a competitive atmosphere, but it is, in theory, only lawyers that they compete with.

3. The profession regulates itself. Professional associations create a bond among those in the profession and add further support to the boundary line separating members from nonmembers. Associations allow members to share information, to establish rules for the profession, and to emphasize a common bond among members. "The cornerstone of the ideology of professionalism is the belief that some professionals in various categories possess skills or knowledge that entitle them to considerable autonomy in the performance of their work."[26]

4. There is a relationship between professionals and clients that is different from what exists between businesses and customers. The client is less able to evaluate the work product because he or she lacks the skill and knowledge of the professional. The client's interests and the public good are presumed to take precedence over the professional's self-interest.

Print has served as a key component in the informational boundaries of the legal profession. The placement of print materials into separate law libraries, as discussed previously, provided a physical presence to the idea of law as a discrete discipline. Further support was provided by bibliographical conventions, such as the West Publishing Company's Key Number System, which seemed to provide the law with a place that had areas of legal knowledge compartmentalized as neatly as rooms in an apartment building and that also separated citizens from the law. This model made it reasonable to view lawyers as specialists in legal information, as persons with control over this legal informational space, and as persons with the authority to provide advice on the use and interpretation of legal information. Finally, the need to master this identifiable body of knowledge created the need for educational institutions that could teach those who desired access to it.

The movement of information electronically appears to have little more respect for institutional and professional boundaries than it has for physical boundaries and national borders. Print, to some extent at least, respected physical boundaries and national borders since distribution of print materials depended upon modes of transportation. It is no longer necessary, however, for knowledge to be in one place to be useful or for it to be physically transported to users. Locations no longer differentiate very successfully since, increasingly, location is irrelevant in obtaining and using information. Print required storage in structures such as books and buildings, that over time became symbols for the law. In cyberspace, illusion often prevails, and what appears to be a single source of information may reside in many different locations.[27] Governments, particularly since the fall of the Soviet Union, seem sensitive to the difficulty of controlling information, but the professions seem barely aware that their territory is being infiltrated in ways that could not have happened previously and that new modes of organizing and accessing information will lead to growing pressure to change boundary lines. As for symbols, cyberspace supports individual control of the work environment and user manipulation of the screen interface. It is more of an individual and group medium than a mass medium, and it is, therefore, not easy to imagine what kinds of unifying professional symbols might emerge from this new environment.

Electronic tools to access legal spaces and legal information reduce the informational distance that previously enhanced the lawyer's role as translator and interpreter.[28] Intricate key number and digest systems are replaced with natural language queries,[29] and interactive software provides some answers to legal concerns. Advances in software design make the screen a more inviting environment and one where clicking a mouse on an icon or speaking into a microphone replaces arcane commands or a complex library arrangement. Perhaps most important, access to an electronic network links one to a large resource of people and to a new kind of community to which he or she can turn for some insight and guidance.

A recent study of the impact of electronic data banks on the German legal profession suggests one kind of impact of the new media on professional boundaries.[30] The study, by Michael Hartmann, concluded that as electronic information services made legal information accessible to trained insurance clerks, there was increased employment competition between lawyers and insurance clerks. He found that, "except for core legal fields with high need for special legal expertise, the use of legal data banks reduces lawyers' employment advantage over competing nonprofessional workers, such as insurance clerks."[31]

The cumulative effect of networks, interactive software, and hypermedia is to make the print-related boundaries that were enjoyed, exploited, and relied on by lawyers more porous. Law will no longer be found in the same place and, indeed, law will no longer be the same kind of place it once was. Law will no longer be an area of "unabashed textuality"[32] as it once was. New sources of legal information, new modes of access to these sources, and new opportunities to represent and decipher legal issues will place pressure on the legal profession and, at a minimum, create a much more competitive environment for practitioners.

Various kinds of physical, institutional, and conceptual boundaries traditionally shaped the flow and use of legal information. In general, however, cyberspace is a place that does not readily support fixed and stable boundaries and divisions, and the effect of the new media thus far has been to break down professional boundaries. Networks have made it possible to distribute information over any border or boundary at electronic speed. At an institutional level, informational distance between virtually all participants in the legal process becomes narrowed. In this sense, even the interactive capabilities of current computers and even the rather primitive expert software that now exists overcome barriers that used to add value to the lawyer's work.

Communication and Conflict

Our emerging electronic culture should not be assumed to be a harmonious or tranquil place. One of the consequences of moving from a manufacturing economy to an informational economy is that there are increasing numbers of information transactions. In such an economy, information is understood to be a valuable and marketable resource. There will be unprecedented low-cost access to large quantities of information, but a focal point of the economy—perhaps *the* focal point of the economy—will be to add value to information and create demand for a useful and marketable informational product.

In an active, often hyperactive, informational environment, where informational products or information about such products can be transmitted around the globe at electronic speed and where new and powerful tools for working with information are being developed, the quantity of information produced and communicated will grow rapidly. The number of conflicts surrounding this information will also grow. For example, contracts and contract disputes will increasingly involve informational products and informational relationships rather than a tangible product.[33] Accidents involving lost, misused, or misleading information will join accidents involving lost, misused, or improperly manufactured products. Questions of ownership of information and rights to information are already becoming the focus of many disputes as information is exchanged and processed in new ways.[34] There is no reason to doubt that increasing numbers of information transactions will be accompanied by an increasing number of disputes arising from those transactions.

The metaphor that still colors many considerations of the new technologies is Orwell's Big Brother, an image suggesting a governmental authority or set of institutions that, in the area of information, is all-powerful. In general, however, states have discovered that they are increasingly unable to control the flow of electronic information and to prevent the disclosure of secrets or the distribution of dissident views. What may, therefore, describe our age more accurately than a single Big Brother is a set of Little Brothers—an image suggesting not power, control, and a unified policy, whether authoritarian or tolerant, but a lack of unity and an ongoing struggle for control and consensus. To continue this metaphor, what is more likely than an age of Big Brother is an era of sibling rivalry, with a frequent questioning of standards and with disputes that continue to arise often over some matter that was resolved only yesterday. In such an environment, territory is staked out and boundary lines are drawn and then something changes and the process starts over again. What was precious yesterday, therefore, may have lost value overnight and be of little concern today, whereas what was valueless yesterday may be valuable today.

In such an era of rapid and continuing change, there is a critical need for individuals with expertise in forming and managing relationships and who are also skilled at dispute settlement. In addition, there will be broadening arenas of conflict, ranging from the local to the international and touching all social and economic institutions. Unlike conflict in previous ages, any conflict in any institution has the potential to have consequences for any other institution in any place since communications links among persons make it difficult for any dispute to be "contained." This is not an environment in which the suppression of rights of expression will be an effective policy, but it is also not an era in which permanent guarantees of broad rights will necessarily be secure. It is an environment in which alliances are easily formed and in which rights will be asserted, but it is also one in which rights will be challenged.

Part of the disputing landscape will be a consequence of new relationships that are formed as links are made between persons and groups that were not in contact previously. The new media not only foster new relationships and novel interactions but encourage a new level of complexity in relationships. Contracts, particularly when agreements are placed in electronic form, will allow activities and relationships to be represented in new ways. Links to networks will allow data to be exchanged automatically and for various facets of the relationship to be monitored continuously.

The legal process has considerable experience in establishing formal contractual relationships, but it has been less focused on the monitoring of such relationships. The lawyer has commonly been "at a distance" from clients and from the places where contractual performance occurs. Lawyers, of course, have experience in dealing with information-oriented disputes, but neither they nor others have experience with such an intensive information-focused environment. For example, we are accustomed to thinking about information-oriented disputes using several traditional categories, such as copyright, the First Amendment, libel and slander, privacy, and obscenity. Most of these can be expected to be growth areas, producing increasing numbers of conflicts. What will be most interesting, however, will be the larger panorama and context in which information disputes will occur, the means used to resolve them, and whether lawyers perceive opportunities in this changing landscape.

An Example: Health Care Reform. Virtually any new commercial activity or governmental endeavor can be expected to include an informational component and to rely heavily on the new technologies. Health care, for example, has not traditionally been a major source of disputes involving information. A core component of health care reform, however, will be computer networks to link offices, clinics, insurers, pharmacies, hospitals, laboratories, and other providers. Information will be shared in novel kinds of ways, which means that users will connect to computers often without being aware of how the information they are acquiring is reaching them, with whom they are sharing information, and where the information is located.

Consider, as just one example, a physician relying on a profile or case history of a patient that has been extracted from many different computers linked together. Who is responsible for overseeing not simply the accuracy of each individual record but the coordination among machines and the design of the picture of the patient that emerges? When the whole is more than the sum of its parts, it is fairly clear who is responsible for the parts, but who is responsible for the whole? Communications links among machines allow for more information to be available and also for more opportunities for disputes to arise. What standard of technical sophistication is to be required of physicians before they are held to be guilty of malpractice in not accessing electronic information? And who is to be responsible for the misuse of information or information technology or its malfunction?

One of the physicians I visited recently has a computerized office. The computers are not linked to insurers or pharmacies, but there is a computer in each examining room and all diagnoses and prescriptions are recorded electronically. The last time I was there, I waited, as usual, alone in the examining room for a few minutes before the doctor came in. The computer was on but I could see that it was not my record on the screen. Somehow, information about the previous patient had not been removed.

A moment later, the nurse entered, cleared the screen, and attempted to call up my records. But the screen locked up and she had to reboot the computer. I watched over her shoulder as she typed in commands and then her password. Something failed, however, and her password did not work. She then called the office manager for help. And, as I listened and watched, the various codes, commands, and passwords were, in effect, demonstrated for me.

There was no great harm done here, but this was a rather small, local operation. Health care reform, under any new system, will include enormous use of new information technologies. It will include data stored on "smart" cards and data stored on computers in offices. At its heart, however, the plan requires extensive and unprecedented reliance on computer networks that move information among many previously unconnected offices and agencies. Under the plan, "information technology assumes a much more important and central role in the organization and delivery of health care,"[35] because information technology becomes "a normal part of the delivery of care rather than some machinery in the basement."[36] The information component of health care reform is so central that one consultant to the Clinton administration called health care reform "the full employment act for health care information officers."[37]

There are considerable benefits to be derived from specialists 500 miles away being able to look at X-rays and from doctors' having access to all prescription records, no matter who prescribed them or where they were filled. In spite of precautions taken, however, it is inevitable that computer networks will leak information more than a metal filing cabinet and that whatever information escapes will travel much further and be involved in other decisions. On the so-called information superhighway, there are no dead ends. Any computer network that carries millions of bits of information will—due to negligence or carelessness, or faulty planning, or accidents of some kind, or intentional misuse—leak information. Thus, although health care reform is oriented around medical care, it is also an unprecedented data storage effort, unprecedented data collection effort, and unprecedented data communication and distribution effort. As all of this traffic moves on the data highway, the accident toll can also be expected to be significant.[38]

Virtually any governmental reform initiative in the future will accelerate the movement of information, the copying of information, and the use of information. Increased conflict is one of the side effects of changes that may very well be in society's interests to make. It is a side effect that has little to do with the subject of a particular reform plan since any proposal for change will incorporate reliance on the new technologies. Such changes may be aimed at health, education, or welfare concerns, but it can be expected that at their core they will rely upon and revolve around the use and delivery of information by new means. As information transactions increase and as new relationships are established, disputes will also increase. The data highway of health or commerce or education can be the source of as much litigation as the paved highways of the physical world.

Lawyers and Informational Value

Where is the legal profession in this far more intense information environment? My purpose is not to look into a crystal ball but to understand some of the stresses that are already beginning to be felt. What is clear is that informational changes occurring in the background will have an impact on what is taking place in the foreground, on what lawyers do and on how they define themselves. The future of the profession is tied, therefore, to how invested it is in an increasingly outmoded information paradigm or whether it will be able to reorient itself in response to a new communications environment, one that may ask lawyers to approach conflict in new ways and one that does not support the status of professions in the same way as occurred in the past.

Capturing Conflict

Conflict, Nils Christie wrote, can be viewed as being a form of property. He suggested that conflict has value and can be captured, manipulated, processed, and exploited. As they work with conflicts, Christie asserted, lawyers "steal" conflicts from the parties being represented.[39] Litigation, according to Christie, typically involves clients' losing control of their conflicts through an intricate process of representation, through a reconceptualization of what is taking place, and through the application of rules.

Implicit in looking at conflict in this manner is that there is competition among lawyers over conflicts. There is, in other words, not simply a struggle for control with clients but economic competition with others, both attorneys and nonattorneys, over who will have jurisdiction and derive value from the conflict. In an era of high and secure professional boundaries, the profession possessed considerable control over opportunities for conflict resolution. It is still true that the state aids the competitive position of lawyers by prohibiting nonlawyers from engaging in the "unauthorized practice of law."[40] The weakening of professional boundaries, however, brings with it increasing competition with others over who will claim jurisdiction over the conflict.

"Unauthorized practice of law" statutes may continue to exist even while new opportunities to access legal information emerge and new forms of nonadversarial conflict resolution are established. The range and impact of unauthorized practice statutes, however, will grow narrower as nonlawyers move closer and closer to legal conflicts. New communications capabilities and new informational sources will open new opportunities to resolve disputes using a variety of out-of-court processes, or even employing online mechanisms that will be developed. As the new media overcome some barriers to accessing legal information, nonlawyers will inevitably have more access to "legal" information. Some skills that used to be recognized "legal" skills also will increasingly be possessed by nonlawyers. A recent study of legal research skills needed by law school graduates, for example, brought a comment by one lawyer that although "associates today are expected to conduct comprehensive legal research, that function also is being handled more by others, including outside services and paralegals."[41] Similarly, a 1986 report by the American Bar Association Commission on Professionalism concluded that "[i]t can no longer be claimed that lawyers have the exclusive possession of the esoteric knowledge required and are therefore the only ones able to advise clients on any matter concerning the law."[42]

What the new media encourage through new modes of organizing and accessing information is a reconsideration of some of the assumptions underlying legal practice. The legal profession cannot simply assume that it should and will be able to control a certain body of information. Marc Galanter and Thomas Palay described one possible scenario:

> Not only should we expect accountants and other professionals to offer legal services, but we anticipate that more so than today the Later Big Firm will stress a multidisciplinary or "diversified" law practice. The firm oriented in this direction will incorporate the labor of other professionals and will supplement its legal services with management consulting, investment counselling, lobbying, and so forth. We noted above the move of some aggressive law firms into such arrangements already. Some foresee that firms will become diversified service firms deploying teams drawn from many disciplines, "more oriented to problem-solving than traditional law firms." Something like this is already happening in accounting firms, where the accounting and auditing core forms a decreasing portion of the firms' work and consulting services an increasing portion.[43]

Lexis Counsel Connect, when viewed in this perspective, is not only an information service but an endeavor oriented around capturing conflict and an attempt to fortify deteriorating professional boundaries. One of the principal aims of Lexis Counsel Connect is to link law firms with in-house counsel in corporations. Corporate counsel can use Lexis Counsel Connect to ask questions about legal problems they are encountering. Indeed, one of the main incentives for lawyers to subscribe to Lexis Counsel Connect is to be able to communicate with corporate counsel, exhibit their expertise in proposing solutions or ways of approaching problems, and ultimately, to secure business and a new client.

Looked at in terms of capturing conflict, Lexis Counsel Connect may be considered to be a new marketplace, one that supports the profession because nonlawyers cannot really participate. Lexis Counsel Connect insists that answering questions posed by corporate counsel does not create a lawyer-client relationship, that it is more like answering a question posed at a professional seminar. Whether or not one can form a lawyer-client relationship on line, the electronic nature of Lexis Counsel Connect creates an ongoing process aimed at the formation of relationships. Since only lawyers can participate in Lexis Counsel Connect, however, opportunities, opinions, advice, alternatives, and perspectives that nonlawyers might perceive in any problem are not available.

Lexis Counsel Connect itself faces an interesting boundary dilemma in determining how accessible and broad-based an informational service it will be. Lexis Counsel Connect members can send e-mail messages to the Internet and to other electronic services with e-mail. Originally, Lexis Counsel Connect members could not use Gopher, the World-Wide Web, or other Internet tools and services. These services have recently been made available. Yet, access to Lexis Counsel Connect is still not possible from the Internet. This is partly related to security concerns, but it also creates a more focused, boundaried, and homogeneous universe. Lawyers and corporate counsel speak to each other in a relatively private place. Yet, in an interconnected world, Lexis Counsel Connect will continually feel pressure to allow members access to more and more information. This means links to more outside sources of information and to more people whose expertise may be desired in particular subject areas. Early on, Lexis Counsel Connect granted a limited right of participation to firm librarians, but it has since restricted librarian participation in many forums. It can, however, expect to receive similar pressure from other nonlawyer professionals who are employed in law-related capacities in firms or corporations.

The dilemma for a service such as Lexis Counsel Connect is that there may ultimately be a conflict between the needs of the potential clients, the corporate counsel, and the law firms. Limiting participation to lawyers creates a focus to discussions and, clearly, corporate counsel and law firm attorneys speak the same language. Such a limitation certainly serves the needs of the law firm members. One might ask, however, whether, as members become more and more aware of the interconnected electronic information environment, pressure will build from the potential clients for greater access to nonmembers and to nonlegal information sources and whether the needs of corporate counsel will be sufficiently addressed in such an exclusive information environment.

Reorienting Legal Practice: An Information-Oriented Approach

In one of contemporary literature's most satirical pieces about lawyers, Kurt Vonnegut writes about a character who worked for a large law firm. The character, at one point,

> recalled what his favorite professor, Leonard Leech, once told him about getting ahead in law. Leech said that, just as a good airplane pilot should always be looking for places to land, so should a lawyer

be looking for situations where large amounts of money were about to change hands.

"In every big transaction," said Leech, "there is a magic moment during which a man has surrendered a treasure, and during which the man who is due to receive it has not yet done so. An alert lawyer will make that moment his own, possessing the treasure for a magic microsecond, taking a little of it, passing it on. If the man who is to receive the treasure is unused to wealth, has an inferiority complex and shapeless feelings of guilt, as most people do, the lawyer can often take as much as half the bundle, and still receive the recipient's blubbering thanks.[44]

I include this reference to Vonnegut not because I necessarily agree with this portrayal of the manner in which lawyers obtain their fees but because the metaphor employed, a treasure, appears to be something tangible. As such, this is not simply a description of how lawyers obtain fees but a representation of how the law in general tends to approach disputes, conflicts, and problem solving. The rule-oriented adversary model of conflict resolution tends to enhance and encourage a treasure-hunting mode in which the treasure, whether money or some other tangible object, is necessarily diminished as it passes through the lawyer's hands.

The digital lawyer may continue to be a seeker of treasures, but treasures in the future will increasingly be in the form of information and knowledge, in relationships for sharing and exploiting information, in opportunities to gain access to and use information that are part of the conflict or that come out of the resolution of the conflict. Dispute resolution researchers have described part of the process of litigation as "narrowing," meaning that the lawyer focuses on information that relates to relevant rules and considers other information to be irrelevant.[45] The digital lawyer faces a novel and more complicated task, also reshaping and characterizing the dispute somewhat differently from the lay person but also being more sensitive than lawyers in the past to the value to be gained in looking at the dispute in broader terms. Thus, although legal workers may continue to be more rule-oriented than other information workers, lawyers, like other information workers, will also be opportunity-oriented and information-oriented in ways that many lawyers have not been in the past.

Print has served the law as both a tool and a symbol. Thus, we store, obtain, and distribute information in print and, as we do, we also see things "in black and white," as information that is fixed to the page, that is uniform and standardized, and that involves a limited number of options. As we use the new technologies, it is important to understand that they, too, represent both a resource to be used and a force that will bring about new ways of thinking and of conceptualizing the practice of law.

In a world of instant communication and impressive capabilities for using information, much of the value of the new information technologies lies in using them to process and recombine information in novel ways. In doing this, and in assisting in this process, the lawyer's function is to guide the relationships that are formed between people and institutions, in a sense to promote the recombining of people and interests using the new technologies' model of information processing as a paradigm. Thus, the digital lawyer also sees a treasure but it is not a treasure, to be "divided up" or "found" or "captured," but one to be processed, cultivated, and expanded.

Under this view, Christie may still be correct in pointing out that conflicts have value, but the survival of the legal profession requires that lawyers understand that "stealing" the conflict, in the sense of placing the parties at a greater and greater distance from each other, is not as rewarding a way to proceed as confronting the dispute, clearly revealing the nature of each party's interests, reshaping the conflict, and working with the parties not simply to settle the case but to endeavor to restore, enhance, or redirect the relationship so that all parties can benefit.

Lawyers presented with an information-oriented dispute today might not look at an informational case any differently from a case involving a tangible product. A "digital lawyer," however, might very well look at such a case in different terms. Such a lawyer would focus on the informational component and would be concerned at least as much with the opportunities presented by the information as with the legal issues presented by the dispute. The shift in outlook that characterizes the digital lawyer may be subtle because all lawyers have a sensitivity to both text and context. Yet, the digital lawyer will be employing a broader range of skills and an outlook that reflects not simply what the new technologies do but the manner in which they do it. In outlook, therefore, the digital lawyer views himself or herself not simply as a person with expertise in law but as an information worker whose focus is law.

An Example. One of the landmark cases of copyright law as it relates to software is the case of *Whelan v. Jaslow.*[46] The plaintiff, Whelan, was a computer programmer who had created software that was used to automate the defendant's dental laboratory. The software, which ran on a minicomputer, satisfied the defendant and the two parties began a joint venture—using Whelan's programming expertise and Jaslow's contacts in the dental service industry—to market the program, called Dentalab, to other dental laboratories. The relationship between Whelan and Jaslow was not harmonious, but the business venture was viable and survived until a significant event in the history of computing occurred, the arrival of the IBM personal computer in 1981.

The Dentalab program, which was owned by Whelan, would not

run on the IBM PC, and Jaslow decided that he could successfully develop and market a dental program by himself for PCs. In creating this program, however, Jaslow not only looked at the source code for Dentalab but modeled many of the screens and functions of the new program on Dentalab. The similarities between the two programs were so stark that the judge ruled that Whelan's rights had been infringed, and she was awarded attorneys' fees and $101,000, the amount of the profits Jaslow had made from sales of his PC program.

In a 1989 book,[47] a noted copyright attorney argued that the decision in this case clarified an important point in copyright law. He also pointed out that this case was "a clash of wills, an emotional tempest based on strongly held convictions. That it was also a complete waste of their time and money was beside the point."[48] Yet, the lost opportunity may be the most important lesson in this case. Although the court did clearly rule that screen displays are protectable, it is equally clear that the business partnership was ruined and economic opportunities were lost. There is, of course, no guarantee that mediation or any dispute resolution process could have successfully restored and refocused the Whelan-Jaslow partnership or that the partnership would have conquered the turbulent 1980s software environment. Yet, no one seemed cognizant of or prepared to do anything about the fact that the value of the information at the heart of this dispute was declining rapidly as time passed.

It may be that the attorneys, and probably the parties as well, saw the Whelan-Jaslow relationship, at the time the litigation commenced, as being over and without any possibility of salvaging. Perhaps it was. Yet, mediators and other experts in dispute resolution might have a different perspective. One difference between litigation and mediation is that mediators recognize that by maintaining lines of communication, by placing few or no limits on what issues are raised, and by placing the burden for resolution on the parties, more often than not the unanticipated occurs and the seemingly unresolvable is resolved.[49] It is of little concern that ideas for how this relationship might have been restored are difficult to imagine at this date. Imagining reasonable outcomes is often a fruitless exercise at the beginning of a mediation. What mediators assume is that the mediation process is able to tap the creativity of the parties and to elicit ideas that were hidden or appeared to be irrelevant. As a result, damaged relationships often are rebuilt or reestablished in ways that had not appeared possible at the start.

The increasing number of law firms and lawyers with mediation and other alternative dispute-resolution skills is consistent with the direction in which lawyering is moving. The difficulty for the nondigital lawyer in the information age is that such a person is less aware of the key function of information workers, which is to add value to information, and less aware of the opportunities presented by space-conquering media. In the past, expertise was measured in terms of accessing, possessing, and applying areas of knowledge. Whoever was perceived to possess the greatest amount of knowledge and could apply it effectively and skillfully was the greatest expert. In such an informational environment, there was value in simply holding onto information and keeping it hidden from others. Much of the contest of law could be viewed as flowing from a perspective that placed value on building one's own storehouse of information.

Digital lawyers, and Lexis Counsel Connect as well, recognize that there is less and less value in accumulating and holding onto information and that the profession needs to move away from the storehouse model. In its place must come a recognition that the possessor of electronic information must use it and add value to it. Thus, Lexis Counsel Connect is trying to create a marketplace for the work product of law firms. This is a use of information that is consistent with an information environment where the time frame in which information remains valuable is diminishing. A 1990 Office of Technology Assessment study observed that "technologies are changing rapidly, both qualitatively and quantitatively. This makes the crafting and refining of software protections akin to aiming at a target that isn't there (or doesn't yet exist)."[50]

Computer consultant Patricia Seybold has recognized that it is not easy to convert a profession of information hoarders into information opportunists. She writes that in industry

> [t]he popular approach is to gather all the data from different departments and corral it into one megalithic repository, where it can be carefully maintained and protected. Then, the idea is, everyone in the company can dip into it according to their station and their "need to know." . . .
>
> If you want people to share information, you have to offer them information that's more valuable than what they're "giving up." But the logic isn't always so clear to those you have to convince, whose judgment may be clouded by ingrained and unexamined assumptions about "how we do business."
>
> Let me give you an example: The distribution division of a large manufacturing firm had established a state-of-the-art, just-in-time inventory management system with one of its largest clients. In gratitude, this client, a major retailer, offered to share its database of item sales for each store.
>
> When the folks in the manufacturer's product marketing department heard that offer they began to salivate, thinking about what they could do with this treasure trove of detailed, micromarket information. But the executives in the sales organization threw out a red flag. "We don't want to get that close to our customers," they said. "That's why we sell through brokers."[51]

This is an interesting admission of a desire to maintain boundaries and of the challenges and opportunities that occur as the new technologies are employed to narrow distances. It reveals that some practices and traditions that have been common and perhaps even useful will be increasingly challenged and be found to be counterproductive.

Encouraging a new attitude toward information and toward the formation of relationships is difficult, but it is something that is permeating many businesses. Banks, for example, understand that they are not simply financial institutions but that they are in the information and communications business, that their product includes access to information for consumers, gathering information about customers, and evaluating information in many different contexts.[52] In a similar vein, the chairman of United Parcel Service, Kent Nelson, has stated that "we've learned that information about a package is often as important as the package itself."[53] Nelson has recognized that he is not simply in the package distribution business but in the information business, that distributing packages efficiently requires that the information about the package be available at all times, and that each shipment provides some kind of useful information to the company, whether about a particular customer or a new need for some kind of service, or whether a marketing strategy is working as designed. Federal Express competes with UPS, not simply on the basis of cost or shipping time but on the informational relationship it establishes with customers. For example, Federal Express provides all of its customers with free software that can be used to connect to the Federal Express computer in Memphis and can inform the shipper of where along the route the package is. The technology, in other words, brings the consumer and business closer together in an attempt by the merchant to strengthen and create relationships. By doing so, it requires that an enterprise "asks this question—What business are we really in?"[54] This is no longer an easy question since "a lot of industries won't be separate in the future. What's cable? What's the post office? What's Federal Express? What's a TV network? These all have something to do with information-on-demand capabilities."[55]

Electronic technology changes one's orientation about information, increases attention to it, and encourages the use of information in ways that were either neglected or not possible before. In an era in which timely information is valuable, one writer has argued:

> The data your company collects through the normal course of business is the fuel that moves the business forward. It's extremely valuable information, and without access to sales, accounting, marketing, and product information, your company probably wouldn't be in business.
>
> Now, many IS managers are discovering that the same information that's so valuable inside the corporation can generate revenue when marketed to outside organizations.
>
> Increasingly, companies that haven't been in the information business are getting into it. Whether you are a consumer products manufacturer, a department store, or a wholesale supplier to the medical

industry, a lot of people want to know more about your customers. And they're willing to pay money to find out.[56]

Another instructive case of a business firm's reconceptualizing its role around information is what used to be a travel firm, Rosenbluth Travel. Rosenbluth Travel had been founded in 1892 in Philadelphia. By 1980, it was a successful company with annual bookings of $20–$30 million. Yet, with deregulation occurring and computer reservations services appearing, it appeared that the value provided by travel agencies was declining. The president of the company, however, saw this as an opportunity to work with information, to orient the company toward cyberspace, and to establish new relationships with clients. According to Rosenbluth, however, the "biggest competitive advantage was to understand that as deregulation changed the rules of travel, we were no longer in the travel business so much as we were in the information business."[57]

Richard Lanham has pointed out that "many areas of endeavor in America pressured by technological change have already had to decide what business they were really in, and those making the narrow choice have usually not fared well. The railroads had to decide whether they were in the transportation business or the railroad business; they chose the latter and gradual extinction."[58] Nicholas Negroponte, director of the media lab at the Massachusetts Institute of Technology, has contended that, in the past, "people thought of themselves as being in the newspaper business, or movies, music and so on. But they're really not anymore. They're in the bit manufacturing business."[59] This has been echoed by Vice President Al Gore, who has asserted that "in the ensuing expansion of the information business, the new marketplace will no longer be divided along current sectoral lines. There may not be cable companies or phone companies or computer companies, as such. Everyone will be in the bit business. The functions provided will define the marketplace. There will be information conduits, information appliances and information consumers."[60] As technology becomes more powerful than it is today, lawyers may also perceive themselves as being in the "bit business." They may be oriented around and expert in one part of the "bit business," the legal part, but there will also be more ambiguity about what is the legal part than exists today.

The recognition that lawyers are in the information business as well as in the legal business is an underlying assumption of Lexis Counsel Connect, but it is an idea that lawyers have much more difficulty accepting than bankers, travel agents, overnight shippers, and other business persons. There are also ethical codes that impose constraints on the lawyer's use of information. Lawyers need to understand, however, that what differentiates them from others, and the distance that may be said to exist between lawyers and non-lawyers, is declining. It is not that lawyers are losing their expertise or not being trained as well, but that the role and expertise of lawyers overlap more with others.

The next generation of lawyers cannot rely on the exclusionary power of state-imposed or print-imposed boundaries to maintain the status, power, and distinction enjoyed by the profession in the past. If lawyers are to survive better than scribes or calligraphers did in the post-Gutenberg world, they need to do more than merely adapt new technologies to traditional practices and processes. The route to success lies in a new model of legal practice, in a new orientation toward and appreciation of electronic information, and in an understanding of the implications of shrinking distances between people and institutions. It is not easy to be confident that the value of the new paradigm and the need for the new paradigm will be recognized. The old paradigm appears to still support the legal profession reasonably comfortably and to provide fairly clear definition to the nature of the lawyer's role and responsibilities. There is also a large infrastructure, including libraries and schools, that will probably resist change.

The key to the future of the legal profession may be discerned in whether the new technologies are used primarily in connection with traditional endeavors and traditional approaches to lawyering or whether they engage lawyers in a new relationship with information and reflect a new understanding of the differences between electronic information and print. The virtual information place of Lexis Counsel Connect is intriguing because it is consistent with the direction the profession needs to move in if it is to preserve a place for itself in the future. Justice Brandeis once noted that the work of lawyers is "limited by time and space."[61] It is on these dimensions that change is now occurring and bringing about a changing dynamic in the practice of law.

8

Hypertext:
Constructing Cyberspace

There is no Final Word. There can be no final version, no last thought. There is always a new view, a new idea, a reinterpretation. And literature, which we propose to electronify, is a system for preserving continuity in the face of this fact. . . . Remember the analogy between text and water. Water flows freely, ice does not. The free-flowing live documents on the network are subject to constant new use and linkage, and those new links become interactively available.

—Theodor Nelson

This book began with some observations about the seamless web, a figure of speech that has often been associated with law. I suggested that the unity and consistency that the metaphor implies probably has never fit the law very well and that there has been increasing recognition of its inappropriateness in recent years. The seamless web assumes that all of the various elements of law share many interests, goals, approaches, practices, ways of thinking, and ways of acting. It conceives of law more as a single large territory with a high and clearly defined external boundary than as being many territories with many internal boundaries. Those who have considered the metaphor of the seamless web in recent years have pointed out that whatever its validity in the past, the direction of change has been toward increased fragmentation of the profession, of decision making that is not guided by general principles, and even of less agreement or consensus over what a lawyer is or does.[1] If there are observable boundaries in the law, either as a body of knowledge or as an institution or as a process or method, they seem currently to be more the boundaries of fief-doms than the boundaries of a profession.

The law as it was configured in print space and as it operated in print space, it has become clear, actually had quite a few seams. Yet, law in print space arguably had a meaningful external boundary, in that one could conceive of law as being different from political, social, religious, and economic institutions. This distinguishing boundary certainly was not as clear as the edge of the printed book or the mar-gin of a printed page, and law has often clearly reflected the influence of economic and political forces. The myth of the law's independent character, however, has been pervasive and it was supported and rein-forced by palpable and tangible symbols. Images that, even in this transition period, still resonate and have meaning, such as impres-sively bound law books or judicial robes or wood-paneled court-rooms, suggest that legal space, like any space, is distinctive in many ways and that the activities that take place in it are different from activities taking place in other kinds of spaces. Indeed, the familiar symbols just mentioned may be considered to be part of the boundary that differentiates law from other institutions and processes. All of these symbols separate, create distance, and focus attention inward, thereby fortifying institutional boundaries and helping to support a perception of a distinct law space.

Legal information no longer resides in as autonomous a space as it did in the print era. Cyberspace can serve a legal purpose one moment and a nonlegal purpose the next. As has already been dis-cussed, electronic space can overcome the constraints of physical space and can often be individualized and refashioned instanta-neously. Such a space does not have to make as many compromises as a physical space in order to accommodate many different needs since it is highly flexible and can be personalized as the user wishes. This is one reason that the survival of many shared cultural symbols is in doubt. Many of the symbolic functions performed by physical spaces are lost when virtual spaces appear different to each user. Thus, electronic space does not contain a clearly defined and physi-cally separate "library" that can serve as a place for interacting with law and that can also be a symbol for those who are subject to law. Many library functions that in the past could only be performed in a particular and specialized physical space can, when information is in electronic form, be performed in any space. Less obviously perhaps, the place for conflict resolution is also shifting, from a centralized physical location and entity—the court house—to a more participa-tory but less focused arena. Physical places that have been assumed to be necessary for many kinds of informational transactions will turn out not to be as necessary as they were in the past. We may, as will be described, need a sense of place but no longer need a physical place to perform many information-oriented functions.

Electronic communication can reach many people, but it is a different kind of mass medium than print, where each reader necessarily sees the same image. The displacement of physical places as centers of attention poses a challenge for any institution where power in some way derives from a physical place. One purpose of Lexis Counsel Connect, for example, is to provide a new context or place for the legal profession and allow a profession made vulnerable by changing informational distances and the loss of symbols and shared spaces to try to exploit virtual places. Yet, the difficulty for the legal profession and for entities such as Lexis Counsel Connect is that the displacement and reorganization that is occurring goes beyond institutions, such as the legal profession, and beyond places, such as libraries, to something that is even more fundamental—the actual concepts and internal organization of the law. Although the communicative powers of the electronic media are able to penetrate through the walls of a building, such as the library or a courthouse, hypertext moves us to reconsider what is on the shelves of the library and in between the covers of books. This touches some issues already discussed, such as how research may be conducted and what are considered appropriate boundaries and sources for legal research, and also some more fundamental concerns, such as how law is conceptualized. The distribution of information electronically, as Paul Kahn has observed, "affects our sense of what is known and can be known, as well as how we organize that knowledge."[2]

The difficulty of substituting virtual boundaries for the physical boundaries that have helped to define institutions and disciplines is highlighted by the hypertextual capability of electronic information. Indeed, hypertext carries our analysis of the vulnerability of print's organizational model deeper, perhaps, than any other quality of the electronic media. Hypertext carries us into the words, sentences, and paragraphs of the book, a symbol of both law and linear organization. Whereas the network may take us beyond the library and even outside the law, hypertext carries us to a deeper internal domain by applying electronic tools to what is between the covers of the book and, in effect, by overcoming the very physical nature of paper and ink. Legal territory is changing in various ways as it adapts to a less tangible existence and as changes occur in who operates in that territory and who has access to it. Yet, what we are witnessing as we travel into cyberspace is not simply a change in the surface terrain, of new roads and capabilities for travel, but of changes that go fairly deep, that affect how we think about information, how we organize it, and even how we perceive institutions, such as the law, that rely on a relationship with information.

Hypertext, perhaps more than any other facet of the new media, leads us into uncharted territory, a place where new kinds of relationships with information will develop for which many readers may find that they have no frame of reference. In this regard, hypertext is probably the most disorienting quality of cyberspace. The other main issues discussed in this book represent enormously important and impressive technological achievements. Although they may not be familiar to all readers, most persons probably have some reasonable frame of reference for understanding networks, interactive machines and graphical forms. It is not easy to get used to getting information instantaneously from a distance or to learn to express oneself in more visual ways, but such qualities are not completely novel or unfamiliar. Hypertext, however, involves not simply learning a new skill but forsaking habits and assumptions about how to look for information and think about sources of information. It challenges basic habits of reading and learning, as well as notions of fixity and finality that we have come to expect of words and ideas in books. It is a tool to access information, but it is also a tool that fragments sources of information. Other qualities of the electronic media allow novel interactions with information sources and permit letters to be lifted from the page so that electrical currents can carry them around the globe. These are qualities that are enormously impressive, but they are not usually disorienting to the user. Hypertext, however, threatens to dismantle the print model even further by releasing the page from its binding and by even allowing a reordering of words, sentences, and paragraphs by each and every user.

What Is Hypertext?

Hypertext is an extension of the interactive capabilities of the electronic media. Interaction implies that there are choices one makes while using electronic information. In reading this book, for example, you probably have turned the pages sequentially, moving from beginning to end or at least from the beginning of one chapter to the end of the chapter. Books have a beginning and an end and a preferred arrangement designed by the author. If you were using a hypertextual version of the information in this book, your route to this point might have been different and your exit point from here might be different. At many stages along the way, you would be presented with choices, and instead of thinking about what comes next or about what is on the next page, you would begin thinking about where you would like to go next.

The opportunities for moving through a text in different ways and for branching out of a text at a particular point and following a set of pointers in a new direction is what makes hypertext a nonlinear form of acquiring information. Hypertext itself is a term coined by Theodor Nelson, who defined it as "non-sequential writing—text that branches and allows choices to the reader, best read at an interactive screen. As popularly conceived, this is a series of chunks connected by links which offer the reader different pathways."[3] Nelson's dream was a system called Xanadu, in which every piece of information was linked to other pieces.

Hypertext is an evolving genre and, as David Johnson pointed out, "hypertext is easier to demonstrate than to describe."[4] Its origins, as the word itself suggests, were in the textual realm and largely focused on linking chunks of text together in a much more flexible manner than is possible with something that exists in a "binding." The focus was on new tools for navigating through text, for creating routes through a work that were obscured or were highly cumbersome with works in print. There was rarely any more thought of including graphical material in such works than there is in including graphics in most printed works. Similarly, the idea of establishing links between the work and some other work existing somewhere else on a computer network was unlikely to occur to anyone other than one of the visionaries of the hypertext movement.

We are rapidly expanding both the method and the meaning of hypertext so that works of hypertext—or hypermedia, as such works increasingly are called—are beginning to exploit all of the electronic capabilities mentioned in this book. Thus, many examples of hypertext, such as the World-Wide Web, use networks to link information on different computers, and this information may be text, graphics, or even sound. The evolution of hypertext into hypermedia may involve exactly the same kind of change in thinking that occurred as "moving pictures" evolved into film and cinema, and as "horseless carriages" evolved into automobiles. In each case, a previous technology served as a linguistic frame of reference for a period of time. In each case, it took some time before the new technology was recognized as being distinct, independent, and deserving of a term that allowed the label applied to early uses to be left behind.

Hypertext's early link to text may account for the footnote's being the most commonly used illustration of something familiar that has some hypertextual qualities. For those who are unfamiliar with the interactive nature of electronic communication, hypertext is often explained as being a kind of extended footnote. Footnotes temporarily move a reader out of the primary text just as a hypertextual link moves one either to a different place in the text or to a different text altogether. The uniqueness of electronic hypertext is that it carries the user far beyond footnotes. With hypertext, one can not only look at a reference but can look at or connect to the source. One can then connect to other sources cited in the first source, and then to sources cited in the second source, and so on. Eventually, one realizes that the original source has been left far behind and may never be returned to.

Footnotes or endnotes are understood to be supplementary— appendages to the main text that may illuminate or explain but are also a digression rather than a detour or a new route to more information. The footnote may cause one to change direction later and consult new sources, but the process of reading through a work is generally not disturbed by looking at a footnote. It may cause a brief change in focus but, in general, one's primary attention remains on the text and on the route through the text that the author created. Footnotes give an author one chance to add commentary, but the reader is typically routed back to the text since the footnote itself cannot have a footnote. Thus, in spite of how interesting footnotes may be, they are also a dead end. They appear where there is no more room for expansion, either at the very bottom of the page or at the end of the book. Indeed, they define where the bottom of the page or the end of the book is. They also typically are distracting since the reader is always aware that he or she will be returning to the text. Hypertext, if it solves the dilemma of where to place comments and references, may also solve a logistical dilemma plaguing print—one that caused an observer to comment that "if footnotes were a rational form of communication, Darwinian selection would have resulted in the eyes being set vertically rather than on an inefficient horizontal plane."[5]

Books have beginnings and endings and the author sets out a preferred route from beginning to end. As David Bolter has written, "the book is a physical unit; its pages are sewn or glued together and then bound into a portable whole. Should not all the words inside proceed from one unifying idea and stand in the same relationship to the reader?"[6] There is no guarantee that the reader will take the route laid out by the author, but the existence of the book as a physical object existing in space makes it fairly likely the route will be followed. Although the footnote helps explain the nature of hypertext, it is at best a primitive example of hypertext and one that does not illuminate very effectively the qualities and capabilities of hypertext in the electronic environment.

Hypertext involves acquiring information in nonlinear fashion. To understand its nature and significance, therefore, it would seem beneficial to look not at examples of linear communication, such as print, but of nonlinear modes of experience. Such examples would not only provide a frame of reference that would make hypertext seem less alien, but would help us comprehend that hypertext is not an extension of print but something that is different from and displacing printed text. Print analogies to hypertext, such as the use of the word *e-mail* in the network context, sends us looking for insight in the wrong direction. Indeed, for hypertext it is not even analogies to print that do this but the very word itself, where *text* is the concept that is modified by *hyper*. The term *hypermedia* is increasingly being used, and *hypertext* none too soon may become an anachronistic term.

Where might one look for examples of nonlinear learning that might clarify the nature of hypertext? The great irony of hypertext is that it is difficult to explain its meaning even though much, if not most, of our learning occurs in nonlinear or hypertextual fashion. Our "serious" learning or "book" learning may occur linearly, but learning that occurs through experience tends not to be of a linear nature. Consider a conversation where one talks about concepts and ideas he or she is interested in. He or she might begin with a certain topic or agenda but, more likely than not, a comment made by the person spoken to will lead to new questions, and the resulting discussion will cause the conversation to move in still another direction. Or consider a visit to an art museum, where there is a very open layout and where, as visitors walk down one corridor, they may see something at a distance and walk over to it. As they turn to go back, they may then see something different down another hall and move toward it. Or imagine a beautiful garden where there are numerous flowers competing for our attention but there is no real beginning or end to the garden. These are the kinds of interactions and information-rich environments that hypertext tries to emulate.

There are probably many other examples that one could provide of common nonlinear learning experiences. Such events occur not as the result of following an itinerary or an agenda established by others but by searching for the answers to one's own questions. Hypertext, therefore, is probably best seen as an attempt to allow us to use electronic information not as we use printed text but as we learn from others and as we learn when we are in control of our environment and able to use the environment to satisfy our own needs.

Discussions of hypertext often refer to the user's "navigating" through a work. The term suggests that we are in some space and that much responsibility for getting from beginning to end falls on the navigator. It is difficult to speak of navigating through a book because there is usually only one preferred route through the book. Hypertext, however, enables users to establish their own paths because choices are available that the physical nature of a book makes difficult, if not impossible.

One of the frequent metaphors used to explain computer communication is the superhighway. I am not sure that the superhighway metaphor is more appropriate than some other frequently used metaphors for cyberspace, but it does have some relevance to the issue of hypertext—an area where it is rarely, if ever, employed. The appropriateness of the metaphor here is that both hypertext and highway travel allow the user or driver to control both the destination and the route. The point of a highway is not to travel it from beginning to end as defined by the road designer but to travel from beginning to end as each traveler defines the beginning and the end. The highway can have many travelers and each may have a different beginning and end.

Hypertext, unlike print, provides alternate and competing paths and routes to information. Because of this, the user becomes a director or creator, a driver or navigator, perhaps even an author, and much less of a subject or recipient of an author's message. The book's physical nature, for example, requires that it be presented to the reader in some order. Conceivably, a book provided on cards or in looseleaf form could be rearranged by the user, and even bound books can contain suggestions by the author for proceeding through the text in different ways depending upon the goals and purposes of the reader. Clearly, however, this is cumbersome when dealing with a product in which the words, letters, and paragraphs are fixed and the "referenced (or linked) materials lie spatially distant from the references to them."[7]

We already have many examples of hypertextual works, but both the novelty and the imperfect design of many of these works cause problems for users. This should not be too surprising. Books are used from an early age, and features of printed works such as tables of contents, page numbers, indexes, and chapter headings—those parts of book design that help readers know their place—need no explanation. Much hypertext is disorienting to new users because text on the screen creates expectations of a print experience and navigating through the hypertextual material proves more difficult, rather than less difficult, than moving through a printed work. Nor have most hypertextual works effectively captured the characteristics of non-print space. Hypertext opens up the opportunity for creating an information-rich space, one considerably richer than the medium of print in that it can be used more flexibly and include sound and images in addition to text. Much of what currently passes for hypertext, however, simply provides information out of context or, more precisely, without any context. It possesses neither the comfortable linear mode of print nor the information-rich space of the physical environment that touches all of our senses. It carries us somewhere, but not anywhere that, for most people, is an adequate substitute for a book or for a nonbook information experience.

We have some way to travel before the potential of hypertext is realized. It is necessary not only to become comfortable and familiar with the concept of hypertext but to provide hypertextual programs with a supporting and appropriate environment. Again, this is largely the role of software that will create a space that does not mimic print but that supports the presentation of information in new modes. It is important to remember that books are more than a collection of words. Our 500 years of experience have taught us a great deal about the value of context in print space. By context I refer to everything about a printed work other than the words. Thus, the vast majority of printed works use serif typefaces rather than sans-serif fonts because the serif helps the eye link small letters and words together. We use combinations of upper- and lowercase letters rather than all capital letters. As mentioned earlier, there is a title page providing information about author, publisher, and publishing history of the book. There is a table of contents providing an indication of the components and mode of organization of the work. There is an index providing a listing of terms, ideas, and concepts contained in the work. There are page numbers that continually provide the reader with some grounding and a sense of how much has been read.

Someone holding and reading a book is always receiving some feedback from the physical object along with the information represented by the words on paper. For example, as the reader turns the pages he or she can feel how quickly he or she is moving through the work. If a book was ever printed in which, for some strange reason, the pages were numbered but one needed a key to know in what order the pages had to be read, it would be quite troublesome for many readers. Similarly, a book without any page numbers would probably be disorienting to many readers even if the pages were arranged in the "right" order.

It is sometimes assumed that the only questions readers are concerned with are the questions "What does this mean?" and "What is the author saying?" Readers also, however, continuously ask the question "Where am I?" It took several generations after Gutenberg for print publishers to realize this and to provide the tools, such as the index and table of contents, that help answer this question. This is a question that readers of a book can answer instantaneously by looking at the thickness of the book, by a glance at the table of contents or index, and by looking at what the last page of the book or article is. What is provided is a sense of place—a coherent and organized place, a place with an accepted logic behind it. This space provides the reader some clues of how much can be accomplished in a certain period of time.

The challenge for hypertextual programs is to provide not merely data or quick access to information but information in some context. This is also the means by which electronic publishers can add value to information and compete with other electronic publishers. There are many computer programs that can be used to create hypertextual "documents" with features for searching text, creating links across files, and allowing the user to type in notes and otherwise personalize the material. These programs allow electronic material to be used in a hypertextual manner and even allow for the incorporation of graphical material and the establishment of network links. These programs contain many capabilities for navigating through text, but they often do not provide a broad enough array of contextual cues that let users feel comfortable and that actually facilitate and enhance the information acquisition process.

The point of hypertext is that it changes many different kinds of boundaries and will force us to think differently about information and about the structure and organization of information. Cases, for example, have always been linked in time to other cases through the West key number system. The West key number system, indeed, can be considered a print version of hypertext. The Digests and Reporters are complicated systems, but they are also, given print's limitations, information-rich environments. With training, a reader obtains a great deal of information from each of the many components of the printed page. They have succeeded, over the past century, in becoming a primary legal research tool because the design of each page communicates a great deal of information.

The design of the Digests and Reporters also focuses attention on the case or opinion as the main object of interest. In print, the cases and the digests are linked by a rather remarkable system, yet each case also exists by itself in time and space. The boundaries of each case are clear even if each key number and headnote emphasizes the importance of a small part of the case. Thus far, as case law has become electronified, little has changed. Both LEXIS and WESTLAW have relatively undeveloped hypertext capabilities[8] and appear to have assumed that the focus of electronic materials will be the same as the focus of print materials. Hypertext, however, does not respect the same boundaries as print. As hypertextual opportunities expand, cases will be incorporated in each other or parts of cases will be appear "inside" of other cases. Just as print led to the development of abridgments and digests, the vastly more flexible electronic medium will allow new representations and portrayals of law and "enable some modes of thought at the expense of others."[9] What will color how we employ cases will be not only our traditions of legal reasoning but our experience with electronic information, an experience that will not be the same as it was in the print world.

Why Is Hypertext Different?

Hypertext is still perceived by many to be either an extension of print or the same as print, albeit with some special features and capabilities for searching through text or moving around text. The continued identification with printing, or at least the continued conceptualization of hypertext as an appendage of text or as a kind of text, rather than as something novel and independent of printing, is reinforced by the existence of many electronic works that contain only words and that one can, if he or she wishes, read as one normally reads a book, namely from beginning to end. This often is done by pressing a key, found on all IBM-style keyboards, that has the words *Page Down* imprinted on it and that moves the user from screen to screen. The labeling of this key in this manner reflects the exceptionally strong appeal of the printed-page metaphor and the exceedingly strong attraction we feel to it. It is a subtle suggestion sitting right on the keyboard that there is little perceived difference between the screen and the page and that moving from one screen of words to another is not very different from turning a page.

Hypertext may not reach maturity until the *Page Down* key is either removed from the keyboard or is programmed for some other use. At that point, we will understand that moving from screen to screen is not the same as turning a page, since the former sets various things in motion that the latter does not. At present, the page metaphor has appeal and exercises considerable power over users. It is a powerful metaphor and its continued pervasiveness inhibits the change in informational habits and orientations that hypertext requires.

Pressing a key may be a tactile experience like turning a page but, at least at present, one often receives none of the feedback that occurs as a page is turned. There is rarely any visual sense of connection or continuity between the new screen and the old. The link between the new screen and the old is purely the informational content that one reads, whereas with print, the information is linked through a whole series of spatial and contextual cues, such as page numbers and chapter or section headers that may appear at the top of the page, as well as the understanding that the pages are literally bound together. If a reader moves from page 1 to page 100 in a book, he or she actually sees that a hundred pages are "skipped" and that some line of argument may be missed. To go from page 1 to page 100 in the WESTLAW database directory, however, as one does when one goes from the main directory screen of WESTLAW to a screen on which other files are listed, skips nothing. Labeling screens as page numbers provides a user with a sense of familiarity but, unlike pages in a book, no real information or feedback is given to the user. In cyberspace, everything is next to everything else or at least can be made to appear to be next to everything else. Many more things can be close to something than is possible with physical entities. Unfortunately, at present the techniques and metaphors employed with electronic information cause almost everything to appear to be at a distance from everything else, something that is also easily achieved in cyberspace and that, in this transition period, seems to occur all too often.

The surface affinity of hypertext to printed text and the modeling of electronic information on printed information should not be surprising. As has already been pointed out, early printed works used typefaces that scribes commonly used and early printers saw value in designing works that looked like handwritten works and, therefore, looked familiar to readers. It is still not easy for many to separate writing from print and, particularly for hypertextual works that are image free, one can expect the aura of print to be influential for some time.

Hypertext, as its design is refined, will bring about a changed understanding of text, a recognition that words can be used in multiple ways, of which the linear is only one. This displacement, dislocation, or deconstruction of the print paradigm is one way of viewing hypertext and its significance. It has been argued that lawyers "ought to be able to read between the lines and to link texts to larger contexts"[10] and this can now be done in novel ways. In addition, however, hypertext will be one of the core tools for new construction in cyberspace. In cyberspace, as users direct the search for information to satisfy their own informational needs, there will no longer be any sense to the idea that information is being "skipped." There may be detours, diversions, and digressions as one seeks needed information, but what is achieved, in the end, is the construction of an information place that meets the needs of information users because everything is close to everything else in a way that is not possible with physical objects, and thus is a place where information can be employed more efficiently than is possible with print materials.

Hypermedia, alien as the genre may seem to many today, will eventually be recognized as the most common, familiar, and typical model of accessing electronic information in the future. Although many may find hypertextual materials today to be less information rich than a printed work, it is not hard to envision a future in which screen clarity, screen design, and network capabilities have advanced and users will desire and prefer information in hypertextual form. Whatever overlapping qualities exist today between hypermedia and print will inevitably become fewer and fewer and, as a consequence, each genre will identify less and less with the other. There may, in cyberspace, be room for something called an electronic book just as there are today "books on tape," but such works will be seen to be distinguishable from hypertext and will be understood to be a form of electronic information that does not exploit the medium's main capabilities and that is not a mainstream use of the medium. We recognize a television program or film as being something that is distinct from transcripts or scripts and, when hypermedia becomes more commonplace and familiar, we will recognize that it, too, is not print in another guise but something quite independent of print even though words may appear on screen.

The inevitable growing appeal of hypermedia and its escape from the gravitational pull of print will, particularly for the law, have less to

do with having whole books in electronic form or with glitzy animations and MTV-like visual techniques than with its ability to satisfy a
more basic need, that of obtaining appropriate and relevant information quickly and efficiently. Hypermedia, with colorful images and
accompanying sound, is being marketed today mainly as an engaging
new technique for education. It may indeed be a viable and desirable
new educational tool. For the law, however, the need it will satisfy has
less to do with education than with the pressing need to move around
cyberspace to access information more quickly and efficiently than in
the past. All of this is necessary to cope with the rather novel and significant difficulties that have coalesced in the expression "information
overload."

What this expression means is not simply that much more information is reaching us than previously but that traditional techniques
for reviewing and using this information are inadequate. We all have
informational habits and expectations that structure our information-
seeking efforts. Much of this relationship with information is based
on assumptions that have largely been structured by the nature of
print technology and our experiences with information in print form.
We understand implicitly how different kinds of information are organized, how they are accessed, how long it takes to access them, and
what economic costs and time demands are involved. Rather suddenly, however, these assumptions are being challenged. More information reaches us from many more sources than ever before and
more quickly than ever before. It has been asserted, for example, that
"the average person in seventeenth-century England covered less
'data' in a lifetime than is typically found in a single issue of *The New
York Times*."[11] The validity of this comment depends upon what "data"
means but it is true that more information is directed to us since others know more about us and our interests, and we also have more
access to novel kinds of information sources. And, since increasing
amounts of this information are in electronic form, more and more of
it can, if one wishes, be stored on one's own computer.

Those who use the Internet, for example, are provided access to
thousands of newsgroups on virtually any topic one can imagine. Virtually anyone who uses e-mail can have every Supreme Court decision delivered to his or her computer automatically a short time after
the case is decided.[12] In the pre-electronic era, the quickest public
access to Supreme Court decisions was provided by the *U.S. Law
Week*, a publication that required about a week to be printed and distributed. Free and quick access to information that was difficult to
obtain in the past makes it tempting to acquire and possess greater
amounts of information, particularly when the information is available at a nominal cost and computers have larger and larger storage
capabilities. Yet, no individual has the time to read all of the information that has, in effect, moved closer to us, just as no individual has

the ability to read all of the newsletters that are offered for subscription through traditional channels or all of the books and journals that are accessible in the library. Cyberspace challenges us to confront new opportunities for using larger and larger amounts of information, and hypertext is one method that will allow larger information resources to be used efficiently. This need for new means of access and use accounted for the earliest description of a hypertext process by Vannevar Bush in 1945. The need for what Bush called Memex was "not so much that we publish unduly in view of the extent and variety of present-day interests, but rather that publication has been extended far beyond our present ability to make real use of the record. The summation of human experience is being expanded at a prodigious rate, and the means we use for threading through the consequent maze to the momentarily important item is the same as was used in the days of square-rigged ships."[13]

In the print era, access to information meant something very different from acquisition of information. Access, typically through libraries, provided the possibility of temporary possession without acquisition or ownership. One who acquired information, however, usually had something more valuable—something that allowed permanent possession, use, and access. Ownership not only provided the owner with access but enabled the owner to exclude others from having access or allowed the owner to impose costs on those wishing to obtain access. For a lawyer, the size of one's library and the nature of one's library space suggested something about one's resources, successes, and capabilities. The library was not only a functional area where information was located but a space that symbolized something about a firm's assets, resources, areas of specialization, and even skills.

It is not surprising that in this transition period acquiring, collecting, and possessing information is still being valued over access, and that ownership of information is still desired above other possibilities. There are many new opportunities to acquire information, and long-standing assumptions about information still shape our responses even though such responses may be more suited to an environment in which information exists in print form. It still, for example, seems generally preferable to possess information than to have access to it. It is also still commonly taken for granted that information that is acquired has the same value as it previously did even though the information may become out of date more quickly and it may no longer fulfill any symbolic function.

When information is in electronic form, acquisition, ownership, and access all are easier than they were in the print era. What is changing, however, when information is in electronic form, and what is much less obvious than the new opportunities for securing information, is the relative value of ownership and access. Unlike in the past, access to some kinds of electronic information may provide more value than ownership and, therefore, may be more desired in the future than ownership or possession. For other kinds of information, access may be indistinguishable from ownership. With physical objects, there may be disputes over ownership but the object has a clear identity and form. With electronic information, however, where one can appear to possess something that exists somewhere else, where one can use something that exists somewhere else, where copying inevitably occurs as information is used, where the user may be unaware of where the original is or even what the original is, and where the original may be changing over time, any assumption that possession is more valuable than access is increasingly open to question.

It is tempting, when information is in electronic form, to make information acquisition a major goal—to acquire, in effect, a "library on one's desk" or a "library on one's disk." The library was the solution to the costs and constraints of acquiring and accessing information one needed in the past, and electronic tools would seem to make it possible for the shared library of the past to be replaced by a larger and privately held library. The ideal "library" of the future, however, will not be a mammoth personal "collection" of information in electronic form, something that shrinks the contents of print space onto a disk, but a set of links or connections to hypertextually connected sources of information. The direction we are moving in is not to re-create the shared public space in a private space but actually to create a much larger shared space with vastly larger resources. As attitudes change, the allure of owning and capturing information will give way to the reality that it is one's skills at using information that will be rewarded and that one needs to participate in the collective international information effort to do this. One may still need a mammoth disk drive to use or work with information but, when the time comes that information across the globe is perceived to be close by, we will gradually lose our fascination with owning the Library of Congress and will be more concerned with how to use it, something that hypertext will assist us in doing.

The hypertext model focuses on links to information located elsewhere as much as on possession of the information itself and brings about a reconsideration of what is valuable about information. In the future, for example, one may gain much more through access than through acquisition and, in such cases, access will be valued more than acquisition. As Bruce Sterling has observed:

> What's information really about? It seems to me there's something direly wrong with the "Information Economy." It's not about data, it's about attention. In a few years you may be able to carry the Library of Congress around in your hip pocket. So? You're never gonna read the Library of Congress. You'll die long before you access one tenth of one percent of it. What's important—increasingly important—is the process by which you figure out what to look at. This is the

beginning of the real and true economics of information. Not who owns the books, who prints the books, who has the holdings. The crux here is access, not holdings. And not even access itself, but the signposts that tell you what to access—what to pay attention to. In the Information Economy everything is plentiful—except attention.[14]

Links become valuable because they provide up-to-date information—and information from people as well as from documents. Electronic information is not revised in stages or in editions, as occurs with printed works, but continuously changes. Hypertext provides the links to such information, and in an electronic environment, the links may be worth more than the information itself. The links provide access to the latest information; when one merely possesses information acquired in the past, however, he or she cannot easily be certain whether or not it has been revised. As one librarian has observed, "there is a growing trend in having *access* to materials rather than *owning* those materials."[15]

Information overload has become a problem because large amounts of information are being brought closer to us, but tools for using and navigating through information have not yet evolved very quickly. Most tools for working with information still have as an ultimate goal to "print" something on paper. Many still assume that one can work efficiently with electronic information even if one approaches the information as one would approach information in print and have the same tools available as one has with printed works. Yet, given the need to highlight information and avoid dwelling on irrelevant information, it may be true, as David Johnson pointed out, that "perhaps the most valuable attribute of any hypertext system is its ability to suppress information."[16]

It is not as easy to use information as it is to store it, which is why our electronic storage media, even more than print spaces, fill up with information that is rarely used. Our focus is still on many of the concerns that made sense in an era when information was tangibly fixed on paper rather than on the kind of processing techniques and access that will be valuable in the future. Possession and ownership are still assumed to be synonymous with value, and the fact that information is in a more dynamic form on an internationally linked network seems of little relevance or significance.

There may still be validity to the belief that one who owns information is richer than one who merely has access to it. Yet, this will change, as will many other assumptions about the value and use of information. Possessing information and acquiring information are no longer as distinguishable as they once were. Access is generally easier than it was in the past since distance is no longer as great a barrier as it once was. We are closer to information than when it was in a physically separate place and in a more unchanging form. Access will now often be preferred because much information is now in a more dynamic form and value may be connected to having the latest and most up-to-date information. The long-term solution to information overload, therefore, is not increased information possession or storing greater and greater quantities of information on one's computer but increased and more efficient information accessibility and management, something that hypertext facilitates and encourages.

In print culture, every book had its own space and identity. Access required that each work be in a discrete location. The use of hypertext in cyberspace requires a new image or conception of information—not of discrete volumes existing on shelves, or of discrete and numbered issues and editions, but of something more organic and dynamic, of bodies of information in which the links contribute to a work in which the whole is much more than the sum of its parts. Such an entity has no fixed form but acquires a form that meets the needs of the user. If there is competition to supply something of value to a user, it is competition that focuses less on delivering the information and more on assisting in the use of the information, on taking the needs of the user into account, on providing multiple views of the information, multiple entry points to the information, and multiple exit points from the information. To think simply of "electronic books" in such an environment is to be very far from the kind of relationship with information that users will come to demand.

The changes in what it means to own information, in what it means to have access to information, and in what it means to organize information are part of a larger set of deep-rooted changes in how we search for, use, and relate to information. Hypertext may look like print, but it requires different skills, offers new opportunities, and poses challenges to the user that are not present with print. The reason for this is that hypertext exerts pressure for change on two of the most significant legacies of Gutenberg's invention—a mass media model of information distribution and a linear route through information directed by the author. More generally, it exerts pressure on how we categorize knowledge, since hypertext is a model in which categories and their boundaries are more fluid than before.

9

Lighting and Enlightening Cyberspace: Copyright and Privacy

Cyberspace. A consensual hallucination experienced daily by billions of legitimate operators, in every nation . . . A graphic representation of data abstracted from the banks of every computer in the human system. Unthinkable complexity. Lines of light ranged in the onspace of the mind, clusters and constellations of data . . .

—William Gibson

And God said: "Let there be there light." And there was light. And God saw the light, that it was good; and God divided the light from the darkness. And God called the light Day, and the darkness he called Night.

—Genesis, I:3

Light. An elemental force. A metaphor for purity and truth, wisdom and vision. A symbol of power. A key to mysteries. A power to heal, warm, reveal, provoke. A link to the earliest moments of time and to the most distant future. At one time, only a force of nature and the divine. And, for our generation, the heart of cyberspace.

Light and its manipulation are cyberspace. Messages moving at the speed of light.[1] Relationships established by beams of light. Hundreds of thousands of lights flashing at us on computer screens. Hundreds of thousands of suns, competing suns, captivating suns, colorful suns, confounding suns, creating suns, cleansing suns, colliding suns, communal suns. Suns with little respect for the past and even less for the present. Suns that bring us to the future and the future to us.

What kind of light is this? flickering? direct? permanent? fleeting? focused? reflective? broad? inviting? inclusive? exclusive? revealing? deceiving? This is a light, we have seen, that can foster illusions. Seeing is believing?[2] Perhaps in natural light. Perhaps on the printed page. In digital light, seeing can be persuasive but we wonder more about what we are seeing. What is illuminated, we hope, is also illuminating. Often, however, it is illusory. We have, as the light spreads, certainly more to see in the light than in the dark. There is no "face in the water"[3] at night and there are no rainbows in the dark.

Streams of light versus ink on paper. This is the main change I have been concerned with and with which the law is being challenged. Our books are both a tool and a symbol—something to read and use, something to hold up and display, something to represent our goals and ideals. Paper? Discrete, boundaried, fixed, authoritative, trustworthy. And light? Powerful, stimulating, shifting, spreading, exposing, expanding, animating, unifying. It raises questions—some new, some old. Who is holding the light? Who is hiding behind it? Does it shine on us all? How can we use it? How long will it last? Is this, indeed, a light without shadows, without boundaries, without a surrounding field of darkness?

This digital light is built on zeroes and ones, on data in binary form. The binary looks familiar. Ones and zeroes, on and off, black and white, guilty and innocent, right and wrong, plaintiff and defendant, winner and loser. The light itself, however, makes us see things differently. The illusions multiply. As the electronic sun shines, it appears to transform. Nothing seems binary. There is no edge. White is joined to black by shades of gray. Precision is aided by "fuzziness."[4] Color is everywhere. There are new perspectives. Backgrounds become clearer. New parties appear. We look at things differently. The electronic light includes colors that even the eye cannot distinguish. Everything is duplicable. Yet one cannot be certain that anything is real. The strength of this world is magic, the apparent escape from the laws of physics. Yet, there is nothing to this world but the laws of physics. Can we ever be more aware of what it will mean if the light goes out?

Thus, challenges and concerns, paradoxes and contradictions. We may not all be happy with this new light. What was secure and safely hidden in the dark may be fragile and vulnerable when exposed to the light. Even the dark can be profitable to those who are familiar with it. What we have, quite clearly, is a new environment, a brighter and more intense environment, one in which new interactions will develop, in which a range of activities become possible, and in which very little is the same as it was before. It will, one might say, be as different as night is from day.

When we hear of the superhighway, of on ramps and off, let us remember the light, and the face of the river, and the web, and the other visions that inform us about this new place. Light may, after all, be the ultimate hypertext and, perhaps, the only seamless web. We can see and touch and also be seen and be touched. A guiding light but not a hiding light. And, of course, the light might go out. "Eternal vigilance," it is said, "is the price of liberty."[5] Do we not quest for an eternal light?

One last observation. Light, at first, can be blinding rather than illuminating. The light shines on us and around us but we are, for a time, still "in the dark" and can see no better than when all was dark. The process of transition is a time of adjustment and activity but not necessarily of seeing clearly. Until we have adjusted, we rely on old and secure habits, on familiar ways of seeing, and move very cautiously. Clearly, this is where we are. But it is not where we will be.

In a New Light

William Gibson, coiner of the term *cyberspace*, titled his most recent novel *Virtual Light*.[6] This suggests the appropriateness of light as a metaphor for the new media and a need for any discussion of the new technologies to be sensitive to light, since it is light that transforms spaces, negates boundaries and borders, and provides the architecture and environment of cyberspace. As the light's rays reach us and touch us, they also link us to many other people and machines that are exposed to the light. It is for this reason that the light can be disorienting and misunderstood, not simply by its brightness but because what was previously absent is now present, what was hidden is now visible, what was distant is now close, and what was separate is now joined.

The image of the light and the power of the light to create new links and relationships should be the frame around any consideration of legal doctrines directly touched by the new technologies. Yet, light does not have the same metaphorical power as, perhaps, an "information superhighway," and the new media's ability to deliver films and entertainment on demand is certainly easier to envision than its ability to inspire and encourage new interactions and relationships. Yet, the focus needs to be on who is newly connected by the highway as much as it is on what is transported on it. The highway is not linear but hypertext, not a route or a road but a web, joining people and groups rather than merely delivering something to them. Light is something that not only permits the individual to see but allows the individual to be seen, and the ramifications of this for any area of law that relies on keeping information separate and at a distance will be profound.

The following discussion focuses on copyright and privacy, but these are merely the legal doctrines that have risen most quickly to the surface of public concern during this transition. These seedlings have sprouted first because their link to information and communication is most intimate, but we should be prepared for the effects of the new technology to spread much more widely. The light of change is shining on corporate law and where corporations are located, on tax law and on who has the power to tax, and on legal ethics, and on what it means to be "admitted" to the bar. It is reflected in areas that appear closer to the natural world than the virtual world, such as environmental law, where "citizens, commissions, agencies, courts, and legislatures are using complex and arcane models and assessments to estimate and evaluate the consequences of a proposed development. The use of these intellectual tools is often hidden from sight, buried within the bowels of the discretionary planning activities of an administrative agency. But the use of cost-benefit analyses, risk assessments, ecosystem and economic models often see the light of day in public administrative hearings, court trials, and legislative inquiries."[7]

The following, therefore, is really about perspective more than it is about policy, and about illustrating how the shape of the new environment and the use of the new environment need to be at the heart of any discussions of new regulatory models.

Copyright

Copyright is probably the focus of more attention and concern than any other area of law touched by the new technologies. Over 1,200 people on the Internet belong to a group called CNI-COPYRIGHT, asking questions and exchanging information on a daily basis about whether particular uses of the new media violate current copyright doctrine or not. It is likely that never before in the almost 300-year history of copyright law have so many people in one "place" had such an extended discussion of how copyright law should be applied. This conference or discussion group is composed of librarians, professors, publishers, lawyers, programmers, and members of many other groups with a concern about copyright. A decade or two ago, copyright would have been a subject that few of these persons would have had any interest in. In an information-oriented economy, however, virtually all professions and occupations are information producers since almost anyone who works with information is increasingly doing so in electronic form and is encouraged to engage in value-adding activities. The existence and size of this particular group is itself evidence of how it is possible to share and distribute information in new ways, and of how concern is raised by new processes for making copies and redistributing information. It is difficult to imagine the circumstances under which, in physical space, such a heterogeneous group might ever have come together. In the manner in which it crosses boundaries, at least, this group may be considered to be a microcosm of law in the new environment.

To this group, and to most others concerned with copyright law, it appears self-evident that the law is being challenged because of the new technologies' ability to make copies more easily and more rapidly than was possible with paper. Several times a day members of the group ask whether copying in a particular context or for some particular purpose constitutes copyright infringement. This is not surprising since more and more of the information we use is in electronic form and we have the option, often at nominal cost, of making and keeping a copy of any information that comes into our possession.

Although deliberate copying of copyrighted products can now occur in questionable and often undetectable ways, it is copying occurring on a different level that may exert pressure not on the details of the statute but on the assumptions we make about intellectual property. These assumptions are eroding not because of piracy or intentional unlawful copying but because our interaction with electronic information routinely involves us in a process of copying and working with copies. As we interact with the new media, our work experience inevitably changes since copying is an act that inevitably takes place on a new scale as one works with information in electronic form.

Copying is an ongoing, necessary, and inevitable component of using electronic information. Saving a file, for example, involves making a copy of what is in memory. Using a file or loading it into memory involves making a copy of what has been stored on disk. Communicating electronically involves sending a copy and not the original. Compared to reading a case in a library, where a copy the publisher has made is read, a case in LEXIS or WESTLAW on the screen is a copy one makes oneself. Indeed, one cannot read anything on screen without first copying something. As Ithiel de Sola Pool recognized, "[t]o read a copyright text is no violation, only to copy it in writing. The technological basis for this distinction is reversed with a computer text. To read a text stored in electronic memory, one displays it on the screen: one writes it to read it. To transmit it to others, however, one does not write it; one only gives the password to one's computer memory. One must write to read, but not to write."[8]

Pamela Samuelson, perhaps the most insightful analyst of copyright issues in the electronic environment, has recognized that it is not simply the degree and frequency of copying that occurs that pressures copyright law to change. There are, in her view, a series of six tools that operate on digital information that "seem likely to change significantly the contours of intellectual property law, especially copyright."[9] These are:

1. Copying
2. Transmission
3. Processing and manipulation
4. Obsolete media categories
5. Reliance on technology to see and use digital works
6. Searching and linking capabilities.[10]

Alvin Kernan has argued that the effects of printing included not simply increases in the number of books produced and the number of uniform and authoritative copies available, but a "print logic" that permeated the culture. This had been a major theme of Marshall McLuhan, who claimed that the world, as seen through the eyes of a literate person, was "connected (abstract figures with fixed boundaries, linked logically and sequentially but having no visible grounds), homogeneous (uniform everywhere), and static (qualitatively unchangeable)."[11] The process of reading silently, for example, which replaced reading aloud, "began to shape mental structures, imparting a sense of the world as a set of abstract ideas rather than immediate facts, a fixed point of view organizing all subject matter into an equivalent of perspective in painting, and the visual homogenization of experience."[12] More generally, sociologist Peter Berger has argued that,

> [o]nce produced, the tool has a being of its own that cannot be readily changed by those who employ it. Indeed, the tool (say, an agricultural implement) may even force the logic of its being upon its users, sometimes in a way that may not be particularly agreeable to them. For instance, a plow, though obviously a human product, is an external object, not only in the sense that its users may fall over it and hurt themselves as a result, just as they may by falling over a rock or a stump or any other natural object. More interestingly, the plow may compel its users to arrange their agricultural activity, and perhaps also other parts of their lives, in a way that conforms to *its* own logic, and they may have been neither intended nor foreseen by those who originally devised it. The same objectivity, however, characterizes the non-material elements of culture as well. Man invents a language and then finds that both his speaking and his thinking are dominated by its grammar.[13]

A new information environment infiltrates our minds as well as our activities, although changes in thought and orientation occur more slowly and less noticeably than changes in behavior. At some point, we not only are presented with information in a new form but begin thinking about information differently because we acclimate ourselves to the new form. Thus, as electronic modes of information acquisition become commonplace, not only do we become able to obtain information from distant places but we stop thinking about distance and begin not to think of information as being in distant places. The concept and relevancy of distance change, and expectations and perspectives change.

We are closer in time as information moves faster, and we are closer in space as information travels significant distances. We are, so to speak, "in the same light" with other elements in the creative process that were previously separated by distance. As this occurs, roles, statuses, and functions that previously had been discrete and separate also move closer and, in some cases, acquire new identities. New relationships are fostered in which entities are dynamic and shifting, are less independent of each other, and interact more frequently.

If the electronic environment is considered in cultural or spatial terms, one finds that the creative process in general changes because many elements in the environment become closer to each other than they were previously. Those working alone can now see others, feel closer to others, and work with others who in the print era were separated in a variety of ways. We cannot assume that we are working as independently as we were before. Indeed, as we become acclimated to the new light, many assumptions that governed what is or would be done or attempted will be seen to be invalid and will change our outlook as well as our behavior. The net effect of a set of impressive new capabilities, therefore, is not simply a set of new rules or a readjustment of old rules but a set of new attitudes and expectations that will provide the frame around a new model of working with information.

As has been described in other chapters, the power of cyberspace is that it can overcome, or can appear to overcome, the limits of the physical environment. We can process information in novel ways because nothing is fixed to anything else. Words and images can be moved and edited, lifted off the screen, and put back down. Humpty Dumpty, as a physical entity, falls and permanently shatters, but an electronic Humpty Dumpty can be put back together again by clicking on some magical "undo" button. Yet, even though much information in electronic form contradicts one of print's most influential features, typographical fixity,[14] electronic words and works at this time are still perceived within the frame of print, the original and most dominant media influence on copyright. Electronic logic clearly is not replacing print logic as quickly as electronic tools are replacing print tools. Our language and our habits of thought color what we see so that although we recognize that there are new means of producing and creating, we also assume that there is an underlying and fundamental connection and similarity between the old and the new, that we have new tools but not necessarily a new environment.

Current copyright law reinforces such thinking by applying the same model to electronic works as it does to the traditionally protected media. The requirement for a copyright is quite simple. Copyright protection is provided for "original works of authorship fixed in any tangible medium of expression, now known or later developed, from which they can be perceived, reproduced, or otherwise communicated either directly or with the aid of a machine or device."[15] Spoken words cannot be copyrighted but words on paper can be, and so can words, sounds, or images encoded on some other medium. Ideas are not copyrightable but the expression of the idea, the representation of the idea in some physical form, is copyrightable. The law has had little difficulty treating the electronic format as a "tangible" medium and the placement of information in electronic form as fulfilling the "fixed" requirement.

But what if information in electronic form—or at least some electronic information—is, indeed, not fixed? What if the very nature of electronic information is to be dynamic and changing? What if the true nature of electronic information is not to be equated with the tangible medium upon which it is stored but is to be evaluated in terms of how it is used? What if our eyes are deceiving us and the words on the screen are not "text" any more than the words coming out of our mouths are text? What if the image one draws on screen is no more permanent than the picture one draws on the sand as a wave rapidly approaches the shore? What if, "unlike the stable and autonomous 'work,' which the law treats as akin to an object, the text is a process?"[16] What if, although it may be difficult to imagine, there are no longer works with fixed boundaries? What if the letters on screen are a fundamental illusion and we should be thinking about such words and letters not in terms of text but in terms of some other genre, such as music or art, or as something totally new? Since digitized information is fungible and a press of a key can turn text into sound or sound into image, can any traditional frame of reference be valid? Copyright is in a difficult and highly challenging period not simply because copying is rampant and enforcement is difficult but because, even though it has not yet been widely recognized, the nature of our relationship with electronic information is vastly different from our relationship with print.

The role of the new media, as I have argued earlier, is not to replace print but to displace it. We undoubtedly will continue to have printed books, but the manner in which they dominate our thinking about information will change. David Bolter has insightfully written that,

> [t]he printed book . . . seems destined to move to the margin of our literate culture. The issue is not whether print technology will completely disappear; books may long continue to be printed for certain kinds of texts and for luxury consumption. But the idea and the ideal of the book will change; print will no longer define the organization

and presentation of knowledge, as it has for the past five centuries. This shift from print to the computer does not mean the end of literacy. What will be lost is not literacy itself, but the literacy of print, for electronic technology offers us a new kind of book and new ways to write and read.[17]

Information has existed in tangible form, in a "fixed" form, for thousands of years, since pictures were drawn on the walls of caves and, more commonly, since writing began. Copyright law, however, has its origins in the much more recent period after printing, a period when the value of words on paper had increased and a time when, for the first time, information was truly "fixed" on paper.[18] In the scribal period, words on paper lacked the authority that was later attained by print because every copy that was made imported errors into the text. There were no final copies or final versions. Indeed, the valuing of and approach to what kind of information was trustworthy and authentic relied on assumptions that were just the opposite of assumptions made today. What tended to be prized as being most authentic was not a recent version but an old version. The reason for this was the recognition that the oldest version would necessarily have the fewest errors in it. In this way, an ancient text would be preferred over a contemporary author since the ancient text was assumed to be more authentic.[19] There was no assumption that anything but the earliest version contained the words that the author had "fixed" on paper.

It was print's ability to provide uniform and standardized copies that created a body of knowledge that could be assumed to be "fixed." Such information was fixed, therefore, not simply in the sense that it existed as ink that adhered to some tangible surface but also in the sense that it was in a form that would remain stable over time. Print "fixed the literary text, by giving it an objective and unchanging reality in its own right. In earlier oral cultures there could be no such thing as an exact text, since the particular form something took at any moment always depended . . . on performance. Even in a manuscript culture a work was seldom or never reproduced *exactly* the same way twice running and so remained always a process, never becoming a completed, static object."[20]

Print, as a form of communication that was secure and had an independent and trustworthy existence in time and space, not only spurred the emergence of copyright law but has served as the paradigm for thinking about copyrighted information. Copyright law applies to nontextual forms of communication, such as music, even though, as will be explained, that form of communication may not be as "fixed" over time. Print logic, in such cases, is applied to and prevails over the experience of musicians who work with information differently from those who work with words.

It has been pointed out by Aaron Keyt, among others, that there is a difference between music logic and print logic—that, for example, "borrowing" has been commonplace among composers and has been viewed "in a different light" from print borrowing or plagiarism. He wrote:

> While copying words from another author's book without some form of acknowledgement is generally considered plagiarism, the music world functions according to different social expectations and has done so for centuries. Composers historically have drawn heavily from folk music and current popular music. In addition, composers often borrow directly from their colleagues. It is this borrowing from colleagues which is most likely to subject a composer to criticism of his ethics (folk music, in contrast, is generally accepted as legitimate source material). . . .
>
> Nonmusicians often ascribe an almost magical quality to the invention of musical material. In reality, generating musical material is much less difficult than structuring it. The creation of musical material can be compared to the collection of scientific data, which may be time-consuming and require great care, but which is still usually within the capabilities of any trained technician. The real genius lies in the organization and interpretation of the data. Judge Learned Hand recognized this when he wrote, "True, it is the themes which catch the popular fancy, but their invention is not where musical genius lies."
>
> The artistic world has developed its own informal rules for borrowing. For example, the musical practice in Handel's time, emphasizing productivity and professional skill over originality of material, permitted borrowing so long as the composer used the material to good effect; the focus was not on the source of the components, but on the quality of the whole. This attitude dates back to antiquity. Classical writers saw the work of their predecessors as a common fund; originality was not seen as creation on a blank slate, but rather as a process of selection, reinterpretation, and improvement. It was only when a writer's use of the fund was uninventive or superficial that he would be taken to task.[21]

Music, when it is not being played but is in the form of notes affixed to paper, presents a tangible and discrete object that appears quite similar to text that is affixed to paper. Copyright law treats such musical notes similarly to text. Indeed, a brief quotation of music may even trigger a violation of copyright's "fair use" provisions more quickly than a brief quotation taken from a novel.[22] Yet, although notes on a piece of music may be printed and look like other forms of print and although copyright law may treat copying from such music similarly to copying from printed text, there are differences. The notes may be fixed to the paper in the same manner that all ink is affixed to paper, yet the paper version of music does not exist by itself as discretely as does a work of literature. Novels, essays, and other textual forms exist only as text. Music on paper, however, coexists with music as sound, and what is most likely to be copied in the case of music is the sound—the melody—rather than the source of the sound—the words on paper. Music, therefore, has a significant existence apart from the printed page and, as a result, is less fixed to the paper version of the composition.

The relationship between musical notes on paper and the melody the notes represent is reminiscent of the relationship between written and spoken speech in the pre-printing era. At that time, documents were more commonly considered something to be listened to than read. To make sense of a document, it would be read aloud rather than inspected. Clanchy notes that medieval authors "questioned the value of writing and that neither they nor their readers took its significance for granted. Did writing exist independently of speech? Was it heard or seen? Was it a record or a picture? . . . Latin letters were a cue for speech, not a substitute for it."[23] The primacy and emphasis on the spoken word derived partly from the lack of trust in handwritten documents and partly in the added value that came from speech. The speaker's intonation and tone of voice added meaning to the text, something that might be considered unnecessary, indeed inappropriate, today, when one assumes that words can *speak* for themselves. Clanchy recognizes that this frame of mind suggests a possible analogy "with musical literacy. Only a minority of the modern population reads music, and those who do so go to concerts, listen to records, or play instruments as well. The paper text of the music is not felt to be a substitute for its performance, even though an expert may hear the music in his mind. Like musical notation, medieval letter script was understood to represent sounds needing hearing."[24]

Authors of text can escape the grasp of the copyright laws by paraphrasing, something that takes the idea but leaves the expression of the idea alone. How does one paraphrase music? How does one separate the idea of a melody from the expression of the melody? How does one create a variation on a theme without running afoul of the copyright laws? Applying the print logic of the copyright law to music has, in the words of one author, been an activity that is similar to placing square pegs into round holes.[25] Charges of copying result in comparisons between notes as they exist on paper as well as listening to how the music sounds. Little attention is paid in such cases to the process of composition or to the music environment.

Just as music has survived this imperfect fit, it might be argued that the electronic media could also live under a regime where many underlying assumptions are not valid. There is, however, a significant difference between music and electronic information in that in recent centuries, music never served as the cultural paradigm for thinking about information and was unlikely to become the dominant societal medium. In copyright law, music logic has always been subject to print logic. The question one must consider with the electronic media is not how such new media can be subjected to print logic but what changes will come about as print logic is displaced and as, inevitably, electronic logic becomes the dominant paradigm. What happens, for example, when it is generally acknowledged that the screen is not paper and that,

> [e]ven as pixeling a written text onto an electronic screen radically destabilizes and volatizes it, so painting on an electronic screen launches the image into existence forever *inpotentia*. Electronic painting exists to be transformed by the viewer. The image you see is but one readout of a digital code that can produce hundreds more. Apply a contrast-enhancement program and you have a different picture; a Fourier transform and you get yet another. The Arnoldian ideal of fixed perfection simply dissolves.[26]

Is it possible to suggest how the balance between copying and access might exist in a legal world governed by "electronic logic"? To do this requires not merely addressing what aspects of current copyright law can operate effectively or be preserved in the new environment but looking at what kinds of constraints and practices would be consistent with the perspective that will dominate in an electronic environment. It requires us to consider what facets of copyright law are tied not merely to print but to "print logic," to see not only what new tools we have but to revisit our expectations and to revise our assumptions about information. Indeed, I use the words *revise* and *revisit* intentionally since the idea of vision is embedded in the etymology of these terms and what is most needed is a new way of seeing.

John Perry Barlow, in a provocative analysis of cyberspace and copyright, writes that

> throughout the time I've been groping around cyberspace, an immense, unsolved conundrum has remained at the root of nearly every legal, ethical, governmental, and social vexation to be found in the Virtual World. I refer to the problem of digitized property. The enigma is this: If our property can be infinitely reproduced and instantaneously distributed all over the planet without cost, without our knowledge, without its even leaving our possession, how can we protect it? How are we going to get paid for the work we do with our minds? And if we can't get paid, what will assure the continued creation and distribution of such work?[27]

A partial answer to this question, at least, is provided by looking at how our relationship with information is shifting. We increasingly confront information whose attraction is that it is dynamic and changing rather than fixed. In a sense, everyone working with a hypertextual document is working with a changed document, one that the reader changes to match his or her interests. If the electronic information is on a network, it is increasingly shared information. It can be possessed for a time and, through copying, acquired in new ways. Yet, unlike information that is static and fixed, the value of any single piece of electronic information often shrinks over time rather than increases over time. Barlow draws an analogy with sharks, who "are said to die of suffocation if they stop swimming, and the same is nearly true of information. Information that isn't moving ceases to exist as anything but potential . . . at least until it is allowed to move again. For this reason, the practice of information hoarding, common in bureaucracies, is an especially wrong-headed artifact of physically based value systems."[28]

It is, therefore, not owning or possessing the information that is valuable but opportunities presented to use and exploit the information that electronic logic encourages. Under this perspective, an electronic product is less a mine that contains a finite amount of value than a resource that can be inexhaustible. It is less a thing, a fixed entity, than the equivalent of an idea, something that over time will be turned into something of even greater value. It is not something that the creator completes and holds onto as much as it is something evolutionary in character that is continually being improved and that the creator continually adds value to. In this shifting view of information, the boundaries of ownership are fraying, but the opportunities for exploiting and adding value are being enlarged. In the words of Peter F. Drucker, "knowledge is power, which is why people who had it in the past often tried to make a secret of it. In post-capitalism, power comes from transmitting information to make it productive, not from hiding it."[29]

Virtually all of current copyright law denies this view of information, and those who today own copyrighted information in electronic form understandably are fighting to protect the value of that information in the same way they would protect information in printed books. The legal definition of fixed is that "a work is 'fixed' in a tangible medium of expression when its embodiment in a copy or phonorecord, by or under the authority of the author, is sufficiently permanent or stable to permit it to be perceived, reproduced, or otherwise communicated for a period of more than transitory duration. A work consisting of sounds, images, or both, that are being transmitted, is 'fixed' for purposes of this title [17 USCS Sects. 101 et seq.] if a fixation of the work is being made simultaneously with its transmission."[30]

What I am suggesting is not a proposal for specific statutory changes but a description of a set of forces that many who are immersed in copyright law will have difficulty seeing, largely because the events are taking place outside of their field of vision. It is not difficult to adjust to changes in a statute or to court decisions that reinterpret a prior holding. It is difficult and disorienting to enter a new place or environment, in this case a place where what one needs to do to protect and add value to information is different from what it was in the place one is accustomed to. Yet, as our economy becomes one in which electronic information is the principal resource to be worked on, this will be the challenge to those who add value to information and wish to market that value.

The origin of copyright law lies more in the experiences with information and with print that occurred in the sixteenth and seventeenth centuries than in an agreed-upon set of ideas about copying.[31] Given this experience, it is not surprising that "copyright law is more geared toward dealing with works that are permanently fixed."[32] In a similar way, the future of copyright and of the value of information may be less tied to current copyright law provisions than to the business practices of entrepreneurs who understand how to manage and exploit information, to develop new products more quickly than others, and to establish relationships with those most likely to use their products.

One of the lessons of hypertext is that the creator/author is in a new relationship with the user/reader. The key lesson of the information economy is that the seller of an electronic product is also in a new kind of information relationship with the purchaser and that the relationship or link with the purchaser is more important than any other part of the transaction. As noted earlier, all sales in which the new technology is employed are designed to capture information about the purchaser. Merchants are no longer interested in anonymous transactions, but it is also no longer necessary to ask the purchaser his or her name to obtain it. One goal of any vendor is to acquire information that has value in itself and might be sold along with other data collected about other purchasers. Equally important, however, is that sellers of information products cannot thrive in the marketplace simply by selling the product once. What is most to be prized is a future sale and a future relationship.

Software transactions are often criticized because of a phenomenon known as "shrinkwrap licenses." Unlike a book, where the exchange of money triggers a sale and the transfer of ownership, software is not really sold.[33] Software is leased to the user rather than sold. It is leased under the conditions of the license, and the license is considered to be automatically agreed to by the act of opening the package. Software is, of course, copyrighted, but the user of software is bound by both copyright law and the terms of the license. It is because of the lease conditions, for example, that manufacturers can insist that software be used on only one machine.

This is a problematic arrangement, particularly since most consumers are unaware of the lease arrangement and generally are not intending to consent to anything when they open a package. There is, however, something instructive in using a lease arrangement rather than a sale in an informational context. This is that a lease suggests a different kind of relationship between lessee and lessor than between seller and buyer. Such an arrangement, at least ideally, suggests a relationship that will continue into the future, a closer and more communicative relationship, and a less discrete relationship.

Licenses, if they actually establish an ongoing relationship, are appropriate to a hypertext world, where links and relationships are among the principal elements of value. The value of information can change as easily through new links being developed as through new information being added to the core document. As space becomes less of a constraint, works in different places can be linked so that they appear to be not two connected works but a single new work. Hypertext erases spatial boundaries and, in the process, challenges ideas, concepts, forms, and practices that have been "in place" for some time.

The sale of a book, a discrete object that exists in space, makes perfect sense. The author of a book is and will remain distant from the reader. The development of alternative arrangements for using electronic material also makes sense, since the electronic material is not as boundaried and there are opportunities for linkages of various kinds. The lease may not be the most appropriate form for obtaining the use of software, but it should not be surprising if a new model develops that builds on the closer relationship between the creator and user.

The new environment, in which there are new links, new opportunities to communicate, and new tools for creating, is one that encourages changes in how we look upon created works and in how we describe and think about them. In earlier periods, for example, individuals "felt that all the literature that existed in their time was a fund of man's knowledge, rather than belonging to its individual authors."[34] This is not the direction in which we are headed, but we also cannot return to an era in which information was located in a discrete container in a fixed medium. Our new media do allow piracy and copying that adds no value, but they also encourage copying that is more integrated in the creative process. They allow linking sources together to create new bodies of information and encourage collections of information to be linked together. As was described earlier in connection with LEXIS and WESTLAW, they allow vastly more combinations to be made than is possible with a physical body of information. The word *body* is appropriate here because the nature of growth is, in many ways, organic. It also occurs through replication, a form of copying that suggests both change and continuity.

It has been suggested that "information economics, in the absence of objects, will be based more on relationship than possession."[35] The use of hypertext encourages such a point of view. It encourages us to think of how to establish new relationships and how to use the new media to add economic value through these new relationships. The ability to form new relationships is the underlying theme of hypertext and the underlying goal of economic enterprises in an electronic environment. The challenge to develop a new regulatory model in such an environment is not merely to control copying but to find a way to see copies as constituting a link between copier and creator and to ensure that this link is rewarding to both.

Shining Lights: Privacy

George Orwell's vision of the loss of privacy assumed both a powerful technology and a powerful state.[36] Indeed, the state was powerful because it was able to control and exploit the technology. As symbolized by Big Brother, the state was able not only to collect information but to restrict the flow of information. Big Brother represented a model of powerful government with total control over a mass medium. The shining light continuously collected information from individuals and also prevented individuals from obtaining information from the state. The individual's identity was defined by the information the state possessed about the individual. Total control over communication meant that the state could even destroy and change records about past events.

This is not the kind of environment fostered by cyberspace. We may frequently question the value, validity, and authenticity of electronic information, but that is because there are multiple or conflicting accounts or interpretations of an event rather than because there is only a single source. The shining light of government does collect information, but it is not the only information-seeking light or even the most aggressive information-seeking light. Economic growth depends on the acquisition, use, and reuse of information by large numbers of institutions. Although there still are large amounts of information distributed simultaneously through mass media channels, there are also new opportunities for individuals and for groups of many different sizes to circulate information widely. The challenge to privacy, in this regard, shares a great deal with the challenge to copyright. In both cases, the shining lights of data acquisition, processing, and distribution are intense and challenge the control of information not because of a single bright light but because of many. These are, as described in the beginning of this chapter, the cumulative suns, and they are also the competing suns.

In Orwell's society, there was no right of privacy or expectation of privacy. In our society, privacy is highly valued and some legal rights of privacy do exist.[37] Yet privacy, in the sense of being able to control information about oneself, is also an eroding condition. There are reasons for still being concerned about the use of governmental power to invade privacy, but the most pervasive challenge facing privacy, like the challenge facing copyright, comes from an electronic information environment that keeps collecting, processing, reprocessing, and selling information at a highly accelerated pace. Orwell is still a force that affects our thoughts about privacy, but the erosion of privacy probably has less to do with the light of government than with the rising economic value of information and with efficient new techniques for collecting, processing, and distributing information.

The movement from an economy oriented around producing tangible goods to one concerned with information and communication leads government to be as concerned with stimulating communication and releasing information as with capturing and controlling it. Democratic government has always suffered from competing tensions, from desiring to use information for political control and for security concerns, while also responding to pressure to provide a free flow of information. The current information marketplace, in which government is still a significant player, is even more intense than before and the tension felt by government is undoubtedly at a peak, since information is both highly valuable and highly volatile, since it can be used to exercise power, and since its value increasingly declines over time rather than increases over time. Profit occurs through acquiring information, adding value to it, and selling it, and this is no longer a task performed only by those in the news business. It represents the business plan of those in the information business, which very well may be a large percentage of all industries.

How should one approach the issue of privacy in such an active environment? Can privacy survive in any form when information is the central economic commodity? Consider three events that received attention from the news media in early 1994.

The first involved Tonya Harding, the Olympic ice skater who enjoyed more than fifteen minutes of fame in the weeks before the Winter Olympics of 1994. Harding's ex-husband had admitted participating in a plot to injure Nancy Kerrigan, the ultimate winner of the Silver Medal in the Olympics. There was considerable media attention devoted to Ms. Harding—to whether she knew about the plot while it was being planned and to whether she would be permitted to skate in the Olympics.

In general, there was nothing unusual about press coverage of Ms. Harding, a celebrity whose life was subjected to the closest scrutiny by the news media. Yet, Ms. Harding was also the victim of an invasion of privacy linked to the new technologies. Ms. Harding had an electronic mail account and, although her mail was not read, her e-mail account was accessed by several members of the press who obtained her password.[38]

In the second case, one that first received media attention in 1993 and is still receiving attention as this is being written, the U.S. government was proposing that a chip be included in communications devices, such as telephones, that would enable the government to "wiretap" encrypted digital communications after obtaining a court order.[39] The word *wiretap* is somewhat anachronistic, not only because much communication is wireless but because digital coding and encryption methods make it impossible for the government to "listen in" to the stream of data moving via fiber optic cables as it might have done in the past.

The Clinton administration has argued that the plan, or Clipper Chip initiative, is needed in order for the government to possess the capability it previously possessed to fight crime. The Clipper Chip proposal would, however, still permit the use of non-Clipper methods to encode or encrypt communications, thus making it impossible to access the communications of anyone, including members of organized crime, using a separate encryption program. The Clipper Chip proposal has been vigorously opposed both by civil liberties groups, which argue that secret communications are not to be feared and that the precedent of allowing the government to oversee how consumer communications devices encrypt communications is a dangerous one, and by many communications companies, who argue that it will be harder to sell their products overseas, since competing foreign products will not contain the Clipper Chip.

The third case revolves around the efforts of a company called EPS (Electronic Postal Service) to do business on the Internet. In early 1994, EPS sent the following notice to many individuals on the Internet:

Electronic Postal Service (EPS) Registration Information

Here's how you can reduce commercial e-mail on the Internet and make money for yourself at the same time.

Electronic Postal Service will pay you money to receive commercial e-mail. EPS estimates you will be paid an average of 6.5 cents per commercial e-mail message. It is estimated that the average commercial e-mail receiver can make $200.00 to $500.00 a year and likely more. There is absolutely no charge, periodic charge, hourly charge or phone charge to receive or review EPS commercial e-mail. The sender bears all of the cost. You are provided with a free EPS mailbox and you may access this EPS mailbox through a toll free phone number so there are no phone line charges.

In addition, as an e-mail receiver, EPS offers you many other new and innovative on-line services such as special interest bulletin boards, special interest conferencing, new services, information

services, full Internet access including network Internet e-mail
remote log-in, file transfer capability and much more.
  To receive more information about EPS and its services, reply by
sending e-mail to our internet address at . . .[40]

Shortly thereafter, journalist Brock Meeks wrote a scathing article
about EPS and its parent company, Suarez Industries. Meeks pointed
out that Suarez was in the direct marketing business under a number
of business names and that some of its business ventures had brought
it into conflict with attorneys general in several states. EPS sued
Meeks for libel, claiming that its plan was legitimate and that paying
people to read advertisements in electronic form made considerable
economic sense, since delivery of information in electronic form
saved the company the expense of paper, printing, and postage.

Ms. Harding's case was a classic invasion-of-privacy case. There was
no ambiguity about the intrusion. The e-mail account was under her
exclusive control, it was designed to be used only by her, she did not
authorize access, and those responsible for the violation were human
beings who were aware that a norm was being violated. The invasion
was committed by journalists, the target of most invasion-of-privacy
suits in recent years. Although this was an invasion of privacy that
involved the new technologies, it was not otherwise an unusual case.

Case 2 is another classic privacy case and one with clear Orwellian
overtones. The state recognizes that its wiretapping capability is diminished by digital communication and assumes that the Clipper Chip proposal will restore its crime-fighting capabilities. The proposal has serious problems associated with it, but even if it was put into place, it
should be understood that the old environment cannot be re-created
and that governmental authority has permanently been displaced. The
state, armed with Clipper and other devices, might appear to be more
powerful and in control of information, and citizens might appear to be
potentially threatened with invasions of privacy at almost any time and
any place. Yet, this exhibition of apparent governmental authority
would be illusory. The Clipper Chip proposal is a sign of the loss of governmental control over information and communication, and this is a
trend that may be slowed down by such legislation but not stopped.

Whereas the first two cases involve clear and obvious invasions of
privacy, the key indicator of what privacy will mean in the future is, I
believe, suggested most clearly by the third case. The long-term threat
to privacy does not originate from widely known and easily identifiable entities such as unscrupulous reporters or Big Brother. It goes
beyond single unlawful intrusions or governmental plans aimed
specifically at privacy interests. Rather, it is the almost continuous
movement of information away from the individual that presents a
much more difficult situation for privacy. Privacy is, perhaps, the
most difficult dilemma of cyberspace because the individual is no

longer simply a victim but a collaborator. Loss of privacy accompanies almost every activity, from making purchases in the supermarket to obtaining medical care. The continuous surrender of personal information in the course of ordinary living is not easily covered by the most commonly used models of privacy. Can we, for example, talk about invasions of privacy when personal information is not obtained surreptitiously or illegally but is given away or sold? As new policies are considered, we may decide that there are circumstances in which information cannot be used by the recipient for any purpose desired regardless of how it was obtained.

The case of EPS, if it is ever in the news, will be referred to as a libel case, not a privacy case.[41] It is a case, however, with considerable overtones of privacy because Suarez Industries is not simply in the direct mail business but in the information business. There is no invasion of consumer privacy that one can easily point to, or at least none as overt as in the Tonya Harding and Clipper Chip examples. Yet, privacy is the issue that permeates the activities of all information acquirers and information distributors, and increasing numbers of businesses fall into this category. It reveals that electronic links may routinely involve an information transaction in which one side provides information and the other a good or service.

Privacy conflicts, and copyright conflicts too, are certain to follow the introduction of a new technology that eliminates boundaries. The link between privacy and space and the dependence of privacy on keeping information physically separate is revealed just by the language we use to talk about privacy. Physical spaces serve often as metaphors to facilitate explanation of privacy interests. The expressions "one's home is one's castle" and "zones of privacy" suggest that privacy can be understood in terms of property and a boundary that separates two spaces. The phrases "invasion of privacy" and "penetration of private space"[42] suggest the image of territory being crossed.

Privacy does not receive the same kind of sustained attention as copyright. Copyright is an area of law that all those who work with information have become aware of. Privacy, which touches all citizens, operates less visibly and touches a less tangible concern. Copyright holders are having difficulty assessing how products of artistic and intellectual efforts can be protected and retain value. Yet, the basic goal of copyright, to foster such enterprises, also seems secure since the new technologies present us with an extraordinary array of tools to create new information products. The basic goal of privacy, to protect the autonomy of the individual by securing some space between the individual and others, seems much more vulnerable. If the continuous running of copying machines challenges copyright, the continuous operation of digital machines linked to purchases and transactions of all kinds shows the vulnerability of privacy.

Can protection of the individual and maintaining the autonomy and dignity of the individual be reconciled with the vastly accelerated movement of information in an electronic environment? Can a space around individuals be secure when everything about the new media tell us that accessing spaces and removing boundaries is what the technology does best? Are new ways of looking at privacy and new techniques for achieving the goals of privacy made possible by the powers of the new media? Most characterizations and conceptions of privacy imply some kind of protected space for the individual.[43] This space can come about in many ways. It can be created by law, as has occurred during the past hundred years. Or it can be a consequence of being left alone, of being in a place where the light is not shining. Thus, privacy seems to be encouraged when the individual can keep the light from shining on him or her or, at the very least, can turn the light off.

But what happens when the light is never off? As I have been suggesting, the light today is not Big Brother's light, since many, not one, are holding lights and the individual upon whom the light is focused may be holding a light as well. This is not the light of totalitarian government, since information moves so quickly and in so many directions that even governmental information previously kept secret is routinely revealed. But the light, or the combination of lights, is intense. How, in this environment, can one be left alone when the light does not go out?

The light shining on the individual is a most difficult challenge since, just as copyright holders no longer can find *the* light that is pirating copies, those concerned with privacy have difficulty finding *the* light collecting and distributing information. Reducing this light, therefore, may be as difficult and frustrating as trying to remove a light by stamping on a lighted area of the ground rather than looking for a switch and a source.

Invasions of privacy that occur as a result of economically valuable information moving over a network may represent the supreme challenge to cyberspace. We may have a right to control information about ourselves, but the ability to control such information is diminishing rapidly. Perhaps one or several shining lights can be blocked but, like pixels on a screen, more lights reappear. This is not to suggest that vigilance over invasions of privacy associated with government and the traditional news media are not warranted. It does suggest, however, that if government served as the original focus of concern for privacy, as evidenced by the Fourth Amendment, and the news media have been an added concern during the past century, the diffusion of information in cyberspace requires new understandings and definitions of privacy. As with copyright, the effort cannot solely be to enforce standards that emerged out of our experience with the print media and with print logic, but to understand how our relationship with information is changing and how informational experiences and relationships are at the heart of the difference between print logic and electronic logic.

Jennifer Nedelsky, in a most perceptive essay, wrote that privacy is about human autonomy and that "what actually makes human autonomy possible is not isolation but relationship. . . . The image of the child developing autonomy teaches us not to mistake interdependence and even dependence as antithetical to autonomy. That image is, of course, very different from and far more helpful than that of a man securely ensconced on his property, whose boundaries are well guarded against intrusion."[44] She adds:

> The question here, as always, is whether the focus on boundaries is the best way for us to understand the sorts of relationships we want to foster. We associate privacy so closely with boundary imagery that I expect a suggestion to abandon boundary will be heard as a rejection of the concept of privacy itself. That is not my intention. The concept of privacy captures, illusively, important values such as people's capacity to decide for themselves some of the ways they will or will not enter into relationship with others. . . . I think we can best foster those values by focusing directly on the expressions and patterns of relationship that foster and express respect for people's needs, rather than on "respecting boundaries," which draws our minds away from relationship. . . . Boundaries structure relationships. But they structure them badly, in part because boundary imagery masks the existence of relationships and their centrality to concepts like property and privacy. When the dominant metaphors turn our attention away from relationships, we cannot give either the relationships or the legal concepts that mask them the critical scrutiny they require.[45]

Any book about the electronic media is about a technology that does not support boundaries, either physical or conceptual. It is about media that establish new relationships with information and that foster new relationships with people and institutions. One of the themes of this book has been that print contributed to the reliance on boundaries since print itself exists discretely in space and relies on margins and boundaries. Print contributed to privacy in the sense that the print environment intensified the focus on the individual and the concern for the individual. It provided an image of an individual, reading silently under the light of a single lamp, that is a symbol of a person wishing to be "let alone." Yet, it is also highly significant that print contributed to the "problem" of privacy in the sense that mass distribution of information brought about the circumstances that led Brandeis and Warren to be concerned with the issue.[46] Print provided us, in other words, with experiences of privacy and also with experiences of invasions of privacy.[47]

Privacy law has developed over the past hundred years in a print or mass media environment—one in which there were clear roles for government, the news media, and the individual, and one that supported the mass media and fostered concern with the individual. The environment of cyberspace is different. The flow of information at electronic speed has already changed the nature of the broadcasting and publishing industries. It has contributed to the fall of governments whose authority relied heavily on controlling information and communication. In spite of what I have suggested thus far, however, it is probably too early to assume that the electronic environment is unconcerned with values associated with individual privacy. Indeed, it is, perhaps ironically, individuals, more than government or the traditional mass media, who have been empowered by the new technologies.

Individuals may have great difficulty controlling the flow of information about themselves, but they also have been provided with new tools for acquiring, processing, and distributing information. The computer is the most powerful creative tool humans have ever produced. It is for this reason that the threat to copyright law is not necessarily a threat to human creativity. It is also for this reason that the threat to privacy law may not end up destroying privacy. It is not too early to be highly concerned about privacy, but it is too early to conclude that privacy in all forms is obsolete. Privacy adheres not merely in a boundaried space but in the ability of the individual to choose and to be autonomous, and the support provided by the new media in these areas needs to be taken into account in any long-term consideration of privacy.

Privacy is not and should not be equated with isolation or, as suggested earlier, with existing alone in the dark. Rather, privacy is a condition that allows the individual freedom to choose when to establish a relationship and when not. There is some significance to the fact that *Roe v. Wade*,[48] the abortion decision that rested on a finding of privacy, was also a finding for the "pro-choice" movement. Privacy needs to be understood as being an inherently pro-choice doctrine in that its goal is to provide the individual with an environment in which he or she can make independent choices. It is by looking at privacy in this light that one can see that there are opportunities for individuals, creative activities, and expressive activities that were not possible in the print environment.

Those who feel that privacy is doomed need to consider the hypertext environment, in which one does not simply read what another has written but can obtain information by making a series of choices. The link between these choices and privacy may be obscure to most, but these choices point to how our new relationship with information places the individual in a new position. The key element of the hypertextual environment is that the reader makes choices in a way that was never possible in the print environment. There is, in short, some reason to be optimistic that there will be greater, not fewer, opportunities for individuals to exercise their autonomy in the future.

It should not be surprising that privacy and copyright are linked by an intriguing focus on and concern for individual choice. The new media may support new entities, such as small and medium-sized groups, and provide less support for institutions oriented around a single widely circulated uniform message. The future of copyright and privacy, however, may be most closely tied to the manner in which the new environment provides opportunities to the individual to be involved in and initiate information-oriented activities.

This connection between the individual, copyright, and privacy has been pointed out recently by Mark Rose. Rose argues that the origins of copyright are linked to recognition of the role of the author and to the "concept of the unique individual who creates something original and is entitled to reap a profit from those labors."[49] Rose points out that "in their quest for a precedent Warren and Brandeis went to copyright law. . . . copyright cases from the earliest days had mingled matters of privacy with matters of property."[50] Copyright is relevant to privacy because

> the institution of copyright stands squarely on the boundary between private and public. . . . Change the rules of copyright—determine, say, that photographs have authors and are protected, or determine that fair use applies more restrictively to unpublished works than to published—and the demarcation between private and public changes. "Private" and "public" are radically unstable concepts, and yet we can no more do without them than we can do without such dialectical concepts such as "inside" and "outside" or "self" and "other."[51]

This is an interesting formulation of the problem facing policy-makers but it may also, in some ways, be a formulation that reflects print logic more than models we will come to accept in the electronic environment. There is, for example, too much reliance on the metaphor of boundaries and of dichotomies such as "inside" and "outside" or "self" and "other." We are continuously faced with choices about the link between our private and public selves, but the new media provide us with opportunities to consider more multifaceted relationships and to look at our relationships in frameworks that may not be possible in physical space.

Although the manner of representing the individual's link to others will not be the same as it was in the print environment, the end result is probably less a nonprivate existence than a different concept of privacy and a different role for privacy. It should not be forgotten that privacy is not always secure in a mass media environment, where information flows generally in one direction and the individual has limited access to organs of communication. In a hypertext environment, we are, almost by definition, all authors. The hypertext environment may not support the image of the reader, sitting alone and reading silently in private, but it does support the image of an individual with power and discretion, an individual who has tools to exploit opportunities for expression and association. Indeed, it is an image of an individual who may have considerably more power and discretion than any individual who simply consumes what the mass media provide.

Our concern with privacy in the future, therefore, must focus as much on preserving a highly active information relationship as it does on protecting a notion of a boundary separating the individual from others. As Richard Lanham has insightfully pointed out, "the central self is threatened not by a lively social self but by the lack of one. . . . If we seek to protect the central self, its rich interiority . . . we shouldn't do it by singling it out, but by focusing on the rich, tense interaction between the central and social self which creates that interiority in the first place. If print created that rich sense of self, it must have done so by intensifying the oscillation, not by shutting it down."[52] In the preservation of the "electronic" self, we will need new metaphors that suggest a flow of information and of change as much as they suggest boundaries and containment. There are many images that satisfy this, from Twain's river mentioned at the beginning of this book to the human form, which continuously is replenished by interaction with the environment. Our struggle to preserve privacy is real and difficult, but we can also expect to be able to exploit many new opportunities for individual empowerment. We are not ready "to give up the sense of who we are,"[53] but we can expect the individual to be nurtured in new ways that will provide us with new perspectives on who we are.

10

Conclusion

Visit the Pentagon or the *New York Times*, and everywhere there are maps, solemnly defining national borders and sovereign territories. No one shows any signs of knowing that we no longer live in geographic time and space, that the maps of nations are fully as obsolete as the charts of a flat earth, that geography tells us virtually nothing of interest about where things are in the real world.

—George Gilder

Consider the experience of anthropologist Edward Hall. While on a research trip to Japan, Hall returned to his hotel one day, went up in the elevator, put his key in the lock, opened the door, and found that although it was the room he had been living in, someone else's belongings were there. Hall took this in for a few moments, all the time feeling uncomfortable, indeed feeling that somehow he must be in the wrong place and that he would be found and accused of being in someone else's room. He then went down to the desk where he was told that his room and his belongings had been moved. He was given a new key, went up to his new room, and found that all of his possessions had been laid out for him in just about the same way he had left them in the first room. There was a marked resemblance to the room and the arrangement and yet, he could feel, much was different as well.[1]

One theme of this book is that, as the new technologies have begun to play an increasingly important role in our society, we, too, in a sense, have been moved. We have not been moved, thus far, to a completely alien environment. Indeed, much seems to have been transported from the old environment to the new. Much communication, for example, still occurs in traditional fashion and much about law appears little changed. Yet, everything in the new space is not exactly where it was before. Everything does not respond as it did in the past and everything is not as it appears on the surface to be. It is difficult to know exactly how different things are and how differently things will operate in the new environment because we often perceive the new environment through the lens of the past. As a result, we miss some things that are there and see other things that are not there. Much, therefore, looks familiar, even while feeling different, a condition that can make this new space disorienting as well as fascinating.

In the new environment, both artifacts of print and artifacts of law may appear not only to be present but to be retaining much of their authority. At the moment, for example, more printed works are being produced than ever before and more lawyers are practicing than ever before. Yet, the process of displacement has only recently begun and both the medium and the profession face ongoing challenges and unstable futures. There are many illusions in the transitional environment, items that are not exactly what they appear to be. Words on the screen, for example, or even words that come out of a "printer," look like words on a printed page but they are not really the same. They do not have the uniform, standardized, authoritative quality of a mass medium. The so-called electronic library has information like a library but it is not organized or used in the same manner as a print collection of tangible books. Seeing is no longer believing, at least when realistic-looking images can be created of scenes that could not exist.

In a variety of ways, our sense of place is different. This should not be surprising since the electronic media treat space and distance so differently from any previous medium of communication. Indeed, one of the principal themes of this book has been to suggest that the new technologies remove the constraints of space and distance as much as they remove constraints of time and speed. They blur boundaries of various kinds and, as a consequence, move various elements of the legal process into a different and, compared to print, less differentiated space.

Hall, as an anthropologist, understood that what was important about his experience went beyond the nature of the artifacts in his new space. He realized that he was not only in an unfamiliar physical place but in a cultural environment he did not completely understand. He was no longer confident in what he could expect to occur in this space. Whose space was this, for example, and might he be moved again? Long-held assumptions about hotels seemed no longer to be valid and he recognized that his relationship with the hotel was different from what he had assumed it to be. He even eventually discovered that his role as tourist/guest/renter had changed.

Hall, as he adapted to his new space, continued to wonder what his new surroundings signified. He eventually left Tokyo, where the first hotel had been located, and moved to Kyoto. He wrote:

> There we were fortunate enough to stay in a wonderful little country inn on the side of a hill overlooking the town. Kyoto is much more traditional and less industrialized than Tokyo. After we had been there about a week and had thoroughly settled into our new Japanese surroundings, we returned one night to be met at the door by an apologetic manager who was stammering something. I knew immediately that we had been moved, so I said, "You had to move us. Please don't let this bother you, because we understand. Just show us to our new rooms and it will be all right." Our interpreter explained as we started to go through the door that we weren't in that hotel any longer but had been moved to another hotel. What a blow! Again, without warning. We wondered what the new hotel would be like, and with our descent into the town our hearts sank further. Finally, when we could descend no more, the taxi took off into a part of the city we hadn't seen before. No Europeans here. The streets got narrower and narrower until we turned into a side street that could barely accommodate the tiny Japanese taxi into which we were squeezed. Clearly this was a hotel of another class. I found that, by then, I was getting a little paranoid, which is easy enough to do in a foreign land, and said to myself, "They must think we are very low-status people indeed to treat us this way."
>
> As it turned out, the neighborhood, in fact the whole district, showed us an entirely different side of life from what we had seen before, much more interesting and authentic. True, we did have some communication problems, because no one was used to dealing with foreigners, but few of them were serious.[2]

Hall understood that what was causing him difficulty was not really the events as much as the interpretation he placed on these events. Space, he realized, was not simply a physical place but an environment affected by the culture in which it was located. Ultimately, he realized that being moved did not have the same significance as moving might have in the United States. Hotel space looked the same, but it was being governed by quite different conventions and values. Indeed, far from according him a low status, he learned that the hotel managers who moved him were treating him quite respectfully. He wrote that "the fact that I was moved was tangible evidence that I was being treated as a family member—a relationship in which one can afford to be 'relaxed and informal and not stand on ceremony.'"[3] The moves reflected an orientation about privacy and a relationship between two parties that might be understandable and acceptable in a familial context but that, at least to him, was not common where there was a commercial relationship.

Changes in our information environment are important for all institutions in society. They may, however, be particularly important

for law. Law is not only a process that touches all other societal institutions but it is, as I have stressed, an institution that is fundamentally oriented around information and communication. When information is whizzing by in the air, or in the wires in the wall, and is
moving much faster than it ever has, when more people and groups
are collecting, producing, and distributing information than ever
before, when information is an animated picture rather than an open
or closed book, legal doctrines, processes, and values that grew up in
the relatively tranquil era of print, and even television, cannot help
but be affected. We are, therefore, likely to encounter some surprises
as novel conflicts are generated and as we endeavor to develop new
norms and standards.

Displacement presents us with many challenging questions, most
of which fall into two categories. There are, first, questions about particular artifacts of the old environment, such as legal doctrines, that
have been transplanted to the new. Technology is changing rapidly,
and it increasingly will be asked whether our legal doctrines and our
ways of using or applying law can be extended to activities in this new
place. During the transition period, we will, with increasing frequency, be asked about revising or stretching familiar doctrines. For
example, can employers and online service providers look at e-mail
messages received by an employee or a subscriber? Or, what kind
of responsibility is assumed by someone who runs an electronic
bulletin board on which copyrighted information is uploaded and
downloaded without the owner's knowledge? Or, since a finding
of obscenity must take into account local community standards,[4]
which community's standards apply when someone in Tennessee
downloads questionable material from an electronic bulletin board in
California?

Such questions will inevitably dominate public discussion about
law in the new environment. There will be important and difficult
questions of this type since, as I have suggested, tranquility and harmony do not appear to be natural conditions of cyberspace. Yet, in
addition to the presence of new objects and the accelerated movement of these objects, there is a second category—one concerning
new values and expectations, new ways of speaking and thinking, new
relationships being formed, new concerns of style and culture. We
need to understand that we are being spoken to in new ways and that
we have new opportunities to speak. As we engage in new activities, it
is not only what we hear and see but assumptions we have long held
that need our attention.

This point has been noted by Roger Chartier, who has written
about changes that occurred in the period after printing was developed. He uses an example from *Don Quixote* to try to make us sensitive to these kinds of changes. He writes that,

[t]o pass the time the night before a battle, Sancho Panza offers to tell stories to his master. The way he tells his tale, interrupting the narration by commentaries and digressions, repeating himself and pursuing related thoughts—all of which serve to place the narrator in the thick of his tale and to tie it to the situation at hand—throws his listener into a fit of impatience. "If that is the way you tell your tale, Sancho," Don Quixote says, interrupting him, "repeating everything you are going to say twice, you will not finish it in two days. Go straight on with it, and tell it like a reasonable man, or else say nothing." A bookish man *par excellence* and to mad excess, Don Quixote is irritated by a tale that lacks the form of his usual readings, and what he really demands is that Sancho Panza's story obey the rules of written style: clear expression, linear development and objectivity. There is an insurmountable distance between the reader's and the listener's expectations and the spoken practice that Sancho Panza is familiar with. Sancho replies, "Tales are always told in my part of the country in the very way I am telling this, and I cannot tell it in any other, nor is it right of your worship to ask me to adopt new customs." Resigned but disgruntled, Don Quixote agrees to listen to a text so different from the ones presented in his precious books. "Tell it as you will," he exclaims, "and since fate ordains that I cannot help listening, go on with your tale."[5]

In our new environment, we too are listening to a tale told in a new way and are experiencing an environment that operates in a manner we are unfamiliar with. We too are encountering an environment to which we "cannot help listening." As we continue to experience new legal sounds and images, we shall gradually begin to hear and see in new ways, and will recognize that the "revolution in information is a revolution of perception"[6] as well as it is one of behavior.

Recognition of this fact may, at this time, be more apparent in the corporate world than in the world of law.[7] For example, Donald Schneider, the chief executive officer of Schneider National, a trucking concern that owns more than 9,000 trucks and has revenues of $1.25 billion, claims that he is not running a trucking company. Schneider asserts that "people get the mistaken impression that our business is running trucks."[8] Rather, he claims, his business is not trucking but information, that "Schneider is really an information system masquerading as a trucking line."[9] Schneider's change in thinking about his firm occurred as he began employing the new technologies to distribute information to his trucks and his drivers. Each tractor-trailer truck comes equipped with a satellite receiver and a small personal computer, and drivers receive a continuing stream of information ranging from road conditions to changes in pickups and deliveries.

Similarly, changing perceptions are at the heart of a Ford Motor Company plant that produces electronic components such as engine controllers, antilock brakes, and speed control devices. All of these products tend to contain microprocessors and would generally be considered to be hardware. Yet, the plant is viewed as being "more of a software business than hardware."[10] The reason for this is that the plant's primary focus is on being able to respond quickly to information and to move "from the era of mass production to mass customization."[11] Ford can do this if it can track every component and share information instantaneously about inventory and orders with suppliers and designers, wherever they are located.

It has not been my intention in this book to measure precisely where in the transition from print to electronic culture we currently are. As I complete this work in the summer of 1994, it seems fair to say not only that "our paradigm of information *has been* the book" (emphasis added),[12] but that our paradigm of information is *still* the book. The presence of new technologies and the influence of new technologies already seem widespread, yet it is also unusual to find someone in the law with expertise in all of the areas of technological change I have discussed. The most public and, in all likelihood, the most significant change thus far has occurred with networking and the ability to interact with and form new spaces that include persons who are widely separated by distance. Our capabilities to interact with machines, to express ourselves visually, and to explore knowledge in nonlinear fashion are lagging somewhat.

For the paradigm of information to be something other than the book, individuals and institutions will have to move further into cyberspace, to employ and become familiar with more than one quality of the new technologies, and to consider opportunities that cannot be imagined in print space. Our activities, one might say, are increasingly cyberspatial, but our attitude toward information remains, quite understandably, oriented more around print than around electronic culture. This will certainly change over time as we come to recognize that this new element in our midst constitutes both a new world view and a set of challenges and opportunities.

The assumption underlying much discussion of cyberspace and law is that cyberspace is an extension of our culture and, therefore, our task is to bring our legal tradition to bear on it. In the background, however, lurks an equally likely possibility, that cyberspace is a quite different culture and one that will bring its values to bear on all of us as we, and our legal tradition, increasingly interact with it. William Mitchell has observed that "a new logic has emerged. The greastest power struggles of cyberspace will be over topology, connectivity, and electronic access—not borders and territory."[13] He adds:

> Romulus, according to Plutarch's Life, plowed a deep furrow to delineate the boundary of Rome and thought the task so important that he killed the interfering Remus. Roman law provided severe punishment for those who tampered with boundary stones, and the Roman

pantheon gave a proud place to Terminus—god of boundaries. Spatial boundaries were important because they marked limits of power and control, and so it is today; the maps negotiated by politicians and drafted by urban planners are patchworks of ownership boundaries, zoning boundaries, and jurisdictional boundaries. Within jurisdictional borders, local laws and customs apply, local power is exerted by some over others, and local police and military forces maintain power by the potential or actual use of violence. But bits answer to terminals, not Terminus; these lines on the ground mean little in cyberspace.[14]

We have done more than tamper with boundaries. The boundaries that are being overturned mean that accessible sources of information can be anywhere, that print's exclusion of the visual is breaking down, and that linear modes of learning about the world are in competition with new nonlinear modes. They mean that interaction with the new media may be as different from the act of reading as the silent and solitary reading of print was from nonsilent and collective reading during the scribal period. They mean that network communication is a "centerless"[15] system, a non-mass medium and nonhierarchical system, fostering interactions and the formation of new relationships more than the distribution of a uniform message. They mean that "print logic" will not govern thinking about hypertextual information. They mean, in other words, that as we encounter cyberspace, we become linked to a light, a sun, that unleashes powerful energies for new and creative visions, vigorous pressure for change, and novel, strong, and even "dizzying"[16] gravitational forces.

Notes

Introduction

1. Samuel Clemens, *Life on the Mississippi* (1880) (New York: Oxford University Press, 1990), chap. 8.

2. Robert E. Calem, "In Far More Gadgets, a Hidden Chip," *New York Times*, January 2, 1994, p. F9.

3. Rose K. Goldsen, *The Show and Tell Machine* (New York: The Dial Press, 1975), p. xi.

4. George Bolling, *AT&T: Aftermath of Antitrust* (Washington, D.C.: National Defense University, 1983), p. 3.

5. H.L.A. Hart, *The Concept of Law* (Oxford: Oxford University Press, 1961), p. 121.

6. David P. Vandagriff, "Taking the Computer Cure," *ABA Journal*, December 1993, p. 59.

7. M. Ethan Katsh, *The Electronic Media and the Transformation of Law* (New York: Oxford University Press, 1989).

8. Ronald K. L. Collins and David M. Skover, "Paratexts," 44 *Stanford Law Review* 509 (1992).

9. Jean Stefancic and Richard Delgado, "Outsider Jurisprudence and the Electronic Revolution: Will Technology Help or Hinder the Cause of Law Reform?" 52 *Ohio State Law Journal* 847, 855 (1991).

10. Peter Martin, "Learning the Law from Littleton to Laser Disks and Beyond," *GNN Magazine*, January 1994.

11. Oliver Wendell Holmes, *The Common Law* (Boston: Little, Brown, 1881), p. 5.

12. Katsh@legal.umass.edu. Information about electronic versions of this book can be obtained on the World-Wide Web from URL: http://www.umassp. edu/legal/Katsh.html.

13. See, for example, Janet Barron, "Putting Fuzzy Logic into Focus," *Byte*, April 1993, p. 111.

14. Michael Hammer and James Champy, "Explosive Thinking," *Computerworld*, May 3, 1993, p. 124.

15. Tom Forester, "Megatrends or Megamistakes? What Ever Happened to the Information Society?" *EFFector Online*, Issue 4.01, December 17, 1992.

16. "Cyberspace. A consensual hallucination experienced daily by billions of legitimate operators, in every nation. . . . A graphic representation of data abstracted from the banks of every computer in the human system. Unthink-

able complexity. Lines of light ranged in the onspace of the mind, clusters and constellations of data. Like city lights, receding . . ." William Gibson, *Neuromancer* (New York: Berkeley Publishing Group, 1984), p. 51.

17. Simeon Garfinkel, "Computer Punks and 'Cyberspace,'" *Christian Science Monitor*, August 21, 1991, p. 13.

18. Donald A. Norman, *Things That Make Us Smart* (Reading, Massachusetts: Addison-Wesley, 1993), p. 243.

19. Robert M. Cover, "The Supreme Court 1982 Term. Foreword: Nomos and Narrative," 97 *Harvard Law Review* 4 (1983).

Chapter 1

1. A search of the LEXIS MEGA file showed 177 references to a "seamless web" (search of LEXIS, MEGA library MEGA file, July 23, 1994). There is considerable ambiguity about the origin of this expression. Frederic Maitland, an English legal historian, appears to have been the first to use the phrase *seamless web* in a law-related context: "Such is the unity of all history that any one who endeavours to tell a piece of it must feel that his first sentence tears a seamless web." Frederic William Maitland, "A Prologue to a History of English Law," 14 *Law Quarterly Review* 13 (1898); see also Frederick Pollock and Frederic W. Maitland, *The History of English Law*, 2d ed. (Cambridge, England: Cambridge University Press, 1899), v. 1, p. 1.

2. Robert C. Berring, "Legal Research and Legal Concepts: Where Form Molds Substance," 75 *California Law Review* 15, 16 (1987).

3. Kenneth J. Kress, "Legal Reasoning and Coherence Theories: Dworkin's Rights Thesis, Retroactivity, and the Linear Order of Decisions," 72 *California Law Review* 369, 389 (1984).

4. Oliver W. Holmes, "The Law," in *Speeches* (Boston, Massachusetts: Little, Brown, 1918), pp. 17–18

5. Harold J. Berman, *Law and Revolution* (Cambridge, Massachusetts: Harvard University Press, 1983), p. 39.

6. Berring, "Legal Research and Legal Concepts," p. 26.

7. *Blessing v. United States*, 447 F. Supp. 1160, 1167 (1978).

8. Persuasion is one of the functions of metaphor. See George Lakoff and Mark Johnson, *Metaphors We Live By* (Chicago: University of Chicago Press, 1980), p. 139.

9. For a discussion of the role and uses of metaphor in law, see James B. White, *The Legal Imagination* (Boston: Little, Brown, 1973), pp. 57–64. ("As [the lawyer] works on an antitrust case or a criminal appeal, the lawyer may say to himself that what he is doing and saying really means something else. . . . The activity of law can be spoken in other terms.") See also Milner S. Ball, *Lying Down Together: Law, Metaphor and Theology* (Madison: University of Wisconsin Press, 1985), pp. 21–36; and Lon L. Fuller, *Legal Fictions* (Stanford, California: Stanford University Press, 1967).

10. See generally M. Ethan Katsh, *The Electronic Media and the Transformation of Law* (New York: Oxford University Press, 1989).

11. See Ronald W. Staudt and Rosemary Shiels, *Chicago–Kent 1993 Large Firm Survey and Statistical Analysis* (Chicago: Chicago-Kent College of Law, 1994). In 1993, 76 percent of the lawyers in the 500 largest law firms in the

United States had a computer workstation on or near their desks. Seven years before, in 1986, the percentage was 7 percent. Ibid. §1.13, at 13.

12. James Martin, *Hyperdocuments and How to Create Them* (Englewood Cliffs, New Jersey: Prentice-Hall, 1990), p. 9.

13. Elizabeth Eisenstein, *The Printing Press as an Agent of Change* (New York: Cambridge University Press, 1979), p. 303. In this classic study of the impact of printing, Eisenstein notes that Church officials hailed printing as a "divine art" and as being "divinely inspired." Ibid., p. 317. Yet, as printing was employed in novel ways and as it became a mass medium, individuals became empowered and were able to challenge the Church in ways that had not been possible in earlier periods. Thus, in 1519, when Martin Luther tacked his complaints about the Catholic Church to the church door in Wittenberg, Germany, the Ninety-Five Theses were also printed and circulated widely. Eisenstein wrote:

> When Luther proposed debate over his Ninety-Five Theses, his action was not in and of itself revolutionary. It was entirely conventional for professors of theology to hold disputations over an issue such as indulgences and "church doors were the customary place for medieval publicity." But these particular theses did not stay tacked to the church door (if indeed they were ever really placed there). To a sixteenth century Lutheran chronicler, "it almost appeared as if the angels themselves had been their messengers and brought them before the eyes of all the people." Luther himself expressed puzzlement, when addressing Pope Leo X six months after the initial event: It is a mystery to me how my theses, more so than my other writings, indeed those of other professors, were spread to so many places. They were meant exclusively for our academic circle here.

Ibid., p. 306 (footnotes omitted).

14. When used in reference to an electronic database, the word *library* may seem to some readers to be an appropriate use of the word. My view is that there are such considerable differences between print libraries and electronic sources of information that the use of the word to describe both sources of information hinders our understanding of these differences and, indeed, prevents many users from adapting to the novel features of the electronic environment. If it is thought that it might be helpful to use the word *library* in some electronic contexts, therefore, it should be made clear that it is only being used as metaphor, as an allusion to something familiar.

15. See William J. Kauffmann and Larry L. Smarr, *Supercomputing and the Transformation of Science* (New York: Scientific American Library, 1993), pp. 118–223. See also James R. Beniger, "Information Society and Global Science," 495 *The Annals of the American Academy of Political and Social Science* 14, 20 (1988). ("Through digitalization and telematics, currently scattered information—in diverse forms—will be progressively transformed into a generalized medium for processing and exchange by a global system. . . . We might expect the implications to be as profound for a global science as the institution of money was for world trade.") For an excellent perspective on the relationship of science and forms of communication, see John M. Ziman, *Public Knowledge: An Essay concerning the Social Dimension of Science* (New York: Cambridge University Press, 1968), p. ix.

16. See Michael Benedikt, "Introduction," in *Cyberspace: First Steps*, ed. Michael Benedikt (Cambridge, Massachusetts: MIT Press, 1991), p. 4.

17. Richard Lanham, *The Electronic Word* (Chicago: University of Chicago Press, 1993), p. 22.

18. Michael Benedikt, "Cyberspace: Some Proposals," in *Cyberspace*, ed. Benedikt, p. 124.

19. See chapter 6.

20. See chapter 8.

21. Richard E. Susskind, *Expert Systems in Law* 8–18 (Oxford: Oxford University Press, 1987); Edwina L. Rissland, "Artificial Intelligence and Law: Stepping Stones to a Model of Legal Reasoning," 99 *Yale Law Journal* 1957 (1990).

22. Harold A. Innis, *Empire and Communications* (Toronto: University of Toronto Press, 1950), p. 33. See also Harold A. Innis, *The Bias of Communications* 33–60 (Toronto: University of Toronto Press, 1951). Marshall McLuhan later developed a famous spatial metaphor for understanding the interaction of media and space. In explaining his global village metaphor, McLuhan stated that "[p]ostliterate man's electronic media contract the world to a village or tribe where everything happens to everyone at the same time." See Edmund Carpenter and Marshall McLuhan, eds., *Explorations in Communication* (Boston: Beacon Press, 1960), p. ix. For an interesting recent examination of media in spatial terms, see J. David Bolter, *Writing Space: The Computer, Hypertext, and the History of Writing* (Hillsdale, New Jersey: Erlbaum Associates, 1991), pp. 15–31.

23. Bolter, *Writing Space*, p. 11.

24. The term *cyberspace* was coined by William Gibson and described in the following manner:

> Cyberspace. A consensual hallucination experienced daily by billions of legitimate operators, in every nation . . . . A graphic representation of data abstracted from the banks of every computer in the human system. Unthinkable complexity. Lines of light ranged in the nonspace of the mind, clusters and constellations of data. Like city lights, receding. . . .

William Gibson, *Neuromancer* (New York: Berkeley Publishing Group, 1984), p. 51.

25. See generally Benjamin Wooley, *Virtual Worlds* (Oxford: Blackwell, 1992); Myron Krueger, *Artificial Reality II* (Reading, Massachusetts: Addison-Wesley, 1991); David Gelernter, *Mirror Worlds* (New York: Oxford University Press, 1991). Bruce Sterling defines cyberspace as "the funhouse mirror of our own society. Cyberspace reflects our values and our faults, sometimes in terrifying exaggeration. Cyberspace is a mirror you can edit. It's a mirror you can fold into packets and send across continents at the speed of light. It's a mirror you can share with other people, a place where you can discover community. But it's also a mirror in the classic sense of smoke-and-mirrors, a place where you might be robbed or cheated or deceived, a place where you can be promised a rainbow but given a mouthful of ashes." Speech by Bruce Sterling to National Academy of Sciences, Convocation on Technology and Education, Washington D.C. , May 10, 1993.

26. Howard Rheingold, *Virtual Reality* (New York: Summit Books, 1991), p. 116.

27. Benedikt, *Cyberspace*, p. 122.

28. See, for example, Carol C. Gould, ed., *The Information Web* (Boulder, Colorado: Westview Press, 1989). The "web" concept is also built into the

World-Wide Web software that exists on the Internet to link a person to sources of information on many other computers around the world.

29. See Vinton G. Cerf, "Networks," *Scientific American*, September 1991, p. 72.

30. National Information Infrastructure Task Force, *The National Information Infrastructure: Agenda for Action Executive Summary*, September 15, 1993, p. 1.

31. Pamela Samuelson, "Digital Media and the Law," *Communications of the ACM*, October 1991, p. 23.

32. Ibid., p. 26.

Any work that can be represented in other media can now be represented in digital form. In this form it can be used in a computer or other data processing unit, whether to be displayed or heard, or to perform some other function. Once in digital form, works protected by copyright are going to become less and less differentiated by type and more and more equivalent to one another because they will now all be in the same medium. This equivalence of works in digital form will make it increasingly easy to create a difficult-to-classify work by combining what have previously been thought of as separate categories of works. (What is an interactive annual report for a company? A literary work? A computer program? An audiovisual work?) Consequently, the elaborate distinctions copyright law has made among different kinds of works will lose much of the meaningfulness they had when media were more differentiated.

33. See James R. Beniger, *The Control Revolution: Technological and Economic Origins of the Information Society* (Cambridge, Massachusetts: Harvard University Press, 1986), p. 25.

34. Marc Galanter, "The Legal Malaise; Or, Justice Observed," 19 *Law and Society Review* 537, 545 (1985).

35. See Collins and Skover, "Paratexts," pp. 510–511. "Paratexts are beginning to enframe the reality that was once largely the domain of print. They influence and shape depositions, presentations of material evidence, expert tests and experiments, reenactments of events and conditions, 'day-in-a-life' accounts, settlement negotiations, and entire trial and appellate proceedings. " Id. But see David Margolick, "At the Bar," *New York Times*, December 11, 1992, p. D18. ("Court reporters, their news seconded by many judges and lawyers, argue that electronic recording is unreliable, cumbersome, and more costly.")

36. For an unusual perspective on the telephone, see Avital Ronell, *The Telephone Book* (Lincoln: University of Nebraska Press, 1989).

37. Nicholas Baran, "Wireless Networking," *BYTE*, April 1992, p. 291; Thomas A. Monheim, "Personal Communications Services: The Wireless Future of Telecommunications," 44 *Federal Comm Law Journal* 335 (1992).

38. Statement of Theodor H. Nelson, "National High-Performance Computer Technology Act of 1989," *Hearings on S. 1067 before the Subcommittee on Science, Technology, and Space of the Senate Committee on Commerce, Science, and Transportation of the United States Senate*, 101st Cong., 1st Sess., 399 (1989).

39. See John R. Pierce, "The Telephone and Society in the Past 100 Years," in *The Social Impact of the Telephone*, ed. Ithiel de Sola Pool (Cambridge, Masssachusetts: MIT Press, 1977), pp. 159–195. It is possible for a message to

spread from one to many through use of the telephone if the message is passed along from one person to another. It is even possible, using this mode, for many people to hear of something in a relatively brief time if each hearer calls more than one person. But this method does not transform the telephone into a mass media instrument or an instrument for reliably and accurately communicating a message to many. Ibid., p. 173 ("In all of their uses, however, the telephone and mass communication are poles apart. . . . Mass communication is from the few to the many; the telephone is always from person to person.") A few uses do exist that arguably employ the telephone in the mass communications business, such as call-in radio programs where the caller is heard by a large audience, or prerecorded messages where the telephone can be linked to a computer to automatically dial many numbers; these examples, however, illustrate atypical uses of telephone technology. See Cameron B. Armstrong and Alan M. Rubin, "Talk Radio as Interpersonal Communication," 39 *Journal of Commumation* 84 (1989).

40. Henry H. Perritt, Jr., "The Electronic Agency and the Traditional Paradigms of Administrative Law," 44 *Admininistrative Law Review* 79, 93 (1992).

41. Ibid.

42. For a description of such a computer, see Maureen Caudill, "Kinder, Gentler Computing," *BYTE*, April 1992, pp. 135–150.

43. "We are merging the PC, phone and fax with this product." Statement of Jacques Clay quoted in Ron Condon, "HP to Launch PC/Phone Hybrid," *Computerworld*, July 4, 1994, p. 42.

44. Katie Hafner and John Markoff, *Cyberpunk: Outlaws and Hackers on the Computer Frontier* (New York: Simon and Schuster, 1991). See also Bruce Sterling, *The Hacker Crackdown* (New York: Bantam Books, 1992); Peter Denning, ed., *Computers under Attack: Intruders, Worms, and Viruses* (New York: ACM Press, 1990), p. xiv. ("The phenomenon of widespread electronic intrusion is very recent. It is made possible by the proliferation of personal computers and their connection to electronic networks.")

45. Starr R. Hiltz and Murray Turoff, *The Network Nation: Human Communication via Computer* (Reading, Massachusetts: Addison-Wesley, 1978).

46. See Henry H. Perritt, Jr., "Tort Liability, the First Amendment, and Equal Access to Electronic Networks," 5 *Harvard Journal of Law and Technology* 65 (1992).

47. Ibid., p. 67.

48. See Johna T. Johnson, "NREN: Turning the Clock Ahead on Tomorrow's Networks," *Data Communications*, September 1992, p. 43. Johnson describes the Internet as a "collection of interlinked commercial and educational networks in the U.S. and overseas." Ed Krol, *The Whole Internet User's Guide & Catalog* (Sebastopol, California: O'Reilly and Assoc., 1994). See also John S. Quarterman, *The Matrix* (Bedford, Massachusetts: Digital Press, 1990), pp. 277–338.

49. This data was obtained from the statistics directory of NIC.MERIT.EDU.

50. Ed Paulson, *The Complete Communications Handbook* (Plano, Texas: Wordware Publishing Co., 1992), pp. 191–193.

51. See academic list files prepared by Diane Kovacs, available via FTP from ftp.cni.org.

52. See generally Henry H. Perritt, Jr., "Market Structures for Electronic

Publishing and Electronic Contracting on a National Research and Education Network: Defining Added Value," in *Building Information Infrastructure*, ed. Brian Kahin (New York: McGraw-Hill, 1992), pp. 344–401. Perritt highlights ten types of values that can be "unbundled, supplied, and assembled through high-speed digital networks": authorship, chunking and tagging, internal pointers, external pointers, presentation, duplication, distribution, promotion, billing, and integrity assurance.

53. Richard J. Solomon, "Computers and the Concept of Intellectual Copyright," in Martin Greenberger, ed., *Electronic Publishing Plus* (White Plains, New York: Knowledge Industry Publications, 1985), p. 238.

54. See Samuelson, "Digital Media and the Law," p. 26; see also Pamela Samuelson, "Digital Media and the Changing Face of Intellectual Property Law," 16 *Rutgers Computer & Technical Law Journal* 323 (1990); Ethan Katsh and Janet Rifkin, "The New Media and a New Model of Conflict Resolution: Copying, Copyright, and Creating," 6 *Notre Dame Journal of Law, Ethics & Public Policy* 49 (1992) (suggesting that mediation might be more appropriate than litigation for resolving copyright problems with electronic communication because it puts decision making in the hands of parties, allows parties to vent emotion, offers greater flexibility in settlement, and protects relationships, and because it is informal, confidential, quicker, and more cost-effective).

55. The difference between commercial online services and the World-Wide Web is that one does not stay connected to World-Wide Web sites as one might stay connected to WESTLAW. The World-Wide Web operates through a process of sending informational requests to the server and receiving information back, although it may appear to the user that he or she is indeed connected to the server.

56. Gord Nickerson, "Networked Resources," *Computers in Libraries*, September 1992, p. 54. ("[Gopher] allows a user to access various types of data on multiple hosts in a seamless fashion using a client-server communications model," and "provides an easy way of organizing both local and remote resources to provide better access for users and to help make the electronic library a reality.") It is "software following a simple protocol for tunneling through a TCP/IP internet." Information accessible through gophers can be discovered through software called VERONICA (Very Easy Rodent-Oriented Net-wide Index to Computerized Archives). Gopher is currently being displaced by the World-Wide Web, which allows access to sounds and images in addition to text.

57. Information about the development and use of the World-Wide Web is available electronically from its developer, CERN—the European Laboratory for Particle Physics in Geneva, Switzerland—at http://info.cern.ch/hypertext/WWW/TheProject.html.

Chapter 2

1. Peter Denning, "A New Paradigm for Science," 75 *American Scientist* 573 (1987).

2. The inefficiency of the fax machine has been described by Nicholas Negroponte as follows:

The notion of "imaging" documents in general and the presence of fax machines in particular are setting back by decades the cause of making information more readable to computers.

Just think of how this inefficiency is part of your own behavior. You type a letter on a word processor, print it on a laser printer and stuff the hard copy into a fax (or use a fax modem). The last step in this chain just deleted the computer-readable format of the text; the recipient can no longer use the text in an information management system that would have access to the content. Yet we all do this because there are more fax machines than coherent electronic mail systems (let alone systems capable of interpreting page description languages).

The fax, a dumb terminal par excellence, perfectly represents the services that result when we do not focus on the intelligence of the network and its ends but instead rely on the lowest common denominator of transceiver. Making such mistakes grossly limits the quality and originality of the products and services that can later arise.

Nicholas Negroponte, "Products and Service for Computer Networks," *Scientific American*, September 1991, p. 113.

3. Charles McClure et al., *The National Research and Education Network: Research and Policy Perspectives* (Norwood, New Jersey: Ablex, 1991); Kahin, ed., *Building Information Infrastructure;* Fred W. Weingarten, "NREN and the National Infrastructure: A Personal Vision," *Internet Research,* Fall 1993, p. 2; J. T. Johnson, NREN, p. 43.

4. See Trotter Hardy, "Electronic Conferences: The Report of an Experiment," 6 *Harvard Journal of Law and Technology* 213 (1993).

5. This is one of the basic themes of V. Mital and L. Johnson, *Advance Information Systems for Lawyers* (London: Chapman and Hall, 1992).

6. Langdon Winner, "How Technology Reweaves the Fabric of Society," *Chronicle of Higher Education,* August 4, 1993, p. B1.

7. Peter Martin, "How New Information Technologies Will Change the Way Law Professors Do and Distribute Scholarship," 83 *Law Library Journal* 633, 641 (1991).

8. The most thoughtful and comprehensive analysis of specific differences between print and electronic publishing and of opportunities for adding value to information once it is in electronic form is Perritt's "Market Structures for Electronic Publishing," in *Building Information Infrastructure,* ed. Kahin, pp. 344–401.

9. This is a concern that has been raised about other new technologies. In a famous passage, for example, Socrates is quoted as decrying the increased reliance on writing in Athens of the fifth century B.C.

If men learn [writing], it will implant forgetfulness in their souls, they will cease to exercise memory because they rely on that which is written, calling things to remembrance no longer from within themselves but by means of external marks; what you have discovered is a recipe not for memory, but for reminder. And it is no true wisdom that you offer your disciples, but only its semblance; for by telling them of many things without teaching them you will make them seem to know much, while for the most part they know nothing; and as men filled not with wisdom, but the conceit of wisdom, they will be a burden to their fellows.

Plato, *Phaedrus,* tr. R. Hackforth (Cambridge, Massachusetts: Harvard University Press, 1952), p. 275a. More to the point and in a phrase quoted less often,

Socrates remarks that "once a thing is put in writing, the composition, whatever it may be, drifts all over the place, getting into the hands not only of those who understand it, but equally of those who have no business with it; it doesn't know how to address the right people, and not address the wrong." Ibid., p. 275e. See also Eric Havelock, *Preface to Plato* (Cambridge, Massachusetts: Harvard University Press, 1963).

10. Michael Heim, "The Erotic Ontology of Cyberspace," *Cyberspace*, ed. Benedikt, p. 73.

11. The relationship between automation, computers, and efficiency is often ambiguous because computers do much more than automate. M. Ethan Katsh, "The Law Librarian as Paratrooper," 83 *Law Library Journal* 627, 628 (1991).

12. Benedikt, *Cyberspace*, p. 14.

13. Lindsay Van Gelder, "The Strange Case of the Electronic Lover," in *Computerization and Controversy*, ed. Charles Dunlop and Rob Kling (Boston: Academic Press, 1991), pp. 364–375. See also Clare Collins, "Friendships Built on Bytes and Fibers," *New York Times*, January 5, 1992, § 1, p. 32; Michael Freitag, "As Computer Bulletin Boards Grow, If It's Out There, It's Posted Here," *New York Times*, April 2, 1992, § 1, p. 38.

14. The new technologies obviously have already affected the ability of firms to coordinate activities in different cities and countries. A recent paper by Villanova Law School student Martin Lessner goes further by raising questions about new alternatives to law firms. He asks:

> [W]hat is the best governing structure, i.e., organizational structure, for the practice of law? Options range from a traditional law firm to a market structure where lawyers practice independently and cooperate with each other only on a task by task basis. Computer technology lowers the transaction costs of working with attorneys of the market, thus providing a lawyer with an attractive alternative to the traditional law firm organization. The advantages of the market include quality as well as cost. Rather than relying solely on affiliate partners and associates in a firm, a lawyer can treat every fellow lawyer in the country as a potential partner. Why should a lawyer commit his efforts exclusively to one firm when it is more efficient (and profitable) to work with fellow lawyers only on an "as needed" basis?"

Martin Lessner, "Information Technology and the Legal Product: Whither the Law Firm and Welcome the Market?" (1992, unpublished).

15. Statement of Sheryl Handler, *Hearings on S. 1067, the National High-Performance Computer Technology Act of 1989, before the Subcommittee on Science, Technology, and Space of the Senate Committee on Commerce, Science, and Transportation of the United States Senate*, 101st Cong., 1st Sess., 399 (1989). Consider also the following: "Today AT&T sends information between Chicago and the East Coast at the rate of 6.6 gigabits (the equivalent of a thousand books) per second. At this pace, the entire Library of Congress could be dispatched in twenty-four hours. Using conventional copper wire and a 2,400 baud modem it would take two thousand years." Walter B. Wriston, *The Twilight of Sovereignty* (New York: Charles Scribner's Sons, 1992), p. 21.

16. The Internet address of the Library of Congress is URL: http://www.loc.gov/. For a discussion of how to view Library of Congress exhibits over the Internet, see Edward J. Valauskas, "Digital Images over the

Internet: Rome Reborn at the Library of Congress," *Database*, April 1994, p. 57.

17. Joshua Meyrowitz, *No Sense of Place* (New York: Oxford University Press, 1985).

18. Ibid., p. 75.

19. Ibid., p. 79.

20. Ibid., p. 7.

21. Ibid., p. 38.

22. Teun A. Van Dijk, "Structures of Discourse and Structures of Power," 12 *Communications Yearbook*. 18 (1988).

23. Katsh, *The Electronic Media*, pp. 198–226.

24. Perritt, "The Electronic Agency."

25. Ronald W. Staudt, "An Essay on Electronic Casebooks: My Pursuit of the Paperless Chase," 68 *Chicago-Kent Law Review* 291 (1992).

26. As will be described later in connection with applying the term *library* to electronic databases, some of the frequently employed metaphors are more confusing than illuminating. One commentator, for example, has criticized the

> "desktop metaphor," that opening screen jumble which is widely thought at the present time to be useful . . . . Why is this curious clutter called a desktop; we have to tell the beginner how it looks like a desktop, since it doesn't (it might as easily be called the Tablecloth or the Graffitti Wall). . . . We are told to believe that this is a "metaphor" for a "desktop." But I have never personally seen a desktop where pointing at a lower piece of paper makes it jump to the top, or where placing a sheet of paper on top of a file folder caused the folder to gobble it up; I do not believe such desks exist; and I do not think I would want one if it did.

Theodor Holm Nelson, "The Right Way to Think about Software Design," in *The Art of Human–Computer Interface Design*, ed. Brenda Laurel (Reading, Massachusetts: Addison-Wesley, 1990).

27. Brenda Laurel, *Computers as Theatre* (Reading, Massachusetts: Addison-Wesley, 1991), p. 32–33.

Chapter 3

1. Robert C. Berring, "Full-Text Databases and Legal Research: Backing into the Future," 1 *High Technology Law Journal* 27, 29 (1986).

2. William G. Harrington, "A Brief History of Computer-Assisted Legal Research," 77 *Law Library Journal* 543 (1984); Jill Abramson, John Kennedy, and Ellen Joan Pollack, "West Publishing: The Empire's New Clothes," 12 *Student Lawyer*, January 1984, p. 17.

3. A typical advertisement is one by LEXIS with the headline: "In Law Practice Today, It's Always the Eleventh Hour: With LEXIS, You Can Make It Ten O'clock." *ABA Journal*, October 1992, p. 9.

4. See Daniel Dabney, "The Curse of Thamus: An Analysis of Full-Text Legal Document Retrieval," 78 *Law Library Journal* 5 (1986); Jo McDermott, "Another Analysis of Full-Text Document Retrieval," 78 *Law Library Journal* 337 (1986); Craig E. Runde and William H. Lindberg, "The Curse of Thamus:

A Response," 78 *Law Library Journal* 345 (1986); Scott F. Burson, "A Reconstruction of Thamus: Comments on the Evaluation of Legal Information Retrieval Systems," 79 *Law Library Journal* 133 (1987).

5. Perritt, "Market Structures for Electronic Publishing," and in *Building Information Infrastructure*, ed. Kahin.

6. David R. Johnson, "A New Era: All Your Expertise in a Database," 4 *Computer Counsel* 1 (1992).

7. P. Martin, "How New Information Technologies Will Change the Way Law Professors Do and Distribute Scholarship," 83 *Law Library Journal* 633, 641 (1991).

8. Joan S. Howland and Nancy J. Lewis, "The Effectiveness of Law School Legal Research Training Programs," 40 *Journal of Legal Education* 381 (1990).

9. Berring, "Full-Text Databases and Legal Research," p. 29. ("[T]he structuring of the literature implies the structure of the [law].")

10. See particularly chapter 8 on hypertext.

11. Sherry Turkle, when interviewing computer users, found that "Escher was a favorite among computer people before *Godel, Escher, Bach* captured a long-standing computer-culture aesthetic by making the point, well known to programmers, that Escher's prints of hands drawing each other or of stairs that continue to rise until they reach their starting point are recursive." Sherry Turkle, *The Second Self: Computers and the Human Spirit* (New York: Simon and Schuster, 1984), p. 220.

12. What is not an illusion is the continuing shrinkage in the amount of space required to store information. In July 1992, for example, a Bell Labs team reported that it had fit 45 billion bits (45 gigabits) of data into one square inch. It was claimed that two copies of *War and Peace* could be stored in an area the size of a pinhead. Elizabeth Corcoran, "Storage Space," *Scientific American*, October 1992, p. 110.

13. The Legal Studies Gopher is located at URL:gopher://klaatu.ucs. umass.edu:70/00/academic/law. Persons with World-Wide Web software can access this through URL:http://www.umassp.edu/legal/home.html

14. Gelernter, *Mirror Worlds*, p. 73; See also W. Daniel Hillis, "What Is Massively Parallel Computing, and Why Is It Important?" *Daedalus* (1990), p. 1.

15. Interestingly, material is often removed from databases by its owners. New electronic information often "replaces" old information. In contrast, in the print library it is common for new information or new editions to "join" old information. The electronic medium, therefore, may be placing a lower value on prior editions of a work than does print. This may simply be a consequence of the ease with which electronic information can be deleted. It may also reflect a difference in how information in tangible form is valued. A more troublesome problem with distributed computing may arise because, at times, only one copy of the work exists. It is, after all, unnecessary for a database to have its own copy of something if the database has access to the computer where the material is located. In theory, a computer could provide only links to other computers and store none of the information it provides to users. A potential problem with this is that if the only copy is removed for some reason, everyone loses access to it. An example of this occurred with Peter Martin's treatise on social security law. This was the first electronic trea-

tise and it appeared on LEXIS. LEXIS removed the treatise from its offerings and, for some time, the treatise was not only "out of print," but out of circulation. The treatise has recently been issued by the Clark, Boardman Company on CD-ROM.

16. Comment made at Third International Conference on Substantive Technology in Law School, Paris, France, July 11, 1994.

17. Benedikt, *Cyberspace*, p. 128.

18. Turkle, *The Second Self*, p. 222.

19. This expression is borrowed from Laurel, *Computers as Theatre*, p. 128.

20. Henry H. Perritt, Jr., "Metaphors for Understanding Rights and Responsibilities in Network Communities: Print Shops, Barons, Sheriffs, and Bureaucracies" (unpublished, 1992).

21. Lakoff and Johnson, *Metaphors We Live By*, p. 3.

22. Tom Erickson, "Working with Interface Metaphors," in *The Art of Human–Computer Interface Design*, p. 66.

23. Lakoff and Johnson, *Metaphors We Live By*, p. 10.

24. Laurel, *Computers as Theatre*, p. 128.

25. Ibid., p. 131.

26. One piece of software that explains how to use LEXIS to new users employs, only partly in a tongue in cheek manner, a "sending out for pizza" metaphor. This metaphor suggests that electronic legal research might have more in common with the process of using the telephone to have an item delivered from a distance, e.g. pizza, than with going to the library. See M. Ethan Katsh and Thomas Bruce, *Rock'n Roll LEXIS: A Hyperactive Approach to Electronic Legal Research* (1992).

27. In an important work about space and culture that touches many of the themes I have raised, Edward Hall notes:

> Man and his extensions constitute one interrelated system It is a mistake of the greatest magnitude to act as though man were one thing and his house or his cities, his technology or his language were something else. Because of the interrelationship between man and his extensions, it behooves us to pay much more attention to what kinds of extensions we create. . . . Because extensions are numb (and often dumb, as well), it is necessary to build feedback (research) into them so that we can know what is happening, particularly in regard to extensions that mold or substitute for the natural environment.

Edward Hall, *The Hidden Dimension* (Garden City, New York: Doubleday and Co., 1969), p. 188.

28. Berring, "Full-Text Databases and Legal Research," p. 54.

29. Kudzu "is a vine whose vigorous growth is legendary in the Southeastern United States, where it covers everything in its path." Jane Smith, "CNIDR: Report from the Kudzu Patch." *Internet World*, September/October 1993, pp. 63–64.

30. Statement of James O'Donnell to *Humanist* list, April 26, 1993, criticizing lack of quality control in management of Gopher sites on the Internet.

31. Although I have focused on LEXIS "libraries," the print orientation is present in WESTLAW also. As mentioned earlier, to see the content of a directory, one must type in the "page" number of the directory. This obviously is a metaphor. Moreover, dividing the directory list into "pages" that have none of the "look and feel" of printed pages has questionable value.

32. Charles A. Goodrum, *Treasures of the Library of Congress* (New York: Harry Abrams, 1991), p. 63.

33. William Stallings, *ISDN: An Introduction* (New York: Macmillan, 1989).

34. Paul Heckel, *The Elements of Friendly Software Design* (New York: Warner Books, 1984); Laurel, *The Art of Human–Computer Interface Design.*

35. A symbiotic relationship exists between software and hardware. Less powerful hardware, for example, cannot support a monitor that can rapidly show images and text together in many colors. If hardware supports only slow transmission rates, less incentive exists to transmit images, because images take longer to transmit than text. As hardware becomes more powerful, however, software can be designed to take advantage of it. Software that puts images, text, and even animation images on the screen can be a more effective communicator than text alone and can be a catalyst and motivator for increased use of the technology.

36. McClure et al., *The National Research and Education Network*, p. 42.

37. Harrington, "A Brief History of Computer-Assisted Legal Research," p. 551.

38. Mitchell Kapor and Jerry Berman, "Building the Open Road: The NREN as Testbed for the National Public Network," in *Building Information Infrastructure*, ed. Kahin, p. 211.

39. Heckel, *The Elements of Friendly Software Design*, p. 10.

40. An interesting examination of the West Digest and classification scheme is John Doyle, "WESTLAW and the American Digest Classification Scheme," 84 *Law Library Journal* 229 (1992).

41. Jon Bing, "Legal Text Retrieval Systems: The Unsatisfactory State of the Art," 2 *Journal of Law and Information Science* 1 (1986).

42. Henry H. Perritt, Jr., *How to Practice Law with Computers* (New York: Practicing Law Institute, 1988), p. 260. The recently implemented WESTLAW natural language search process (WIN) includes a thesaurus.

43. An example of a design feature that is very helpful and illustrates an understanding of the needs of users is contained in WESTLAW'S Westmate for Windows software. Although WESTLAW's DOS software and LEXIS' DOS software provide an essentially blank screen on which to type in a search, Westmate for Windows contains a list of the connectors on the screen. If the user is familiar with boolean searching but not familiar with WESTLAW's particular syntax, he or she can choose a connector simply by clicking with a mouse. In other words, the software allows the user to employ connectors and to limit searches without having to remember abbreviations or the order in which the connectors and key words must appear.

44. Katsh, *The Electronic Media and the Transformation of Law*, pp. 198–226.

45. "Self-Help Guides on Law Grow into Big Business," *New York Times*, September 25, 1992, p. B16.

46. I do not want to minimize the inherent differences between searching with words and searching with categories and digests. There will be different results using print and electronic means, as others have pointed out. See Dabney, "The Curse of Thamus"; Jo McDermott, "Another Analysis of Full-Text Document Retrieval"; Runde and Lindberg, "The Curse of Thamus"; Burson, "A

Reconstruction of Thamus." What has not been pointed out is how much extra training and how much poor searching have occurred because inadequate attention has been paid to software.

47. Gelernter, *Mirror Worlds*, p. 8.

48. Lawrence Teslet, "Networked Computing in the 1990s," *Scientific American* (1991), p. 90.

49. Sheila E. Desert, "WESTLAW Is Natural v. Boolean Searching: A Performance Study," 85 *Law Library Journal* 713 (1993); Richard A. Leiter, "WIN: 'It's the Natural Way,'" *Information Alert*, November/December 1992, p. 1.

50. When the natural language approach available in EZACCESS is chosen, EZACCESS will become more functional.

51. Some additional hardware is required to configure an IBM-compatible 486 class machine.

52. Some have argued that lack of understanding of legal databases' content will deter potential users who are not trained in the legal area. There is some truth to this. However, well-designed software can provide assistance to those users. Current software is almost universally abysmal in terms of informing any user, expert or novice, about what is in a particular database or file.

53. Dabney, "The Curse of Thamus"; McDermott, "Another Analysis of Full-Text Document Retrieval"; Runde and Lindberg, "The Curse of Thamus"; Burson, "A Reconstruction of Thamus."

54. Quarterman, *The Matrix*, p. 40.

55. Statement of Thomas R. Bruce to Third International Conference on Substantive Technology in the Law School, July 11, 1994.

56. EFF is accessible via http://www.eff.org. CPSR is accessible at http://cpsr.org/homl.

57. "No doubt as a matter of history [the] step from the pre-legal to the legal may be accomplished in distinguishable stages, of which the first is the mere reduction to writing of hitherto unwritten rules. . . . what is crucial is the acknowledgement of reference to the writing or inscription as *authoritative*, i.e. as the *proper* way of disposing of doubts as to the existence of the rule." Hart, *The Concept of Law*, p. 92.

58. Judith Perolle, "Conversations and Trust in Computer Interfaces," in *Computerization and Controversy*, ed. Charles Dunlop and Rob King (Boston: Academic Press, 1991), p. 355.

59. Virginia Wise, "Managing Information Inflation," in *Expert Views on Improving the Quality of Legal Research Education in the United States* (St. Paul, Minnesota: West Publishing Co., 1992), p. 125.

60. Ronald Rice, "Mediated Group Communication," in *The New Media: Communication, Research, and Technology*, ed. Ronald Rice (Beverly Hills, California: Sage Publications, 1984), p. 158.

61. Wise, "Managing Information Inflation," p. 122.

62. Kevin Kelly, *Out of Control* (Reading, Massachusetts: Addison-Wesley, 1994), p. 25.

63. Collins and Skover, "Paratexts."

64. Ball, *Lying Down Together*, p. 122.

65. For an exploration of multidimensional approaches to legal reasoning, see Timothy P. Terrell, "Flatlaw: An Essay on the Dimensions of Legal Reason-

ing and the Development of Fundamental Normative Principles," 72 *California Law Review* 288 (1984).

Chapter 4

1. Gen. 3:7.
2. Eisenstein, *The Printing Press as an Agent of Change*, pp. 80–88.
3. George Sarton, *Six Wings* (Bloomington: Indiana University Press, 1957), p. 116.
4. See generally Katsh, *The Electronic Media and the Transformation of Law*.
5. Michael T. Clanchy, *From Memory to Written Record: England 1066–1307* (Cambridge, Massachusetts: Harvard University Press, 1979).
6. Ibid., p. 20.
7. Helen Cam, "An East Anglican Shire-Moot of Stephen's Reign," 34 *English Historical Review* 570 (1924).
8. Clanchy, *From Memory to Written Record*, p. 210.
9. J. David Bolter, *Turing's Man* (Chapel Hill: University of North Carolina Press, 1984), p. 224.
10. Message from Stephen L. Haynes to *cni-copyright* list, April 27, 1993.
11. Heim, "The Erotic Ontology of Cyberspace," in *Cyberspace*, ed. Benedikt, p. 77.
12. Hart, *The Concept of Law*, p. 92.
13. John Markoff, "Turning the Desktop PC into a Talk Radio Medium," *New York Times*, March 4, 1993, p. 1.
14. "Getting a Read on the Customer," *Information Week*, May 3, 1993, p. 22; Christina Del Valle, "They Know Where You Live—And How You Buy," *Business Week*, February 7, 1994, p. 89.
15. Paul Saffo, "Future Tense: Personal Computers Will Make Solitude a Scarce Resource," *InfoWorld*, December 23, 1991, p. 37.
16. Shoshana Zuboff, *In the Age of the Smart Machine* (New York: Basic Books, 1988), p. 10.
17. Anthony D'Amato, "Can/Should Computers Replace Judges?" 11 *Georgia Law Review* 1277 (1977).
18. See chapter 7.
19. Susskind, *Expert Systems in Law*.

Chapter 5

1. Clanchy, *From Memory to Written Record*.
2. Ibid., p. 209.
3. Ibid., p. 262.
4. John D. Calamari and Joseph M. Perillo, *The Law of Contracts* (St. Paul, Minnesota: West Publishing Co., 1987), pp. 391–460.
5. Beacon Expert Systems, *Negotiator Pro* (Brookline, Massachusetts).
6. Patricia Brumfield Fry, "X Marks the Spot: New Technologies Compel New Concepts for Commercial Law," 26 *Loyola Los Angeles Law Review* 607 (1993).

7. Benjamin Wright, "EDI Applications." Statement made to LEXIS Counsel Connect Conference on Law of the Electronic Road, May 18, 1994.

8. Boris Kozolchyk, "The Paperless Letter of Credit and Related Documents of Title," 55 *Law and Contemporary Problems* 39 (1992).

9. Ian MacNeil, *The New Social Contract* (New Haven, Connecticut: Yale University Press, 1980), p. 15.

10. See chapter 8.

11. Andy Reinhardt, "Managing the New Document," *BYTE*, August 1994, p. 91.

12. Wright, "EDI Applications."

13. J. Martin, *Hyperdocuments and How to Create Them*, p. 9.

14. Michael Schrage, *Shared Minds: The New Technologies of Collaboration* (New York: Random House, 1990).

15. Glover T. Ferguson, Jr., "What Groupware Means for Business," *Information Week*, December 6, 1993, p. 64.

16. Ibid.

17. MacNeil, *The New Social Contract*, p. 4.

18. Calamari and Perillo, *The Law of Contracts*, p. 2.

19. J. C. Smith, "The Unique Nature of the Concepts of Western Law," 46 *The Canadian Bar Review* 191, 202 (1968).

20. Bernard J. Hibbitts, "'Coming to Our Senses': Communication and Legal Expression in Performance Cultures," 4 *Emory Law Journal* 873 (1992).

21. MacNeil, *The New Social Contract*, p. 1.

22. Richard E. Speidel, "Article 2 and Relational Sales Contracts," 26 *Loyola Los Angeles Law Review* 789 (1993).

23. Stewart Macaulay, "Elegant Models, Empirical Pictures, and the Complexities of Contract," 11 *Law and Society Review* 507 (1977).

24. Robert W. Gordon, "Comment: Macaulay, Macneil, and the Discovery of Solidarity and Power in Contract Law," 1985 *Wisconsin Law Review* 565, 569 (1985).

25. Message posted on Counsel Connect concerning computer contracting, June 13, 1993.

26. Ibid., September 15, 1993.

27. Ibid., September 16, 1993.

28. MacNeil, *The New Social Contract*, p. 19.

29. Henry Sumner Maine, *Ancient Law* (1861), p. 141.

30. Geoffrey Sawer, *Law in Society* (Oxford: Oxford University Press, 1965), p. 67.

31. Fritjof Capra, *The Turning Point* (New York: Bantam Books, 1982), p. 87.

32. Kevin Kelly, *Out of Control* (Reading, Massachusetts: Addison-Wesley, 1994), p. 27.

33. This is suggested in David R. Johnson, *Building and Using Hypertext Systems in the Practice of Law* (Washington, D.C.: Wilmer, Cutler and Pickering, 1989), p. 15.

34. Charles W. Mooney, Jr., "Property, Credit and Regulation Meet Information Technology: Clearance and Settlement in the Securities Market," 55 *Law and Contemporary Problems* 131, 157 (1992).

35. Ibid., p. 148.

36. Bart Kosko, *Fuzzy Thinking: The New Science of Fuzzy Logic* (New York: Hyperion, 1993), pp. 4–5.

Chapter 6

1. Marshall McLuhan, *Understanding Media* (New York: McGraw-Hill, 1964), p. 23.
2. Condon, "HP to Launch PC/Phone Hybrid," p. 42.
3. George Gilder, "Life after Television, Updated, " *Forbes ASAP,* February 23, 1994.
4. See generally Eisenstein, *The Printing Press as an Agent of Change.*
5. It is estimated that between 12 and 20 million books were printed before 1500 and that 150 and 200 million copies were printed in the sixteenth century. Lucien Febvre and Henri-Jean Martin, *The Coming of the Book* (London: NLB, 1976), p. 262. Rudolph Hirsch estimates that 40,000 titles (approximately 10 million books) were published in the fifteenth century and that by the middle of the sixteenth century, 150,000 titles had been published in more than 60 million copies. Rudolph Hirsch "Printing and the Spread of Humanism: The Example of Albrecht Von Eyb," in *The Printed Word,* ed. Rudolph Hirsch (London: Variorum Reprints, 1978), p. 25.
6. Eisenstein, *The Printing Press as an Agent of Change,* pp. 80–88.
7. See generally Katsh, *The Electronic Media and the Transformation of Law.*
8. Ibid., pp. 247–265.
9. Samuel Y. Edgerton, *The Renaissance Rediscovery of Linear Perspective* (New York: Basic Books, 1975).
10. Ernst Ph. Goldschmidt, *The Printed Book of the Renaissance* (Cambridge: Cambridge University Press, 1950), p. 27.
11. Bernard Diamond, "Psychic Pressure," *Juris Doctor,* December 1976, p. 42.
12. Eisenstein, *The Printing Press as an Agent of Change,* p. 261.
13. Ibid., p. 258.
14. Ibid., pp. 67–70.
15. Ibid., p. 56.
16. Edward Tufte, *Envisioning Information* (Chester: Graphics Press, 1990), p. 121.
17. Goldschmidt, *The Printed Book of the Renaissance,* p. 57.
18. Febvre and Martin, *The Coming of the Book,* p. 263.
19. Ibid.
20. Kenneth M. Sheldon, "You've Come a Long Way, PC," *BYTE,* August 1991, p. 336.
21. The human eye can see only about 5 million colors, so some of the different colors that could be shown on screen would not seem to be different to the eye. Since the number of pixels on a monitor may be less than a million, it is not even possible to show all the possible colors on one screen. If one wanted to do so, one could assign a different color to every pixel.
22. I am not claiming that the text-graphics issue accounted for all of this difference. There were different marketing and licensing strategies and differ-

ences in price as well. Part of the reason, however, that Macintosh machines cost more than IBM (or IBM clone) machines is that they needed more power to do essentially the same job.

23. Donis A. Dondis, *A Primer of Visual Literacy* (Cambridge, Massachusetts: MIT Press, 1973), p. xi.

24. Ibid., p. 1.

25. E. H. Gombrich, *Art and Illusion* (Princeton, New Jersey: Princeton University Press, 1961), p. 172.

26. Pamela McCorduck, "How We Knew, How We Know, How We Will Know," in *Literacy Online*, ed. Myron C. Tumin (Pittsburgh: University of Pittsburgh Press, 1992), p. 246.

27. Katsh and Rifkin, "The New Media and a New Model of Conflict Resolution."

28. William Mitchell, *The Reconfigured Eye: Visual Truth in the Post-Photographic Era* (Cambridge, Massachusetts: MIT Press, 1992); William Mitchell, "When Is Seeing Believing?" *Scientific American* (February 1994), p. 68.

29. White, *The Legal Imagination*.

30. Rodney A. Smolla, *Free Speech in an Open Society* (New York: Knopf, 1992), p. 3.

31. McCorduck, "How We Knew," in *Literacy Online*, p. 253.

32. Tufte, *Envisioning Information*, p. 31; Selwyn Raab, "A Weakness in the Gotti Case: Major U.S. Witnesses Viewed as Unreliable," *New York Times*, March 14, 1987, p. 1.

33. James W. Dabney, "Animation Is Invading Courtrooms," *National Law Journal*, February 1, 1993, p. S1.

34. See chapter 9. See also Katsh, *The Electronic Media and the Transformation of Law*, pp. 172–181.

35. Collins and Skover, "Paratexts."

36. Ibid.

37. McLuhan, *Understanding Media*, p. 158.

38. Presentation by Bruce Collins about the Supreme Court Opinion Network, *Graylyn Conference Report* (Dayton: Mead Data Central, 1991).

39. "US Supreme Court Installs Miles 33 OASYS," *Typeworld*, July 1, 1992, p. 1.

40. Laura S. Fitzgerald, "Towards a Modern Art of Law," 96 *Yale Law Journal* 2051 (1987).

41. Harold J. Berman, "The Background of the Western Legal Tradition in the Folklaw of the Peoples of Europe," 45 *University of Chicago Law Review* 553, 563 (1985).

42. Norman, *Things That Make Us Smart*, p. 53.

43. Ibid., p. 55.

44. Pamela Gray, "Scaling Up to a Three Dimensional Graphic Trace" (unpublished, 1993), p. 1.

45. D. R. Johnson, *Building and Using Hypertext Systems*, p. 2.

46. Stephen Jay Gould, "A Tale of Three Pictures," *Natural History*, May 1988.

47. Terrell, "Flatlaw."

48. Ibid., pp. 291–292.

49. Ibid.

50. "Escaping this flatland is the essential task of envisioning information—for all the interesting worlds (physical, biological, imaginary, human) that we seek to understand are inevitably and happily multivariate in nature. Not flatland." Tufte, *Envisioning Information*, p. 12.

51. Edgerton, *The Renaissance Rediscovery of Linear Perspective*, pp. 164–165.

52. Marshall Brain, "Stop Bit," *BYTE*, April 1992, p. 368.

Chapter 7

1. Evan Schwartz, "Software Valets That Will Do Your Bidding in Cyberspace," *New York Times*, January 9, 1994, p. F11.

2. Jim Meyer, "The Portable Lawyer," 77 *American Bar Association Journal* 62 (September 1991).

3. Peter Morrison, "Arizona Courts Introduce Automated Legal Help," *The National Law Journal*, August 9, 1993, p. 12.

4. Ibid.

5. David R. Warner, Jr., "A Neural Network-Based Law Machine: Initial Steps," 18 *Rutgers Computer & Technology Law Journal* 51 (1992); David R. Warner, Jr., "Toward a Simple Law Machine," 29 *Jurimetrics Journal* 451 (1989).

6. *The Seybold Report on Desktop Publishing*, November 8, 1993, p. 3.

7. Wayne MacPhail, "The Information Revolution: The Function of the Journalist in a Multimedia World" (unpublished, 1993), p. 9.

8. See chapter 5. See also Benjamin Wright, *The Law of Electronic Commerce* (Boston: Little, Brown and Co., 1991).

9. See Ejan Mackaay, "Lawyering and Litigating in Cyberspace," address to the Eleventh Colloquy on Legal Data Processing in Europe, October 4, 1993; John M. Cunningham, "What Is a High Tech Lawyer? An Essay in Self-Definition," 10 *Computer Lawyer* 23 (1993).

10. See, for example, Perritt, *How to Practice Law with Computers*; Mital and Johnson, *Advanced Information Systems for Lawyers*.

11. What began in 1993 as Counsel Connect became Lexis Counsel Connect in February 1994. The name of the service can be a little confusing since Lexis Counsel Connect is still wholly owned by American Lawyer Media. What was anticipated in the partnership were opportunities for subscribers to either service to take advantage of informational sources offered by the other and, through the use of software interfaces and communications links, to create an entity that, for users at least, appeared to be a single, albeit multifaceted, information source.

12. Lexis Counsel Connect's contract includes the following:

I. GENERAL RULES REGARDING USE OF SYSTEM

A. Authorized Users. In order to be an authorized user, an individual must be (i) a lawyer employed by a member law firm, (ii) a lawyer employed in the legal department of a member company and acting as counsel to that company, or (iii) a librarian or someone similarly situated who is employed by a member company or firm (who may access the system to monitor but not contribute to discussion groups other than those intended for nonlawyers), or (iv) a sponsored guest, approved by Lexis Counsel Connect, who has agreed to abide by all applicable rules. Sponsored guests include information providers and non-lawyers whose views and participation will, in the judgment of Lexis Counsel Connect, provide substantial value to members. Each member law firm or corporation agrees to provide a copy of the membership agreement and these rules to each authorized user and to monitor and require their strict compliance.

13. David R. Johnson, "Building a Facility Lawyers Want to Use," *New Jersey Law Journal*, March 8, 1993, p. 2.

14. David H. Maister, "What Makes a Firm?" *The American Lawyer*, December 1993, p. 32.

15. A competitor to Lexis Counsel Connect called Law Journal Extra began operations in October 1994.

16. Steven Brill, "The New Value, The New Leverage, The Next Revolution," *New Jersey Law Journal*, March 8, 1993, p. 1.

17. Steven Brill, "LEXIS Counsel Connect: The Road Ahead," *New Jersey Law Journal*, March 8, 1993, p. 1.

18. David R. Johnson, "On the Path to Electronic Collegiality," *The American Lawyer: LEXIS Counsel Connect Supplement*, April 1993, p. 1.

19. Frances H. Foster, "*Isvestia* as a Mirror of Russian Legal Reform: Press, Law, and Crisis in the Post-Soviet Era," 26 *Vanderbilt Journal of Transnational Law* 675 (1993).

20. Dan Burk, "Patents in Cyberspace: Territoriality and Infringement on Global Computer Networks," 68 *Tulane Law Review* 1 (1993).

21. Katsh and Rifkin, "The New Media and a New Model of Conflict Resolution." See also Samuelson, "Digital Media and the Law," at 23, and Samuelson, "Digital Media and the Changing Face of Intellectual Property Law."

22. Katsh, *The Electronic Media and the Transformation of Law*, pp. 198–226.

23. Only a "profession has the recognized right to declare . . . 'outside' evaluation illegitimate and intolerable." Eliot Freidson, *Profession of Medicine* (New York: Dodd, Mead, 1970), pp. 71–72. See also American Bar Association, *In the Spirit of Public Service: A Blueprint for the Rekindling of Lawyer Professionalism* (Chicago: American Bar Association, 1986); Eliot Friedson, *Professional Powers: A Study of the Institutionalization of Formal Knowledge* (Chicago: University of Chicago Press, 1986). Rayman Solomon, "Five Crises or One: The Concept of Legal Professionalism, 1925–1960," in *Lawyers' Ideals/Lawyers' Practices*, ed. Robert Nelson, David Trubek, and Rayman Solomon (Ithaca, New York: Cornell University Press, 1992), pp. 144–173.

24. Andrew Abbott, "Jurisdictional Conflicts: A New Approach to the Development of the Legal Professions," 1986 *American Bar Foundation Research Journal* 187 (1986), p. 192.

25. See Barlow F. Christensen, "The Unauthorized Practice of Law: Do Good Fences Really Make Good Neighbors—or Even Good Sense?" *American Bar Foundation Research Journal* 159 (1980); Deborah L. Rhode, "Policing the Professional Monopoly: A Constitutional and Empirical Analysis of Unauthorized Practice Prohibitions," 34 *Stanford Law Review* 1 (1981); Thomas R. Andrews, "Nonlawyers in the Business of Law: Does the One Who Has the Gold Really Make the Rules?" 40 *Hastings Law Journal* 577 (1989).

26. Stanley Aronowitz, "The Impact of Computers on the Lives of Professionals," in *Literacy Online*, ed. Tumin, p. 122.

27. The Legal Information Institute of Cornell Law School has proposed that persons accessing the Legal Information Institute computer be provided with a menu listing the Rules of Professional Conduct for each of the fifty states. Conceivably, however, each of the state codes could be stored in a different place, although the user would have no ability to discern this. Message from Thomas Bruce to *Teknoids* list, July 2, 1993.

28. Clark D. Cunningham, "The Lawyer as Translator, Representation as Text: Towards an Ethnography of Legal Discourse" 77 *Cornell Law Review* 1298 (1992).

29. Desert, "WESTLAW Is Natural v. Boolean Searching."

30. Michael Hartmann, "Legal Data Banks, the Glut of Lawyers, and the German Legal Profession," 27 *Law and Society Review* 421 (1993).

31. Ibid., p. 190.

32. Richard Volpato, "Legal Professionalism and Informatics," 2 *Journal of Law and Information Science* 206, 215 (1991).

33. Raymond T. Nimmer and Patricia Ann Krauthaus, "Information as a Commodity: New Imperatives of Commercial Law," 55 *Law and Contemporary Problems* 103 (1992).

34. Katsh and Rifkin, "The New Media and a New Model of Conflict Resolution."

35. Statement of Alan Dowling, *Predicasts*, Vol. 14, No. 19, September 27, 1993.

36. Ibid.

37. Ibid.

38. The administration has indicated some awareness of this issue and claims that new standards will be designed. But protecting privacy in a wired-up environment may be as difficult a task as persuading a physician to make a house call. Both may be nice to have, but both may cost too much. Privacy in a wired-up environment requires retraining people not simply on how to use the technology but on how to deal with leaks and how to prevent leaks. It requires not merely setting standards but enforcing them and persuading workers that the standards are important.

It is hard to be optimistic that government and the health care industry are up to this task. In a recent survey, fewer than half of 870 corporate chief information officers considered security to be an extremely important issue in their companies. Although 60 percent of those involved with banking rated security as being extremely important, the number fell to 27 percent for health care companies and 29 percent for insurers. There are some grounds, it seems, to the comment by one person surveyed that "we are technically smart but procedurally stupid." "In Their Own Words: IS Managers on Security," *Information Week*, October 4, 1993, p. 48.

39. Nils Christie, "Conflicts and Property,"17 *British Journal of Criminology* 1 (1977).

40. *Supra*, n. 25.

41. Anne Stein, "Job Hunting? Exude Confidence," *American Bar Association Journal* (November 1993), p. 40.

42. Quoted in James Podgers, "Legal Profession Faces Rising Tide of Non-lawyer Practice," *American Bar Association Journal* (December 1993), p. 51.

43. Marc Galanter and Thomas Palay, *Tournament of Lawyers: The Transformation of the Big Law Firm* (Chicago: University of Chicago Press, 1991), p. 124.

44. Kurt Vonnegut, *God Bless You, Mr. Rosewater* (New York: Dell Publishing Co., 1965), p. 8.

45. Carrie Menkel-Meadow, "The Transformation of Disputes by Lawyers: What the Dispute Paradigm Does and Does Not Tell Us," *Missouri Journal of Dispute Resolution* 24 (1985).

46. 609 F. Supp. 1307 (E.D. Pa. 1985), aff'd. 797 F.2d 1222 (3d Cir. 1986), cert. denied 479 U.S. 1031 (1987).

47. Anthony Clapes, *Software, Copyright, and Competition* (Westport, Connecticut: Greenwood Press, 1989), p. 99.

48. Ibid.

49. Sam Kagel and Kathy Kelly, "The Anatomy of Mediation: What Makes It Work," 1990 *Journal of Dispute Resolution* 201 (1990).

50. U.S. Congress, Office of Technology Assessment, "Computer Software and Intellectual Property," background paper (1990), p. 2.

51. Patricia B. Seybold, "Data-Hoarding Habit Dies Hard," *Computerworld*, September 6, 1993, p. 33.

52. Wriston, *The Twilight of Sovereignty*.

53. Kent Nelson, "The Re-Education of UPS," *Information Week*, March 1, 1993, p. 56. See also Linda Wilson, "Stand and Deliver," *Information Week*, November 23, 1992, p. 32.

54. Lanham, *The Electronic Word*, p. 23.

55. "Interview with Bill Gates," *Computerworld*, June 22, 1992, p. 32.

56. Alice LaPlante, "Turning Corporate Data into Profitability: Other Companies Want Your Data and They're Willing to Pay for It," *InfoWorld*, October 18, 1993, p. 63.

57. Hal Rosenbluth, "Tales from a Nonconformist Company," *Harvard Business Review*, July/August 1991, p. 26.

58. Lanham, *The Electronic Word*, p. 8.

59. Quoted in Evan Ramstad, "Bits Cornerstone of Techno-Convergence," *Springfield* (Massachusetts) *Sunday Republican*, October 31, 1993, p. F1.

60. Speech by Albert Gore, January 11, 1994.

61. Louis Brandeis, "The Opportunity in the Law." Address delivered to Harvard Ethical Culture Society, May 4, 1905, cited in *The Legal Profession: Responsibility and Regulation*, ed. Geoffrey C. Hazard, Jr. and Deborah L. Rhode (Mineola, New York: Foundation Press, 1985), p. 15.

Chapter 8

1. Mark G. Yudof, "Like It or Not, We're Post-Modern Lawyers," *Texas Lawyer*, February 14, 1994, p. 20.

2. Paul Kahn, "Joining the Network of Ideas: The Impact of Digital Information on the Organization of Knowledge," *Annual Review of the Institute for Information Studies* 1 (1990).

3. Theodor Nelson, *Literary Machines* (Swarthmore, Pennsylvania: author, 1981), p. 2.

4. David Johnson, *Building and Using Hypertext Systems in the Practice of Law*, p. 1.

5. Abner Mikva, "Goodbye to Footnotes," 56 *University of Colorado Law Review* 647, 648 (1985).

6. Bolter, *Writing Space*, p. 7.

7. George P. Landow, *Hypertext: The Convergence of Contemporary Critical Theory and Technology* (Baltimore: Johns Hopkins University Press, 1992), p. 5.

8. Peter Martin, "Hypertext for Tomorrow." Speech to the ABA Technology in Law Practice Conference, March 12, 1992.

9. "Interview with Alan Kay," *Computerworld*, June 22, 1992, p. 30.

10. Elizabeth Fajans and Mary R. Falk, "Against the Tyranny of Paraphrase: Talking Back to Texts," 78 *Cornell Law Review* 163 (1993).

11. Jerry Mechling, "Introduction," *Annual Review of the Institute for Information Studies* (1990), p. ix.

12. Through Project Hermes, Supreme Court decisions are distributed electronically to various sites. Subscribers to a service of the Cornell Law School Legal Information Institute can receive information about every decision issued by e-mail.

13. Vannevar Bush, "As We May Think," *Atlantic Monthly* 176, July 1945, pp. 101–108.

14. Bruce Sterling, "Free as Air, Free as Water, Free as Knowledge." Speech to the Library Information Technology Association, June 1992.

15. Andrea Keyhani, "The Online Journal of Current Clinical Trials: An Innovation in Electronic Journal Publishing," 16 *Database* 14, 15 (1993).

16. David Johnson, *Building and Using Hypertext Systems in the Practice of Law*, p. 28.

Chapter 9

1. Transmission capacity of optical fibers has increased tenfold every four years since 1975. Emmanuel Desurvire, "Lightwave Communications: The Fifth Generation," *Scientific American*, January 1992, p. 114.

2. "A Picture Is Worth a Thousand Lies: Electronic Imaging and the Future of the Admissibility of Photographs into Evidence," 18 *Rutgers Computer and Technology Law Journal* 365 (1992).

3. See Introduction for quotation referring to "face in the water" in Clemens, *Life on the Mississippi*, chap. 8.

4. Kosko, *Fuzzy Thinking*.

5. This is a paraphrase of a statement made by John Philpot Curran, "Speech upon the Right of Election" (1790), in *Speeches of the Right Honorable John Philpot Curran*. Dublin: John Duffy, 1865.

6. William Gibson, *Virtual Light* (New York: Bantam Books, 1993).

7. Richard Brooks, "Intellectual Technology: The Dilemma of Environmental Law," 15 *Rutgers Computer and Technology Law Journal* 411, 411–413 (1989).

8. De Sola Pool, *Technologies of Freedom*, p. 214.

9. Pamela Samuelson and Robert J. Glushko, "Electronic Communications and Legal Change: Intellectual Property Rights for Digital Library and Hypertext Publishing Systems," 6 *Harvard Journal of Law and Technology* 237, 240 (1993).

10. Ibid.

11. Marshall McLuhan and Bruce R. Powers, *The Global Village* (New York: Oxford University Press, 1989), p. 45.

12. Alvin Kernan, *Printing Technology, Letters and Samuel Johnson* (Princeton, New Jersey: Princeton University Press, 1987), p. 51.

13. Peter Berger, *The Sacred Canopy* (New York: Doubleday Anchor Books, 1969), p. 9.

14. Richard A. Lanham, "Digital Rhetoric: Theory, Practice, and Property," in *Literacy Online*, ed. M. C. Tumin (Pittsburgh: University of Pittsburgh Press, 1992), p. 222.

15. 17 USCS Sec. 102(a).

16. Robert H. Rotstein, "Beyond Metaphor: Copyright Infringement and the Fiction of the Work," 68 *Chicago-Kent Law Review* 725, 726 (1993).

17. Bolter, *Writing Space*, p. 2.

18. Mark Rose, *Authors and Owners: The Invention of Copyright* (Cambridge, Massachusetts: Harvard University Press, 1993); Lyman Patterson, *Copyright in Historical Perspective* (Nashville: Vanderbilt University Press, 1968).

19. A. J. Minnis, *Medieval Theory of Authorship* (London: Scolar Press, 1984), p. 11.

20. Kernan, *Printing Technology*, pp. 49–50.

21. Aaron Keyt, "An Improved Framework for Music Plagiarism Litigation," 76 *California Law Review* 421, 425 (1988). See also Rotstein, "Beyond Metaphor," p. 725.

22. Erick Bohlman, "Squeezing the Square Peg of Digital Sound Sampling into the Round Hole of Copyright Law: Who Will Pay the Piper?" 3 *Software Law Journal* 797 (1992).

23. Clanchy, *From Memory to Written Record: England 1066–1307*, 2nd. ed. (Oxford: Blackwell, 1993), p. 284.

24. Ibid., p. 285.

25. Bohlman, "Squeezing the Square Peg of Digital Sound Sampling into the Round Hole of Copyright Law."

26. Lanham, *The Electronic Word*, p. 107.

27. John Perry Barlow, "The Economy of Ideas: A Framework for Rethinking Patents and Copyrights in the Digital Age," *Wired*, March 1994, p. 85.

28. Ibid., p. 89.

29. "The Post-Capitalist Executive: An Interview with Peter Drucker," *Harvard Business Review*, May–June 1993, p. 120.

30. 17 USCS Sec. 101.

31. Katsh, *The Electronic Media and the Transformation of Law*.

32. Samuelson and Glushko, "Electronic Communications and Legal Change."

33. David L. Hayes, "Shrinkwrap License Agreements: New Light on a Vexing Problem," 9 *Computer Lawyer* 1 (1992).

34. Marc Drogin, *Anathema! Medieval Scribes and the History of Book Curses* (Totowa, New Jersey: Allanheld and Schram, 1983), p. 18.

35. Barlow, "The Economy of Ideas," p. 128.

36. George Orwell, *1984* (New York: Harcourt, Brace, 1949). See Peter Stansky, ed., *On Nineteen Eighty-four* (San Francisco: W. H. Freeman and Co., 1983); Irving Howe, ed., *1984 Revisited* (New York: Harper and Row, 1983);

Whitney French Bolton, *The Language of 1984* (Knoxville: University of Tennessee Press, 1984); William Steinhoff, *The Road to 1984* (London: Weidenfeld and Nicolson, 1975).

37. Joel R. Reidenberg, "Privacy in the Communications Information Economy: A Fortress or Frontier for Individual Rights?" 44 *Federal Communications Law Journal* 195 (1992).

38. Dorothy Giobbe, "Unlawful Entry: Detroit Free Press Sportswriter Apologizes after Using Tonya Harding's Private Password to Gain Entry into the Olympic Skater's Electronic Mailbox," *Editor and Publisher*, March 5, 1994, p. 11. The reporters obtained access after discovering that Harding's birthdate was her password.

39. The Clipper Chip proposal has received a great deal of attention in the news media. Two of the clearest statements of what the Clipper Chip does and of why some groups oppose it are Whitfield Diffie, "Key Escrow: Its Impact and Alternatives," statement before the Subcommittee on Technology and the Law of the Senate Judiciary Committee, May 3, 1994; and Stewart A. Baker, "Don't Worry, Be Happy: Why Clipper Is Good for You," *Wired Magazine*, June 1994, p. 100. Other statements and information about the Clipper Chip proposal and about the administration's Digital Telephony proposal are accessible electronically from the Electronic Frontier Foundation Internet site: gopher.eff.org.

40. Message from Suarez Corporation to Library Gopher List, March 25, 1994.

41. See, for example, Rosalind Resnick, "Cybertort," *National Law Journal*, July 18, 1994, p. 1. The EPS suit against Meeks was settled out of court in August 1994.

42. Robert Post, "The Social Foundations of Privacy: Community and Self in the Common Law Tort," 77 *California Law Review* 970 (1989).

43. This is explicit in some characterizations of privacy ("a kind of space that a man may carry with him into his bedroom or into the street." Milton Konvitz, "Privacy and the Law: A Philosophical Prelude," 31 *Law and Contemporary Problems* 272, 279 [1960]) and implicit in others, such as "the right to be let alone" or "intrusion" (William Prosser, "Privacy," 48 *California Law Review* 383 [1960]).

44. Jennifer Nedelsky, "Law, Boundaries, and the Bounded Self," 30 *Representations* 162, 169 (1990).

45. Ibid., pp. 177–178.

46. Privacy law is about 100 years old and, therefore, is even younger than copyright law. Its origins lie in a law review article by two Boston lawyers, Louis Brandeis and Samuel Warren. Brandeis and Warren were concerned with the activities of the press in seeking information about Warren's family. They considered privacy to be the "right to be let alone." Samuel Warren and Louis Brandeis, "The Right to Privacy," 4 *Harvard Law Review* 193 (1890).

47. Katsh, *The Electronic Media and the Transformation of Law*, pp. 189–197.

48. 410 U.S. 113 (1973).

49. Rose, *Authors and Owners*, p. 2.

50. Ibid., p. 140.

51. Ibid. pp. 140–141.

52. Lanham, *The Electronic Word*, pp. 219–220.

53. Rose, *Authors and Owners*, p. 142.

Chapter 10

1. Edward Hall, *Beyond Culture* (Garden City, New York: Doubleday, 1976), pp. 58–59.

2. Ibid., pp. 60–61.

3. Ibid. p. 65.

4. *Miller v. California*, 413 U.S. 34 (1973).

5. Roger Chartier, ed., *The Culture of Print* (Princeton, New Jersey: Princeton University Press, 1987), p. 7.

6. Anthony Smith, "On Audio and Visual Technologies," in *The Written Word: Literacy in Transition*, ed. Gerd Baumann (Oxford: Clarendon Press, 1986), p. 191.

7. "Nowhere has the effect of computer technology been felt more greatly than in the business community." Gregory E. Perry and Cherie Ballard, "A Chip by Any Other Name Would Still Be a Potato: The Failure of Law and Its Definitions to Keep Pace with Computer Technology," 24 *Texas Tech Law Review* 797 (1993).

8. Quoted in Marc Levinson, "Riding the Data Highway," *Newsweek*, March 21, 1994, p. 54.

9. Ibid.

10. Statement of Richard A. Chow-Wah, in John Holusha, "Industry Is Learning to Love Agility," *New York Times*, May 25, 1994, p. D1.

11. Ibid.

12. Robert Berring, "Power and Paradigm," in *Highlights: A Selection of Presentations (1991–1993) from the Conference on Teaching Research in Private Law Libraries* (Dayton, Ohio: Mead Data Central, 1993), p. 73.

13. This quotation is taken from Chapter 4 of William Mitchell's *City of Bits* (Cambridge, Massachusetts, MIT Press, 1995). There are no page number references because the source I used was the electronic version of the book, which can be found at URL:http://alberti.mit.edu/arch/4.207/texts/city-of-bits-toc.html.

14. Ibid,

15. Paul Leinberger and Bruce Tucker, *The New Individualists* (New York: HarperCollins, 1991), p. 346.

16. Ibid., p. 350.

Bibliography

Abbott, Andrew. "Jurisdictional Conflicts: A New Approach to the Development of the Legal Professions." *American Bar Foundation Research Journal* 187 (1986).

Abbott, L. W. *Law Reporting in England 1485–1585.* London: The Athalone Press, 1973.

Abramson, Jill, John Kennedy, and Ellen Joan Pollack. "West Publishing: The Empire's New Clothes." 12 *Student Lawyer*, January 1984, p.17.

Altman, Irwin. "Privacy Regulation: Culturally Universal or Culturally Specific?" 33 *Journal of Social Issues* 66 (1977).

American Bar Association. *In the Spirit of Public Service: A Blueprint for the Rekindling of Lawyer Professionalism.* Chicago: American Bar Association, 1986.

Andrews, Thomas R. "Nonlawyers in the Business of Law: Does the One Who Has the Gold Really Make the Rules?" 40 *Hastings Law Journal* 577 (1989).

Armstrong, Cameron B., and Alan M. Rubin. "Talk Radio as Interpersonal Communication." 39 *Journal of Communication* 84 (1989).

Arnold, Terri Finkbine. "Let Technology Counteract Technology: Protecting the Medical Record in the Computer Age." 15 *Hastings Communication/Entertainment Law Journal* 455 (1993).

Aronowitz, Stanley. "The Impact of Computers on the Lives of Professionals." In *Literary Online*, ed. Myron C. Tumin. Pittsburgh: University of Pittsburgh Press, 1992.

Arthur, Paul, and Romedi Passini. *Wayfinding: People, Signs, and Architecture.* New York: McGraw-Hill.

Bagdikian, Ben. *The Information Machines.* New York: Harper and Row, 1971.

Baker, Stewart A. "Don't Worry, Be Happy: Why Clipper Is Good for You," *Wired Magazine*, June 1994, p. 100.

Ball, Milner S. *Lying Down Together: Law, Metaphor and Theology.* Madison: University of Wisconsin Press, 1985.

Ball, Milner S. "The Play's the Thing." 28 *Stanford Law Review* 81 (1975).

Barlow, John Perry. "Electronic Frontier Bill o' Rights." 36 *Communications of the ACM* 21 (1993).

Barlow, John Perry. "The Economy of Ideas: A Framework for Rethinking Patents and Copyrights in the Digital Age." *Wired*, March 1994, p. 85.

Baran, Nicholas. "Wireless Networking." *BYTE*, April 1992.

271

Barrett, Edward, ed. *The Society of Text.* Cambridge, Massachusetts: MIT Press, 1989.

Barrett, Edward, ed. *Text, ConText, and HyperText.* Cambridge, Massachusetts: MIT Press, 1988.

Barron, Janet. "Putting Fuzzy Logic into Focus." *Byte.* April 1993.

Baumann, Gerd, ed. *The Written Word: Literacy in Transition.* Oxford: Clarendon Press, 1986.

Benedikt, Michael, ed. *Cyberspace: First Steps.* Cambridge, Massachusetts: MIT Press, 1991.

Beniger, James R. *The Control Revolution: Technological and Economic Origins of the Information Society.* Cambridge, Massachusetts: Harvard University Press, 1986.

Beniger, James R. "Information Society and Global Science." 495 *The Annals of the American Academy of Political and Social Science* 14 (1988).

Bennett, Colin J. *Regulating Privacy: Data Protection and Public Policy in Europe and the United States.* Ithaca, New York: Cornell University Press, 1992.

Berger, Peter. *The Sacred Canopy.* New York: Doubleday Anchor Books, 1969.

Berman, Harold J. "The Background of the Western Legal Tradition in the Folklaw of the Peoples of Europe." 45 *University of Chicago Law Review* 553 (1985).

Berman, Harold J. *Law and Revolution.* Cambridge, Massachusetts: Harvard University Press, 1983.

Bernstein, Jeremy, *The Analytical Machine*, 2d ed. New York: William Morrow and Co., 1981.

Berring, Robert. "Collapse of the Structure of the Legal Research Universe: The Imperative of Digital Information." 69 *Washington Law Review* 9 (1994).

Berring, Robert C. "Full-Text Databases and Legal Research: Backing into the Future." 1 *High Technology Law Journal* 27 (1986).

Berring, Robert C. " Legal Research and Legal Concepts: Where Form Molds Substance." 75 *California Law Review* 15 (1987).

Berring, Robert. "Power and Paradigm." In *Highlights: A Selection of Presentations (1991–1993) from the Conference on Teaching Research in Private Law Libraries.* Dayton, Ohio: Mead Data Central, 1993.

Bigelow, Robert. "The Lawyer's Role in the Computer Age." 16 *Rutger's Computer and Technology Law Journal* 289 (1990).

Bing, Jon. "Legal Text Retrieval Systems: The Unsatisfactory State of the Art." 2 *Journal of Law and Information Science* 1 (1986).

Blake, Judith, and Lee Tiedrich. "The National Information Infrastructure Initiative and the Emergence of the Electronic Superhighway." 46 *Federal Communications Law Journal* 397 (1994).

Blume, Peter. "Credit Reporting and Data Protection: Efficiency versus Privacy." 1 *The International Computer Lawyer* 12 (1993).

Bohlman, Erick. "Squeezing the Square Peg of Digital Sound Sampling into the Round Hole of Copyright Law: Who Will Pay the Piper?" 3 *Software Law Journal* 797 (1992).

Bolling, George. *AT&T: Aftermath of Antitrust.* Washington, D.C.: National Defense University, 1983.

Bolter, J. David. *Turing's Man.* Chapel Hill: University of North Carolina Press, 1984.

Bolter, J. David. *Writing Space: The Computer, Hypertext, and the History of Writing*. Hillsdale, NJ: Erlbaum Associates, 1991.

Bolton, Whitney French. *The Language of 1984*. Knoxville: University of Tennessee Press, 1984.

Brain, Marshall. "Stop Bit." *BYTE*, April 1992.

Branscomb, Anne. *Who Owns Information?* New York: Basic Books, 1994.

Brenner, Susan W. "Computers and Common Law: Precedent as Information." 35 *Res Gestae* 550 (1992).

Brenner, Susan W. "Of Publication and Precedent: An Inquiry into the Ethnomethodology of Case Reporting in the American Legal System." 39 *DePaul Law Review* 461 (1990).

Bresnick, David. "The Lawyer as Information Manager." 12 *Legal Studies Forum* 275 (1988).

Breyer, Stephen. "The Uneasy Case for Copyright: A Study of Copyright in Books, Photocopies, and Computer Programs." 84 *Harvard Law Review* 281 (1970).

Brill, Steven. "LEXIS Counsel Connect: The Road Ahead." *New Jersey Law Journal*, (March 8, 1993), p. 1.

Brill, Steven. "The New Value, the New Leverage, the Next Revolution." *New Jersey Law Journal* (March 8, 1993), p. 1.

Brooks, Richard. "Intellectual Technology: The Dilemma of Environmental Law." 15 *Rutgers Computer and Technology Law Journal* 411 (1989).

Bunker, Matthew D., Sigman L. Splichal, Bill F. Chamberlin, and Linda M. Perry. "Access to Government-Held Information in the Computer Age: Applying Legal Doctrine to Emerging Technology." 20 *Florida State University Law Review* 543 (1993).

Burk, Dan. "Patents in Cyberspace: Territoriality and Infringement on Global Computer Networks." 68 *Tulane Law Review* 1 (1993).

Burson, Scott F. "A Reconstruction of Thamus: Comments on the Evaluation of Legal Information Retrieval Systems." 79 *Law Library Journal* 133 (1987).

Bush, Vannevar. "As We May Think." *Atlantic Monthly* 176, July 1945, pp. 101–108.

Calamari, John D., and Joseph M. Perillo. *The Law of Contracts*. St. Paul, Minnesota: West Publishing Co., 1987.

Calem, Robert E. "In Far More Gadgets, a Hidden Chip." *New York Times*, January 2, 1994, p. Fp.

Cam, Helen. "An East Anglican Shire-Moot of Stephen's Reign." 34 *English Historical Review* 570 (1924).

Capra, Fritjof. *The Turning Point*. New York: Bantam Books, 1982.

Carey, James. "Harold Adams Innis and Marshall McLuhan." 17 *Antioch Review* 5 (1967).

Carpenter, Edmund, and Marshall McLuhan, eds. *Explorations in Communication*. Boston: Beacon Press, 1960.

Carter, John, and Percival Muir, eds. *Printing and the Mind of Man*. London: Cassell, 1967.

Castells, Manuel. *The Informational City*. Oxford: Basil Blackwell, 1989.

Caudill, Maureen. *In Our Own Image: Building an Artificial Person*. New York: Oxford University Press, 1992.

Caudill, Maureen. "Kinder, Gentler Computing." *BYTE*, April 1992.

Cerf, Vinton G. "Networks." *Scientific American*, September 1991, p. 72.

Chartier, Roger, ed. *The Culture of Print*. Princeton, New Jersey: Princeton University Press, 1987.

Chaytor, Henry John. *From Script to Print*. London: Sedgwick and Jackson, 1966.

Christensen, Barlow F. "The Unauthorized Practice of Law: Do Good Fences Really Make Good Neighbors—or Even Good Sense?" *American Bar Foundation Research Journal* 159 (1980).

Christie, Nils. "Conflicts and Property." 17 *British Journal of Criminology* 1 (1977).

Clanchy, Michael T. *From Memory to Written Record: England 1066–1307*. Cambridge, Massachusetts: Harvard University Press, 1979.

Clanchy, Michael T. *From Memory to Written Record: England 1066–1307*. 2nd ed. (Oxford: Blackwell, 1993).

Clapes, Anthony. *Software, Copyright, and Competition*. Westport, Connecticut: Greenwood Press, 1989.

Clark, Aubert. *The Movement for International Copyright in Nineteenth Century America*. Washington, D.C.: Catholic University Press, 1960.

Clemens, Samuel. *Life on the Mississippi*. New York: Oxford University Press, 1940.

Collins, Clare. "Friendships Built on Bytes and Fibers," *New York Times*, January 5, 1992.

Collins, Ronald K. L., and David M. Skover. "The First Amendment in an Age of Paratroopers." 68 *Texas Law Review* 1087 (1990).

Collins, Ronald K. L. and David M. Skover. "Paratexts." 44 *Stanford Law Review* 509 (1992).

Condon, Ron. "HP to Launch PC/Phone Hybrid." *Computerworld*, July 4 1994.

Coover, Robert. "And Hypertext Is Only the Beginning." *New York Times*, August 29, 1993, Sec. 7, p. 8.

Corcoran, Elizabeth. "Storage Space." *Scientific American*, October 1992.

Cover, Robert M. "The Supreme Court 1982 Term. Foreword: Nomos and Narrative." 97 *Harvard Law Review* 4 (1983).

Cunningham, Clark D. "The Lawyer as Translator, Representation as Text: Towards an Ethnography of Legal Discourse." 77 *Cornell Law Review* 1298 (1992).

Cunningham, John M. "What Is a High Tech Lawyer? An Essay in Self-Definition." 10 *Computer Lawyer* 23 (1993).

Curran, John Philpot. *Speech upon the Right of Election*. 1790.

Cutrera, Terri A. "Computer Networks, Libel and the First Amendment." 11 *Computer/Law Journal* 555 (1992).

Dabney, Daniel. "The Curse of Thamus: An Analysis of Full-Text Legal Document Retrieval." 78 *Law Library Journal* 5 (1986).

Dabney, James W. "Animation Is Invading Courtrooms." *National Law Journal* (February 1, 1993), p. S1.

D'Amato, Anthony. "Can/Should Computers Replace Judges?" 11 *Georgia Law Review* 1277 (1977).

Davies, Wendy, and Paul Fouracre, eds. *The Settlement of Disputes in Early Medieval Europe*. Cambridge: Cambridge University Press, 1986.

Davis, Natalie Zemon. *Society and Culture in Early Modern France*. Stanford, California: Stanford University Press, 1975.

Delany, Paul, and George Landow, eds. *Hypermedia and Literary Studies.* Cambridge, Massachusetts: MIT Press, 1991.

Del Valle, Christina. "They Know Where You Live—And How You Buy." *Business Week*, February 7, 1994.

De Mulder, R. V., M. J. van den Hoven, and C. Wildemast. "The Concept of Concept in 'Conceptual Legal Information Retrieval.'" 3 *Law Technology Journal* 12 (October 1993).

Denning, Peter. "A New Paradigm for Science." 75 *American Scientist* 573 (1987).

Denning, Peter, ed. *Computers under Attack: Intruders, Worms, and Viruses.* New York: ACM Press, 1990.

Desert, Sheila E. "WESTLAW Is Natural v. Boolean Searching: A Performance Study." 85 *Law Library Journal* 713 (1993).

de Sola Pool, Ithiel. *Technologies of Freedom.* Cambridge, Massachusetts: Harvard University Press, 1983.

Desurvire, Emmanuel. "Lightwave Communications: The Fifth Generation." *Scientific American*, January 1992, p. 114.

Diamond, Bernard. "Psychic Pressure." *Juris Doctor* (December 1976), p. 42.

Diffie, Whitfield. "Key Escrow: Its Impact and Alternatives." Statement before the Subcommittee on Technology and the Law of the Senate Judiciary Committee, May 3, 1994.

Dijksterhuis, Eduard. *The Mechanization of the World Picture.* Oxford: Oxford University Press, 1961.

Dondis, Donis A. *A Primer of Visual Literacy.* Cambridge, Massachusetts: MIT Press, 1973.

Dowling, Alan. *Predicasts*, Vol. 14, No. 19, September 27, 1993.

Doyle, John. "WESTLAW and the American Digest Classification Scheme." 84 *Law Library Journal* 229 (1992).

Drogin, Marc. *Anathema! Medieval Scribes and the History of Book Curses.* Totowa, New Jersey: Allanheld and Schram, 1983.

Dunlop, Charles, and Rob King, eds. *Computerization and Controversy.* Boston: Academic Press, 1991.

Dunn, Donald J. "Why Legal Research Skills Declined, Or When Two Rights Make a Wrong." 85 *Law Library Journal* 49 (1993).

Dzeiewit, H. S., J. M. Graziano, and C. J. Daley. "The Quest for the Paperless Office—Electronic Contracting: State of the Art Possibility but Legal Impossibility?" 5 *Computer and High Technology Law Journal* 75 (1989).

Edgerton, Samuel Y. *The Renaissance Rediscovery of Linear Perspective.* New York: Basic Books, 1975.

Eisenstein, Elizabeth. *The Printing Press as an Agent of Change.* New York: Cambridge University Press, 1979.

Englund, Steven R. "Idea, Process, or Protected Expression? Determining the Scope of Copyright Protection of the Structure of Computer Programs." *Michigan Law Review* (1990).

Fajans, Elizabeth, and Mary R. Falk. "Against the Tyranny of Paraphrase: Talking Back to Texts." 78 *Cornell Law Review* 163 (1993).

Febvre, Lucien, and Henri-Jean Martin. *The Coming of the Book.* London: NLB, 1976.

Ferguson, Glover T., Jr. "What Groupware Means for Business." *Information Week*, December 6, 1993.

Fiore, Quentin. "The Future of the Book." In *The Future of Time*, ed. Henri Yaker, Humphry Osmond, and Frances Cheek. Garden City, New York: Doubleday, 1971.

Fitts, Michael A. "Can Ignorance Be Bliss? Imperfect Information as a Positive Influence in Political Institutions." 88 *Michigan Law Review* 917 (1990).

Fitzgerald, Laura S. "Towards a Modern Art of Law." 96 *Yale Law Journal* 2051 (1987).

Flaherty, David H. "On the Utility of Constitutional Rights to Privacy and Data Protection." 41 *Case Western Reserve Law Review* 831 (1991).

Flaherty, David H. *Protecting Privacy in Surveillance Societies*. Chapel Hill and London: The University of North Carolina Press, 1989.

Forester, Tom. "Megatrends or Megamistakes? What Ever Happened to the Information Society?" *EFFector Online*, Issue 4.01. December 17, 1992.

Foster, Frances H. "*Isvestia* as a Mirror of Russian Legal Reform: Press, Law, and Crisis in the Post-Soviet Era." 26 *Vanderbilt Journal of Transnational Law* 675 (1993).

Freedman, Warren. *The Right of Privacy in the Computer Age*. New York: Quorum Books, 1987.

Friedhoff, Richard Mark. *Visualization: The Second Computer Revolution*. New York: Harry N. Abrams, 1989.

Freidson, Eliot. *Profession of Medicine*. New York: Dodd, Mead, 1970.

Friedson, Eliot. *Professional Powers: A Study of the Institutionalization of Formal Knowledge*. Chicago: University of Chicago Press, 1986.

Freitag, Michael. "As Computer Bulletin Boards Grow, If It's Out There, It's Posted Here." *New York Times*, April 2, 1992.

Fry, Patricia Brumfield. "X Marks the Spot: New Technologies Compel New Concepts for Commercial Law." 26 *Loyola of Los Angeles Law Review* 607 (1993).

Fuller, Lon L. *Legal Fictions*. Stanford, California: Stanford University Press, 1967.

Galanter, Marc. "The Legal Malaise; Or, Justice Observed." 19 *Law and Society Review* 537 (1985).

Galanter, Marc, and Thomas Palay. *Tournament of Lawyers: The Transformation of the Big Law Firm*. Chicago: University of Chicago Press, 1991.

Gardner, Anne von der Lieth. *An Artificial Intelligence Approach to Legal Reasoning*. Cambridge, Massachusetts: MIT Press, 1987.

Garfinkel, Simeon. "Computer Punks and 'Cyberspace.'" *Christian Science Monitor*, August 21, 1991.

Gavison, Ruth. "Privacy and the Limits of Law." 89 *Yale Law Journal* 421, 430 (1980).

Gelernter, David. *Mirror Worlds*. New York: Oxford University Press, 1991.

"Getting a Read on the Customer." *Information Week*, May 3, 1993.

Gibson, William. *Neuromancer*. New York: Berkeley Publishing Group, 1984.

Gibson, William. *Virtual Light*. New York: Bantam Books, 1993.

Gilder, George. *Life after Television*, rev. ed. New York: W. W. Norton, 1994.

Gilder, George. "Life after Television, Updated." *Forbes ASAP*, February 23, 1994.

Ginsburg, Jane C. "Copyright without Walls? Speculations on Literary Property in the Library of the Future." 42 *Representations* 53 (1993).

Ginsburg, Jane C. "No 'Sweat'? Copyright and Other Protection of Works of Information after *Feist v. Rural Telephone* [111 S. Ct. 1282]." 92 *Columbia Law Review* 338 (1992).

Giobbe, Dorothy. "Unlawful Entry: Detroit Free Press Sportswriter Apologizes after Using Tonya Harding's Private Password to Gain Entry into the Olympic Skater's Electronic Mailbox." *Editor and Publisher,* March 5, 1994.

Glance, Natalie S., and Bernardo A. Huberman. "The Dynamics of Social Dilemmas." *Scientific American,* March 1994, p. 76.

Goldschmidt, Ernst Ph. *The Printed Book of the Renaissance.* Cambridge: Cambridge University Press, 1950.

Goldsen, Rose K. *The Show and Tell Machine.* New York: The Dial Press, 1975.

Gombrich, H. E. *Art and Illusion.* Princeton, New Jersey: Princeton University Press, 1961.

Goodrich, Peter. *Reading the Law.* Oxford: Basil Blackwell, 1986.

Goodrum, Charles A. *Treasures of the Library of Congress.* New York: Harry Abrams, 1991.

Goody, Jack. "Alternative Paths to Knowledge in Oral and Literate Cultures." In *Speech and Written Language: Exploring Orality and Literacy,* ed. Deborah Tannen. Norwood, New Jersey: Ablex Publishing Co., 1982.

Goody, Jack. "Literacy and the Non-Literate." *Times Literary Supplement* (London), May 12, 1972, pp. 539–540.

Goody, Jack, ed. *Literacy in Traditional Societies.* Cambridge: Cambridge University Press, 1968.

Gordon, Robert W. "Comment: Macaulay, Macneil, and the Discovery of Solidarity and Power in Contract Law." *Wisconsin Law Review* 565 (1985).

Gordon, Wendy J. "On Owning Information: Intellectual Property and the Restitutionary Impulse." 78 *Virginia Law Review* 149 (1992).

Gormley, Ken. "One Hundred Years of Privacy." *Wisconsin Law Review* 1335 (1992).

Gould, Carol C., ed. *The Information Web.* Boulder, Colorado: Westview Press, 1989.

Gould, Stephen J. "A Tale of Three Pictures," *Natural History,* May 1988.

Graham, "Our Tong Maternall Marvelously Amendyd and Augmentyd: The First Englishing and Printing of the Medieval Statutes at Large, 1530–1533." 13 *UCLA Law Review* 58 (1965).

Gray, Pamela. "Sealing Up to a Three-Dimensional Graphic Trace." Unpublished, 1993.

Greenwood, Ernest. "Attributes of a Profession." 2 *Social Work* (1957), pp. 44–47.

Grendler, Paul F. "The Advent of Printing." In *Censorship: 500 Years of Conflict.* New York: The New York Public Library, 1984.

Gruner, Richard S. "Instructional Hypertext: Using Non-sequential Text to Represent and Analyze Real Property Interests." Presentation to Third International Conference on Substantive Technology in the Law School, Paris, July 11, 1994.

Guilshan, C. "A Picture Is Worth a Thousand Lies: Electronic Imaging and the Future of the Admissibility of Photographs into Evidence." 18 *Rutgers Computer and Technology Law Journal* 365 (1992).

Hafner, Katie, and John Markoff. *Cyberpunk: Outlaws and Hackers on the Computer Frontier.* New York: Simon and Schuster, 1991.

Hall, Edward. *Beyond Culture.* Garden City, New York: Doubleday, 1976.

Hall, Edward. *The Hidden Dimension.* Garden City, New York: Doubleday and Co., 1969.

Halpern, Sheldon W. "Rethinking the Right of Privacy: Dignity, Decency, and the Law's Limitations." 43 *Rutgers Law Review* 539 (1991).

Hambleton, James. "Managing Information and Libraries in the Electronic Era." 81 *Law Library Journal* 545 (1989).

Hammer, Michael, and James Champy. "Explosive Thinking." *Computerworld,* May 3, 1993, p. 124.

Hammer, Michael, and James Champy. *Reengineering the Corporation.* New York: HarperCollins, 1993.

Hammond, Grant R. "Electronic Technology: Law and the Legal Mind." 26 *Cornell International Law Journal* 167 (1993).

Hardy, Trotter. "Electronic Conferences: The Report of an Experiment." 6 *Harvard Journal of Law and Technology* 213 (1993).

Hardy, Trotter. *A New Jurisdiction for Cyberspace: A Transcript of Newjuris, An Electronic Conference Held September–October, 1993.*

Hardy, Trotter. "Project CLEAR's Paper Choice: A Hypertext System for Giving Advice about Legal Research." 82 *Law Library Journal* 209 (1990).

Harrington, William G. "A Brief History of Computer-Assisted Legal Research." 77 *Law Library Journal* 543 (1984).

Hart, H.L.A. *The Concept of Law.* Oxford: Oxford University Press, 1961.

Hartmann, Michael. "Legal Data Banks, the Glut of Lawyers, and the German Legal Profession." 27 *Law and Society Review* 421 (1993).

Havelock, Eric. *The Greek Concept of Justice.* Cambridge, Massachusetts: Harvard University Press, 1978.

Havelock, Eric. *Preface to Plato.* Cambridge, Massachusetts: Harvard University Press, 1963.

Hayes, David L. "Shrinkwrap License Agreements: New Light on a Vexing Problem." 9 *Computer Lawyer* 1 (1992).

Hazard, Geoffrey C., Jr., and Deborah L. Rhode, eds. *The Legal Profession: Responsibility and Regulation.* Mineola, New York: Foundation Press, 1985.

Heckel, Paul. *The Elements of Friendly Software Design.* New York: Warner Books, 1984.

Hibbitts, Bernard J. "'Coming to Our Senses': Communication and Legal Expression in Performance Cultures." 4 *Emory Law Journal* 873 (1992).

Hillis, W. Daniel. "What Is Massively Parallel Computing, and Why Is It Important?" *Daedalus* (1990), p. 1.

Hiltz, Starr R., and Murray Turoff. *The Network Nation: Human Communication via Computer.* Reading, Massachusetts: Addison-Wesley, 1978.

Hirsch, Rudolph. "Printing and the Spread of Humanism: The Example of Albrecht Von Eyb." In *The Printed Word,* ed. Rudolph Hirsch. London: Variorum Reprints, 1978.

Hixson, Richard. *Privacy in a Public Society.* New York: Oxford University Press, 1987.

Hofstadter, Samuel, and George Horowitz. *The Right of Privacy.* New York: Central Book Company, 1964.

Holmes, Oliver Wendell. *The Common Law.* Boston: Little, Brown, 1881.

Holmes, Oliver Wendell. *Speeches.* Boston: Little, Brown, 1934.

Holusha, John. "Industry Is Learning to Love Agility." *New York Times,* May 25, 1994.

Hoover, James L. "Legal Scholarship and the Electronic Revolution." 83 *Law Library Journal* 643 (1991).

Howe, Irving, ed. *1984 Revisited.* New York: Harper and Row, 1983.

Howland, Joan S., and Nancy J. Lewis. "The Effectiveness of Law School Legal Research Training Programs." 40 *Journal of Legal Education* 381 (1990).

Hylton, Keith N. "Asymmetric Information and the Selection of Disputes for Litigation." 22 *Journal of Legal Studies* 187 (1993).

Innis, Harold A. *The Bias of Communications.* Toronto: University of Toronto Press, 1951.

Innis, Harold A. *Empire and Communications.* Toronto: University of Toronto Press, 1950.

"Interview with Alan Kay." *Computerworld,* June 22, 1992.

"Interview with Bill Gates." *Computerworld,* June 22, 1992.

"In Their Own Words: IS Managers on Security." *Information Week,* October 4, 1993.

Ives, E. W. "A Lawyer's Library in 1500." 85 *Law Quarterly Review* 104 (1969).

Jaszi, Pater. "Toward a Theory of Copyright: The Metamorphoses of 'Authorship.'" *Duke Law Journal* 455 (1991).

Johnson, Bonnie McDaniel, and Ronald E. Rice. "Reinvention in the Innovation Process: The Case of Word Processing." In *The New Media: Communication, Research, and Technology,* ed. Ronald E. Rice. Beverly Hills, California: Sage, 1984.

Johnson, David R. "Building a Facility Lawyers Want to Use." *New Jersey Law Journal,* March 8, 1993, p. 2.

Johnson, David R. "Building and Using Hypertext Systems." 17 *Law Practice Management,* May–June 1991, p. 28.

Johnson, David R. *Building and Using Hypertext Systems in the Practice of Law.* Washington, D.C.: Wilmer, Cutler and Pickering, 1989.

Johnson, David R. "A New Era: All Your Expertise in a Database." 4 *Computer Counsel* 1 (1992).

Johnson, David R. "On the Path to Electronic Collegiality." *The American Lawyer: LEXIS Counsel Connect Supplement,* April, 1993, p. 1

Johnson, Gregory L. "Electronic Contracts: Are They Enforceable under Article 2 of the U.C.C?" 4 *Software Law Journal* 247 (1991).

Johnson, Johna T. "NREN: Turning the Clock Ahead on Tomorrow's Networks." *Data Communications,* September 1992.

Kagel, Sam, and Kathy Kelly. "The Anatomy of Mediation: What Makes It Work." 1990 *Journal of Dispute Resolution* 201 (1990).

Kahin, Brian, ed. *Building Information Infrastructure.* New York: McGraw-Hill, 1992.

Kahn, Paul. "Joining the Network of Ideas: The Impact of Digital Information on the Organization of Knowledge." *Annual Review of the Institute for Information Studies* 1 (1990).

Kaplan, Benjamin. *An Unhurried View of Copyright.* New York: Columbia University Press, 1967.

Katsh, M. Ethan. "The Electronic Media and the First Amendment." *Trial*. July 1990, p. 34.

Katsh, M. Ethan. *The Electronic Media and the Transformation of Law*. New York: Oxford University Press, 1989.

Katsh, M. Ethan. "The Electronic Media and the Transformation of Law." In *Proceedings of the Conference on Teaching Legal and Factual Research in Private Law Libraries*. Dayton: Mead Data Central, 1991.

Katsh, M. Ethan. "The First Amendment and Technological Change." 57 *George Washington Law Review* 1459 (1989).

Katsh, M. Ethan. "Law and Media." In *Encyclopedia of the American Judicial System*. New York: Charles Scribner and Sons, 1987.

Katsh, M. Ethan. "Law in a Digital World: Computer Networks and Cyberspace." 38 *Villanova Law Review* 403 (1993).

Katsh, M. Ethan. "The Law Librarian as Paratrooper." 83 *Law Library Journal* 627 (1991).

Katsh, M. Ethan. "The Transformation of Law and Its Consequences for Legal Research." In *Graylyn Conference Report*, ed. Donald Dunn. Dayton: Mead Data Central, 1991.

Katsh, Ethan, and Janet Rifkin. "The New Media and a New Model of Conflict Resolution: Copying, Copyright, and Creating." 6 *Notre Dame Journal of Law, Ethics and Public Policy* 49 (1992).

Kauffmann, William J., and Larry L. Smarr. *Supercomputing and the Transformation of Science*. New York: Scientific American Library, 1993.

Kelly, Kevin. *Out of Control*. Reading, Massachusetts: Addison-Wesley, 1994.

Kernan, Alvin. *The Death of Literature*. New Haven, Connecticut: Yale University Press, 1990.

Kernan, Alvin. *Printing Technology, Letters and Samuel Johnson*. Princeton, New Jersey: Princeton University Press, 1987.

Keyhani, Andrea. "The Online Journal of Current Clinical Trials: An Innovation in Electronic Journal Publishing." 16 *Database* 14 (1993).

Keyt, Aaron. "An Improved Framework for Music Plagiarism Litigation." 76 *California Law Review* 421 (1988).

Kidder, Tracy. *The Soul of a New Machine*. Boston: Little, Brown and Co., 1981.

Kleiman, Matthew. "The Right to Financial Privacy versus Computerized Law Enforcement: A New Fight in an Old Battle." 86 *Northwestern University Law Review* 1169 (1992).

Klein, S. S. "Your Right to Privacy: A Selective Bibliography." 12 *Legal Reference Series Quarterly* 217 (1992).

Konvitz, Milton. "Privacy and the Law: A Philosophical Prelude." 31 *Law and Contemporary Problems* 272, 279 (1960).

Kosko, Bart. *Fuzzy Thinking: The New Science of Fuzzy Logic*. New York: Hyperion, 1993.

Kozolchyk, Boris. "The Paperless Letter of Credit and Related Documents of Title." 55 *Law and Contemporary Problems* 39 (1992).

Kress, Kenneth J. "Legal Reasoning and Coherence Theories: Dworkin's Rights Thesis, Retroactivity, and the Linear Order of Decisions." 72 *California Law Review* 369 (1984).

Krol, Ed. *The Whole Internet User's Guide & Catalog*. Sebastopol, California: O'Reilly and Assoc., 1994.

Krueger, Myron. *Artificial Reality II*. Reading, Massachusetts: Addison-Wesley, 1991.

Kuhn, Thomas. *The Structure of Scientific Revolutions*. Chicago: University of Chicago Press, 1970.

Kurzweil, Raymond. *The Age of Intelligent Machines*. Cambridge, Massachusetts: MIT Press, 1990.

Lakoff, George, and Mark Johnson. *Metaphors We Live By*. Chicago: University of Chicago Press, 1980.

Landow, George P. *Hypertext: The Convergence of Contemporary Critical Theory and Technology*. Baltimore: Johns Hopkins University Press, 1992.

Lanham, Richard A. *The Electronic Word: Democracy, Technology and the Arts*. Chicago: University of Chicago Press, 1993.

Laperriere, Rene, and Rene Cote, Georges A. Le Bel, Pauline Roy, and Kerim Benyekhlef. *Crossing the Borders of Privacy: Transborder Flows of Personal Data from Canada*. Ottawa: Department of Justice, 1990.

LaPlante, Alice. "Turning Corporate Data into Profitability: Other Companies Want Your Data and They're Willing to Pay for It." *InfoWorld*, October 18, 1993.

Larson, Magali Sarfatti. *The Rise of Professionalism: A Sociological Analysis*. Berkeley: University of California Press, 1977.

Laurel, Brenda. *Computers as Theatre*. Reading, Massachusetts: Addison-Wesley: 1991.

Laurel, Brenda, ed. *The Art of Human–Computer Interface Design*. Reading, Massachusetts: Addison-Wesley, 1990.

Lauritsen, Marc. "Delivering Legal Services with Computer-Based Practice Systems." 23 *Clearinghouse Review* 1532 (1990).

Leinberger, Paul, and Bruce Tucker. *The New Individualists*. New York: HarperCollins, 1991.

Leiter, Richard A. "WIN: 'It's the Natural Way.'" *Information Alert*, November/December 1992.

Lessner, Martin. "Information Technology and the Legal Product: Whither the Law Firm and Welcome the Market?" 1992, unpublished.

Levinson, L. Harold. "Independent Law Firms That Practice Law Only: Society's Need, the Legal Profession's Responsibility." 51 *Ohio State Law Journal* 229 (1990).

Levinson, Marc. "Riding the Data Highway." *Newsweek*, March 21, 1994.

Levy, Steven. *Hackers*. Garden City, New York: Doubleday, 1984.

Levy, Steven. "The King of Software." *Macworld*, September 1991, p. 67.

Littman, Jessica. "Copyright as Myth." 53 *University of Pittsburgh Law Review* 235 (1991).

Lowe, David. "Co-operative Structuring of Information: The Representation of Reasoning and Debate." 23 *International Journal of Man–Machine Studies* 97 (1985).

Macaulay, Stewart. "Elegant Models, Empirical Pictures, and the Complexities of Contract." 11 *Law and Society Review* 507 (1977).

Mackaay, Ejan. "Economic Incentives in Markets for Information and Innovation." 13 *Harvard Journal of Law & Public Policy* 867 (1990).

Mackaay, Ejan. "Lawyering and Litigating in Cyberspace." Address to the Eleventh Colloquy on Legal Data Processing in Europe, October 4, 1993.

Mackaay, Ejan, Daniel Poulin, Jacques Fremont, Paul Bratley, and Constant Deniger. "The Logic of Time in Law and Legal Expert Systems." 3 *Ratio Juris*. 254 (1990).

MacNeil, Ian. *The New Social Contract*. New Haven, Connecticut: Yale University Press, 1980.

MacPhail, Wayne. "The Information Revolution: The Function of the Journalist in a Multimedia World." Unpublished, 1993.

Maine, Henry Sumner. *Ancient Law*. 1861.

Maister, David H. "What Makes a Firm?" *The American Lawyer*, December 1993, p. 32.

Maitland, Frederic William. "A Prologue to a History of English Law." 14 *Law Quarterly Review* 13 (1898).

Margolick, David. "At the Bar." *New York Times*, December 11, 1992.

Markoff, John. "Turning the Desktop PC into a Talk Radio Medium." *New York Times*, March 4, 1953.

Martin, James. *Hyperdocuments and How to Create Them*. Englewood Cliffs, New Jersey: Prentice-Hall, 1990.

Martin, Peter. "The Future of Law Librarians in Changing Institutions, or the Hazards and Opportunities of New Information Technology." 83 *Law Library Journal* 419 (1991).

Martin, Peter. "How New Information Technologies Will Change the Way Law Professors Do and Distribute Scholarship." 83 *Law Library Journal* 633 (1991).

Martin, Peter. "Hypertext for Tomorrow." Speech to the ABA Technology in Law Practice Conference, March 12, 1992.

Martin, Peter. "Learning the Law from Littleton to Laser Disks and Beyond." *GNN Magazine*, January 1994.

McCarty, L. Thorne. "Artificial Intelligence and the Law: How to Get from There to Here." 3 *Ratio Juris* 189 (1990).

McClure, Charles, et al. *The National Research and Education Network: Research and Policy Perspectives*. Norwood, New Jersey: Ablex, 1991.

McDermott, Jo. "Another Analysis of Full-Text Document Retrieval." 78 *Law Library Journal* 337 (1986).

McGrath, Thomas A., III. "The Rise and Fall (and Rise?) of Information-Based Insider Trading Enforcement." 61 *Fordham Law Review* 127 (1993).

McLuhan, Marshall. *The Gutenberg Galaxy*. Toronto: University of Toronto Press, 1962.

McLuhan, Marshall. *Understanding Media*. New York: McGraw-Hill, 1964.

McLuhan, Marshall, and Bruce R. Powers. *The Global Village*. New York: Oxford University Press, 1989.

Mechling, Jerry. "Introduction." *Annual Review of the Institute for Information Studies* (1990).

Meeks, Marjorie, "Alter[ing] People's Perceptions: The Challenge Facing Advocates of Ancillary Business Practices." 66 *Indiana Law Journal* 1031 (1991).

Menkel-Meadow, Carrie. "The Transformation of Disputes by Lawyers: What the Dispute Paradigm Does and Does Not Tell Us." *Missouri Journal of Dispute Resolution* 24 (1985).

Meyer, Jim. "The Portable Lawyer." 77 *American Bar Association Journal* 62 (September 1991).

Meyrowitz, Joshua. *No Sense of Place*. New York: Oxford University Press, 1985.

Mikva, Abner. "Goodbye to Footnotes." 56 *University of Colorado Law Review* 647 (1985).

Miller, Philip H. "Life after FEIST: Facts, the First Amendment, and the Copyright Status of Automated Databases." 60 *Fordham Law Review* 507 (1991).

Miller, Philip H. "New Technology, Old Problem: Determining the First Amendment Status of Electronic Information Services." 61 *Fordham Law Review* 1147 (1993).

Minnis, A. J. *Medieval Theory of Authorship*. London: Scolar Press, 1984.

Minow, Martha. "Telling Medical Stories: Sharing Information among Doctors, Patients, and Families." *Utah Law Review* 903 (1992).

Mital V., and L. Johnson. *Advanced Information Systems for Lawyers*. London: Chapman and Hall, 1992.

Mitchell, William. *City of Bits*. Cambridge, Massachusetts, MIT Press, 1995.

Mitchell, William. *The Reconfigured Eye: Visual Truth in the Post-Photographic Era*. Cambridge, Massachusetts: MIT Press, 1992.

Mitchell, William. "When Is Seeing Believing?" *Scientific American*. February 1994, p. 68.

Monheim, Thomas A. "Personal Communications Services: The Wireless Future of Telecommunications." 44 *Federal Communications Law Journal* 335 (1992).

Mooney, Charles W., Jr., "Property, Credit and Regulation Meet Information Technology: Clearance and Settlement in the Securities Market." 55 *Law and Contemporary Problems* 131 (1992).

Moore, Barrington. *Privacy: Studies in Social and Cultural History*. London: M. E. Sharpe, 1984.

Morgan, John, and Peter Welton. *See What I Mean: An Introduction to Visual Communication*. London: Edward Arnold, 1986.

Morrison, Peter. "Arizona Courts Introduce Automated Legal Help." *The National Law Journal* (August 9, 1993), p. 12.

Munneke, Gary A. "Dances with Nonlawyers: A New Perspective on Law Firm Diversification." 61 *Fordham Law Review* 559 (1992).

National Information Infrastructure Task Force. *The National Information Infrastructure: Agenda for Action Executive Summary*, September 15, 1993, p. 1.

Nedelsky, Jennifer. "Law, Boundaries, and the Bounded Self." 30 *Representations* 162 (1990).

Negroponte, Nicholas. "Products and Service for Computer Networks." *Scientific American*, September 199, p. 113.

Nelson, Kent. "The Re-Education of UPS." *Information Week*, March 1, 1993.

Nelson, Theodor. *Literary Machines*. Swarthmore, Pennsylvania, author, 1981.

Nelson, Theodor H., statement of. "National High-Performance Computer Technology Act of 1989." *Hearings on S. 1067, the National High-Performance Computer Technology Act of 1989 before the Subcommittee on Science, Technology, and Space of the Senate Committee on Commerce,*

Science, and Transportation of the United States Senate, 101st Cong., 1st Sess., 399 (1989).

Nickerson, Gord. "Networked Resources." *Computers in Libraries*, September 1992.

Nimmer, Raymond T., and Patricia Ann Krauthaus. "Information as a Commodity: New Imperatives of Commercial Law." 55 *Law and Contemporary Problems* 103 (1992).

Norman, Donald A. *Things That Make Us Smart*. Reading, Massachusetts: Addison-Wesley, 1993.

Note. "The Message in the Medium: The First Amendment on the Information Superhighway." 107 *Harvard Law Review* 1062 (1994).

O'Connor, Sandra Day. "Civil Justice System Improvements." Speech to American Bar Association, December 14, 1994.

Ong, Walter. *Interfaces of the Word: Studies in the Evolution of Consciousness and Culture*. Ithaca, New York: Cornell University Press, 1977.

Ong, Walter. *Orality and Literacy*. London: Methuen, 1982.

Ong, Walter J. *Rhetoric, Romance, and Technology*. Ithaca, New York: Cornell University Press, 1971.

Orwell, George. *1984*. New York: Harcourt, Brace, 1949.

Palmer, Robert C. "The Origins of the Legal Profession in England." 11 *Irish Jurist* 126–146 (1976).

Patterson, Lyman. *Copyright in Historical Perspective*. Nashville, Tennessee: Vanderbilt University Press, 1968.

Paulson, Ed. *The Complete Communications Handbook*. Plano, Texas: Wordware Publishing Co., 1992.

Perritt, Henry H., Jr. "The Electronic Agency and the Traditional Paradigms of Administrative Law." 44 *Administrative Law Review* 79 (1992).

Perritt, Henry H., Jr. "Electronic Records Management and Archives." 53 *University of Pittsburgh Law Review* 963 (1992).

Perritt, Henry H., Jr. "Format and Content Standards for the Electronic Exchange of Legal Information." 33 *Jurimetrics Journal* 265 (1993).

Perritt, Henry H., Jr. "Government Information Goes On-Line." 92 *Technology Review* 60 (1989).

Perritt, Henry H., Jr. *How to Practice Law with Computers*, 2nd ed. New York: Practicing Law Institute, 1988.

Perritt, Henry H., Jr. "Metaphors for Understanding Rights and Responsibilities in Network Communities: Print Shops, Barons, Sheriffs, and Bureaucracies." Unpublished, 1992.

Perritt, Henry H., Jr. "Tort Liability, the First Amendment, and Equal Access to Electronic Networks." 5 *Harvard Journal of Law and Technology* 65 (1992).

Perry, Gregory E., and Cherie Ballard. "A Chip by Any Other Name Would Still Be a Potato: The Failure of Law and Its Definitions to Keep Pace with Computer Technology." 24 *Texas Tech Law Review* 797 (1993).

Pickover, Clifford A. *Computers, Pattern, Chaos and Beauty*. New York: St. Martin's Press, 1990.

"A Picture Is Worth a Thousand Lies: Electronic Imaging and the Future of the Admissibility of Photographs into Evidence." 18 *Rutgers Computer and Technology Law Journal* 365 (1992).

Pierce, John R. "The Telephone and Society in the Past 100 Years." In *The*

Social Impact of the Telephone, ed. Ithiel de Sola Pool. Cambridge, Massachusetts: MIT Press, 1977.

Plato. *Phaedrus,* tr. R. Hackforth. Cambridge, Massachusetts: Harvard University Press, 1952.

Ploch, Donald R., Bethany K. Dumas, Grayfred B. Gray, Bruce J. MacLennan, and John E. Nolt. "Readability of the Law: Forms of Law for Building Legal Expert Systems." 33 *Jurimetrics Journal* 189 (1993).

Pollock, Frederick, and Frederic W. Maitland. *The History of English Law* 1. 2d ed., 1899.

Post, Robert. "The Social Foundations of Privacy: Community and Self in the Common Law Tort." 77 *California Law Review* 970 (1989).

"The Post-Capitalist Executive: An Interview with Peter Drucker." *Harvard Business Review,* May–June 1993, p. 120.

Pritchard-Schoch, Theresa. "WIN–WESTLAW Goes Natural." *Online,* January 1993, p. 101.

Prosser, William. "Privacy." 48 *California Law Review* 383 (1960).

Quarterman, John S. *The Matrix.* Bedford, Massachusetts: Digital Press, 1990.

Raab, Selwyn. "A Weakness in the Gotti Case: Major U.S. Witnesses Viewed as Unreliable." *New York Times,* March 14, 1987.

Ramstad, Evan. "Bits Cornerstone of Techno-Convergence." *Springfield Sunday Republican,* October 31, 1993.

Reidenberg, Joel R. "Electronic Communications and Legal Change. Rules of the Road for Global Electronic Highways: Merging the Trade and Technical Paradigms." 6 *Harvard Journal of Law and Technology* 287 (1993).

Reidenberg, Joel R. "Privacy in the Information Economy: A Fortress or Frontier for Individual Rights?" 44 *Federal Communications Law Journal* 195 (1992).

Reisman, David. *The Oral Tradition, The Written Word and the Screen Image.* Yellow Springs, Ohio: Antioch Press, 1956.

Resnick, Rosalind. "Cybertort." *National Law Journal* (July 18, 1994).

Rheingold, Howard. *The Virtual Community.* Reading, Massachusetts: Addison-Wesley, 1993.

Rheingold, Howard. *Virtual Reality.* New York: Summit Books, 1991.

Rhode, Deborah L. "Policing the Professional Monopoly: A Constitutional and Empirical Analysis of Unauthorized Practice Prohibitions." 34 *Stanford Law Review* 1 (1981).

Rice, Ronald. "Mediated Group Communication." In *The New Media: Communication, Research, and Technology,* ed. Ronald Rice. Beverly Hills, California: Sage Publications, 1984.

Rissland, Edwina L. "Artificial Intelligence and Law: Stepping Stones to a Model of Legal Reasoning." 99 *Yale Law Journal* 1957 (1990).

Robertson, Bernard. "Marshalling Information Prior to Litigation." 13 *Cardozo Law Review* 705 (1991).

Ronell, Avital. *The Telephone Book.* Lincoln: University of Nebraska Press, 1989.

Rose, Mark. *Authors and Owners: The Invention of Copyright.* Cambridge, Massachusetts: Harvard University Press, 1993.

Rosenbluth, Hal. "Tales from a Nonconformist Company." *Harvard Business Review* (July/August 1991), p. 26.

Ross, Andrew. *Strange Weather: Culture, Science, and Technology in the Age of Limits.* New York: Verso, 1991.

Rotenberg, Marc. "Communications Privacy: Implications for Network Design." 36 *Communications of the ACM* 61 (1993).

Rothfeder, Jefferey. *Privacy for Sale: How Computerization Has Made Everyone's Private Life an Open Secret.* New York: Simon and Schuster, 1992.

Rotstein, Robert H. "Beyond Metaphor: Copyright Infringement and the Fiction of the Work." 68 *Chicago-Kent Law Review* 725 (1993).

Runde, Craig E., and William H. Lindberg. "The Curse of Thamus: A Response." 78 *Law Library Journal* 345 (1986).

Saffo, Paul. "Consensual Realities in Cyberspace." In Peter Denning ed., *Computers Under Attack: Intruders, Worms, and Viruses.* New York: ACM Press, 1990.

Saffo, Paul. "Future Tense: Personal Computers Will Make Solitude a Scarce Resource." *InfoWorld*, December 23, 1991.

Samuelson, Pamela. "Digital Media and the Changing Face of Intellectual Property Law." 16 *Rutgers Computer and Technical Law Journal* 323 (1990).

Samuelson, Pamela. "Digital Media and the Law." *Communications of the ACM* (October 1991), p. 23.

Samuelson, Pamela. "Is Information Property?" 34 *Communications of the ACM* 15 (1991).

Samuelson, Pamela. "Legally Speaking: Digital Media and the Law." 34 *Communications of the ACM* 23 (1991).

Samuelson, Pamela, and Robert J. Glushko. "Electronic Communications and Legal Change: Intellectual Property Rights for Digital Library and Hypertext Publishing Systems." 6 *Harvard Journal of Law and Technology* 237 (1993).

Sarton, George. *Six Wings.* Bloomington: Indiana University Press, 1957.

Sawer, Geoffrey. *Law in Society.* Oxford: Oxford University Press, 1965.

Schrage, Michael. *Shared Minds: The New Technologies of Collaboration.* New York: Random House, 1990.

Schwartz, Evan. "Software Valets That Will Do Your Bidding in Cyberspace." *New York Times*, January 9, 1994.

"Self-Help Guides on Law Grow into Big Business." *New York Times*, September 25, 1992.

Selya, Bruce. "Publish and Perish: The Fate of the Federal Appeals Judge in the Information Age." 55 *Ohio State Law Journal* 405 (1994).

The Seybold Report on Desktop Publishing, November 8, 1993.

Sheldon, Kenneth M. "You've Come a Long Way, PC." *Byte*, August 1991.

Shiels, Rosemary. "Law School Experience in Pervasive Electronic Communications." 5 *Journal of Computing in Higher Education* 122 (1994).

Simon, Herbert. "Applying Information Technology to Organization Design." *Public Administration Review* (May/June 1973), p. 271.

Smith, Anthony. "On Audio and Visual Technologies." In *The Written Word: Literacy in Transition*, ed. Gerd Baumann. Oxford: Clarendon Press, 1986.

Smith, Anthony. *Goodbye Gutenberg.* New York: Oxford University Press, 1980.

Smith, Anthony. "The Influence of Television." 114 *Daedelus* 1 (1985).

Smith, J. C. "The Unique Nature of the Concepts of Western Law." 46 *The Canadian Bar Review* 191 (1968).

Smith, Jane. "CNIDR: Report from the Kudzu Patch," *Internet World*, September/October 1993.

Smolla, Rodney A. *Free Speech in an Open Society*. New York: Knopf, 1992.

Solomon, Rayman. "Five Crises or One: The Concept of Legal Professionalism, 1925–1960." In *Lawyers' Ideals/Lawyers' Practices*, ed. Robert Nelson, David Trubek, and Rayman Solomon. Ithaca, New York: Cornell University Press, 1992.

Solomon, Richard J. "Computers and the Concept of Intellectual Copyright." In Martin Greenberger, ed., *Electronic Publishing Plus*. White Plains, New York: Knowledge Industry Publications, 1985.

Solum, Lawrence B. "Legal Personhood for Artificial Intelligences." 70 *North Carolina Law Review* 1231 (1992).

Speidel, Richard E. "Article 2 and Relational Sales Contracts." 26 *Loyola of Los Angeles Law Review* 789 (1993).

Stallings, William. *ISDN: An Introduction*. New York: Macmillan, 1989.

Stansky, Peter, ed. *On Nineteen Eighty-four*. San Francisco: W. H. Freeman and Co., 1983.

Staudt, Ronald W. "Does the Grandmother Come with It? Teaching and Practicing Law in the 21st Century." 44 *Case Western Law Review* 479 (1994).

Staudt, Ronald W. "An Essay on Electronic Casebooks: My Pursuit of the Paperless Chase." 68 *Chicago-Kent Law Review* 291 (1992).

Staudt, Ronald W. "Legal Mindstorms: Lawyers, Computers and Powerful Ideas." 31 *Jurimetrics Journal* 171 (1991).

Staudt, Ronald W., and Rosemary Shiels. *Chicago-Kent 1993 Large Firm Survey and Statistical Analysis*. Chicago: Chicago-Kent College of Law, 1994.

Stefancic, Jean, and Richard Delgado. "Outsider Jurisprudence and the Electronic Revolution: Will Technology Help or Hinder the Cause of Law Reform?" 52 *Ohio State Law Journal* 847 (1991).

Stein, Anne. "Job Hunting? Exude Confidence." *American Bar Association Journal* (November 1993).

Steinhoff, William. *The Road to 1984*. London: Weidenfeld and Nicolson, 1975.

Sterling, Bruce. "Free as Air, Free as Water, Free as Knowledge." Speech to the Library Information Technology Association, San Francisco, June 1992.

Sterling, Bruce. *The Hacker Crackdown*. New York: Bantam Books, 1992.

Stock, Brian. *The Implications of Literacy*. Princeton, New Jersey: Princeton University Press, 1983.

Stoll, Clifford. *The Cuckoo's Egg*. New York: Doubleday, 1989.

Susskind, Richard E. *Expert Systems in Law*. Oxford: Oxford University Press, 1987.

Susskind, Richard, "Expert Systems in Law: A Jurisprudential Approach to Artificial Intelligence and Legal Reasoning." 49 *Modern Law Review* 168 (1987).

Susskind, Richard. "Expert Systems in Law and the Data Protection Adviser." 7 *Oxford Journal of Legal Studies* 145 (1987).

Tarter, Blodwen. "Information Liability: New Interpretations for the Electronic Age." 11 *Computer/Law Journal* 481 (1992).

Terrell, Timothy P. "Flatlaw: An Essay on the Dimensions of Legal Reasoning and the Development of Fundamental Normative Principles." 72 *California Law Review* 288 (1984).

Teslet, Lawrence. "Networked Computing in the 1990s." *Scientific American* (1991), p. 90.

Toffler, Alvin. "The Future of Law and Order." *Encounter,* July 1973, p. 15.

Tribe, Laurence. "The Constitution in Cyberspace: Law and Liberty beyond the Electronic Frontier." Keynote address at the First Conference on Computers, Freedom and Privacy, March 26, 1991.

Trubow, George B. "Protecting Informational Privacy in the Information Society." 10 *Northern Illinois University Law Review* 521 (1990).

Tuerkheimer, Frank M. "The Underpinnings of Privacy Protection." 36 *Communications of the ACM* 69 (1993).

Tufte, Edward R. *Envisioning Information.* Cheshire, Connecticut: Graphics Press, 1990.

Tufte, Edward R. *The Visual Display of Quantitative Information.* Cheshire, Connecticut: Graphics Press, 1982.

Tumin, Myron C., ed. *Literacy Online.* Pittsburgh: University of Pittsburgh Press, 1992.

Turkle, Sherry. *The Second Self: Computers and the Human Spirit.* New York: Simon and Schuster, 1984.

Tyson, Gerald, and Wagonheim, Sylvia, eds. *Print and Culture in the Renaissance.* Newark: University of Delaware Press, 1986.

Uncapher, Willard. "Trouble in Cyberspace." *The Humanist,* September–October 1991.

Unger, Roberto. *Law in Modern Society.* New York: Free Press, 1978.

U.S. Congress, Office of Technology Assessment. "Computer Software and Intellectual Property." Background paper. 1990.

U.S. Congress, Office of Technology Assessment. *Intellectual Property Rights in an Age of Electronics and Information.* Washington, D.C.: U.S. Government Printing Office, 1986.

"U.S. Supreme Court Installs Miles 33 OASYS." *Typeworld,* July 1, 1992.

Valauskas, Edward J. "Digital Images over the Internet: Rome Reborn at the Library of Congress." *Database,* April 1994.

Vandagriff, David P. "Taking the Computer Cure." *ABA Journal.* December 1993.

Van Dijk, Teun A. "Structures of Discourse and Structures of Power." 12 *Communications Yearbook* 18 (1988).

Van Gelder, Lindsay. "The Strange Case of the Electronic Lover." In *Computerization and Controversy,* ed. Charles Dunlop and Rob Kling. Boston: Academic Press, 1991.

Volpato, Richard. "Legal Professionalism and Informatics." 2 *Journal of Law and Information Science* 206 (1991).

Vonnegut, Kurt. *God Bless You, Mr. Rosewater.* New York: Dell Publishing Co., 1965.

Walter, Marilyn. "Retaking Control over Teaching Research." 43 *Journal of Legal Education* 569 (1993).

Walter, Priscilla A., and Sussman, Eric H. "Protecting Commercially Developed Information on the NREN." 10 *Computer Lawyer* 1 (1993).

Warner, David R., Jr. "A Neural Network-Based Law Machine: Initial Steps." 18 *Rutgers Computer & Techology Law Journal* 51 (1992).

Warner, David R., Jr. "Toward a Simple Law Machine." 29 *Jurimetrics Journal* 451 (1989).

Warren, Samuel, and Brandeis, Louis. "The Right to Privacy." 4 *Harvard Law Review* 193 (1890).

Weingarten, Fred W. "NREN and the National Infrastructure: A Personal Vision." *Internet Research*, Fall 1993, p. 2.

Westin, Alan. *Privacy and Freedom*. New York: Atheneum, 1967.

White, James B. *The Legal Imagination*. Boston: Little, Brown, 1973.

Wiener, Norbert. *The Human Use of Human Beings*. Boston: Houghton Mifflin Co., 1950.

Wilson, Linda. "Stand and Deliver." *Information Week*, November 23, 1992.

Winner, Langdon. "How Technology Reweaves the Fabric of Society." *Chronicle of Higher Education* (August 4, 1993).

Wise, Virginia. "Managing Information Inflation." In *Expert Views on Improving the Quality of Legal Research Education in the United States*. St. Paul, Minnesota: West Publishing Co., 1992, p. 125.

Wooley, Benjamin. *Virtual Worlds*. Oxford: Blackwell, 1992.

Wright, Benjamin. "Authenticating EDI: The Location of a Trusted Record-keeper." 4 *Software Law Journal* 173 (1991).

Wright, Benjamin. "EDI Applications." Statement made to LEXIS Counsel Connect Conference on Law of the Electronic Road, May 18, 1994.

Wright, Benjamin. *The Law of Electronic Commerce*. Boston: Little, Brown and Co., 1991.

Wriston, Walter B. *The Twilight of Sovereignty*. New York: Charles Scribner's Sons, 1992.

Yager, Ronald R. "New Paradigms for Reasoning with Uncertain Information." 13 *Cardozo Law Review* 1005 (1991).

Yates, Frances. *The Art of Memory*. London: Routledge and Kegan Paul, 1966.

Yudof, Mark G. "Like It or Not, We're Post-Modern Lawyers." *Texas Lawyer*, February 14, 1994.

Ziman, John M. *Public Knowledge: An Essay Concerning the Social Dimension of Science*. New York: Cambridge University Press, 1968.

Zimmerman, Diane. "Information as Speech, Information as Goods: Some Thoughts on Marketplaces and the Bill of Rights." 33 *William & Mary Law Review* 665 (1992).

Zimmerman, Diane. "Requiem for a Heavyweight: A Farewell to Warren's and Brandeis's Privacy Tort." 68 *Cornell Law Review* 291 (1983).

Zuboff, Shoshana. *In the Age of the Smart Machine*. New York: Basic Books, 1988.

Index

291

340.0285/ KAT

S.L.